Music
OF THE WORLD

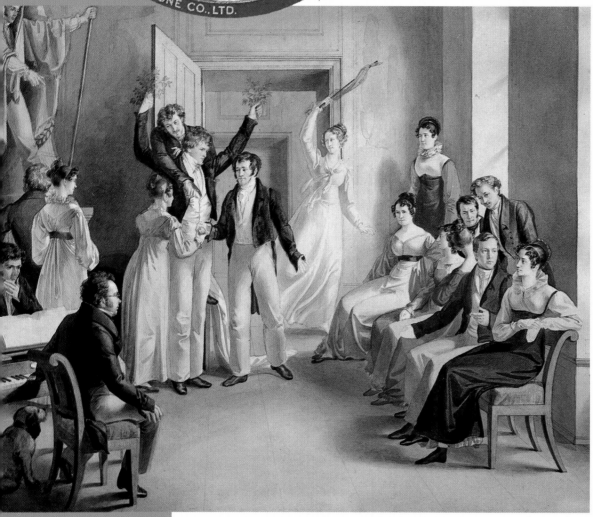

Music

OF THE WORLD

ALAN BLACKWOOD

A QUARTO BOOK

Published by Prentice-Hall, Inc.
A Division of Simon & Schuster
Englewood Cliffs, New Jersey 07632

10 9 8 7 6 5 4 3 2 1

ISBN 0-13-588237-0

This book was designed and produced by
Quarto Publishing plc.
6 Blundell Street
London N7 9BH

Senior Editor: Christine Davis
Editor: Emma Callery
Designer: Hugh Schermuly
Illustrator: David Kemp
Picture Manager: Sarah Risley
Picture Researcher: Liz Eddison
Publishing Director: Janet Slingsby
Art Director: Moira Clinch
Assistant Art Director: Philip Gilderdale

Typeset by ABC Limited, Bournemouth
Manufactured in Singapore by Chroma Graphics Limited
Printed by Leefung Asco Printers Limited, Hong Kong

Contents

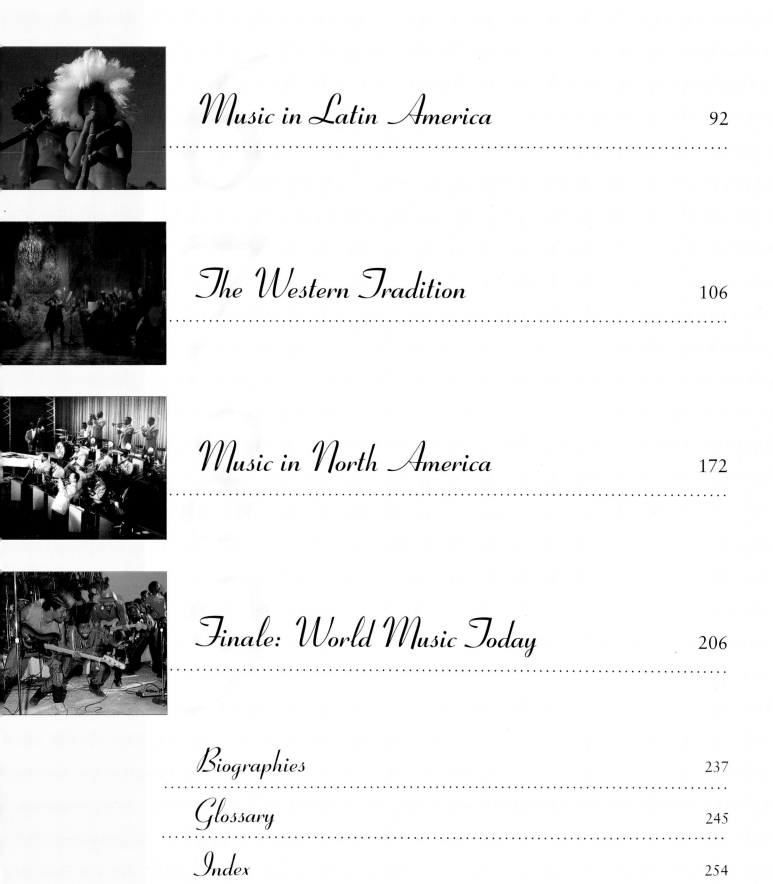

ACKNOWLEDGEMENTS

Quarto would like to thank the following for permission to reproduce copyright material.

T = Top C = Centre B = Below L = Left R = Right

p10–11 C.M. Dixon. p12 C.M. Dixon. p13 C.M. Dixon. p14 "Dat's Jazz". p15 The Hutchison Library. p17 C.M. Dixon. p18 C.M. Dixon. p19T C.M. Dixon; B C.M. Dixon. p20 Patrick Skinner/Joel Photographic Library. p21T "Dat's Jazz"; B Liba Taylor/The Hutchison Library. p22L The Mansell Collection; R E.T. Archive. p23T John Hatt/The Hutchison Library; B E.T. Archive. p24 Alain Le Garsmeur. p25 C.M. Dixon. p26 Alain Le Garsmeur. p27 The Hutchison Library. p28 Alain Le Garsmeur. p29 John Hatt/The Hutchison Library. p30–31 C.M. Dixon. p32 The Bridgeman Art Library. p33T E.T. Archive; B C.M. Dixon. p34 The Hutchison Library. p35 C.M. Dixon. p36L The Mansell Collection; R C.M. Dixon. p37T The Bridgeman Art Library; B The Mansell Collection p39 C.M. Dixon. p40–41T The Egyptian State Tourist Office; p41B Charlie Nairn/The Hutchison Library. p42 The Hutchison Library. p43T Darryl Williams/The Dance Library; p43B C.M. Dixon. p44–45 Michael Macintyre/The Hutchison Library. p47 C.M. Dixon. p48 The Hamlyn Group Picture Library. p49 Michael Macintyre/The Hutchison Library. p50 Michael Macintyre/The Hutchison Library. p51T J.G. Fuller/The Hutchison Library; B J.G. Fuller/The Hutchison Library. p52 Michael Macintyre/The Hutchison Library. p53 The Mansell Collection. p54L W. Hughes/G.S.F. Picture Library; R Australian Overseas Information Service. p55T Maurice Harvey/The Hutchison Library; B The Royal College of Music. p56 Carlos Freire/The Hutchison Library. p57T Michael Macintyre/The Hutchison Library; B Michael Macintyre/The Hutchison Library. p58 Michael Macintyre/The Hutchison Library. p59T J.G. Fuller/The Hutchison Library; B Indonesian Embassy. p61 The Hutchison Library. p62–63 Michael Macintyre/The Hutchison Library. p64 C.M. Dixon. p65T G.S.F. Picture Library; p66 C.M. Dixon. p67L The Hutchison Library; R Mischa Scorer/The Hutchison Library. p68 Jenny Pate/The Hutchison Library. p69 C.M. Dixon. p70L Michael Macintyre/The Hutchison Library; R C.M. Dixon. p71T C.M. Dixon; B Michael Macintyre/The Hutchison Library. p72 Christina Dodwell/The Hutchison Library. p74 The Hutchison Library. p75 C.M. Dixon. p77 The Hutchison Library. p78–79 Derek Richards/The Dance Library. p80 The Hutchison Library. p81 Derek Richards/The Dance Library. p83 The Hutchison Library. p84 Juliet Highet/The Hutchison Library. p85T The Hutchison Library; B The Hutchison Library. p86 The Hutchison Library. p87 The Hutchison Library. p88T The Hutchison Library; B The Hutchison Library. p89T The Hutchison Library; B The Hutchison Library. p90 The Hutchison Library. p91 The Hutchison Library. p92–93 W. Jesco von Puttkamer/The Hutchison Library. p94 Moser Taylor/The Hutchison Library. p95 Moser Taylor/The Hutchison Library. p96 The Hutchison Library. p97 The Hutchison Library. p98T C.M. Dixon; B C.M. Dixon. p99 The Hutchison Library. p101 The Hutchison Library. p102 Aquarius Picture Library. p103:T Michael Macintyre/The Hutchison Library; C The Mansell Collection; B Darryl Williams/The Dance Library. p104 The Hutchison Library. p105 Val & Alan Wilkinson/The Hutchison Library. p106–107 Bildarchiv Preussischer Kulturbesitz, Berlin. p108 The Mansell Collection. p109 C.M. Dixon. p110 The British Library. p111 Archivo Mas/Escorial. p112 E.T. Archive. p113T C.M. Dixon; B C.M. Dixon. p114 C.M. Dixon. p115T The Mansell Collection. p116 The Mansell Collection. p117 The Bridgeman Art Library. p118 The Swiss Tourist Library. p120 The Bridgeman Art Library. p121 E.T. Archive. p122 The Mansell Collection. p123 The Mansell Collection. p124 The Bridgeman Art Library. p125T E.T. Archive; B The Bridgeman Art Library. p128 E.T. Archive. p129 The Bridgeman Art Library. p130 The Bridgeman Art Library. p131 E.T. Archive. p132T Musee d'Orsay; B Stuart Robinson/Aquarius Picture Library. p133T Martyn Goddard/English Chamber Orchestra; p134L The Bridgeman Art Library; R E.T. Archive. p135 The Mansell Collection. p137T Aquarius Picture Library. p138 The Mansell Collection. p139 Mozarteum. p140T The Bridgeman Art Library; B The Dance Library p141TL E.T. Archive; TR E.T. Archive; B The Dance Library. p142 Archive. p144 E.T. Archive. p145 E.T. Archive. p147 The Mansell Collection. p148 Theatrical Museum, Munich. p149T E.T. Archive; BL Opera Company of Philadelphia; p150 E.T. Archive. p151L E.T. Archive; R The Mansell Collection. p152T E.T. Archive; B The Bridgeman Art Library. p153B E.T. Archive. p154 The Mansell Collection. p155 E.T. Archive. p156 The Dance Library. p157T The Mansell Collection; B E.T. Archive. p158 C.M. Dixon. p159L The Mansell Collection. p160 Keith Barrett/Opera Company of Philadelphia. p162 E.T. Archive. p163 E.T. Archive. p164 E.T. Archive. p165T The Mansell Collection; B Quarto. p166 The Mansell Collection. p167 E.T. Archive. p168 E.T. Archive. p169 E.T. Archive. p171 The Mansell Collection. p172–173 "Dat's Jazz" p174 The Mansell Collection. p175 The Mansell Collection. p176 The Mansell Collection. p177 The Mansell Collection. p178L C.M. Dixon; R G.S.F. Picture Library. p179T John Hatt/The Hutchison Library; B John Egan/The Hutchison Library. p180 "Dat's Jazz". p181L "Dat's Jazz". R Joel Photographic Library. p182T Alan Blackwood; B C.M. Dixon. p183L Sylvia Pitcher/Joel Photographic Library. p184 Aquarius Picture Library. p185 "Dat's Jazz". p186 British Film Institute. p187 "Dat's Jazz". p188L "Dat's Jazz"; R "Dat's Jazz". p189 "Dat's Jazz". p190T Aquarius Picture Library; B Aquarius Picture Library. p191T Aquarius Picture Library; B. Aquarius Picture Library. p192 "Dat's Jazz". p193 "Dat's Jazz". p194 Aquarius Picture Library. p195 John Downman/The Hutchison Library. p196T Aquarius Picture Library; B Aquarius Picture Library. p198L The British Film Institute; R The British Film Institute. p199T Aquarius Picture Library; B "Dat's Jazz". p201 "Dat's Jazz". p203 Valerie Wilmer. p205 Dover Books. p206–207 Alain Le Garsmeur. p208 Aquarius Picture Library. p209 Capital Radio. p210 Mowtown Records. p211L Aquarius Picture Library; R Aquarius Picture Library. p212L EMI Archives; R Mary Evans Picture Library. p213T Liz Eddison; B "Dat's Jazz". p214 Aquarius Picture Library. p215 Carlos Freire/The Hutchison Library. p216 "Dat's Jazz". p217 Universal Edition. p218 The Scottish Opera. p219 Houston Grand Opera/Jim Caldwell. p220T The Hutchison Library; B The Hamlyn Group Picture Library. p221T "Dat's Jazz"; B "Dat's Jazz". p222 David Brown. p223 "Dat's Jazz". p224 David Browne. p225 The Hutchison Library. p226T David Browne; B David Browne. p227 David Browne. p228T Alex von Koettlitz; B Alex von Koettlitz. p229L Harold Holt; R Antonia Reeve Photography. p230 The Hutchison Library. p231 Dave Brinicombe/The Hutchison Library. p233 Quarto. p235 "Dat's Jazz". p237L Aquarius Picture Library; R Quarto. p238 Dover Books. p239 The Mansell Collection. p240TL Dover Books; TR The Mansell Collection; B Valerie Wilmer. p243 "Dat's Jazz". p245 Dover Books.

Every effort has been made to trace and acknowledge copyright holders. Quarto would like to apologise if any omissions have been made.

Foreword

A character in one of Noël Coward's plays says it is surprising how potent cheap music can be. It is really no surprise at all. The potency of music, 'cheap' or otherwise, has been recognized since prehistoric times. Take the words of many a popular song, perhaps trite and hackneyed in themselves, then give them back to their tune and hear how instantly they take off, on what somebody else has called the 'wings of song'. That's the power, the sheer magic of music.

This is one of the themes running through my book. I hope that in the course of it I will be able to explain something of the anatomy of music, the pitched notes and scales, the melodies, rhythms, harmonies, forms and styles, that are music's sinews and flesh. If I can also convey something of the special marvel and mystery of music, that has excited or comforted people of every age, colour, race and creed, so much the better.

A second major theme of this book is that of the 'unity in diversity' to be found in music around the world. This can easily be demonstrated in the case of musical instruments. For all their apparent differences and divergences, from age to age and place to place, they nearly all adhere to the same few acoustical principles and methods of playing. But this same underlying unity applies with equal force to the music itself. From chapter to chapter of this book, as we move through history from one civilisation to another, and from continent to continent, we find music serving the same common ends; as the accompaniment to ceremony and ritual, as an aid to work and routine, and as the expression of the same universal and unchanging human emotions of love, joy, happiness, anger, sorrow and grief. Indeed, moving from the general to the particular, we need only get a little way beneath the skin of most musical cultures to find similar melodic twists and turns, similar insistent little rhythms, cropping up again and again, usually in relation to much the same situations and moods.

The universality of music leads me to a point which may be a bit of a 'bee in my bonnet', but which often acts against music's best interests. Through the pages of this book, the reader will meet many terms and names that categorize the music of a particular time or place. Some of these (polyphony, renaissance, baroque, classical, romantic, *raga*, *kabuki*, gamelan, jazz, swing, boogie, rock 'n' roll, bop, reggae) have real meaning and are therefore useful, sometimes necessary to know about. Many others, especially those spawned by today's frenetic world of pop and rock music, are not much more than 'buzz' words, and what little meaning they may have often changes almost from day to day. Useful or not, such categories, labels, terms, have a nasty way of pigeon-holing music, of hindering our acceptance and enjoyment of music on its own terms. Unfortunately, they are difficult to avoid.

I have had much help in the writing of this book, not least from the other books I commend for further reading or reference on page 253. I would like also to say thank you to Lois Darlington of Stern's African Record Centre in London, to Gordon Martin of the music department of Wandsworth Libraries, and to my in-house editor, Christine Davis.

Alan Blackwood
London, May 1991

1

Introduction: The Spirit of Music

Musicians and priests at
a sacrifice, from a Greek
painted wooden panel
c. 500 B.C.

Introduction: The Spirit of Music

The word *Turangalîla* is Sanskrit, the classical language of India. It is the title of a symphony by the French composer Olivier Messiaen, inspired by ancient Hindu myths and mysticism. Benjamin Britten's church opera *Curlew River* is based on a traditional Japanese No play. Japanese composer Toru Takemitsu's *November Steps,* however, is a type of concerto for traditional Japanese instruments and modern symphony orchestra. Another Briton, David Fanshawe, went to Africa to record many of the tribal songs and dances included in his rock-inspired *African Sanctus.*

So, with this century, music can be described as a universally shared experience. This book travels the world and goes back in time, showing that in many respects this has always been the case. Music around the world has as many, if not more, points in common than it has points of difference; and while music can have the most private meaning for each person, it can also unite, filling each and every listener with a sense of that shared experience that is beyond the power of mere words.

Bowl of a Greek cup of about 500 BC, inscribed with the image of a young woman dancing to the strains of the auloi, a pair of reed pipes. The player has a band fastened round his face, which presses against his cheeks and helps him to blow.

THE MAGIC OF MUSIC

For most of history, music has been elevated to the highest place in society. In some communities it was the special preserve of the shamans or witchdoctors. It intensified magical and religious ritual. It was the essential ingredient of public ceremony and celebration. It served occasions of grief. It was there for public or private fun. It marked the days. People's lives revolved around music.

No wonder that for thousands of years music was held in awe and sometimes in fear across the world. It comes more naturally and instinctively than any other form of expression, and it can exercise such a grip on the emotions, soothing or driving us to a frenzy, that people have believed it to be a form of magic and the supernatural. Some believed it was the medium – conjured out of thin air by the beat of a drum, the strumming of a harp, the brazen note of a trumpet, the plangent tones of a flute – through which the spirits spoke to them. For others, it was a divine gift, transported from heaven to earth by a bridge that arched across the sky like a wonderful rainbow. For the ancient Greeks, a very poetic race of people, it was a gift of the Muses, daughters of the supreme god Zeus, who inspired men and women to dance and sing. The word itself 'music' (from *mousiké,* meaning 'art of the Muses') comes from them.

Roman mozaic of the second or third century AD, from a villa near Palermo, Sicily, of the Greek Orpheus charming the animals with the sound of his voice and lyre. The power of music on the mind, psyche or soul has been recognized from the earliest times.

NOTES ON A COSMIC SCALE

The ancient Greeks who built the Parthenon and other great monuments of the ancient world, also shared a widespread belief about music that was far more interesting and marvellous than the mythical Muses. They believed in a Harmony of the Spheres, an idea that did not die with them. According to this notion, the sun, the moon and the planets revolved like spinning tops, each of these producing its own musical note determined by the speed of its revolution. Together, these notes created a cosmic musical scale or 'harmonia'. It might not be possible to hear these wonderful sounds, but they were present everywhere, holding life itself in sway. These ideas were linked with other ideas about numerology, or 'the efficacy of numbers' as it was called. According to these theories the universe was ordered by arithmetical proportions, a kind of cosmic geometry. The philosopher and mathematician Pythagoras was one among many scholars and mystics of his time who tried to find a common ground between the Harmony of the Spheres and the theories of numerology. In pursuit of this grand, if nebulous line of inquiry, Pythagoras investigated certain basic facts about acoustics, the science of sound. It might not be possible to get closer than did Pythagoras to unravelling the mysteries of the universe through music, but an examination of some of the scientific facts that we have discovered about sound will certainly lead to a better understanding of the nature of music itself.

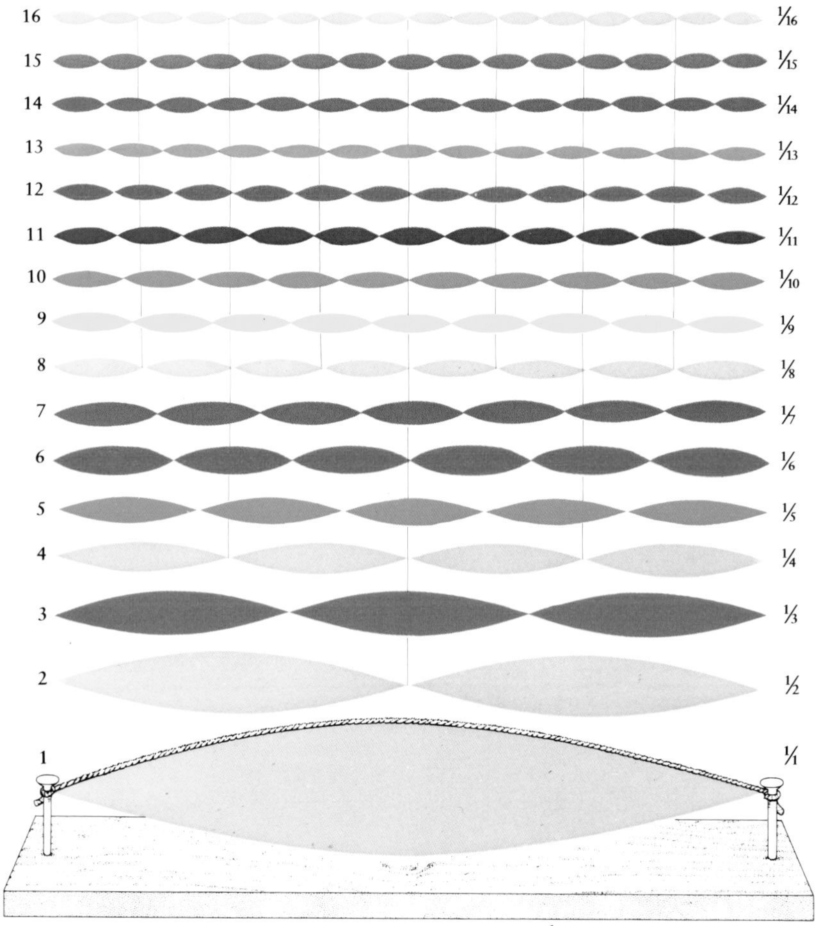
16 1/16
15 1/15
14 1/14
13 1/13
12 1/12
11 1/11
10 1/10
9 1/9
8 1/8
7 1/7
6 1/6
5 1/5
4 1/4
3 1/3
2 1/2
1 1/1

Above: Diagram of a string vibrating simultaneously along the whole of its length and in fractions of that length. The resulting harmonics are known also as 'upper partials' or 'overtones'.

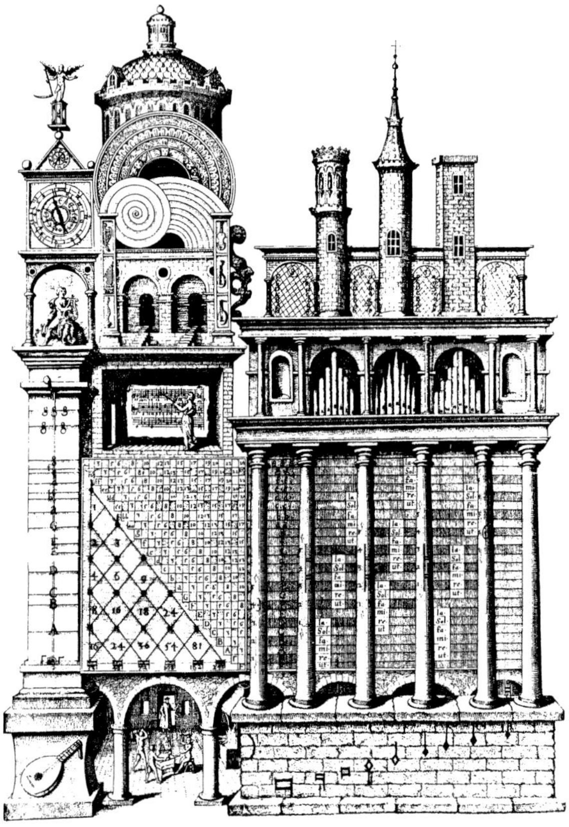

Right: The Temple of Music by the seventeenth-century physician and astrologer Robert Fludd, in which he fancifully relates the principles of pitch and harmony to the mathematical proportions of architecture.

SOUND AND NUMBER

Sound is energy, in the form of vibrations that are transmitted through the air (or it might be water or some other medium) as 'waves' or pulsations. When these waves reach our ears, our eardrums (membranes only a tiny fraction of a millimeter thick) vibrate in sympathy, and our nerves and brain interpret them as sounds or noises.

One easy way to create aural vibrations, and to see what is happening, is by plucking, hitting or stroking a tightly stretched length of string or cord. The cord vibrates, and the resulting sound is heard. Pythagoras probably did much of his work with a monochord, the basic piece of equipment for such experiments, a single string stretched and supported above a sounding board. He knew that the speed or rate of vibration of the string (its frequency) was directly related to the pitch (highness or lowness) of the sound it produced. The more rapid the rate of vibrations, the higher the pitch of the note. He knew also that the frequency and consequent pitch of the sounds were, in turn, related to the length of the vibrating string. From this knowledge, he could work out the ratios between the lengths of the string and the intervals of pitch. It must have been tempting for him, and other thinkers working along the same lines, to believe that they had indeed found the link between the celestial 'harmonia,' the 'efficacy of numbers', and perhaps the key to the secrets of the universe.

HARMONICS

The ratios between vibrating lengths of a string and pitch intervals lead directly to the matter of harmonics (as distinct from musically contrived harmonies, which are discussed later in this section). A string vibrates both as a whole, and in sections (a half, thirds, quarters, fifths, and so on). The distinguishable pitch is called the fundamental, and it is produced by the vibrations of the string's whole playing length. But the vibrating sections are simultaneously producing sounds of successively higher pitch. These are the harmonics. They can sometimes be made to sound more clearly by touching the string very lightly at just the right point. The same thing applies to a vibrating or pulsating column of air in a tube. It vibrates along the whole playing length of the tube, and in sections, so giving the fundamental and all the higher pitched sounds simultaneously. In this case, 'overblowing' can make some of the other harmonics sound.

The way in which the fundamental and other harmonics blend helps give a note its quality, timbre or tone. To take one example, a violin and a clarinet might be sounding a note of exactly the same fundamental pitch; but their timbre, or tone, can still be easily distinguished. This occurs partly on account of their size, shape, construction and design, and partly because of their varying harmonics.

ORGANIZING SOUND

'Organized sound' is as good a definition of music as any. The musician organizes and uses rhythm, melody, harmony and form, much as a writer follows certain rules of spelling, grammar and syntax, or a painter observes the precepts of proportion, perspective, color and line.

RHYTHM Rhythm is the backbone of music, the beat that measures its progress. Almost everybody has a sense of rhythm. A person may be tone deaf, unable properly to distinguish one note from another, but when the band starts playing and the drums start beating, they'll clap their hands or stamp their feet along with everyone else. Some psychologists believe that this innate sense of rhythm is instilled into us by the beating of our mother's heart while we are still in the womb. It is certainly the case that the most effective rhythms fall within the normal compass of

RHYTHM

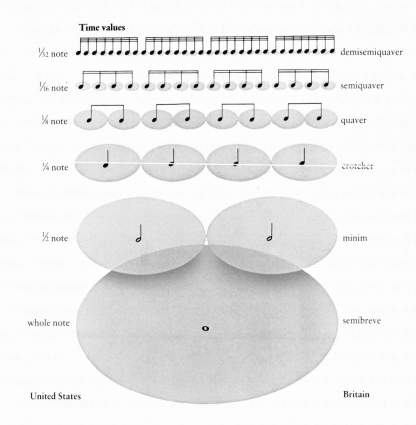

Time values

1/32 note	demisemiquaver
1/16 note	semiquaver
1/8 note	quaver
1/4 note	crotchet
1/2 note	minim
whole note	semibreve

United States · · · **Britain**

Most rhythms are based on a steady beat, divided into regular measures (or bars) of two, or multiples of two, beats (duple time), or three, or multiples of three, beats (triple time), to the bar. Notes of different duration make up a rhythmic pattern within such a framework. Above are the notes representing these duration values, American names on the left and British ones on the right. Each type of note has its corresponding rest or interval of silence, so that even if no note is sounded in a bar, the overall rhythmic beat is maintained. In time signatures, the first (top) figure indicates the number of beats to a bar, and the second (bottom) figure indicates whether they are long or short beats (i.e., 2 means half-note or minim, 4 means quarter-note or crotchet, 8 means eighth-note or quaver). So we can have 2/2, 2/4, 4/4 (common time), 3/4, 6/8, and so on.

Left: Modern Nigerian musicians rejoice in the beat of the drums and the intoxication of rhythm.

KEYS AND SCALES

The Western diatonic system of keys and scales based on the principle that each scale follows a uniform sequence of pitch intervals, whatever its starting note – unlike the old modes, each of which had its own special sequence. The pitch adjustments needed to maintain this sequence through the keys are made by raising

by a semitone (sharpening) or lowering by a semitone (flattening) certain notes. Below are the key signatures and notes of the twelve major scales written out in the treble clef. The scales of F sharp major and G flat major are different in notation but are the same in practice, representing a kind of overlap between the

sharp scales and the flat ones. Note that each major scale has its corresponding minor one; and that these follow their own uniform sequence of intervals. Note also that exactly the same principles apply to music written in the bass and alto or tenor clefs.

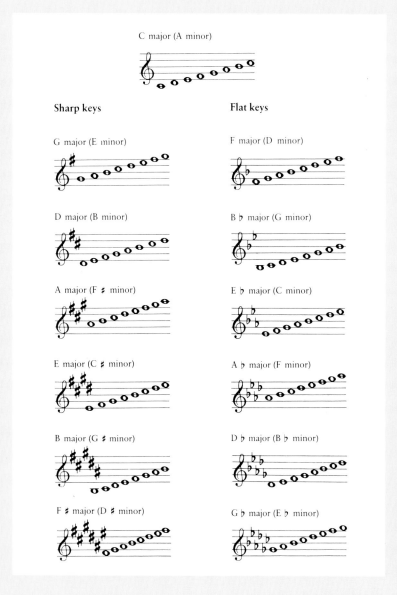

heartbeats, from fast to slow. There is no need to return to the womb, however, to recognize the many ways in which rhythm governs our lives and impinges upon our consciousness. It exists everywhere; in the functioning of our bodies, in the passing of the seasons, the phases of the moon and tides. Everything depends on rhythm, and music most of all.

MELODY Whether it is the chanting of ancient epic poems or dirges, the unfolding of a lovely melody by Mozart or Schubert, or the snappy tune of a song, melody is a succession of notes of varying pitch. At the same time, any melody or tune must exist within the framework of a certain 'tonality'; its notes must be related to a kind of ABC of pitched notes for it to have true musical meaning. The basis for nearly all melody, therefore, is a scale, a pre-existing order of pitched notes, from which the notes of the melody are selected.

This book will look at many different systems of scale: the pentatonic, consisting of five notes, and corresponding, in most cases, to the black keys of a piano; the special type of Indian scales or ragas; the eight-note modal scales which were used for hundreds of years in medieval European music; the diatonic system of twelve major and twelve minor scales which are the basis for most of the best-known melodies or tunes; and such recent developments as twelve-note scales, forming the basis of dodecaphonic music.

Incidentally, 'melody' tends to be regarded as being superior to a 'tune.' This may be because the former is often spoken of in terms of some larger, grander work, like an opera, symphony or sonata, whereas tunes belong to self-contained songs, marches, and the like. Tunes, in fact, can be just as good as melodies. In addition, theme is often used to describe a melody or tune that keeps being repeated, like the theme song of a film, and motif describes a short melodic phrase of three or four notes.

HARMONY Although harmonics and harmony are not the same thing, there is a clear connection between them. For people almost everywhere, the natural harmonics of a vibrating string or column of air in a pipe or tube have suggested certain basic pitch relationships and therefore harmonies. These may be combined to form chords, the simultaneous sounding of two or more notes of different pitch, or they may form part of the weaving together of separate melodic lines called polyphony.

In much simple folk music, harmonies remain fairly static, and they are often not much more than an appendage to the melody. In European and Western 'art' music, on the other hand, harmony grew rapidly in importance, especially once the diatonic system of major and minor keys and scales had been adopted. The diatonic system presents musicians with clearly perceived sets of chords, based primarily on the first, third and fifth notes of each scale (corresponding to the most important pitch intervals in any natural harmonic series). Moreover, the scales allow musicians to transfer or modulate melodies and harmonies from one scale and key to another.

Diatonic harmonies include notions of consonance (a generally euphonious blend of notes) and dissonance (considered as a clash rather than a blend of notes), and there are firm rules about how harmonies should proceed, each harmony leading by an ordered progression to the next. Harmonies of this kind are often of great significance in the shaping of a melody. Indeed, the relationship between many melodies and their harmonies can be so close that even when the melody alone is played, the appropriate harmonies can still be 'heard', guiding the melody alone along. At the same time, different sets of harmonies applied to the same melody can make it sound entirely different.

Despite the textbook rules on harmony, many composers have broken them whenever they've wanted to, and even created new harmonic systems of their own. In the course of this book, such terms as 'atonality,' 'bitonality,' 'polytonality,' 'microtonality' will be discussed as they become relevant.

....

FORM   Children love the repetition in the telling of fairy tales and in nursery rhymes. They represent predictability and security. Conversely, they also love contrasting moments of shock, which make the adrenalin flow. Repetition and contrast, a balance between the expected and the unexpected, are inherent to music. They are the province of musical form. The simplest tune, with its repeated phrases, its ebb and flow, has its own form. The most beautiful, most subtle, most complex music depends equally upon it. Music without form can hardly be said to exist.

It is tempting to compare musical form with the design of a piece of furniture, the construction of a building, the composition of a painting. The difference is that music only exists in time. Musical form, therefore, is really a progression of episodes; repetitions and contrasts within individual rhythms and melodies, perhaps these, in turn, taking their place in the progress of some larger, unfolding pattern or plan.

There are numerous examples of musical form. Two of the simplest are binary or two-part form, in which one melody is followed by another, and ternary or three-part form, in which melody A is followed by melody B, before a return to A. Many songs follow these patterns. Rondo form has the same melody returning many times over. Variation form, which changes in a succession of ways the notes of an initial melody or other idea, is very widespread. In Western music, it has tested the imagination and ingenuity of some of the greatest composers. The special jazz form of the blues is important, because it is the starting point for much of today's pop music. Then there are the intricacies of canon and fugue, or the welding together in sonata form of many contrasting ideas into a whole. The developments over the years are manifold.

Wall-mosaic from Pompei, dating from around the first century AD, showing actors preparing for a play. One of the actors appears to be playing reed pipes similar to those shown on page 12.

MUSICAL INSTRUMENTS

*E*verything so far discussed is theory, but without musical instruments, there can be no music. Using the acoustic principles outlined above, they fashion the 'clay' of mere noise into the musical sounds of pitch, tone and volume, and into the percussive beats of rhythm. A selection of instruments from around the world may, at first sight, seem to present a bewildering variety of objects of different design, shape and size. In fact, it is a case of unity in diversity. They will nearly all be found to adhere to four basic types, whose acoustic principles go back thousands of years into prehistory.

From a strictly scientific point of view, musical instruments are classified into types as follows. Chordophones (stringed instruments) produce their sounds by means of a vibrating string or strings; aerophones (wind instruments) produce their sounds from a vibrating or pulsating column of air in a tube; membranophones (mostly drums) have a tightly stretched skin or membrane that vibrates to produce sounds, and idiophones are a wide variety of instruments, ranging from wood blocks to bells, whose whole fabric vibrates to produce sounds.

It is, however, quite usual to rearrange such a classification into the more familiar one of strings, woodwind, brass and percussion, as the instruments of a concert orchestra are commonly organized. In addition, there are also the keyboard group of instruments, the more recently developed electronic instruments and, of course, the human voice.

STRINGED INSTRUMENTS The Emperor Nero, who was a musician, is supposed to have played his fiddle while Rome burned. If by 'fiddle' an instrument something like a violin is meant, then the story is highly improbable. It is far more likely that the profligate emperor played a harp or lyre. Whatever the case, 'fiddles,' harps and lyres are all examples of stringed instruments. Their vibrating strings give them their basic strumming or humming qualities of sound.

The pitch of their notes is determined by several factors: the effective playing length of their strings (that section of their length that is actually vibrating); their degree of tautness; their thickness. The strength and tone of sound produced by the strings themselves is, however, very weak. So, stringed instruments also need a frame or resonator that vibrates in sympathy with the strings, to augment their

Facing page: Bell in the tower of the thirteenth-century church of the Virgin Mary, Crete, with the clapper held steady by a rope. Bells are one of the most numerous types of idiophone.

Right: Roman mural from Herculaneum, known as 'The Music Lesson'. The instrument is a large lyre. The tuning pegs can just be seen, running along the top bar.

Below: Highly stylized figure of a harpist from the ancient Cycladic civilization of the Greek islands, dating from about 2300 B.C.

volume and improve their tonal quality. Generally speaking, the longer and thicker the strings, and the larger the frame or resonating area, the deeper in pitch will be the range of notes produced.

Harps have a string of a different length or thickness for each pitched note. But most stringed instruments have a limited number of strings, usually of the same length, but tuned to different degrees of tautness. Many more notes can be obtained by 'stopping,' that is, shortening their effective playing length with the fingers.

Another distinction among stringed instruments is between those whose strings are activated by plucking with the fingers (or a plectrum), such as harps, lutes, the Indian sitar, guitars and zithers, and those whose strings are scraped by a bow, which is the case with the medieval rebec and modern violin and its

successively deeper-toned relatives, the viola, cello and double-bass (though their strings may also be plucked).

WOODWIND INSTRUMENTS The Greek philosopher Aristotle warned that the sound of the flute or pan pipes had a seductive and corrupting effect, especially upon women! Whether or not he was right about that, a mellow, caressing quality of tone is characteristic of many woodwind instruments. Originally, they were all made from wood. Today, however, some are made of metal. This does not matter much. It is their design and methods of playing that chiefly distinguish them from brass instruments.

The biggest distinction among woodwind instruments, which has much to do with their tone, is the method of blowing and creating the vibrating column of air in the

A piper ceremonially patrols the walls of Braemar Castle in the heart of the Scottish highlands. It is the Scottish bagpipes which are best-known today around the world; but many versions of this special type of reed wind instrument have existed across Europe, North Africa and the Middle East.

tube or pipe. With pan pipes, whistles, flutes and recorders, the player simply blows across one end of the tube, or across a hole in its side. With other woodwind types, the player's breath activates a thin reed or reeds, whose own vibrations are amplified and modified by the length and bore (diameter) of the tube. The clarinet has a single reed. The various types of shawm, oboe and bassoon have two little reeds that vibrate against each other.

Pan pipes have a tube of a different length, and perhaps also of a different bore, for each note (as a harp has a different string for each note). The great majority of woodwind instruments, though, have a single tube with holes. Opening and closing them alters the effective playing length of the tube, so producing notes of different pitch. With recorders, you do this with your fingers. With most other woodwind instruments, opening and closing the holes is achieved with the aid of keys and pads, to designs dating back to the nineteenth-century German flautist Theobald Boehm.

In European and Western music, the woodwind family provides a very wide range of both pitched notes and tone. Progressing from the highest to the lowest in range of pitch they are: piccolo, flute, clarinet (and bass clarinet), oboe (and cor anglais), bassoon (and double-bassoon).

The saxophone is a reed instrument, but not strictly a woodwind. There is more information about this on page 192.

....

BRASS INSTRUMENTS The very word brass suggests a clamorous or a brazen sound. Such instruments are played by pursing the lips against one end of a tube and blowing at just the right strength or intensity to create sound vibrations inside it. Judged by this method of playing, ram's horns, and even some kinds of seashell, can loosely be classed as brass instruments. The name, though, specifically applies to instruments made from brass or from some other metal. These instruments are, essentially, a long tube (straight or coiled) with a conical (gradually widening) bore, ending in a much wider flare or 'bell.' And all modern brass instruments have a cupped mouthpiece designed to facilitate the method of playing described above.

Traditional brass instruments, consisting of the tube and nothing more, can only sound a limited number of notes. These are the fundamental, or leading notes and, if the player is able to purse his or her lips and alter the breath pressure correctly, some of the

other notes in their own harmonic series. This explains why bugle calls and tunes for old hunting horns have only three or four notes, all in the same key.

The way to give brass instruments more notes is to vary the playing length of the tube. For a long time, the only instrument that could do this was the old sackbut or trombone, with its sliding section of tube. Other brass instruments were sometimes supplied with extra sections of tubing called 'crooks.' Today's trumpets and horns have valves that cut off or introduce extra lengths of tube as they are depressed or released.

In a modern orchestra or band, trumpets, trombones, horns and tubas offer between them a good range of pitched notes, and a good range also of tone, from the bright, piercing note of the trumpet to the much more rounded and mellow sound of the horn.

Above: Traditional New Orleans jazz band accompanying a funeral. To the left, a clarinet, to the right trombones, and in the middle a sousaphone, a type of tuba specially designed for marching bands (see also page 179). Note its wide-open bell.

Above left: Priest sounding a conch shell. These large marine shells can be classed as a basic type of brass instrument, because of the way the player has to purse his lips and blow.

Continued on page 24

Music, Magic and Mysticism

Satanism, witchcraft and sorcery; necromancy and black magic; ghosts, phantoms and spirits; divination and fortune-telling: the whole strange, chilling, sometimes colorful, sometimes lurid world of the occult has been marvelously expressed through music, with its own gamut of magical and mystical connotations.

Beliefs in the supernatural powers of music were widespread in ancient times, a fascinating theme which recurs many times throughout this book. As already mentioned, it was the apparent mystery of music, the summoning of sounds like spirit voices out of thin air, that made it such an awesome experience. Much of this awe, wonder, or sometimes even fear, resided in the instruments themselves, many of which were made from animal (including human) bone, hide or skin. Hitting, scraping or blowing into them summoned the spirit of the dead animal or person and also bestowed upon the player his strength or prowess. The

Above: Fifteenth-century woodcut of the Dance of Death, its grim imagery reflecting the plagues of the Middle Ages, and inspiring music by Liszt and other composers.

Right: The signs of the zodiac, from a fifteenth-century French manuscript. Holst's Planet Suite gives musical expression to some of the age-old notions of astrology.

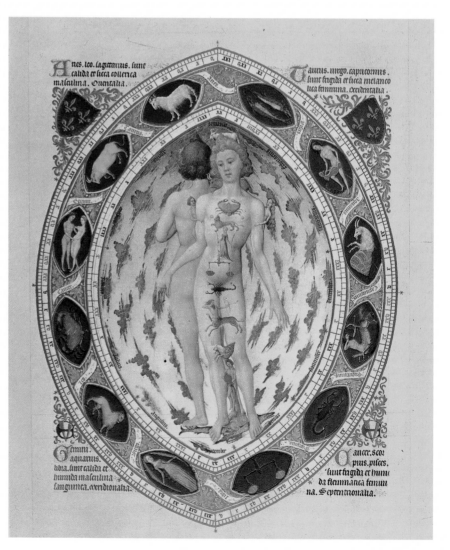

appearance of an instrument was also significant; for example, the phallic shape of a bone or bamboo flute associated it with fertility.

Drums were always held in special awe. Seen as equally sacred or terrifying as the spirits themselves, they were often hidden away by the priests or shamans. In China, large gongs sounded to disperse evil spirits were given splendid names, such as Sir Earthquake and Sir Tiger. Even Bathing in one of them was recommended for the good of the soul. Christianity was not aloof from such beliefs: originally, church bells were rung not simply to call people to worship, but to dispel evil, and their casting of them was steeped in superstition. The blood of an ox was sometimes added to the molten metal. According to one old story, a girl flung herself into the molten metal because an astrologer told her the bell needed a virgin's blood. Church bells are still blessed and named by bishops.

Turning to mysticism, another recurring theme is the wonderful one of the Harmony of the Spheres (see page 13), uniting music with the cosmos – a notion that has never actually been disproved. Some harmonic intervals, notably the perfect fifth (for example, C to G on the piano), are supposed to unite us with the rest of life and the universe, while others, such as the augmented fourth (such as C to F sharp), will damage to the soul. Indeed, the latter interval was once condemned by the Church as *Diabolus in Musica* (the Devil in Music).

Many famous musical works have been inspired by occult themes (these will be looked at in more detail later in the book). Weber's opera *Der Freischütz*, Wagner's *Parsifal*, Tchaikovsky's ballet *Swan Lake*, Stravinsky's *The Firebird*, Mussorgsky's orchestral *Night on the Bare Mountain*, Saint-Saëns' *Danse Macabre*, Liszt's 'Mephisto Waltzes', Alexander

Scriabin's 'Black Mass' Sonata, all dwell upon Satanism and witchcraft. At a more light-hearted level, so do Engelbert Humperdinck's fairy-tale opera *Hansel and Gretel* and Paul Dukas' symphonic poem *The Sorcerer's Apprentice*.

Tartini's 'Devil's Trill' Sonata apparently came to him in a dream. Mozart's opera *Die Zauberflöte* focuses on the occult mysteries of ancient Egypt, while the chilling world of phantoms and ghosts is introduced in two more operas, Wagner's *The Flying Dutchman* and Britten's *The Turn of the Screw*, as well as Falla's ballet *El Amor Brujo* and Ravel's piano suite *Gaspard de la Nuit*. Astrology inspired Gustav Holst's brilliant orchestral suite *The Planets*, Constant Lambert's ballet *Horoscope*, and composer and bandleader John Dankworth's *Zodiac Suite*.

Left: Music in the service of magic; a ritual band in Haiti.

Above: Stage design for the ballet Giselle (music by Adam), which evokes the chill realm of spirits and ghosts.

PERCUSSION INSTRUMENTS Just as rhythm is probably the oldest element in music, so are the percussion family probably the oldest of all instruments. The word percussion, however, is deceptive. It can mean the mighty knock of clapper on metal to produce the joyous clamor of bells, or it can mean the ghostly whisper of a cymbal stroked lightly with a brush. In fact, there is more diversity among percussion than among other groups of instruments, since they include both membranophones and idiophones. One good way to divide them is between those instruments with 'definite pitch' (those sounding a note or notes easily identified by pitch) and those of 'indefinite pitch' (where the pitch of their sound is difficult or impossible to establish).

Many drums have definite pitch, this being determined by the tautness of their skin and the area or volume of the frame or resonator that they cover. In tribal societies, they were often used for communication, because their throbbing sound carries well over distances. They were also used in Greek and Roman galleys, to beat time for the oarsmen. Kettledrums (timpani) are the prime

percussion in an orchestra, being tuned to the key of each piece of music. Xylophones and glockenspiels, of course, are instruments of definite pitch, each block of wood or bar of metal sounding its own note. Bells, too, are usually tuned to a note of a particular pitch, though really big ones sound so many of their harmonics that it is sometimes difficult to pick out their fundamental note.

Percussion instruments of indefinite pitch include side and bass drums, gongs, cymbals, tambourines, triangle, the Latin American maracas, Spanish castanets, wood blocks, scrapers and clappers. In a symphony orchestra, the percussion section is often called 'the kitchen sink department' because it accommodates all these extras, as well as such devices as the wind machine, which is not really a percussion instrument at all (see also page 133).

KEYBOARD INSTRUMENTS The black and white keys of a piano are a familiar sight. They look like notes of music on parade, lined up, waiting to be commanded by a touch of the pianist's fingers. At face value, the piano and other keyboard instruments would seem to form a neat little instrumental class of their

Ceremonial percussionists from the small Himalayan state of Bhutan. The large drum, being struck with the curved stick, is a membranophone. The bronze cymbals are idiophones.

own. In fact, they are a quite disparate bunch, taking certain features from most of the instrumental types already discussed, while adding mechanical ones of their own.

Harpsichords and pianos have arrangements of strings quite like a harp, with the addition of frames and sounding boards to augment and fashion their tone. To this extent, they can be thought of as stringed instruments. In the case of harpsichords, the keys activate a mechanism that plucks the strings, so that they may be considered a type of semi-mechanical harp. With pianos, however, the keys activate hammers that strike the keys, so that they may be thought of as either stringed or percussion instruments. The little keyboard of the celesta operates hammers that strike metal bars, like a mechanical xylophone or glockenspiel, so the celesta can be classed unequivocally as a percussion instrument.

The keyboard of an organ is a different matter entirely. Depressing the keys activates a mechanism that admits air under pressure into a range of pipes. The organ, therefore, is really a type of wind instrument. Large church or concert organs can have hundreds of pipes, ranging in size from a small whistle to monsters bigger than gun barrels. The notes that the bigger pipes produce are so deep in pitch that their soundwaves can sometimes be detected by the ear as individual pulsations. So as to produce notes of varying tone as well as pitch, the pipes are classed either as flue pipes (designed much like a recorder) or reed pipes (closer in design to a clarinet). To sound such a mighty array, the organist operates a whole console, a kind of musical flight-deck, with several keyboards or manuals, a pedal keyboard and stops, which are pulled out or pushed in to select various groups of pipes.

The harmonium and piano accordion (with keyboards) and the harmonica or mouth organ (without one) are three fairly recent spin-offs from the true organ. In each case, thin metal strips that vibrate to produce the notes take the place of pipes.

. . . .

ELECTRIC AND ELECTRONIC INSTRUMENTS All the instruments looked at so far are based on acoustic principles which have been applied for thousands of years. This century, though, the mold has been broken by electric and electronic instruments. Associated words and terms such as 'electro-acoustic' and 'electrophonic' can be a bit confusing and indeed, different authorities do not always use them in exactly the same way. However, some fairly clear distinctions can be made.

In one way or another, electric, or more precisely, electrically-aided instruments still adhere to existing instrumental types. Early experiments included the Neo-Bechstein piano, whose strings were wired up to an amplifier. Today, the most familiar instruments of this type are semi-acoustic and electric guitars, whose vibrating strings are either electrically amplified or converted into electrical impulses before being projected through an amplifier.

True electric or electronic instruments dispense entirely with traditional methods. They generate their sounds purely by electronic means using such devices as oscillators, which produce electric signals or impulses. In

Fourth-century Roman image of the hydraulus or water-organ. Both the Greeks and Romans made these instruments, in which water pressure maintained a supply of air to the pipes. This one appears also to have a simple keyboard below the pipes.

turn, these are modified and amplified electronically. The main distinction here is between instruments that still imitate traditional musical sounds, such as the electric organ and electric piano, and those that create entirely new qualities of sound. These latter include the pioneering Theremin and Ondes Martenot (both named after their inventors), and the modern synthesizer which builds up sounds.

....

THE VOICE Our own voices are so familiar to us, so much a part of ourselves, that we can easily overlook them. Yet the human voice rings out through the long and rich story of

Portable electronic organ as part of the line-up of a modern Jamaican pop group. The sounds may be new, but the keyboard, with its arrangement of black and white keys, has been a familiar sight in Western-style music for hundreds of years.

music around the world. Nor is there any need to be a Callas or a Caruso to make good use of our own vocal equipment: a mother crooning to her baby, or a bunch of revelers having a sing-song around a pub piano, are doing justice to their voices without a scrap of training. Similarly, many successful stars of popular and pop music do not have good voices by academic standards. The secret of their success lies in the use they make of their voices in projecting their personalities.

The source of sound is the vocal cords, two small membranes within the larynx (the Adam's apple), located in the upper part of the throat. When these are slack, breath to and from the lungs passes straight through them. But when they are tightened, breath makes them vibrate; and the tighter they become, the faster they vibrate. The faster they vibrate, the higher in pitch are the sounds. Like the strings of a piano or violin, the vocal cords do not make much sound on their own account. The chest, throat and neck, head, nose, mouth, tongue, teeth, even the sinus cavities around the nose, all act as resonators, giving strength, tone and variety to the vocal sounds. These anatomical factors lend voices more flexibility and subtlety than any other instrument. In speech and in song, there is a tremendous vocal variety around the world.

One obvious distinction is between men's and women's voices. Young boys and girls have voices which are similar in pitch and tone. But at around puberty, a boy's larynx and vocal cords toughen up more than a girl's. Then his voice begins to break, deepening in pitch. The female voice can also become deeper and richer in tone with age, so that, in most cases, it is easy to tell a woman's voice from a girl's. But the changes are not usually anything like the same as in the male voice.

The changing vocal properties produce the various ranges of pitched notes (the vocal tessituras) from high to low: soprano (treble for a boy), mezzo-soprano (half-soprano), contralto (alto), tenor, baritone, bass. A grown man can cultivate a high-toned voice; such singers are called counter-tenors.

MUSIC'S VARIETY

....

*F*rom the grandest ceremony, the most solemn rite, to the most intimate or the most riotous occasion, music has always been on hand. What is interesting is the way people, perhaps separated by thousands of miles or by centuries in time, have employed much the same types of music for the same

functions. Our basic needs and predilections seem to remain much the same, whoever and wherever we are.

. . . .

THE REALM OF SONG The voice in song, with or without instrumental accompaniment, is the music of personal feeling and expression. There are many beautiful songs or ballads for groups of singers; but because of its essentially intimate character, the heart of song lies with the solo voice. Many songs are a part of folk music, discussed on page 28. Others, from the ballads of the medieval troubadours to the songs of Schubert, are art songs, though probably never intended for the formal and serious-minded atmosphere of today's concert recitals. Another treasury of song comes from this century's great songwriters, mostly American, operating in the commercial world of popular and dance music. They may have worked for money, but the best of their songs go straight to the heart of personal feeling and sentiment. As for content, love songs and drinking songs must be by far the most numerous around the world, which says a lot for our priorities and requirements! Beyond

that, people of all nationalities, races and creeds have sung songs of happiness and songs of whimsy (including one famous song about a flea), songs of sorrow, persecution, old age and death.

Above all else, song demonstrates the almost magical power of music to illuminate or give wing to the spoken or written word.

Song of a very different kind has always had a place in magical and religious ritual. This usually takes the form of the chanting of sacred texts. A very good example is the style of chant still regularly heard in Jewish synagogues, a tradition going back thousands of years to Old Testament times. The most important feature of religious singing or chanting is a strict observance of rules and conventions, as part of an unchanging ritual. Sometimes this may extend to the exact time and place of performance. To recite a prayer, to invoke the spirits, at the wrong time or place could be regarded as blasphemy. By much the same token, if the performers, singers or instrumentalists make a mistake, the whole ceremony may have to begin again, for fear of offending the gods.

The joy and pleasure of song, expressed by this choir from Mongolia. The accompanying instruments are an interesting blend of East and West. The women in the foreground are playing types of Chinese folk lute, while a double bass can be seen at the back of the stage.

CEREMONIAL SOUNDS Splendid sounds, from wind and brass instruments to drums, cymbals and bells, are the stuff of ceremony, the sounds for great palaces and churches or the open air. One of the oldest surviving instruments is a big silver trumpet, found in the tomb of the Egyptian pharaoh Tutankhamun. After three and a half thousand years its note is as clear as ever, the unchanging sound of fanfare and ceremony down the ages. Traditionally, brass and drums were also the instruments of warfare. They stiffened the sinews before the fray, while the sharp rattle of drums and the piercing note of bugles and trumpets took the place of verbal commands amid the noise and confusion of battle itself. Away from the battlefield, the huntsman's horn still echoes across woods and fields in many parts of the world. In days gone by, town watchmen also sounded their horns to mark the hour or to announce from the city walls the approach of strangers.

Another group of musicians from Bhutan, this time playing types of the huge horns or trumpets heard also in neighbouring Tibet and Nepal. Horns and trumpets have always featured in ceremonial music around the world.

FOLK MUSIC Voices and instruments find common cause in the vast domain of folk music. Here the word 'folk' means a whole race or community of people, and folk music has grown out of their collective way of life. It is music of the people and by the people and consists mostly of song and dance, the most popular communal activities. Work songs, to accompany and alleviate the burden of such tough jobs as hauling on ropes, breaking rocks or harvesting crops, are also a part of folk music.

The mark of a true, living, folk music tradition is that the music is changing, evolving all the time, often with numerous versions of the same song or dance. Today, old folk music traditions are rapidly dying out, along with traditional and localized ways of life. Arrangements of such music, however attractive, are more like museum pieces than the real thing. Instead, new, urban types of folk music are taking their place. Political protest movements, even the chants of sport fans, are the raw material of today's folk music.

ART MUSIC What is called 'art' music does not just imply music taking elaborate or difficult forms. The rhythms and dancing of many tribal societies can be extremely complicated. Art music is a product of civilizations usually with a highly stratified social or class order, including an intellectual élite. The ancient civilizations of China and India were organized in this way, and both cultivated an élite art music. However, when confined to a certain class, such art music can become over-refined, constrained by too many rules and conventions, and incapable of much further worthwhile development.

European, or Western, art music has avoided this fate. Its dynamic growth, coupled with the dynamic character of Western civilization as a whole, and its willingness to absorb outside influences, whether they be Arabic, Chinese, Japanese, Javanese, black American or Latin American, has kept it vital and alive. Opera, oratorio, symphony, concerto, sonata, the genius of Bach, Handel, Mozart, Beethoven, Wagner, Brahms, Tchaikovsky, Verdi, Debussy and Stravinsky, now the inheritance of musicians and music-lovers of every race and creed, form a large section of this book.

THE INTERPRETATION OF MUSIC

*M*usic is a performing art – something which is easily forgotten when music is on tap from the moment we wake up to the moment we go to sleep again. Until the advent of the phonograph, every performance of a piece of music was a unique event. The performance of live music still is. A vital part of this experience is the musicians' interpretation of how the music should be played – fast or slow, loud or soft, happy or sad. In the days when everybody made their own music, it was hardly given a thought for much of the time. Somebody had a fiddle or a flute, someone else knew the words of a song, and off they went into some folk song or dance just as the mood took them. In contrast, the performance and interpretation of art music is quite a different matter. The notes and other instructions of a printed score are seldom blindly obeyed. Just as no two actors will play the part of Hamlet in the same way, so no two conductors will direct the same account of a Beethoven symphony. Books, magazines, radio and television programs frequently deal with the fascinating and sometimes vexatious questions about how a piece of music should be sung or played, about how closely a performance should stick to the letter of the score, or how deeply the players should probe the inner spirit or meaning of the music that lies behind the little black dots, circles and strokes of the notes themselves.

....

IMPROVISATION Much European art music, in fact, at one time required the performer to add little runs, trills and other figurations to the music as written. It is only a short step from this to improvisation, the art and skill of making up music on the spur of the moment. Indeed, the scores of many concertos have gaps in the music – cadenzas – where originally the soloist was expected to improvise on the themes and other musical material already played. Bach, Mozart and Beethoven were just three great European composers who, from all accounts, were masters of this art. Indian musicians, too, are expected to improvise within the strict forms of a raga. And no jazz musician is worth his salt if he cannot improvise upon a melody, a harmonic chord sequence or a rhythm.

....

STYLE Style in music means a variety of things. It can mean the style of a musical period or of a type of music, involving matters of form, harmony, and instrumentation. Every composer has a style which fits into the music belonging to his or her period, and is also his or her personal idiom. Then there are styles in performance, involving interpretation. The way the great Polish pianist Paderewski played a Chopin nocturne, with all the mannerisms of seventy years ago, would not please many listeners today. In the world of pop music, the styles of six months ago are probably already out of date. All these things, to quote an old popular song, help to make the music go round and round.

Indian dancer from Rajasthan, with very small tinkling bells attached to her hands, similar to crotals. Dance – rhythm in movement – has expressed festivity or ritual since time immemorial.

Music of the Middle East

2

Music of the Middle East

The Middle East has meant different things at different times. Historically, North Africa, Persia (Iran), Turkey (Anatolia or Asia Minor), even the lands of classical or ancient Greece have been included. Much of the land is desert or barren mountain. Yet some of the first civilizations prospered there, next to the life-giving waters of the rivers Tigris, Euphrates and the Nile. Evidence of these ancient communities dates back to as long ago as 10,000B.C., but the climatic disasters of about 3600B.C., recorded in the Bible as the time of the Deluge and of Noah's Ark, destroyed them. Current knowledge of middle-eastern civilization, including its music, dates from after that time.

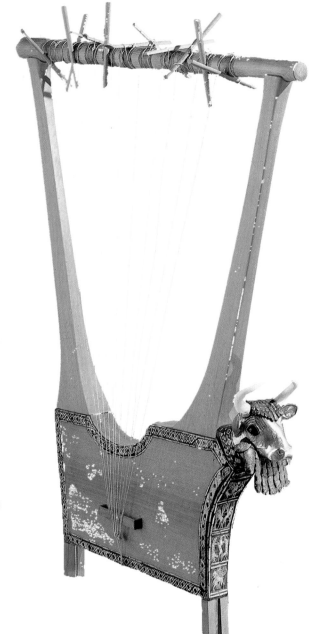

Magnificent reconstructed lyre from the site of the ancient Chaldean city of Ur, dating from about 2500 B.C. These instruments are described in more detail on page 34. Note the pegs for tightening the strings.

MESOPOTAMIA

Mesopotamia means 'between the rivers' – the Tigris and Euphrates. This was the land of the Sumerians, Hittites, Assyrians and Babylonians. Cuneiform script, one of the earliest forms of writing, the shining palaces of Nineveh, and the Hanging Gardens of Babylon, one of the Seven Wonders of the Ancient World, were among the achievements and glories of these civilizations, whose fortunes waxed and waned from about 4000B.C. to 500B.C.

Thanks to the hot, dry climate of the region, some excellent examples of their musical instruments have been preserved more or less intact. These and stone carvings on walls and pillars indicate that the Mesopotamian people had a good selection of musical instruments – harps and lutes, pipes, horns and trumpets, drums and the ubiquitous sistrum, which consisted of a metal rattle. Clearly, music was very important in Mesopotamian civilization, and musicians enjoyed an exalted place in society. In times of war, as when the Assyrian armies captured Babylon about 850B.C., captive musicians were rarely put to the sword or harmed in anyway. They were regarded as highly prized spoils of war rather than enemy prisoners.

In fact, the musicians and scholars of Babylonia must have been remarkable people. The three wise men of the Christian Nativity probably came from Babylonia, or Chaldea as it was also known. They studied astronomy and astrology (the two subjects were virtually the same in those days), and it seems likely that they first conceived the notion of a Harmony of the Spheres, a wonderful cosmic music, unifying the universe. Their ideas about

which is of particular interest. Egyptian deities were frequently associated with animals – the crocodile, cobra, falcon, jackal, ram; they were also associated with the sound of various instruments. The god Osiris, protector of the dead, was 'Lord of the Sistrum.' Its tinkling tones must often have accompanied the chanting of prayers by priests and priestesses.

Much is known about the look of Egyptian instruments and how they were played from the numerous specimens unearthed by archeologists and from the thousands of assiduously detailed wall and papyrus paintings and drawings. But, once again, current knowledge stops tantalizingly short of the one thing we would all like to know – what was the music that they actually played and sang? Hieroglyphics of what is probably a work song, to judge by the regularly repeated symbols, are in existence, but the sound of it is anybody's guess. Scholars have puzzled over the design of instruments, and closely scrutinized pictures of performing musicians and singers, seeking some clue to the systems of tuning, scales, melodies, rhythms and harmonies in both Mesopotamia and Egypt. But while the carved images and vivid paintings remain, the sounds of the music died on the air all those thousands of years ago.

Left: Figure on an eighth-century B.C. Phoenician ivory casket. The pipes may be a type of reed woodwind or trumpets. Playing wind instruments in pairs was a common practice in the ancient world.

Below: Egyptian women playing long-necked lutes at a banquet, from a tomb painting at Thebes, dating from about 1400 B.C.

numerology, and the special significance of the number seven, may also have led them to the seven-note scale (plus the eighth or octave note), which, in various forms, runs through so much musical history.

What kinds of melodies these Mesopotamians played and sang, what kind of rhythms they marched or danced to, is, unfortunately, a closed book. Archeologists have identified one cuneiform tablet as a type of hymn or song, with what are probably both the words and some rudimentary notation signs, but scholars have not been able to decipher them.

EGYPT

The land of the pharaohs, stretching the length of the River Nile from the Mediterranean Sea down into the Sudan, was closely linked with the kingdoms of Mesopotamia by frequent migrations, wars and alliances. Yet, for over four thousand years, its civilization remained unique. The pyramids, the mighty temples at Karnak and elsewhere, and its hieroglyphics, are proof of that.

The Egyptians called music 'joy' and 'gladness,' and symbolized it by a blossoming lotus flower. They loved music for entertainment and pleasure, but it is its religious use

MUSIC AND ARCHAEOLOGY

There are thousands of paintings, stone reliefs, clay and metal models and other images of antique musical instruments in existence. Thanks to archaeology, some specimens of the real thing have also come down to us.

For students of musical antiquity, the most exciting archaeological site has been the so-called Royal Cemetery at Ur, ancient city of Babylonia or Chaldea. Among the other priceless items recovered from this site were eight lyres, or fragments of lyres, dating from around 2500B.C. The largest is over 3ft. (1m) tall. The resonating boxes are gilded and carved in the shape of bulls or bulls' heads – this being a

sacred animal in much of the ancient Middle East. The fact that these lyres were buried with their owners indicates just how much they must have been valued and loved. In one case, the owner's skeletal fingers were found still touching the slack and withered strings. The same site also contained a pair of slender silver pipes, 12ins (30cms) long and each with four finger holes.

Another great moment in archaeology was the opening up of the Egyptian pharaoh Tutankhamun's tomb, which revealed, among all its other treasures, two trumpets similar to the Jewish hasosra, mentioned on page 36. These are 23in. (58cm) and 20in. (50cm) long, one made of bronze and

the other of silver.

As famous as the Royal Cemetery at Ur is the archaeological site at Knossos on the island of Crete, capital city of the once flourishing Minoan civilization. Here some clay bells were found, the oldest known examples of the instrument, dating from around 2000B.C. At Nimrud (the ancient Assyrian capital of Kalakh), a collection of hand bells has been unearthed, this time of bronze, and dating from about 700B.C.

JEWISH MUSIC

From about 2000B.C., when Abraham settled in Canaan, until the time of the Roman Empire, the story of the Jewish people – the biblical Children of Israel – belonged to the history and culture of the ancient Middle East. What distinguished the Jews from their far more powerful neighbors and sometimes their enemies, the Egyptians, Assyrians and Babylonians, was their exclusive way of life. And whereas the other civilizations of the ancient Middle East came to an end, this time-honored Jewish way of life has survived to the present day.

Much of their long history can be heard in the music of the synagogue, particularly in the special kind of religious chanting known as cantillation. During the time that the Jewish people were dispersed among other races and nations, after the sacking of Jerusalem by the Romans in A.D.70, cantillation styles have varied between one community and another, and innovations have crept in. But the essential style can still be heard in a musical tradition stretching back thousands of years, perhaps even carrying some faint echo of the chants of those Egyptian priests and priestesses otherwise lost to us.

Hebrew cantillation not only stretches a long way back, it forms a vital link between the music of the ancient world and the traditions of European music. Using a 'free rhythm' following the inflections of the words being sung to, it consists of fairly brief melodic phrases or motifs, rather than clearly recognizable melodies or tunes. In the synagogue, it is shared between the rabbi and his congregation, the rabbi intoning a phrase, the congregation responding with the same phrase or sequel to it. One other interesting point: Hebrew cantillation is not notated, it has to be memorized. But hand signals remind singers of certain motifs and the general musical direction of the chanting. It is these features which were carried over into plainsong, the earliest important form of European music, which is looked at later in this book.

Sounding the shofar, *or ram's horn, a Jewish ritual going back to Bible times (see also pages 38-39).*

THE LEGACY OF GREECE
....

The ancient or classical Greek civilization, which flourished from the eighth to the first centuries B.C., spread from Greece to parts of Asia Minor (Turkey), and numerous colonies around the Mediterranean Sea. The art and architecture, philosophy, poetry, drama and music of this civilization are considered to be the cornerstone of the Western way of life. But through trade and war, the Greeks were closely tied to the Middle East, and they owed much to the earlier civilizations of Mesopotamia, Egypt, and the remarkable Minoan culture on the neighboring island of Crete.

The Greeks loved music. They sang in choirs, at weddings, funerals and religious festivals (such as the one in honor of Dionysus, the god of wine), and formed the indispensable chorus, singing and dancing at theatrical performances. They sang and danced in the countryside to the fluting tones of the syrinx or pan pipes. There were also many minstrels, singing of legendary heroes and events, often to a lyre accompaniment (interestingly, the words 'lyric' and 'lyrical' come from the Greek lyre and its own song-like associations). But, as Plato and Aristotle made clear in their writings, the Greeks also believed that music had a psychological or spiritual meaning far beyond the actual business of rhythm and pitched notes. It could act on the mind and body for good or ill. They spoke of *nomoi* (laws), according to which specific rhythms, modes and instrumental timbres were deemed suitable for different occasions, or were thought to induce certain moods or states of mind in the listener. In other words, the Greeks tried to codify what we all know to be the case; that there are styles or qualities in music that can make or mar any occasion, also that certain rhythms, harmonies, vocal styles and instruments can appeal to or affect the listener in a wide variety of ways.

A good deal about the organization (the 'organized sound') of classical Greek music can also be inferred from the writings of such philosophers and scholars as Aristoxenus, who lived during the fourth century B.C. The thinking of the Babylonians or Chaldeans, and Pythagoras, regarding the mathematics of sound, lay behind the music. Broadly speaking, most scholars believe classical Greek art music to have been organized in the following manner. The basis of their scales, or modes, were tetrachords (units of four pitched notes),

which generally conformed to the principal notes of a natural harmonic series. When joined together, the tetrachords made up *systema*, or longer sequences of notes, which were more akin to musical formulae, presenting an abstract sequence of pitch intervals rather than actual notes. It was the *tonoi* (from the singular *tonos*, meaning to tighten a string or to tune it) which translated these 'systems' into specific sequences of modes or scales of pitched notes called *harmoniai*.

There is still a good deal of guesswork about how the ancient Greeks put all this theorizing into practice, as well as how they sang and danced. As with the Egyptians, examining their instruments, pictures and other images still leaves us with many questions unanswered. Examples of ancient Greek words and music (using alphabetical signs) only reveal other fragments of the story. But their musical theory is very interesting because of the ways it links up with the medieval modes of early Western music.

Fourth-century Byzantine-Greek marble image of Christ in the guise of Apollo, playing a lyre. Such interesting imagery symbolizes the change from the old Greco-Roman religions to Christianity, and the part played by the Greek modes in the early music of the Church.

Continued on page 40

Music in the Bible

From the opening Book of Genesis right through to Revelations, from the rams' horns that demolished the walls of Jericho to the harp that soothed the brow of Saul, the Bible is full of references to sound and music. These relate in very interesting ways to the whole story of music in the ancient Middle East. The Bible itself, of course, has been the inspiration for a succession of musical compositions.

Below: The Walls of Jericho come tumbling down to the sound of seven rams' horns, in this nineteenth-century engraving.

Below right: Fifteenth-century German altarpiece of Seven Angels with Seven Trumpets (Revelations 8).

One of the most dramatic events in the Bible is the destruction of the walls of Jericho (Joshua 6), brought about, so we are told, by the raucous blast from seven rams' horns and a great shout from the Israelite army. The ram's horn, or *shofar*, is still used in Jewish ritual. There are dozens more references throughout the Old Testament to musical instruments, providing an interesting commentary on the music of the ancient world. Jubal is hailed (Genesis 4) as 'the ancestor of those who play the harp and pipe'; Moses is commanded by the Lord to make 'two trumpets of beaten silver' (Numbers 10). These were probably examples of the *hasosra*, a type of trumpet about 24 in (60 cm) long with a bell-shaped end. They are depicted in many Babylonian and Assyrian stone carvings, and specimens were also found in the tomb of the pharaoh Tutankhamun. Two other instruments that feature in the Scriptures are the *halil*, a woodwind reed instrument,

FALLING DOWN OF THE WALLS OF JERICHO.

sometimes described as a primitive clarinet, and the *sabka*, a bow-shaped harp, represented in many Egyptian tomb paintings.

The Old Testament is also full of references to music-making among the Israelite people. The greatest known musician, not just of Israel, but of the whole of the ancient Middle East, was the charismatic King David. He appears playing the harp or small sets of bells in illuminated manuscripts, in hundreds of stained-glass windows and on hundreds more stone capitals. His playing and singing (Samuel I, 16) soothes the ailing Saul, reminding us of what Confucius, Aristotle and others had to say of music's healing powers (see page 35). Elsewhere, David leads his people in dirges or songs of deliverance. He is also credited (Amos 6) with the invention of musical instruments, and he almost certainly was the author of many of the psalms.

In addition to King David, there is Aaron's sister Miriam (Exodus 15), who leads a dance of joy and thanksgiving after the Crossing of the Red Sea, playing the tambourine or *tof*. This is another familiar instrument of the ancient Middle East, traditionally played by women. And there is the anonymous minstrel (Kings II, 3), who inspired the prophet Elisha to call down the power of the Lord against the Moabites.

The Scriptures have in their turn inspired many great musical works. Apart from *Messiah*, Handel wrote other oratorios on biblical themes, including *Saul, Israel in Egypt* and *Judas Maccabaeus* (with its chorus, 'See the Conquering Hero Comes'). The German Passions of Schütz and Bach are oratorio-like settings of the gospel accounts of Christ's trial and crucifixion. Even Beethoven, not usually thought of in the context of religion, wrote one oratorio, *Christus am Ölberge* (Christ on the Mount of Olives). Mendelssohn composed *Elijah*,

and Elgar *The Apostles*, which features the *shofar*. Walton's vivid *Belshazzar's Feast* recalls the story (Daniel 5) of the feasting and dancing interrupted by the fateful writing on the palace wall. Britten's *Noye's Fludde*, the oratorio *Le Roi David* by the Swiss-French composer Arthur Honneger (1892-1955), Vaughan Williams' ballet *Job*, Saint-Saëns' opera *Samson et Dalila*, Richard Strauss's *Salome* (though based mainly on Oscar Wilde's play) and Schoenberg's *Moses und Aaron* all testify to the continuing fascination of the Bible for composers.

Top: Nicolas Poussin's The Triumph of David. *One of the instruments, incongruously, is a Roman cornu.*

Above: Dancing around the Golden Calf (Exodus 32) to the tap and jingle of a tambourine, or tof.

Instruments of the Middle East

Some ancient middle eastern instruments, such as the *sistrum* and the *shofar,* are now obsolete or reserved only for special occasions. Many more can still be heard and are the ancestors of such familiar instruments of our own day as the violin, guitar, oboe, trumpet and kettledrums.

WIND INSTRUMENTS

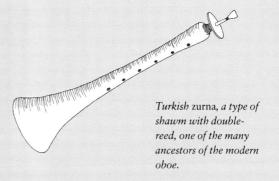

Turkish zurna, *a type of shawm with double-reed, one of the many ancestors of the modern oboe.*

PERCUSSION

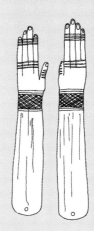

Pair of Egyptian ivory clappers, of about 1500 B.C. In addition to their use as percussion instruments, wall and papyrus paintings show them being used to scare birds.

Egyptian long-necked lute, usually held across the player's waist, the strings plucked with the right hand.

Egyptian angled harp, dating from about the same time as the ivory clappers above. Similar harps existed in ancient Babylonia and Assyria.

STRINGED INSTRUMENTS

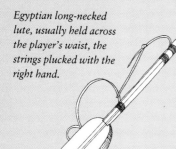

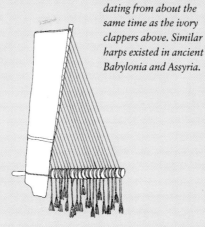

Rebab, *a folk fiddle (played with a bow), still quite common in North Africa, and one of the many ancestors of the violin.*

Instruments are not drawn to scale

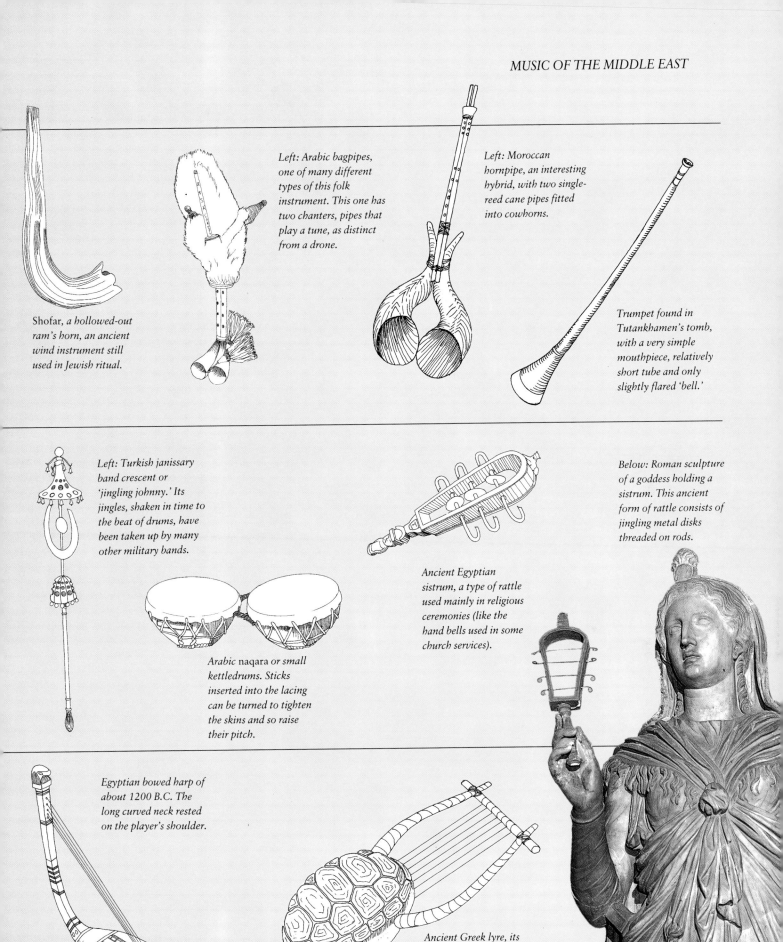

Shofar, *a hollowed-out ram's horn, an ancient wind instrument still used in Jewish ritual.*

Left: Arabic bagpipes, one of many different types of this folk instrument. This one has two chanters, pipes that play a tune, as distinct from a drone.

Left: Moroccan hornpipe, an interesting hybrid, with two single-reed cane pipes fitted into cowhorns.

Trumpet found in Tutankhamen's tomb, with a very simple mouthpiece, relatively short tube and only slightly flared 'bell.'

Left: Turkish janissary band crescent or 'jingling johnny.' Its jingles, shaken in time to the beat of drums, have been taken up by many other military bands.

Arabic naqara *or small kettledrums. Sticks inserted into the lacing can be turned to tighten the skins and so raise their pitch.*

Ancient Egyptian sistrum, *a type of rattle used mainly in religious ceremonies (like the hand bells used in some church services).*

Below: Roman sculpture of a goddess holding a sistrum. This ancient form of rattle consists of jingling metal disks threaded on rods.

Egyptian bowed harp of *about 1200 B.C. The long curved neck rested on the player's shoulder.*

Ancient Greek lyre, *its soundbox or resonator decorated with a large tortoiseshell.*

39

THE WORLD OF ISLAM

The call of the muezzin (or *mu'addin*, someone who proclaims) is a most evocative sound, instantly calling to mind the domes and minarets of the mosque with its gorgeous blue and gold mosaics and elaborate arabesques – indeed everything relating to the art and culture of Islam. This world religion – its name means 'Submission to God's Will' – was founded in Arabia early in the seventh century by the Prophet Mohammed. Two centuries later it already claimed most of the Middle East and North Africa, and in the process it united many older cultures into what is today known as the Arab world.

ARABIC TRADITIONS Traditional Arabic music consists mostly of songs and incantations. Two styles from Arabia itself are the ancient Bedouin *huda*, a form of singing whose

CRUSADERS AND TURKS

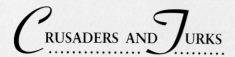

The Crusades were a series of military campaigns by European Christian armies to recover the Holy Land of Palestine (the old lands of the Bible) from the occupying, mainly Turkish, forces of Islam. They took place over a period of nearly 200 years, from 1095 to 1291, and ended in failure. In a much broader context, they can be seen as a triumph for Arabic-Islamic culture, not least where music is concerned.

In the main text, it has been noted how Arabic instruments, such as the stringed *rebab*, and Arabic musical styles, first entered Europe by way of the Moors in Spain. The Crusades, albeit from a different geographical standpoint, reinforced this cultural invasion. Christian knights and soldiers brought home from Palestine and neighboring territories Arabic instruments and a liking for Arabic melody and rhythm. As a result, during the later European Middle Ages, there was a flowering of new or improved instruments of Arabic origin; the bowed stringed rebec; tambourines and drums; lutes, zithers and dulcimers; new types of reed woodwind, and long, slim trumpets with flared bells. Crusading armies began marching to Turkish percussion and pipes, so heralding a new chapter in military music. Then there were the troubadours and trouvères, those colorful and chivalric minstrels of medieval France, some of whom, like Richard Coeur de Lion, had fought in the Crusades and whose style of song carried strong Arabic overtones.

Through the Moors in Spain, through the Crusades, and through the later incursions of the Ottoman Turks, Arabic-Islamic art and music flowed into Europe, influencing and enriching Western music for nearly a thousand years.

intonation and rhythm suggest the peculiar lumbering gait of the camel, and the *buka*, a type of funeral lament. This vocal music was based on scales or modes encompassing many more pitch intervals than exist in conventional Western music, including fractions of a semi-tone called microtones. Such pitch intervals, and the improvisatory nature of the singing, give Arabic song a large measure of its character. To this must be added its nasal sound, whereby the sounds of the voice are projected down through the nose as well as out of the mouth. Old instruments accompanying this traditional style of song have included a kind of tambourine *(duff)*, a frame-drum *(gīrbāl)*, vertical flute *(nāy* or *qussāba)*, and oboe or shawm (known in Arabia as the *mizmār*, but given several other names throughout the Arab world).

ISLAMIC MUSIC With the rapid spread of Islam came that large degree of cultural unity already spoken of. Islamic art and scholarship

Left: Courtyard of a large Egyptian mosque, with the solitary figure of a muezzin, one of the specially trained singers who call the faithful to prayer.

began to take on the character and features by which it is still known throughout the world. From a study of Greek manuscripts, and their own researches, such illustrious Arabic scholars as Al Kindi and Ibn Sina (Avicenna) had a full understanding of the mathematics of sound and of pitched notes. They applied their knowledge to new systems of modes, or scales, for use throughout the Islamic world. Certain instruments, too, came to symbolize Islamic and Arabic art music. Among them was the long-necked lute, which may have originated in Persia, and came to be known either as the *ūd* or, throughout North Africa, as the *qitārā*.

Modes and instruments had mystical implications. Each mode was associated with certain times of day, days of the week, seasons of the year, astrological signs; and the four strings of the *ūd* represented the four seasons, the four phases of the moon, the four alchemical elements, and the four bodily humors, or states of mind.

Below: Algerian woman, in traditional Muslim yashmak or veil, with a large but very simple one-stringed lute, of the type found all over North Africa.

Sudanese religious mendicant, or dervish, dancing himself into a trance-like state. The dervishes are a fairly rare sight these days, always attracting a crowd.

INCANTATIONS, SONGS AND DANCES
Mohammed and other early leaders of Islam had their reservations about music, believing that it could too easily distract the faithful from their devotions. Nonetheless, music has played a prominent part in Islamic worship. Mohammed himself ordained the calls to prayer at specified hours by a muezzin to assert the Islamic faith in lands where there were other far older religions and cults. These calls from the minaret soon grew into quite elaborate musical exercises. The chanted prayers, too, which are in several sections, could inspire some very fine vocal improvisation. Muezzins, therefore, were often highly trained and skillful vocalists and important members of every mosque. With their 'free rhythm' and intonation based on the inflections of the words, these calls to prayer also have points in common with the far older Jewish style of cantillation which, of course, also originated in the ancient Middle East.

Away from the mosque, Islam has inspired other kinds of music. Songs and choruses, accompanied perhaps by flutes and drums and traditionally sung by pilgrims on their way to the holy city of Mecca in Arabia, stand alongside devotional songs associated with the holy month of Ramadan, performed in the cool and peace of the evening after each day's fasting.

Most remarkable are, or have been, the dancing dervishes. The word 'dervish' comes from an old Persian word meaning a poor man or beggar, and Muslim dervishes traditionally took vows of poverty, similar to those of certain Christian, Hindu and other religious orders. They performed ecstatic dances to flutes, fiddles and drums, whirling themselves round and round, to invoke or to express a divine or mystical experience. These rather sensational displays, though, have been condemned by orthodox and conservative Muslims and can only rarely be seen where they might be put on for tourists.

THE MOORS IN SPAIN The influence of Islamic scholarship and art, especially on Christian Europe, has been very strong. From the eighth to the fifteenth centuries, all or much of Spain was occupied by the Islamic Moors of North Africa, and through their science, art and music, they made their presence known and felt far beyond the borders of Spain itself.

In music, Moorish instruments, such as the stringed and bowed Arabic *rebab*, and the twists and turns of Arabic melody, found their way into medieval European music, including the songs of the troubadours and other minstrels, discussed on page 111. Some scholars also suggest a Moorish influence behind English morris dancing. On the face of it, morris dancing seems as English as cricket on the village green, but musical historians cite the way in which the dancers of an old Moorish dance, the 'moresca,' attach small bells to their legs as evidence of a possible link between the two.

Naturally enough, the Moorish and Arabic musical influence rings out most clearly and strongly in Spain's own special flamenco song and dance. There is some dispute about the derivation of the name 'flamenco' which, in a roundabout way, may refer to the time when the old region of Flanders in northern France and Belgium belonged to Spain. But hardly anyone questions the Moorish-Arabic character of the actual music and dancing. Its homeland is the southern province of Andalusia, that part of Spain where the Moors stayed for the longest time. Its basis is a type of singing called *cante hondo* ('deep' or 'serious song'), with its characteristic Arabic repetitions on one note, florid vocal figurations, and pitch intervals. Other similarities lie in the nasal quality of some of the singing, the rhythmic patterns tapped or stamped out by the dancers, and the strumming of the guitar, an instrument derived from types of middle-eastern lute. This thrilling music seems to carry with it the very breath of North Africa.

Two aspects of Moorish rule in Spain. Above: the heritage of flamenco music and dance, here performed by the Paco Pena dance company. Right: Detail of the carving of an eleventh-century casket from Cordoba, combining Arabic and Spanish styles. The figure on the left strums a lute, ancestor of the guitar.

Music of the Far East

3

The Korean kayakeum, a form of long zither.

Music of the Far East

The Far East is separated from the Middle East by the vastness of central Asia that for thousands of years kept these regions of the ancient world almost entirely apart. Yet they share important musical characteristics. Oriental scholars followed lines of inquiry into the nature of musical sound remarkably close to those of ancient Mesopotamia and Greece. Also, in both parts of the world, the skillful performer has always been music's guiding light. Ways of playing a piece, of subtle improvisations upon established forms, are what have counted most.

There is, however, one musical ideal that is strongly associated with the Far East. This is to produce the maximum effect with the minimum means. It is, in fact, an esthetic ideal often found in oriental art; in the brush strokes of Chinese calligraphy, or the carefully chosen objects and patterns in a Japanese Zen Buddhist garden. It gives to much oriental music its chamber-like qualities, its concentration on the tone of individual instruments or notes, with all the spiritual meaning they are supposed to convey.

The austere serenity of a Japanese Zen Buddhist garden, in which every object invites deep contemplation. The same concentration on essentials is an aspect of much oriental music.

CHINA

*W*hen Marco Polo returned home in about 1297, nobody would believe his account of his years in far distant Cathay. Yet China already boasted a civilization and a way of life at least as old as the pyramids of Egypt. From the sixteenth century, as Europeans opened the sea routes to the Far East, so the treasures of Chinese civilization, the beautiful ceramics, paintings, metal and stone work, became the wonder and envy of the West. 'Chinoiserie' became a craze. Modern China, with a thousand million people, may no longer be a place of such mystery and wonderment, but its venerable past, and the sophistication of Chinese thought and esthetics, live on in its art and its music.

MUSIC AND CHINESE PHILOSOPHY

China's ancient musical past can be traced back to some bronze bells, stone chimes and small clay wind instruments (similar in shape and size to an ocarina), thought to date from around 2000BC. The earliest surviving written records relating to music, the *Li Chi*, a collection of ritual verses, and the *Shih Ching*, the texts of over three hundred songs, date from about 1100BC. The antiquity of these musical traditions is brought home to us when we reflect that European or Western music did not begin for well over another thousand years after that.

Chinese philosophers and musicians studied the mathematics of musical sound, just as Pythagoras did, and thought about music along lines very similar to those of the ancient Greeks (see pages 14 and 35). Indeed, a short time before Plato and Aristotle, China's own two most celebrated philosophers, Lao-tzu (the half legendary founder of Taoism;) (*c.* 604–531BC) and Confucius (K'ung Fu-tzu;) (551–479BC), were stressing music's moral values, both for the individual and as an aid to the good ordering and regulation of government. On a more metaphysical or mystical level, they believed music should be in tune with the deeper harmonies of the universe, with the rhythms and cycles of nature, and with what they conceived to be the balance between heaven and earth, between female and male forces, the *yin* and the *yang*.

PITCHES AND SCALES

The theoretical basis for Chinese art music were the twelve *lü*, the 'standard' or 'fundamental' pitches. So much importance was attached to them for the

Sixth-century image of a Chinese deity or 'celestial being', playing a type of long-necked lute, which appears to be a cross between a true Chinese ruan *and an Indian* tambura.

teaching of music that they were at one time laid down in government records, just like weights and measures. These *lü* correspond approximately to a twelve-note chromatic scale (that is, all the notes on a piano keyboard between one note and the same note an octave higher) and were worked out by acoustical methods. Legend has it that they were the cries of the phoenix, the mythical bird re-born from the ashes of a fire. According to Chinese metaphysics, they were ordered, half of them representing the female *yin*, and half the male *yang*, so that a perfect balance of spiritual forces was maintained.

Individual scales were selected from the master notes or tones of the *lü*. Best known of these is the five-note pentatonic scale, corresponding in pitch relationships to the black notes on a piano keyboard. This type of scale, and the tunes based on it, are thought of as being typically Chinese. In fact, the pentatonic scale was widely used in the ancient world, and still is in many folk music traditions. The Chinese, however, invested their pentatonic scale with great extra-musical significance. Its five notes stood variously for earth, metal, wood, fire, water; center, east, west, south, north; salt, bitter, sour, acrid, sweet; yellow, white, blue, red, black; or the planets Saturn, Venus, Jupiter, Mars, Mercury.

THE SOUNDS OF INSTRUMENTS In addition to bronze bells, stone chimes and clay wind pipes already mentioned, other time-honored types of Chinese instrument include the lute or *p'i p'a*; two types of long zither, the *ch'in* and *she*; flutes, such as the bamboo *ch'ih*, and pan pipes; the mouth organ or *sheng* (which has nothing to do with today's mouth organ or harmonica); and trumpets (including some remarkable types constructed like a telescope). In addition, there was an enormous variety of cymbals, gongs, drums, clappers and scrapers, and many more bells of widely differing shape and size.

For thousands of years, all of these instruments were treated with great reverence and invested with mystical or metaphysical meaning. They 'spoke' with the accents of the materials they were made from, which evoked the spirits of one or other of the seasons, or of such natural phenomena as wind, fire, water, thunder and earth. So, the silken strings of the *ch'in* and *she* zithers evoked the spirit or essence of summer and of fire, while the pan pipes sang of spring and mountain air.

The Chinese above all loved bells, gongs, cymbals, stone chimes and wood blocks. As idiophones, they were made from a single material, and so 'spoke' with a particularly strong, undivided and emphatic voice. Also, they could be assembled in groups: Chinese musicians could combine the mystical tone of the instruments with the broader metaphysics they attached to pitch intervals and scales.

When the importance of Chinese musical mysticism and metaphysics is combined with the huge significance placed on individual tones, the fact that the emphasis on melody is placed far above rhythm and harmony is explained. The longer each note was sounded, the longer and more complete the intervals of silence surrounding them, and the greater the attention given to each, so the deeper was the message received by the listener.

MUSIC AT COURT Music at this elevated level belonged to temple ritual or to the imperial court. Court music (*ya-yüeh* or 'elegant music') also reflected the extreme formality of imperial and aristocratic life. There was music for banquets, official receptions, festivals, the emperor's birthday and military parades. Although this has been the

ORIENTAL TEMPLE BELLS

The French poet Charles Baudelaire said that bells 'excavate heaven.' No doubt he was thinking of bells ringing in churches and cathedrals. But the bells of China, Korea, Japan and elsewhere in the Far East have just as splendid a history.

There were probably bells of various kinds (including the very small, tinkling, spherical type known as crotals) as long ago as 3000 B.C. In ancient China, bells played a vital part in theoretical studies, establishing scales and pitch relationships. The spread of Buddhism, to China, Korea and Japan, in the third century A.D., raised bells to a place of spiritual and mystical importance, as did the spread of Christianity in Europe. Buddhists likened the deep, sonorous boom of large bells to the sound of the sacred syllable 'Om.' This encouraged the casting, in bronze or iron, of larger and larger bells, some of which weighed well over 70,000 kg (150,000 lbs). Housed in monasteries and temples, these mighty bells differ from Western-type models. In general, they are more elongated than European bells with their distinctive flared rims. Also, the great bells of the Orient do not usually have a clapper. They hang stationary and are struck on their rim with a hammer.

A true oriental specialty is small wind bells, strung out like necklaces along the eaves of many temples and pagodas. These do have little clappers, which strike the bells as the wind blows across them. Like the strings of the aeolian harp, which vibrate in the wind, it is a pleasing fancy to think of them as speaking with the voice of the wind.

Antique Chinese stone image of a god playing the ch'in, *a traditional type of Chinese long zither, similar to, but simpler than, the Japanese* koto.

case in royal courts and households everywhere, in the imperial Chinese court, formalities did not stop with styles or categories of music appropriate to this or that occasion. The number of musicians, singers and dancers involved, and how they were arranged around a room or courtyard, corresponded to the hierarchy of court life just as clearly as clothes and uniforms. The emperor enjoyed quadrophonic sound, with his musicians placed around him according to the four cardinal points of the compass. Lords were allowed musicians at three compass points, while lesser mandarins and other court officials had to be content with just a small group of instrumentalists and singers in one corner of the room.

Such rigid formalities did not indicate a totally closed and inward-looking society. From about the first century AD, Buddhist missionaries arrived in China, bringing with them the music of India, Burma and other parts of Asia. Within a few centuries, the Islamic world had also made its presence felt. A generally tolerant Chinese court and society quite happily accepted these outsiders, and musicians, singers and dancers came from places as far away as Persia and Samarkand. Yet while China's size allowed it to absorb outside influences easily, the antiquity of its art and

institutions tended to stifle change.

....

CHINESE OPERA Opera in China, like opera in the West, has been a combination of drama and music. Beyond that, the history of Chinese opera and Western opera have little in common. To begin with, opera has always had a much broader meaning for the Chinese than for Westerners, since it is virtually synonymous with all kinds of theater. For centuries, in its various forms, it was the chief entertainment of all the Chinese people, from the emperor to the humblest of his subjects.

Court opera was extremely formal, with written librettos or scripts, and a form of notated music. The music was generally slow and dignified, with great emphasis on melody and subtle instrumentation. Indeed, the same basic song might be repeated, with variations, throughout a five- or even a six-hour performance. A particularly aristocratic and formalized kind of opera, *k'un ch'ü*, specialized in male falsetto singing.

Away from the imperial court and the homes of the aristocracy, there were multifarious types of folk opera, categorized by region and local dialect rather than as the work of any particular poet or musician. These kinds of regional opera were usually presented by itinerant troupes, like the mummers and

The formal grace and beauty of old Chinese court opera. The musicians on stage are playing a variety of lutes, including the p'i p'a; also the long zither, or ch'in.

jongleurs of medieval Europe (see page 111), often at times of local religious festivals. They relied on improvisation, often engaged in plenty of slapstick, and the pace was comparatively brisk.

What is known as Peking Opera is a relatively recent (late eighteenth century) amalgam of many aspects of all these styles. It has continued the venerable traditions of Chinese opera, notwithstanding all the social and political eruptions of this century, right up to the present day. The repertory is divided mainly between *wen*, love stories or domestic dramas, and *wu*, the more swashbuckling

part in Chinese opera.

CHINESE SONG In addition to opera, China has a long tradition of song, much of it provided by troupes of minstrels. One very popular entertainment of this type is usually translated as 'the extended tale.' These are narratives of historical or legendary sagas, and they can be very extended indeed, spread over two or three months, with episodes of an hour or two at a time, like some long-running television series. There are also much shorter sung ballads, or drum songs, so-called because the singer usually accompanies himself with

By comparison with the performance on the previous page, a lively moment in Chinese folk opera. Note the two giant trumpets symbolically raised behind the dancer, as well as the large drum to the right of the stage.

adventures of soldiers or brigands. Both types rely heavily on stock situations and characters, such as an old man and woman, a hot-blooded young soldier, a virtuous wife, and a flirtatious girl (female parts being traditionally taken by men or boys, since, until recently, there were no mixed companies of players). There are very few stage props in Peking Opera, but the appearance of the players, their special make-up, their gestures and facial expressions, and the types of melody they sing, all contribute strongly towards a sense of place and action. Performances are accompanied mainly by percussion instruments, including clappers, which have always played a prominent and important

clapper and drum.

JAPAN

Japan's geographical situation has very largely shaped its history. Its relative proximity to China, Manchuria and Korea has exposed it to strong foreign influences. Its separation from the Asian mainland, however, has allowed it to distance itself from its oriental neighbors and maintain a language and way of life unmistakably its own. The recorded history of Japanese music is not nearly so ancient as that of China. Nevertheless, it still pre-dates Western music by hundreds of years. More bronze bells date back probably to the third century BC, while tomb figurines, depicting musicians playing a variety of instruments, date from the fourth century AD. However, for the next few hundred years, there are some interesting parallels between the development of Japanese music and early Western music. While the main stimulus to Western music came from classical Greece, the older instrumental and theoretical traditions of China provided the basis for Japanese music. And while early Western music was much beholden to the Church, so Japanese music was largely shaped by Shintoism and then Buddhism.

Today, Japan is the most westernised Oriental nation, with a dynamic economy (that in many activities far outstrips other parts of the industrialised world), high-tech industries and its densely-packed cities. Yet the Japanese people have managed to keep alive their great cultural heritage, especially that of music and theater.

COURT MUSIC The Japanese word for court music, *gagaku*, means exactly the same as its Chinese equivalent, 'elegant music;' and this old aristocratic music of Japan had a good deal in common with that of China. The instruments were much the same (allowing for different names and some modifications in design), and the Japanese borrowed the basic Chinese scale of twelve *lü*, though the system of modes they extracted from it was their own. The Japanese also encompassed their court music with just as many rules and conventions. *Gagaku* musicians received special training and formed themselves into élite schools or guilds. The music itself was classified according to instrumentation, mode and rhythm. Compositions were also defined as 'small pieces,' 'middle pieces' and 'great pieces,' according to how long they lasted.

The character of Japanese court music was steady, relaxed and graceful. Instrumentalists were expected to have the skill and experience to make it all look and sound easy, without showing off. Singers likewise had to sing naturally and with perfect control, and not indulge in any artifice, such as too much vibrato. In performance, the musicians usually began slowly, in free rhythm, gauging each other's mood and style, like a small group of intellectuals settling down to a good conversation. Then they would establish their tempo and the performance would proceed in its steady and graceful style.

SHINTO AND BUDDHISM The Japanese imperial court patronized the two major religions of Shinto and Buddhism, and their music became closely associated with *gagaku* court music.

Shinto ('The Way of the Gods'), involving ancestor and nature worship, was the far more ancient of the two, its origins lost in myth and legend. Music at court and in special shrines and tabernacles featured gongs, stick drums, jingles and high-pitched flutes, and was often accompanied by ritual dancing.

Buddhism reached Japan, by way of Korea, during the fifth or sixth centuries. Its musical specialty was chanting, or *shōmyō*, based on a catalogue of short melodic phrases or motifs. Though each was unchanging and codified by name, they could be strung together in various ways to form larger passages of chant. Such a system of chanting, coupled with free rhythm, has prompted some scholars to believe that there may have been some common musical ground between Buddhist *shōmyō* chant and ancient Hebrew cantillation (see page 34). After all, Buddhism began in northern India, which is much closer to the Middle East than to the Orient.

Above: Large, double-headed ceremonial drum housed in the Meiji Shinto shrine, Tokyo. Large gongs and bells are also housed in Shinto and Buddhist shrines.

Below: Japanese priest, head concealed beneath his wicker helmet, playing the traditional type of bamboo flute, or shakuhachi.

Performance of a No *play in Kyoto, Japan. The formality of this type of theater can be gathered from the placing of the actors and musicians. Instruments include drums and flutes.*

THE CHRISTIAN CENTURY It is worth noting that during the sixteenth and seventeenth centuries, Portuguese Christian missionaries reached Japan, bringing with them such Western instruments as virginals and viols. There are even records of small keyboard organs being made in Japan. But the missionaries were then persecuted and expelled, bringing the 'Christian Century' to an end, and little more is heard of Western music for another two hundred years or more.

NO THEATER Japan, like China, has had a strong and rich tradition of musical theater. Indeed, in terms of variety, Japanese musical theater probably offers more than its giant mainland neighbor.

The classical *No* or Noh theater is the most refined and sophisticated form of all Oriental theater and drama. The name means 'ability' – ability to convey the deepest and the most elevated dramatic situations with the greatest economy of means. No theater dates from the fourteenth century, and the work of two actor-musicians, Kiyotsugu Kan'ami and his son Motokiyo Zeami. The character of the drama, usually centered around some kind of intense personal crisis, is very similar to classical Greek tragedy, as is the empty or near empty stage, and the masks worn by the actors. The spartan setting and the deadpan masks are intended to focus and concentrate the drama in the minds of the audience, and to invest every word, every gesture with a maximum of significance.

The music backs this up. The *shite*, or principal actor, alternately speaks his lines, sings and dances, and every note, every movement is pregnant with meaning. There is also a small chorus who sing in unison, and there are accompanying flutes and drums. The percussionists are highly skilled at combining free rhythm with a strict metrical beat, an effect designed to heighten the dramatic tension still more. A novel feature are large clay vases often placed beneath the stage, to give added resonance to words and music.

It has to be said that the pace of No theater can sometimes seem labored and slow, unless the significance of every dramatic and musical point is fully understood.

PUPPET THEATER Traditional Japanese puppet theater has something of the same dignity and restraint as No theater, but on a smaller scale. Dating from the sixteenth century, two very old traditions – those of storytelling to flute accompaniment and puppetry – are combined. The Samurai warrior's code of honor and duty inspires much of the theater's repertory.

Musically, the most striking feature of Japanese puppet theater, in its early days at any rate, was the accompanying samisen, a relatively modern lute-like instrument. In the hands of a skilled player, it provided a novel range of instrumental effects; plucked notes (pizzicato), arpeggio runs up and down the notes of a mode, portamento or a certain sliding from one note to another, and the sounding of chords.

KABUKI THEATER 'Kabuki' literally means 'unusual;' but in practice, it means 'popular.' Also dating from the sixteenth century, it is more of a cross between opera, pantomime and circus. It is based on stylized dances, probably Shinto in origin, but popularized or vulgarized to make them more openly erotic. Indeed, the erotic nature of early kabuki performances led to a ban on women on stage, which lasted into this century. The kabuki popular theater repertory is wide, ranging from historical adventures to domestic drama. Far more striking – and in contrast to No theater – is the fast pace of much of the action. There is also plenty of color, dancing and music. Many productions have musicians, singers and instrumentalists, both on stage and off-stage. Dances are accompanied by drum and flute, or by voice and samisen. Songs, with samisen accompaniment, may help to set the mood of a scene, or they may serve as a kind of musical soliloquy, expressing the private thoughts and feelings of one of the characters in the play. Drums, gongs, bells and clappers announce the start of the proceedings and also punctuate other episodes in the performance.

JAPANESE INSTRUMENTAL MUSIC Both the samisen and the end-blown, or vertical, flute (shakuhachi), widely used in Japanese theater, are highly regarded in their own right, and there is a large repertory of solo music for both of them. But in the field of instrumental music, pride of place must go to the koto, and to the special body of music (sokyoku) it has inspired. This long zither is basically similar to the Chinese ch'in or she; but it can fairly be taken as the living symbol of Japanese art music. For hundreds of years, the koto was the favorite instrument of the imperial court and the aristocracy, its playing cultivated by high-ranking ladies, much as ladies in renaissance and baroque Europe played the portative organ or harpsichord. Various schools of koto playing modified the design and construction of the instrument (so that it exists in several forms), and each school also developed its own systems of tuning and playing methods. In the seventeenth century, much of the repertory was notated and codified, though, as with almost all Asian music, it should always be memorized and played by ear. There are songs with special koto accompaniment, and a special chamber music ensemble (sankyoku) features samisen and flute and a koto player, who may also sing. There is also a substantial repertory (danmono) of pieces for solo koto.

Continued on page 56

THE ORIENTAL FACTOR

'Chinoiserie,' the Western fascination with Chinese and other oriental arts and crafts, has a strong echo in music. At the start of the nineteenth century, Weber wrote his incidental music to a play about the legendary Chinese Princess Turandot. He included in it the characteristic oriental pentatonic (five-note) scale, which Hindemith later amplified with much relish in his Symphonic Metamorphoses of Themes by Weber.

The same tale of the cruel princess finally conquered by love was the subject of Puccini's last and perhaps greatest opera, as well as the lesser-known opera by Feruccio Busoni. Puccini had earlier turned to Japan in Madame Butterfly, a touching and tragic counter-weight to Gilbert and Sullivan's comic lampoon of Japanese culture in their popular operetta, The Mikado.

Mahler's song-cycle Das Lied von der Erde (The Song of the Earth) is a setting of Chinese poems (in German translation), with more echoes of those same pentatonic notes breaking through in places. Debussy, fascinated all his life by oriental art and music, wrote one of his most impressionistic piano pieces, Poissons d'or, after seeing a Japanese lacquered screen decorated with golden fish. Hans Christian Andersen's story of the Chinese clockwork nightingale inspired Stravinsky's opera The Nightingale, with its many evocative touches. The same composer later set some Japanese lyrics for soprano and piano. Britten's own love for oriental art and music comes out in his chamber opera Curlew River, based on Japanese No theater, and in his ballet The Prince of the Pagodas. At a much deeper level, oriental religion and philosophy run through the musical thinking of the American John Cage.

The English soprano Eva Turner in a scene from Turandot.

The Music of Australasia

Australasia – Australia, New Zealand, Tasmania and contiguous islands – has its own unique fauna, in the shape of the kiwi, the kangaroo, the platypus and other marsupials. It is also a cultural mix of the near prehistoric and the mechanized bustle of the twentieth century. All this contrast and variety is echoed in Australasian music.

Before European colonization in the eighteenth century, the way of life of Australia's Aborigines had probably changed little in tens of thousands of years. Their music-making, like that of the Amazonian Indians and other communities left undisturbed until recent times, tempts us to believe we really are hearing musical sounds of the remotest past. This may or may not be the case, but what is certain is that Aboriginal music is not simple. Singing, linked to magical ritual, is paramount. Some of it, usually beginning on a high note and descending to a low one, and punctuated by howls, grunts, snorts and whistles, may sound primordial, but other singing includes a kind of organum (singing in parallel intervals apart) and polyphony. Some vocalists can even manage to sing two notes at once. There are also polyrhythms (the simultaneous use of two or more metric beats).

Aboriginal instruments, made from wood, bark, bamboo, seed pods, reptile or fish skins, include clappers, 'concussion sticks' to beat on the ground and bull-roarers. Best known, of course, is the *didgeridoo*, which has become in its way as much a symbol of Australia as the kangaroo and the boomerang. It is a pipe, of varying length, fashioned from a tree branch already partially hollowed out by termites. Skilled players can sound its basic drone and vocalize or verbalize at the same time, making it a kind of 'talking' instrument. Some also employ 'circular breathing', taking in short breaths through the nose while continuing to blow out through the mouth – a technique shared by just a few other remarkable wind players around the world.

The Maoris of New Zealand belong to a quite different race

Above left: Sunrise at Ayers Rock, for thousands of years sacred to the Aborigines.

Above: A very large didgeridoo, played by a member of the Aboriginal Island Dance Theatre.

of people, the Polynesians, inhabitants of many of the Pacific island groups. Their singing and dancing is much more extrovert and vigorous. The *haka*, for example, is a war-like 'posture' dance with shouted phrases and responses, accompanied by bellicose gestures and grimaces. The *poi*, by contrast, is a much gentler dance performed by women swinging colored bangles around their heads. There are also *karakia*, rapid magical incantations delivered in a monotone, whose 'singers' must be word perfect or, so it is believed, they can bring disaster. Maori instruments include a resonating wooden gong, trumpets made from shells or wood, used for signaling, and flutes and whistles, some made from the teeth of certain whales or sharks. It is worth mentioning that on other Polynesian islands they have nose flutes, played in this way because of the ancient belief that breath from the nose has more spiritual power than that emanating from the mouth.

The life of the early colonists in Australia and New Zealand, as in North America, left little time for music, though the Australian settlers did produce such fine songs as *Waltzing Matilda*, which has long been the country's unofficial national anthem. Since then, Australia and New Zealand have both made their mark in world music. Nellie Melba, Joan Sutherland and Kiri Te Kanawa have each in turn conquered the world of opera. Composers Percy Grainger (1882-1961) and Arthur Benjamin (1893-1960) settled in Europe and left their homeland behind in musical terms; Malcolm Williamson (born 1931) has also lived in England for nearly forty years, but Don Banks (born 1923) returned home to preside over music at Canberra University after studying in Europe. The Sydney Opera House, one of the most original structures of modern times, symbolizes the vitality of music in Australia today.

Above: Maori dancer from New Zealand. Maori festive and ceremonial dancing is among the most lively and colorful to be seen.

Below: Percy Grainger as a young man. There is a museum dedicated to him in Melbourne, his native city.

Percy Grainger

MONGOLIA AND TIBET

．．．．．．．．．．．．．．．．．．．．．．．．．．．．．．．．

Land-locked Mongolia and Tibet stand on the fringes of China. One is now a republic, the other is politically a part of China; but both have an ancient way of life that owes little or nothing to any neighboring country, while sharing some common ground.

The original Mongols were among the great nomads of prehistory, moving westward to the Ural Mountains and beyond, eastward to the Bering Strait and, almost certainly, over the strait and on across the American continent. Their religion was shamanistic, a belief in a world peopled by spirits. Their music, what remains of it, is a relic of all this. It is primarily vocal, although some of it is best described as semi- or quasi-vocal, with nasal recitation, featuring very rapid, high-pitched utterances, growlings and other stylized imitations of animals and such natural phenomena as rain, wind and running water. This extraordinary kind of solo vocalizing also involves the simultaneous sounding of two notes, the fundamental pitch of the note and one of its harmonics, achieved by a special fashioning of the mouth. Mongolian instruments include a type of spiked fiddle,

Tibetan Buddhist trumpeters in their saffron robes. Compare them with the Bhutanese players on page 28.

various whistles and the Jew's harp. This miniature instrument, twanged against the teeth and lips, has no special connection with Jewish music, and nobody is quite sure how it got its name. Different versions of the Jew's harp have existed for centuries in many parts of Asia and Europe.

The music of Tibet has more variety. Much of it is connected with its religion, nominally Buddhist, but shot through with remnants of ancient shamanistic beliefs. In the monasteries high up among the eternal snows of the Himalayas, the hours are marked by chanting, just as they were in the monasteries of medieval Christendom (see page 108), though Tibetan Buddhist chanting sometimes comes closer to a deep murmuring than the gentle melodic flow of medieval plainsong. Ritualized types of 'mystery' drama, with various Buddhist or shamanistic connotations, are performed outside monasteries, just as the medieval morality or mystery plays were usually staged by the doors of a church or cathedral. The actors wear costumes and masks, dance and mime to chanting and to such instruments as hand bells, gongs and exceptionally long ceremonial trumpets that emit an almost unearthly deep tone.

SOUTHEAST ASIA

Southeast Asia straddles an area of tropical land and sea from the borders of India and China to the northern shores of Australia. For all the differences, ethnic, cultural and religious, to be found in such a large and scattered region, its peoples share a common identity through much of their music. The gongs, bells, cymbals and other idiophones that feature in so much Chinese and Japanese music-making, achieve a kind of apotheosis with them. From the golden temples and pagodas of Rangoon and Bangkok to the palm-fringed shores of Sarawak and Java, this 'gong-chime' culture, as it is sometimes called, unites them all. Most of the idiophones are tuned to definite or near-definite pitch, and in performance engage in a sometimes clamorous, sometimes sweet-toned polyphony. Many of them also present an amazing sight. Xylophones and metallophones (xylophones with metal bars) are molded into the shapes of peacocks, dragons or sea serpents. Gongs are suspended between ornately carved figures or hang from bars fashioned into the image of more mythical beasts and birds. Nowhere else in the world has music joined hands with such a fabulous menagerie.

KOREA

The large peninsula of Korea has for most of its recorded history been a cultural and sometimes a military stepping stone between China, Manchuria and the adjacent islands of Japan. The influence of China and of Buddhism have left an indelible mark on Korean architecture, art and music; and most of its musical instruments – zithers, flutes and reed woodwinds, gongs and drums – are basically Chinese, too, as are its traditional court and theater song and dance.

There are, however, features of Korean music that link it to the nomadic Mongols of prehistory. One or two specimens of a traditional type of Korean gong, quite small and almost flat, have been found among the American Eskimos and in Finnish Lapland, as further evidence of the Mongol migrations referred to above. This Mongolian connection probably accounts also for the ancient Korean shamanistic religions and cults, with their own special chanting and dancing. The best-known type of Korean folk dance (known as the 'farmer's dance'), very animated, with much frenzied beating on small drums, has no known parallel in China or Japan.

Above: Korean musician in traditional court dress, playing a fiddle similar to many such oriental bowed instruments. Note the bow itself, and the way she holds it.

Left: Burmese dancer displaying a typical formalized posture and poise. Note the angle of her right hand and thumb, just two of the hundreds of postures and gestures such dancers must learn.

The Gamelan Orchestra

Anybody who thinks percussion instruments are only for beating time should listen to a gamelan orchestra or band. Such ensembles usually include one or two stringed or wind instruments, but consist mainly of drums and special types of gong and xylophone. The music is like no other and has devotees all over the world.

A gamelan ensemble on the Indonesian island of Bali, making a wonderfully exotic sight as well as sound.

*I*n 1889 Paris staged a great international exhibition, with the newly built Eiffel Tower as its focal point. One of the novelties was a Javanese gamelan orchestra, and among the thousands who stopped to listen was the twenty-seven-year-old Claude Debussy. Its tones and rhythms entranced him, and they soon entered his own music.

The word gamelan means 'struck with a hammer.' A few stringed and woodwind instruments are sometimes included and occasionally there is singing also, but gamelan music of Java and neighboring islands is predominantly for percussion instruments. It is the finest flowering of the 'gong-chime' culture of Southeast Asia already mentioned (see page 57).

According to legend, the Javanese god Sang Hyang Guru used gongs to summon other deities, thus initiating this ancient music – it dates back at least to the second century A.D. Today's gamelan ensembles may have up to seventy-five percussion instruments, belonging to about twenty different types, of both indefinite and definite pitch. There are gongs of various sizes. The largest ones, called *ageng*, are about 35 1/2 in (90 cm) in diameter. Types of xylophone include the *saron* and *gender*, both with bronze bars, and the *gambang*, with wooden ones. The *bonang* consists of bronze 'kettles' or 'pots' placed on a horizontal frame. In addition, there are the *kendang*, barrel or double-headed drums, played with the hands. The casting of the gongs and other percussion instruments requires great skill and experience. Traditionally, the work was accompanied by offerings of food and flowers to the spirits, intended to prevent them from disturbing the difficult task of molding the metal to exactly the right pitch and timbre.

Gamelan music is classed as 'loud' or 'soft' according to the combination of instruments used. It is highly polyphonic, drawing together many individual rhythmic and melodic parts. There are two kinds of scale, distinguished mainly by different pitch intervals. There is, however, no standard system of tuning in Javanese music, and each ensemble uses its own version of these scales. Rhythmically, the music is divided into phrases (sounded by the gongs), sometimes with changes of tempo, where the key player is the drummer, who guides the pace and mood of the music. This role is similar to that of the tabla player in the performance of ragas – a reminder of Java's historical links with India.

Gamelan music sometimes accompanies ritual dancing or the shadow puppet shows for which

A gamelan drummer. The instrument is a cylindrical, double-headed drum, played with the hands.

Java is also famous, but really it is a kind of part-musical, part-mystical communion among the players, and is not intended as a performance for a passive audience. That did not matter to Debussy and other composers (including Britten), who in common with music-lovers around the world have been entranced by the 'symphonies' of exotic bells created by the gamelan orchestras.

Bonang player. The gong chimes or pots are tuned to the notes of a scale.

Instruments of the Far East

Bells, gongs, stone chimes and other idio-phones form the most characteristic instru-mental group from this part of the world, reflecting the oriental interest in the pitch and tone of individual sounds. Among stringed in-struments, especially, there is much similarity between Chinese and Japanese types.

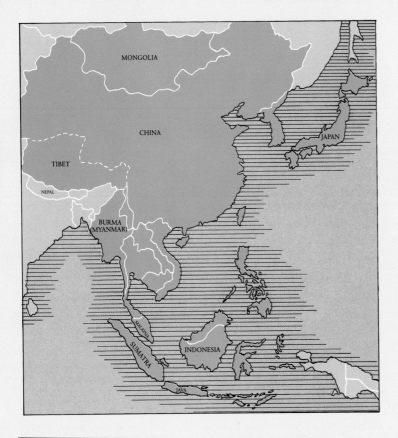

PERCUSSION

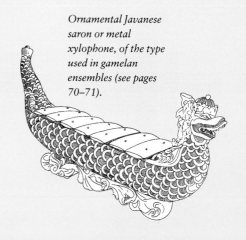

Ornamental Javanese saron or metal xylophone, of the type used in gamelan ensembles (see pages 70–71).

WIND INSTRUMENTS

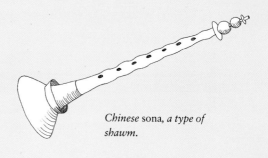

Chinese sona, *a type of shawm.*

STRINGED INSTRUMENTS

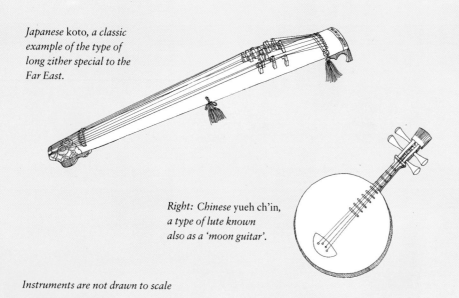

Japanese koto, *a classic example of the type of long zither special to the Far East.*

Right: Chinese yueh ch'in, *a type of lute known also as a 'moon guitar'.*

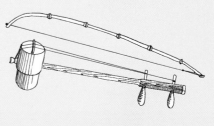

Very simple two-stringed fiddle, from China.

Instruments are not drawn to scale

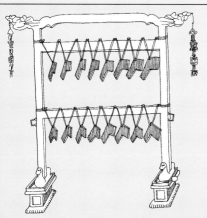

Chinese pien ch'ing or stone chimes, each the same shape but of different thickness, to produce tones of varying pitch.

Chinese bell in ceremonial stand.

Burmese gong suspended between two mythological figures.

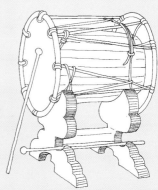

Japanese kakko or double-headed drum.

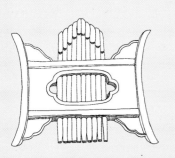

Japanese p'ai hsiao or bamboo panpipes.

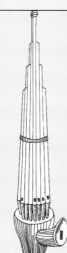

Chinese sheng or mouth organ, a set of bamboo pipes attached to an air chamber.

Chinese instrument-maker fashioning long-necked lutes.

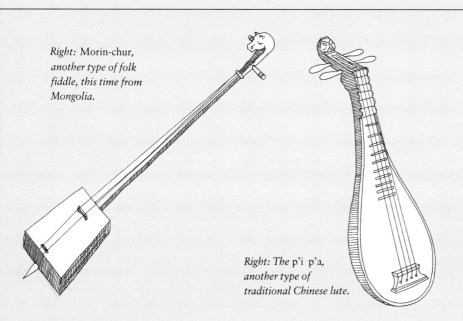

Right: Morin-chur, another type of folk fiddle, this time from Mongolia.

Right: The p'i p'a, another type of traditional Chinese lute.

The Indian Subcontinent

4

Indian musicians beside the Ganges.

The Indian Subcontinent

The densely packed Indian subcontinent is divided into India (by far the largest and most populous nation), Pakistan, Nepal, Bhutan, Sikkim, Bangladesh and Sri Lanka. Religious and political strife prompted the creation of some of these countries; and, unfortunately, the same or similar religious and racial enmities, between Hindus, Muslims, Sikhs, Tamils and Sinhalese, still lurk dangerously close to the surface of everyday life, sometimes erupting in tragic and destructive violence. But for all the differences and conflicts that have brought about these political divisions, India and its closest neighbors have much in common and share thousands of years of cultural history; and in art and music, there is far more holding them together than keeping them apart.

Facing page: More Himalayan ceremonial trumpeters (see also page 56), this time in Kashmir, India's most northerly province.

Below: Twelfth-century sculpture of a female drummer, from the Deccan region of south India.

INDIAN MUSIC

Indian civilization is at least as old as those of the ancient Middle East and China. The Indus Valley civilization, as revealed by the sites of Mohenjo-Daro and Harappa (now both in Pakistan), dates back to about 4000BC, and probably had links, by land and sea, with Sumeria in Mesopotamia and with ancient Egypt. This civilization was destroyed by the invasion of an Indo-Aryan race of people from the region of southern Russia in about 1300BC. They pushed the Indus Valley people, or Dravidians, into the southern tip of India and established a new culture, based on the language and script of Sanskrit and a collection of sacred hymns and poems called the *Vedas*. This Vedic period, from about 1000 to 500BC, established the tenets of Hinduism. All that followed – the advent of Buddhism in what is now Nepal, other invasions, by the Asiatic Huns, the armies of Islam, subjugation by the Portuguese, French and British – has not displaced Hinduism for hundreds of millions of Indian people. This religion, and the art and music that goes with it, today represent one of the oldest living cultural traditions.

A word or two about the Hindu caste system is relevant here. In many respects, this ancient system of dictating a person's station in life by caste was a tyranny, and the Indian government has now formally abolished it. In the arts, though, it often worked well. Sub-castes of artists, dancers and musicians operated like hereditary schools or guilds, with all the pride and sense of tradition that went with them. It is largely due to these artistic sub-castes that the illustrious heritage of Indian art, and especially of music, has been so lovingly preserved.

THE CHARACTER OF THE MUSIC The long history of Indian music has not involved the rapid changes of form and style that are found in the much shorter history of Western music. Indian musicians have rarely, if ever, sat down and composed new and individual pieces of music. Instead, they see their art as one of improvisation; of continually re-working or re-creating systems of melody and rhythm that were established in principle a thousand or more years ago. They also see music in much the same light as their Hindu religion; as a constantly shifting relationship between diversity and an ultimate unity. The first time a piece of Indian music is heard, it might sound rather monotonous. But as the idiom becomes familiar, so it is possible to detect some of the intricate patterns of notes and rhythms, never quite the same from one passage of the music to the next, that make up the whole, the final unity.

MUSIC AND RELIGION According to ancient Indian precepts, music, poetry and dance are all rolled into one divine dramatic scheme or dramaturgy. They are only different aspects of the same divine presence and one cannot be considered without the others. Even so, music may be regarded in this mystical scheme of things as the first among equals, because of its supposed cosmic importance. This idea partly overlaps that of the Harmony of the Spheres, whose roots, together with a sacred view of music, may well lie in the ancient Middle East.

The Indian Sanskrit word for 'sound,' *nada*, also means 'breath' and 'fire.' In this triple meaning, it suggests cosmic energy, the primal cause or source of creation, symbolized by the most famous of all Hindu images, that of the god Shiva performing his cosmic dance. The idea of sound to Indians, therefore, is much the same as 'light' in the account of creation in the Old Testament of the Bible.

Indian mystics and philosophers also recognize two kinds of sound: *ahada nada*, which is audible sound; and *anahada nada*, the normally unheard but all-pervading sound of the cosmos. In this philosophy, there is a parallel with the notion of the Harmony of the Spheres (see page 110), which may well have entered India either by way of ancient Mesopotamia, or with the Aryans and their contacts with the Greeks of classical antiquity.

BHARATA NATYA-SASTRA Much of India's ancient musical mysticism and theorizing is contained in a book or treatise called the *Bharata Natya-Sastra* (or 'The Doctrine of Dramaturgy by Bharata'). Its author was a Brahman priest and sage of whom very little is known, even when he lived, which may have been during the third century AD, or several centuries earlier. But his celebrated work explains much of the theory and practice of India's performing arts, particularly of music.

As with Plato and Aristotle in classical Greece (see page 35), and Lao-tzu and Confucius in China (see page 47), Bharata expressed the belief that music should not just echo emotions or other states of mind, but should induce them. He named eight such moods or emotions, equating each with a deity and a color. There is, for example, the conjunction between Love, Vishnu and Green; Heroism, Indra and Orange; and Wonder, Brahma and Yellow.

MODES AND SCALES Bharata also deals with the subject of Indian modes or scales, probably already fairly well established by his time (whenever that may have been). The foundation for these is the *swaras*, a scale of seven basic pitched notes, roughly equivalent to a Western scale, less the eighth or octave note. These notes are associated in mythology with such animal sounds as the peacock's cry

and the trumpeting of the elephant. A particular mode or scale can begin on any of the notes, following the sequence around from there (similar in arrangement to the old Greek modes). Most important of all, for an understanding of Indian music, the notes of a mode, in whatever sequence they are presented, allow for performers to introduce microtones between them. Some Indian theorists recognize up to sixty-six such microtones, or *srutis*, but very few listeners could ever distinguish between such finely graded intervals of pitch. The standard number of basic notes plus microtones in any particular mode or scale is twenty-two. Such scales are called ragas.

RHYTHM Rhythm features much more strongly in Indian music than in the classical music of China and Japan. The Indian approach to rhythm is also quite different from that of Western music. In the West, the metrical beat of a rhythm usually drives the music along, whereas in Indian music there is an overall rhythmic scheme, like some large arch or roof, beneath which individual bars and beats fit into place.

The commanding rhythmic unit is called the tala. This word is fancifully derived from the first two letters of two mythological dances: the masculine tandava, performed by the god Shiva, and the feminine lasya, performed by his consort Parvati. It is more directly connected with the word *tali*, meaning a clap of the hands. A tala is a total number of beats, an anga is a 'limb,' a measure or bar, within the tala, and a matra is a single beat within an anga.

There are about forty standard talas in use today, providing the rhythmic pattern for a piece of music, as a raga provides for melody. Students learn these patterns by a system of mnemonics (memory aids in the form of recited syllables). In performance, they may introduce all kinds of rhythmic subtleties based upon them.

INDIAN INSTRUMENTS

The sites of Mohenjo-Daro and Harappa tell a good deal about the Indus Valley civilization, but not, unfortunately, very much about their music. Archeologists have discovered one or two rattles and whistles, a conch shell that may have been used as a kind of trumpet, and a clay figurine of a woman playing a small drum held under one arm. They have also recovered some examples of the Indus Valley script, and identified one of the signs as probably representing a very early type of harp, found also in Sumeria. Unfortunately, although this adds to the evidence of a link between the Indus Valley people and the civilizations of ancient Mesopotamia, nothing more is known about the instrument itself.

The instruments that have served Indian music so well for over two thousand years nearly all date from, or after, the time of the Aryan occupation, with the other Asiatic influences that the Aryans brought with them. One very important point to make about them is their relationship to the voice. For the Indian people, the voice was the first musical instrument, bestowed on mankind by the gods, and most other instruments are supposed to imitate or emulate the sound of the voice in one way or another. The primacy of the voice in Indian musical thinking, it should be added, also explains the emphasis on melody or pitched sounds. Harmony, as it is understood in Western music, has no place in the classical or art music of India.

. . . .

STRINGS Stringed instruments (*tata*, or 'stretched') predominate in most Indian ensembles. The sitar, a type of long-necked lute, is the most famous of them. It probably came originally from Persia, since its name is a corruption of the old Persian word for 'three-stringed.' The various types of Indian sitar, however, have many more strings than that, six or seven main ones, plus more sympathetic strings beneath them, and they can all be tuned to a particular scale or raga. Some are plucked

with a plectrum to play the melody; others provide a more or less continuous drone. One characteristic feature of the sitar, and of many other Indian stringed instruments, is the large gourd (traditionally the hollowed-out rind of the dried fruit) attached to one end of the instrument's long neck, which functions as an extra resonator.

The sarod, shorter than the sitar, is modeled on an ancient stringed instrument from Afghanistan. The long-necked tambura has four to six strings only, which are stroked, not plucked, to create a background drone effect. Small pieces of quill or silk are sometimes inserted beneath them, to add a soft buzzing sound to the drone. The vina, or veena, also a plucked stringed instrument, is

Right: Nepalese fiddle player. The instrument is similar to a sarinda. *The way he holds it and uses the bow is quite different from modern Western practice.*

Below: Sitar player. This type of long-necked lute is the universal symbol of Indian classical music.

The Persian Connection

If ever talk of a country standing at a 'cultural cross-roads' really meant something, then it did in the case of ancient Persia (modern Iran). The mountainous land of Persia joined hands with the civilizations of Mesopotamia to the west and the Indian subcontinent to the east and south. At one time, Persia controlled the greatest empire of the ancient world, stretching from the banks of the Nile and the shores of Greece to India itself. At other times, it was overrun by such conquerors as Alexander the Great and Genghis Khan. All the time, it served as a bridge between the scholarship and art of East and West, as well as possessing its own distinctive culture.

The links with India are particularly interesting. It is probable that ancient types of Mesopotamian harp arrived in India via Persia. There is stronger evidence that cylindrical drums and sticks entered India from Persia; also types of lute and flute, whose origins are noted in the main text.

The Sassanid Empire, lasting from the third to the seventh centuries A.D., was a golden age for Persian music, made all the more interesting by foreign musical influences. Sassanid stone reliefs, mosaics, murals and decorated silver cups and bowls, give a very clear picture of the rich variety of instruments to hand,

many from Egypt and Mesopotamia, and others, such as pan pipes, which came from countries as far away as China. Musicians, too, were imported from abroad by the courts of the Sassanid kings. One such was the legendary Greek female harpist Azade. From the other direction came troupes of singers and dancers from India. The dancers may have belonged to the gypsy race, whose migration from India across the Middle East

and into Europe is discussed on page 75.

From the seventh century, the eastward advance of Islam brought a fresh wave of Arabic music to India.

Fine example of the ranasringa, *the ceremonial horn of southern India.*

closer to a zither (see page 48) in construction and method of playing. Some types have two large gourds, one at each end of the long fingerboard.

Indian music also employs a variety of bowed fiddles, including the sarangi and sarinda. Because the strings are bowed and so can sustain a note for a longer period of time than strings that are plucked, they come closest to imitating the voice in performance.

WIND Indian wind instruments (*susira*, or 'tubular') include many types of flute and bagpipe. But the best-known wind instruments belong to other categories. In Persia, the shahnai means 'king flute,' clearly indicating its provenance. It is, however, a woodwind instrument with a double reed, and so related to the shawm and the modern oboe rather than the flute. The pungi is another reed instrument, which may have come originally from Egypt. In its Indian form, it has a calabash or gourd close to the mouthpiece, and has long been a favorite with snake charmers.

The tirucannam trumpet of southern India differs from most other types of trumpet, being comparatively short but with a fairly large bore. As such it resembles, and may have some connection with, the kind of trumpets depicted on ancient Assyrian stone carvings and Egyptian paintings. Some musicians can play two of these trumpets at the same time, though with the intention of making more noise rather than sounding two different notes. The more spectacular ranasringa is a brass or copper type of horn, made in three curved sections, which can be fitted together to form either a serpentine or a crescent shape. These large horns, with great carrying power, were used traditionally to herald a fair, religious festival or some other celebration.

The tirucannam and ranasringa are folk instruments, rarely seen in the refined company of the sitar and its companions.

PERCUSSION There are many types of Indian drum (*avanaddha* or 'covered'). Far and away the most important are the two relatively small drums that make up the *tabla-banya* (one to the right of the player, the other to the left), the essential accompaniment to almost every kind of Indian classical or art music. Both are a type of kettledrum and can be tuned to different pitches. The tabla player, using hands and fingers, can produce a fascinating and sometimes quite hypnotic pattern of rhythm and tone. Idiophones (*ghana* or 'solid') include bells, cymbals and gongs.

There is also the jaltarang, which is not a single instrument but a number of small porcelain bowls. Each of them contains a different amount of water, each bowl producing notes of different pitch. The bowls may be struck lightly with bamboo sticks, in the manner of a water xylophone, or the player may stroke their rims with a wet finger. Wine glasses will produce the same sort of soft, glowing sound. Played this way, the jaltarang is like a simple version of Benjamin Franklin's glass harmonica (see page 175).

DIVERSITY OF THE MUSIC

*I*ndia's seven hundred million people speak dozens of regional languages and dialects, as well as the official Hindi language. At the same time, nearly eighty per-cent of them still live in small towns and vil-lages, each forming its own tightly-knit little community. Consequently, both Indian folk and art music exists in hundreds of local forms and styles. Whole books are devoted to the music, song and dance of a particular region, from Kashmir in the north to Kerala in the south, from Gujarat in the west to Assam in the east. Generally, there is a broad distinction to be made between the music of southern India (Carnatic) and northern India (Hindu-stani), though even this division is blurred by many local divergencies, while other musical features crop up almost everywhere.

SONG Indian singers accustom their ears and tune their voices from childhood to microtones, which are fractions of a semitone (see page 16), and learn to sing with a degree of subtlety and expressiveness that few Western singers can emulate. Taking India as a whole, the country's vast repertory of song (*gita*) is one of the richest and most diverse of any country in the world.

Among religious and devotional songs, or song-cycles, the most famous is the classic *Gita-govinda*, a cycle of twenty-four songs based on a twelfth-century Sanskrit poem about the love of the god Krishna for his consort and mistress Radha. Some passages from it are beautiful examples of the expression of erotic love in Indian music.

Turning from particular songs to vocal forms, the *bhajan* is a more popular type of religious song or hymn that can be sung in any of India's vernacular tongues or dialects. *Thumris* and *ghazals* are more urbanized song styles, devotional or secular in character. Among Indian Muslims, there is the *qawwali*,

a type of choral song inspired by Sufi themes (the Sufis being an Islamic mystical sect). There is also the tradition of *tarranum* singing which is different again – it is closer to a kind of musical recitation, or chanted poetry.

DANCE Dance and music share the same term, *sangita*, and for many Indians that im-age of Shiva performing his cosmic dance is a constant reminder of the inseparability of the two.

Indian dancing concentrates far more than Western dance and ballet on posture, as distinct from movement. Positions of the limbs and joints, angles of the head, gestures of the hand (*mudras*), so graphically portrayed in Indian religious sculpture, all have deep mysti-cal or emotional meaning. Foot movements, too, are very important, often obeying com-plex rhythmic patterns called *jatis*, which the dancer can learn by a system of syllabic mnemonics similar to those of a drummer.

The best-known type of south Indian or Carnatic dance is the statuesque *bharata natyam*, which is danced to love songs. The north Indian or Hindustani *kathak* is gener-ally more energetic, with thrilling rhythmic dialogues between dancer and drummer. Then there is the *kathakali*, or dance-drama. The tradition of dance theater goes back a long way in Indian history, the *kathakali* itself inheriting many antique themes and styles. Usually five or six dancers, in elaborate costumes and headdresses, act out stories from Hindu mythology. The music may include songs from the *Gita-govinda*. In addition to two singers, there are a drum, gong and cymbals, both to accompany the dancers and mark the various episodes.

Kandian drummers of Sri Lanka, much in evidence on such festive occasions as the Perahera Day parade. Their double-headed drums with strong lacing symbolize the vigor of Kandian dance.

Continued on page 72

Indian Classical Dance

Perhaps the longest and richest tradition of movement and dance to be found anywhere in the world today belongs to the Indian subcontinent. At its best, it is an art form that communicates with astonishing sophistication and subtlety; Indian classical dance is a unique and beautiful blend of dance, drama and religious mysticism.

Above: This dancer embodies all the poise of Indian classical dance to her very fingertips.

Right: Much the same posture, enshrined in stone in this twelfth-century temple sculpture.

The physical character of Indian classical dance comes across very strongly in the many Hindu temple carvings of gods and goddesses, with limbs and torsos disposed in acts of sinuous movement. Its grace and delicacy are beautifully conveyed in temple murals and in thousands of beautiful miniature paintings.

Indian classical dance has a history of well over 2,000 years. Its principles are enshrined in the concepts of *natya*, embracing the whole art of theater, and more specifically in *sangita*, concerning the closely related arts of music and dance. The dance is traditionally performed barefoot, which has much to do with its special physical character. It is also, as explained in the main part of the text, much more statuesque or 'sculptural' than most Western folk dance or ballet. This, it should be noted, applies to much other oriental dance. Dance steps can be important; but more important still are matters of posture and gesture, by which the dancer communicates an esthetic idea, or a state of mind or feeling.

We can gain some insight into both the spirit and the technique of Indian classical dance by considering some of its many terms. To begin with, the body is divided into major and minor parts. The major parts (*anga*) are the head, torso, arms and legs. The minor parts (*upanga*) include the anatomy of the face, nose, chin, eyebrows and so on.

Turning to the dancing itself, there is a wide division between what we can regard as pure or abstract dance (*nritta*) and the more theatrical notion of mime (*nritya*). Following from this, *abhinaya* is to do with the whole art of mimetic dance. Another distinction can be made between the style of *tandava*, which conveys strength and virility (historically associated with the Hindu god Shiva) and *lasya*, suggesting love and other more tender emotions (associated with

Shiva's wife Parvati).

Sattwika or *satvik* means emotional expression, while *angika* is formal or esthetic display. *Aharya* is to do with stage presentation, costume and choreography, and *vaciva* or *vacik* is the accompanying art of song, instrumentation and rhythm. Going into even greater detail, there is the study of *ankur*, dealing with attitudes and angles of the head, use of the eyes and other facial expressions, and *mudra*, listing the hundreds of gestures made with the hands and fingers, each pregnant with meaning.

The main types of Indian classical dance – the antique and formal *bharata-natyam*, the *kathakali* mime play, *manipuri*, *odissi*, and *kathak* – are fascinating to watch even with no knowledge

Right: An athletic member of Sri Lanka's famed Kandy Dancers.

Below: Another study of Indian classical dance, with instrumental ensemble in attendance.

of their rich and ancient heritage. However, the experience is greatly enhanced if at least something is understood of the underlying concepts, the skills and training involved, and the mythological dramas and legends that the dancers are re-enacting.

Double pipes in the border country of Pakistan and Afghanistan. These kinds of double woodwind pipes, so widespread in the ancient world, point to the historical importance of Afghanistan and adjacent Iran (Persia) as a cultural link between the Middle East and the Indian subcontinent.

RAGAS At the very heart of Indian music is the raga. This word describes both the type of scale, mode or melodic outline, and the type of performance based upon it. The classical raga, then, is to Indian music what the symphony is to Western music, though the two forms of music are otherwise far apart in concept and performance. There are hundreds of ragas, in terms of scale or mode, though only about 130 are regularly used. Each has its own name, and its own mystical or metaphysical attributes; each is supposed to 'color the mind' with a particular mood or emotion; and each is considered appropriate to a certain season of the year or time of the day or night.

Every performance, usually by three or four string players, plus the indispensable tabla player, is, basically, a set of variations upon a chosen raga. At its best, it raises to its highest peak the age-old Indian tradition of improvisation within the limits of established form and convention. The raga itself is sounded right at the start, like the musical raising of a curtain – the musicians sense or establish its mood in an opening episode in free rhythm. Then the tabla player sets in motion the first basic rhythm, and the variations begin. At certain key points, the rhythmic patterns change and the tempo increases, so that the variations increase both in complexity and excitement, ending in a sudden relaxation of mood and effort. The players may also vocalize, in which case they can engage in marvelous passages of imitative music between voice and instruments.

PAKISTAN

*P*akistan was created a separate nation in 1947, at the same time that India gained her independence from British rule. It is a Muslim country, while India remains predominantly Hindu. From a musical point of view, these religious and political divisions are not so important. What is significant is Pakistan's geographical position. Its region of Baluchistan extends culturally and historically into Iran (Persia), the Pathan region extends into Afghanistan, and the Punjab stretches into India. Pakistan is, therefore, a reminder of the many musical connections between India and the lands of the ancient Middle East.

Some of the musical instruments to be found in Pakistan, such as the frame drum or *duff*, are themselves a very interesting halfway house between the Middle East and India. But in the realm of song, Pakistan has a number of distinctive forms and styles, not quite the same as anything to be found in neighboring India. For example, the region of Sind is the place to hear *kafi* music, songs based on Islamic mystical poems. Punjabi music, is notable for its *mahiya* or improvised song, sometimes taking the responsorial form of a soloist singing a verse, answered by a chorus or simply by everybody else present. This much looser and more relaxed type of communal singing is often heard at weddings and other festive occasions.

BANGLADESH AND BENGAL

*A*t the time of Indian independence, Bangladesh at first became East Pakistan, but it gained its own independence in 1971. The important thing, historically and culturally, is that it includes much of the old Indian province of Bengal, which has a rich musical heritage. Indeed, Bengal's most famous scholar, Nobel prize-winner Rabindranath Tagore (1861–1941), revived old folk

Indian Temple Dancers

Shapely girls and women carrying out duties in temples and at shrines were a common sight in the ancient world. Well-known examples are the Egyptian handmaidens who assisted in the temples of Isis, and the famous Vestal Virgins of Imperial Rome. India had its devadasis, girls who sang and danced in the temples, especially those dedicated to Surya, the god of sun and light, the Hindu equivalent to the Greek Apollo. The girls mostly came from upper-class families and were chosen both for their looks and their musical

talents. After training in music and dance, they were consecrated, or 'married' with great ceremony to Surya or some other deity. In addition to performing in the temples, they became highly honored members of society, their presence eagerly sought at weddings, births and other social occasions for the good luck they were supposed to bring.

On a less spiritual plane, many of them also became courtesans. It was this aspect of their careers, probably coupled with a general lowering of moral tone, that eventually caused

trouble, first with Christian missionaries and then with the British raj. It was not only strait-laced British officials and their wives who attacked the devadasis. Mahatma Gandhi, chief architect of Indian independence and no great friend of the British, condemned many Indian temples as 'no better than brothels.' Today, the way of life and art of the devadasis is almost a thing of the past, but for a thousand years or more, they helped to keep alive styles of Indian music and dance that might otherwise have been forgotten.

song and dance in a new school or genre of music called *Rabindra-sangeet*. Other fine old art and folk music traditions have been retained in Bangladesh and Bengal, nearly all in the form of song. *Kirtan* are devotional songs, based on the *Vaisnava padavali*, a collection of Hindu poetry; and *Baul* songs are the preserve of a curious local mystical sect, sung by mendicants who sometimes dance and play a drum as they sing. Bangladesh and Bengal occupy the delta region of the River Ganges, and all this water has inspired many boating songs. *Bhatiali* are boatsmen's songs, their tempo and mood echoing the slow progress of boats over the broad, often sluggish delta waters. *Sari* are much more lively and are traditionally sung during boat races.

Below: Nepalese Sherpa priest punctuates his reading of the scriptures with jingle and bell. Small hand bells and jingles are associated with religion and ritual in many parts of the world. Note also the conch shell behind the priest

NEPAL

The kingdom of Nepal, with the small contiguous states of Sikkim and Bhutan, stands between the plains of the River Ganges and the massive southern wall of the Himalayas. Mount Everest itself bestrides the border with Tibet. It was the homeland of Prince Siddhartha Gautama, the Buddha. To this day, Nepal remains a self-contained little nation, linked to Tibet and India, owing something to both, but is by no means a carbon copy of either.

Nepal's still thriving band of minstrel-musicians have their own kind of hierarchy, a local variant of the Indian caste system. Each group is distinguished by the instruments played or the songs and dances performed. The music, as might be expected, is an interesting cross between the music of central Asia and of India. One of their instruments, the long-necked *damyan* or lute, probably originated in Afghanistan, and the Nepalese *manirimdu* ritual dances have close Tibetan connections. The latter are very similar to the Tibetan monastery dance dramas described on page 56, and are performed by the famous mountain-climbing Sherpas of Nepal, who belong in the same racial group as the Tibetans and Mongolians.

SRI LANKA

At the other end of India is the large tropical island of Sri Lanka (Ceylon), sometimes likened in shape to a pendant gemstone, in view of its valuable trade in rubies and sapphires. Sri Lanka's historical and cultural ties with mainland India are very close; but the country cherishes its own customs and culture, colored far more by the Buddhist rather than the Hindu religion.

In music, Sri Lanka's history can be traced right back to a group of songs, probably created by the Yakkha or Vedda peoples of near prehistoric times, and lovingly preserved in the oral tradition. They are especially interesting to musical historians because of their melodies based on a very limited range of pitched notes. But the indigenous (that is, Sinhalese) music of Sri Lanka is associated primarily with dancing. Drums figure largely among its instruments. As in India, dancers sometimes learn their intricate steps by a system of mnemonics, and as well as the beat of the drums, they may accompany themselves with hand cymbals and wear ankle bracelets or bells. Some of their steps and movements (as well as their costumes and masks) may go right back to those same prehistoric times and to Yakkha devil dances. Other dance routines are derived from the ritualized acting out of ancient Hindu myths and legends, including stylized representations of such local animals as monkeys, peacocks and elephants.

Today, the Kandyan Dance, named after the ancient royal capital of Kandy, with its beautiful old palace and large ornamental lake up in the hills, represents the best of Sri Lanka's rich and varied national tradition. The dancers usually perform in groups of five or six, sometimes singing as well as dancing, and accompanying themselves with drums, cymbals and other percussion instruments in the ways just described. A good time to see these colorful and athletic dancers, and their drummers, is during the annual Perahera Buddhist festival, when the casket of the Buddha's tooth is paraded through the streets of Kandy, accompanied by a procession of gorgeously attired elephants.

INDIA AND THE GYPSIES

So, some of the influences on Indian music have come from Persia and elsewhere in the ancient Middle East. But over the centuries, India has extended its own musical influences beyond its borders. Hinduism spread to much of southeast Asia, taking the sounds of Indian music with it; and Buddhist missionaries performed a similar service for Indian music in parts of China and Japan. Then there have been the Gypsies. For a long time, people believed this nomadic and self-contained race, setting up encampments and moving on again across much of Europe, came originally from Egypt (hence 'gypsy'). But it is now virtually established that they came from India first. Their veneration of animal life, and their love of fortune-telling, reflect aspects of Hindu life. They have also been noted for their special kind of music-making, which breathes with the spirit of much traditional Indian music. There is no doubt that this music found its way into indigenous musical styles in those parts of Europe where their influence was strongest. There is still a fine old tradition of gypsy music in Hungary and Romania, which people, Liszt and Brahms among them, have sometimes mistaken for the native Magyar folk music. Similarly, something of the fire and passion of Spanish flamenco song and dance may also be attributed to the Gypsies and so, back through history, to the music of India.

Sri Lankan piper before the famous Buddhist Temple of the Tooth in the old capital of Kandy.

Instruments of the Indian Subcontinent

The best-known instruments of India and her closest neighbors are the sitar, vina and other stringed instruments. These belong almost exclusively to Indian classical music, and form a class or group apart from the hundreds of folk instruments of this region of Asia.

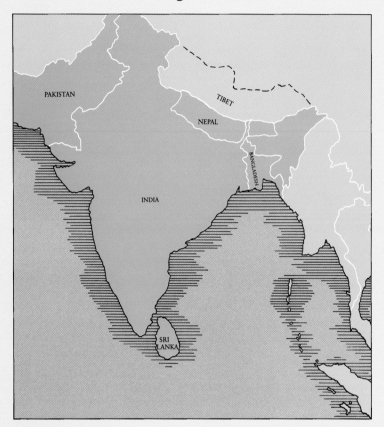

Stringed Instruments

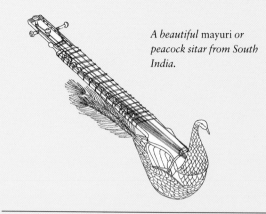

A beautiful mayuri *or* peacock sitar *from South India.*

Wind Instruments

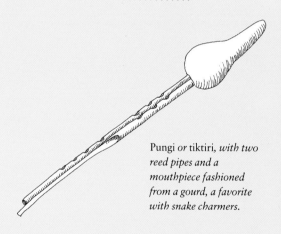

Pungi *or* tiktiri, *with two reed pipes and a mouthpiece fashioned from a gourd, a favorite with snake charmers.*

Double-headed barrel drum from the Madras area. It is usually hung around the neck so that each hand can play one of the heads.

Tabla drum. These small hand drums are almost always played in pairs, each tuned to a different pitch.

Percussion

Right: Traditional barrel drums being played at a wedding in South India.

Below: Indian example of a jew's-harp, with vibrating metal strip or tongue. Played against the mouth, the name may be a corruption of 'jaw's harp.'

Instruments are not drawn to scale

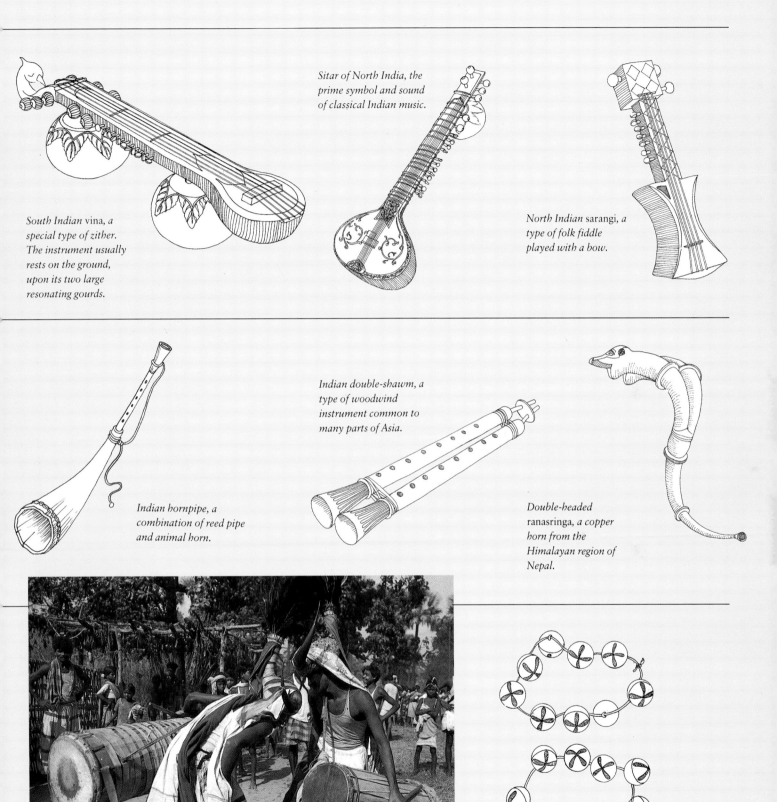

South Indian vina, *a special type of zither. The instrument usually rests on the ground, upon its two large resonating gourds.*

Sitar of North India, the prime symbol and sound of classical Indian music.

North Indian sarangi, *a type of folk fiddle played with a bow.*

Indian double-shawm, a type of woodwind instrument common to many parts of Asia.

Indian hornpipe, a combination of reed pipe and animal horn.

Double-headed ranasringa, *a copper horn from the Himalayan region of Nepal.*

Jinglebells worn around the ankles of Indian dancers.

African Music

5

Drummers in Zambia.

African Music

The history and music of North Africa, from its Arabic roots to the great flowering of Islamic art in the Middle Ages, has already been traced in Chapter 2. But the true music of Africa, the music of tribal song and dance, belongs south of the Sahara Desert. This was the Africa long spoken of by European explorers as the 'Dark Continent.' Its coastlines were already charted by the Portuguese navigators Bartolomeo Diaz (*c.*1450–1500) and Vasco da Gama (*c.*1469–1524) at the end of the fifteenth century; but most of its vast interior of dry grassland or savanna, and impenetrable rain forest, remained a closed book, a dark mystery, to outsiders until this century. The traditional music of its peoples is the subject of this chapter.

Ancient mimetic ritual (see also pages 90-91) re-enacted by tribesmen in Zaire, the heart of tropical Africa. Note the group of drummers on the left, essential to such ritualistic dancing.

BACK INTO PREHISTORY

The majority of the native inhabitants of equatorial and southern Africa are spoken of collectively as belonging to the Bantu race. Although they are not really a single group or race of people, their tribal way of life and music can be looked at as a whole. Because their society was, with the exception of Swahili, pre-literate (with no written form of language and therefore no records), it is impossible to reconstruct much of their history. It is true that archeologists and anthropologists have found stone tools at sites

Another scene of ritual magic. The strangely clad figure in the foreground is dancing both to drums and hand claps.

in East and South Africa which are thought to be a million years old and are, therefore, some of the oldest evidence of human activity. Evidence of some of the earliest types of musical instrument – the use of scrapers and rattles dating back 30,000 years – also comes from Africa. Beyond that, there is little to show how African tribal societies might have evolved and developed over the thousands of years leading to this century. On the other hand, the main characteristics of their tribal life, and the very important place of music in it, have been well documented.

MUSIC IN TRIBAL LIFE

*I*n tribal societies, there is no such thing as 'art.' Life is strictly utilitarian. Each individual has his or her role to play, every activity, every object and item, from pots and pans to totems and masks, has its own particular function. This applies to music, too, for there is no music of an exclusive aristocracy or an intellectual élite. Nor does music exist, except perhaps incidentally, purely for pleasure and entertainment. It may be enjoyable, but it almost always has a specific purpose in the life and routine of the tribe.

Via shamans and witch doctors, music serves as a communication with the spirit world (as important a function as any other

in most tribal societies). It is a more practical means of audible communication and signaling. It marks the days and seasons, and accompanies work. It is, in a very real sense, life set to music. This is what gives so much African music its marked qualities of spontaneity, vitality and vigor. At the same time, such music is not intended for an audience, for passive listening. To understand it fully, to get the most out of it, it is necessary to join in.

AFRICAN INSTRUMENTS

*W*hen judged by Western, Indian, Chinese or Japanese standards, many of the musical instruments of tribal Africa may appear primitive and crude – but there is certainly nothing crude about the way some of them, drums especially, are played. Also, they are of tremendous interest from the point of view of musical history, since most of them have probably not changed very much, in design and construction, in ten or twenty thousand years. Most of them are fashioned directly from the plants and animals of the natural environment, showing a remarkable ingenuity in using the materials at hand – wood, fiber, animal bone and hide. They are living evidence of how many stringed instruments, woodwind, brass and percussion, probably came into existence.

Continued on page 84

African Instruments

Leaving aside the Islamic north of the continent, drums and other percussion predominate in the gallery of traditional African instruments, representing the African people's unique sense of rhythm, and the strong links they have forged between rhythm and speech. There are, however, some interesting examples of early stringed and wind instruments.

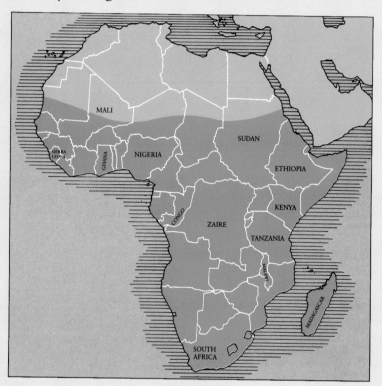

WIND INSTRUMENTS

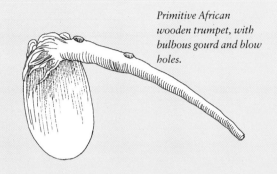

Primitive African wooden trumpet, with bulbous gourd and blow holes.

STRINGED INSTRUMENTS

Simple 'stick' zither from the Congo region, with large resonating gourd attached.

PERCUSSION

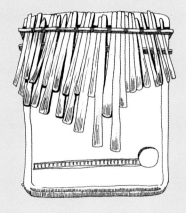

South African mbira or Sansa an idiophone, also known as a "thumb piano". The little metal or cane bars are plucked with fingers and thumbs.

"Footed drum" are intended literally to stand on their own "feet" or supports. Many African examples, like this one, are modelled on the human torso.

Instruments are not drawn to scale

Side-blown horn from Malawi being played. The marking on the animal horn is clearly visible.

Carved wooden horn from West Africa. Note the prominent mouthpiece.

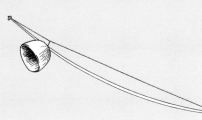

Right: Nigerian 'raft' zither, yet another instrument using a large gourd to lend volume and tone to the strings.

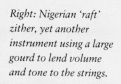

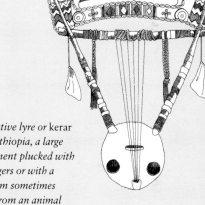

Left: African musical bow with cupped resonator made from half a gourd or coconut shell.

Decorative lyre or kerar from Ethiopia, a large instrument plucked with the fingers or with a plectrum sometimes made from an animal claw.

Congolese slit drum. The attached stick is moved vigorously up and down the slit.

Nigerian wooden clapper bell, handsomely carved with the figure of a kneeling woman.

Xylophone from Sierra Leone, with wooden bars and gourd resonators beneath.

Left: Kalungu or 'talking drum.' The pitch of the drum is adjusted by tightening or slackening the lacing.

Africa's Talking Drums

There are hundreds of connections between music and the sounds of speech. Instruments such as conch shells, Jew's harps and mirlitons have been used to mask the voice and to give it mysterious, half-musical properties in magic and ritual. In a totally different context, the composers Mussorgsky and Janácek modeled much of their

an excellent means of communication, often deployed in relays, over long distances or through stretches of jungle difficult or dangerous to cross on foot.

Some talking drums are used in pairs, a low-pitched (male) and a higher-pitched (female) drum; and sometimes a piece of stone or iron might be held against

which can span up to an octave in pitch, are especially good at reproducing the vocal glides found in the Yoruba language of West Africa.

The awe in which drums are held, as the voices of spirits as well as the instruments of the 'jungle telegraph,' surrounds them with all kinds of magic and myth. They are often

THE DRUMS Drums are the kings among African instruments. They come in many shapes, sizes and forms, taking in both membranophones and idiophones. Pitch and tone are important in many cases. Drums with stretched-skin heads (membranophones) can be grouped according to their shape: cylindrical and barrel (which may have a drum head at each end), and conical. There are 'talking drums' which, as their name suggests, come closest to emulating African speech patterns, their pitch being quickly adjusted by tightening or loosening a cord around their body. The membrane of friction drums is vibrated by hand or by revolving a stick that pierces the membrane. Types of kettledrum include the large, pot-shaped ngoma that is usually placed on the ground for convenience of playing. Some shields, made of hide tightly

Talking drum players, Nigeria.

music directly on the inflections of spoken language.

Nowhere have such connections been stronger and closer than in parts of Africa, where for thousands of years 'talking drums' have reproduced the inflections, pitch and pace of speech to a quite remarkable degree. Talking drums are thus

the drumhead, changing its tone rather than its pitch to suggest also syllabic sounds. Even more effective are so-called hourglass drums, whose pitch can be changed instantly by squeezing or releasing the body by means of leather lacing or cord, so tightening or slackening the skin of the drumhead. Such drums,

hidden away, as they are considered to be too sacred to look upon except by the initiated, and can only be moved at night. On the other hand, anybody taking refuge in a drum house or yard can not be touched until they move on again, just like someone seeking sanctuary in a church.

stretched over a frame, are also used as drums. And there are the slit drums, idiophones this time, which are made by hollowing out a tree trunk or smaller length of wood through a slit along one side.

OTHER PERCUSSION INSTRUMENTS The close relationship in African music between rhythm, tone and pitch is continued with other idiophones. African xylophones have wooden bars or blocks. They may be strapped to a frame, with gourds or other resonating objects attached beneath them, or they may simply be portable wooden bars that can be laid across the player's legs or placed over a hole in the ground, depending on their size. Though such items may sound a contradiction in terms, wooden bells are found in parts of Africa. However, they are bells only to the extent that they are hollowed out and carved into a bell shape, with a clapper inside them.

There is one type of idiophone that is almost unique to Africa. This is the mbira, sometimes also known as the sansa, or more colloquially as the 'thumb piano.' It consists of a number of small strips or tongues of cane (in a few cases of metal) fastened above a wooden sounding board. The player plucks them with his thumbs to sound a sequence of pitched or semi-pitched notes. In some examples of the mriba, the little cane or metal strips look like the tuned forks in music boxes, though the sound they make is closer to the twang of a Jew's harp.

Rattles and jingles, hand held or tied around the legs and ankles, proliferate.

....

STRINGED INSTRUMENTS One of the simplest types of African stringed instrument is the bow (as in bow and arrow). In addition to being either plucked or stroked with a stick, one traditional way of playing them is to grip one end of the string with the teeth, so that the player's mouth acts as a resonator. Other bows have gourds or nut shells as resonators, and more closely resemble simple types of fiddle.

It seems likely that at some time in the distant past these simple musical bows also led to very early types of bowed harp, with five or

six strings. Existing examples look very similar to paintings and carvings of ancient Egyptian and Mesopotamian bowed or angled harps. African lyres, including the very large obukano, with their strings stretched inside a frame, may also have some remote historical link with examples in the ancient Middle East (see pages 32-34).

Lutes, or lute-like instruments, have their string or strings stretched over the neck and circular or oblong resonator, though the ramkie of southern Africa has a shorter neck and is closer in appearance to a folk guitar than a typical lute.

Above: A fine example of an mbira, sansa *or* thumb piano, *as described in the accompanying text, from Kenya.*

Right: A pair of African marimbas, large xylophones with resonators beneath the bars. These two also have the names of notes chalked on them, suggesting a link with Western-style music.

Instruments similar to a zither exist in many forms. For example, there is the so-called stick zither, with a single string. An unusual way of playing it means the player has to blow or draw in his breath across one end of the string to set it vibrating. The strings, or sometimes thin pliable canes, of raft zithers are stretched over a raft-like frame, whereas the strings of trough zithers are stretched over a hollowed-out section of wood, or a section of wood cut from the trough. The strings may, in some cases, be a single length of cord laced back and forth across the trough or board. There are also examples of what are called ground zithers. Here, a string is stretched over two posts set in the ground. A third post is then attached to a board placed over a hole in the ground, which is the resonator.

WIND INSTRUMENTS Many whistles, flutes and sets of pan pipes are made from lengths of bone or from cane. One interesting variant combines a length of cane (with holes for note-stopping) with a gourd or similar object. The cane is inserted into the gourd, which also provides the player with his mouthpiece.

Horns, like the Hebrew shofar (see page 36), may be fashioned directly from cow, antelope or buffalo horn, or elephant tusk. Two other traditional kinds of African tribal wind instrument are more obscure, even bizarre. Mirlitons, or kazoos, are instruments designed to modify the sound of the voice. Humming into a paper and comb is a simple example of such a device. One kind of African mirliton looks like an ordinary section of horn, but inside there is a vibrating membrane made from the protective silk cocoon most spiders spin around their eggs. So-called buzz disks are another curiosity. The wooden discs, probably with a serrated edge and holes, are threaded with lengths of cord. When the cord is tightly twisted, they can be made to spin around, producing a buzzing or whirring sound. Like the bull-roarers described on page 54, they reverse the normal principle of wind instruments. Buzz disks disturb the air, and not the other way around. Also, like bull-roarers, they are not normal instruments of rhythm or melody. Their sound has magical and ritual connotations.

RHYTHM AND MELODY

*R*hythm, whether beaten out by the drums, clapped by the hands, or played on idiophones such as African xylophones or 'thumb pianos', is often seen as the heart and soul of African tribal music.

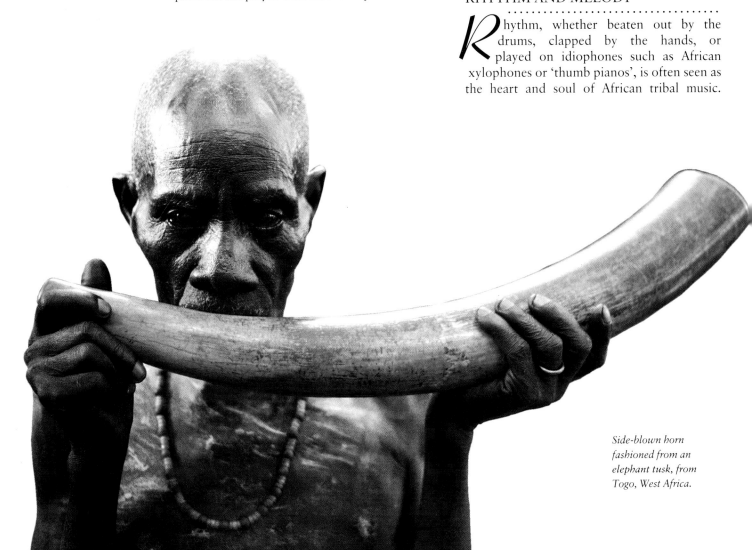

Side-blown horn fashioned from an elephant tusk, from Togo, West Africa.

However the beat is made, the use of rhythm has reached great levels of sophistication in African music making. Polyrhythms – two or more rhythms of different metrical beats sounding against each other – are an outstanding feature of their music. To the Africans themselves, though, the actual rhythm of the drums is only half the story; their tone and pitch are equally significant. In the Bantu languages, the pitch and tone of the voice is very important, and since nearly all African tribal music is regarded as an extension of spoken language, these sound properties are inseparable from rhythm.

African tribal music does, nonetheless, have its own melodies which are based on scales, as they are almost everywhere in the world. However, the concept of pitched notes is an interesting and a singular one in this context. The notes are not so much thought of as being high or low in pitch, but as small or large. So, most scales are considered in descending order, progressing from the less to the more important notes. The octave is recognized as a very important interval of pitch, as are the intervals of the fourth and the fifth (in terms of Western notation). Most scales, though, are penta- hexa- or heptatonic, that is, consisting of five, six or seven notes, respectively. Actual melodies usually begin on a high note and descend in pitch to a lower and more important one. Their progress is also determined by the intonation of the words which are being sung.

SINGING AND SONG

For all the hypnotic beating of drums, African music is full of song. It serves the community and all the diverse sections within it. There are songs to celebrate weddings and births, songs to mourn sickness or death. There are songs for girls and for boys, for women and for men. Work songs demonstrate the utilitarian aspect of African music at its most effective. They lift the burden of such labors as threshing or pounding grain, hauling logs or lifting loads, by turning them into another musical occasion. Interestingly, there are also songs of a political nature. The

Northern Nigerian tribesman with large drum. This part of Nigeria, bordering the Sahara, is the home of hausa music, old ceremonial music played mostly on drums and trumpets.

Continued on page 90

West African Odyssey

Through the iniquitous horror and shame of the slave trade developed the music of jazz and of Latin America, and, by extension, much of the popular music of today. The starting point for this enormous body of music was the rich and varied music and ceremony of the peoples who inhabited the West African coast.

Above: Massive funeral drums (membranophones) belonging to the Ashantis of Ghana.

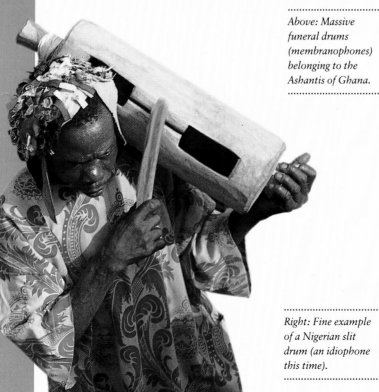

Right: Fine example of a Nigerian slit drum (an idiophone this time).

Around the Gulf of Guinea are the areas once known as the Ivory Coast, the Gold Coast and the Slave Coast. The last-named is of great importance to students of music, since it was from these West African shores that thousands of black slaves began their grim voyage across the Atlantic during the eighteenth and nineteenth centuries, taking with them the music that was to contribute much to the tango and the rumba (see pages 102 and 105), ragtime and the blues.

This musical tradition, perhaps the richest in Africa, was formed in the old empire of Benin and among the Yoruba-speaking people, that is, in present-day Ghana, Togo, Benin and Nigeria. Among the ancient instruments belonging to the region are many of those already described in the main text: a great variety of drums, including the 'talking drums' whose changing pitch and rhythm echo the inflections of speech (see page 84); raft zithers; sansas or 'thumb pianos', and xylophones, the biggest in Africa, with wooden bars or beams up to 60 in (150 cm) long placed across a resonating pit. Other old West African instruments include iron bells (not cast, but made from beaten and soldered metal sheets) and percussion pots, which are struck across the top of the neck with the flat of a leather or wicker-work fan to produce a hollow, semi-pitched sound.

As intriguing as some of these old instruments are, it has been the variety and richness of West

African musical life which, with its Afro-American links, is so interesting and significant. No other part of the continent can offer as much. The great public entertainments, celebrating births, marriages, a seasonal holiday or a tribal coronation include mime, dance, song and displays of instrumental virtuosity. Also featuring gorgeous costumes, they are a cross between Renaissance pageant and opera-ballet, and are no doubt one source of Carnival from Rio to New Orleans.

Turning from public display to secret ritual, the *vodun* or spirit worship of West Africa has inspired a large repertory of chants in esoteric dialects. The *ono* (secret society of night-hunters) have filled the tropic night with the whirr of bull-roarers and the half-vocal hum and buzz of mirlitons – like nocturnal stirrings of jungle life – as well as the inexorable beat of the drums. Across the Atlantic, the voodoo cults of Haiti and elsewhere in the Caribbean continue these dark and secret traditions.

An old colonial French word, *griot*, focuses attention on yet another colorful band in the broad spectrum of West African music.

Traditionally, griots are professional musicians, combining the roles of town-crier and public jester. They sing or declaim both news and gossip and may also engage in political or personal satire and lampoon. Their musicianship, skillful improvisations and quick wit and banter are reincarnated in West Indian calypso, reggae and rap, and the same tradition is evident in the ebullience of such musicians as Louis Armstrong and Fats Waller.

....
Above: Mounted Nigerian musicians, playing the long, slim kakaki *ceremonial trumpets that belong to the Hausa musical tradition (see also page 87).*
....

Below: A group of Yoruba drummers at a recent festival, again in Nigeria.
....

Dinka girl singing in a wedding procession. The Dinka people of Sudan are noted for their wedding festivities, with singing and dancing that may continue for six or seven days.

phonic, with the singers divided into groups. A favorite type of polyphony has one group after the other taking up the same melody, following each other around, in the form of a canon. Sometimes the groups might interpolate the successive notes of a melody, one against the other, which is similar to an old vocal device known in Western textbooks as a hocket. At other times, the groups of singers might all sing the melody together, but certain pitch intervals apart, as in medieval organum (see page 110). Also common in Africa is the responsorial song, where one lead singer or group declaims a refrain, to be answered by the rest with the same refrain or a response to it.

Much of this is common to almost every tribal group throughout equatorial and southern Africa. There are, however, local specialities. The diminutive Pygmies of the rain forests, from Gabon in the west to Uganda and Tanzania in the east, have a type of song which interpolates a whistle or flute with the voice, in a kind of instrumental-vocal hocket. Several whistles or flutes might join in, each sounding a note of different pitch. The Bushmen of South Africa are noted for their style of yodelling.

MOVEMENT AND DANCE

African singers clap their hands, sway or shake their bodies, or stamp their feet, as they sing – how different from the statuesque ladies and gentlemen of a church or concert choir! This is song and dance rolled into one. But dance with a clearer identity and purpose of its own does have a vital place in African tribal life. Indeed, just as the types of African percussion, stringed instruments, horns and pipes already discussed provide an insight into the probable origins of many instrumental types, so the spirit and purpose of many African tribal dances reach back to the same prehistoric times. They are informed by sympathetic magic, the belief that by representing or rehearsing a certain event you can cause it to happen. The images in cave paintings of wild animals pierced by spears and arrows are famous examples of this.

MIMETIC DANCE Mimetic rituals – acting out, miming, imitating an action or event – are best illustrated by hunting dances. In these, one or more members of the tribe represent some animal prey, while the remainder take the part of the hunters. A rainmaking dance

people of a tribe might voice their praise, approval or disapproval of a chief or witch-doctor through song, in a way they would not dare to do as individuals. Music might also take some of the sting out of quarrels and disputes: chanted insults are usually less offensive than spoken ones.

VOCAL POLYPHONY Most of this song is a communal activity. Everyone learns from childhood the chants and rhythms handed down from one generation to the next. Beyond that, the singing has an impromptu freshness and spontaneity – all the more remarkable considering the number of voices usually involved. It also includes vocal styles and techniques that are distinguished by academic names in other societies and cultures. African tribal singing is primarily poly-

Two more tribal dancers from Zaire. The camera has caught all the compulsive vigor and intensity of traditional African dance.

begins with the shaman priest or witchdoctor sprinkling a few drops of water on the ground. Then the dancers patter their feet in imitation of the first heavy drops of rain from a storm cloud. Finally, they stamp or patter about much more rapidly, also twisting and turning, their flying skirts and beads imitating the patter and rush of steadily falling rain. In contrast, for a dance of mourning, the participants move slowly and solemnly around a tree, as they accompany, in thought and action, the dead person on his or her journey to join the spirits. A short descending phrase, chanted over and over again, accompanies their dance. Another very interesting dance is more symbolic than openly mimetic. The chief of the tribe throws a newly cut gourd higher and higher into the air as he dances. The gourd holds within it new energy and strength, and as long as he catches it, this strength and energy will invigorate the chief himself and the life of the tribe. If, alas, he drops it, the energy will be lost to the earth.

Not all African dance is so pregnant with magical meaning. The step dances of the Zulus, the leaps and strides of the Sothos, the pure acrobatics of some Pygmy dancers (whose reputation in this field was known to the ancient Egyptians), are all examples of the sheer love of rhythm and movement manifested by the whole black African race.

The Music of Madagascar

The large tropical island of Madagascar (the Malagasy Republic) off the east coast of Africa is a real mixture of musical cultures. Historians and anthropologists believe that the native population is not much connected with any of the African races, but is descended from people who made the not inconsiderable voyage in outrigger canoes right around the Indian Ocean from somewhere in southeast Asia.

This proposition is backed up by the existence of such local instruments as the valiha, a type of tube zither (a section of cane tube with the strings stretched around it), variations of which are found in many parts of the Far East. Some dirges and other traditional Madagascan forms of song also carry echoes of the kind of tribal singing heard in New Guinea and parts of present-day Indonesia.

The Arabic-Islamic influence, coming down the East African coast from Arabia, has given the island many more of its instruments, including a kind of double-reed oboe, the type of lute known as the ud, the tambourine, and double- and single-headed drums.

Over the centuries, of course, the music of mainland Africa has also left its mark, in such instruments as stick zithers from Ethiopia, and a variety of rattles; also in forms of responsorial singing and hand-clapping.

Overlaying all this has been the European influence, from the time of the early Portuguese explorers, through the work of Christian missionaries, to the period of French colonization at the end of the nineteenth century. To this day, in odd corners of the island, such curiosities as old harmoniums and examples of hurdy-gurdies bear witness to these past intrusions of the white man.

Music in Latin America

6

Amazonian Indian boys
playing traditional urua-
type *flutes.*

Music in Latin America

Latin America covers the whole of Central and South America. It is called 'Latin' because much of it was conquered and colonized by Spain and Portugal, whose languages are based on Latin and are still spoken almost everywhere. Historically, the key date is 1492, when Christopher Columbus first set foot on American soil. This divides the history of the region into Pre-Columbian and Post-Columbian.

In reality, the situation is not nearly so clear cut as that. The Spanish conquistadors soon destroyed the Pre-Columbian civilizations of the Incas, Aztecs and others, but they did not penetrate very far into the vast Amazonian interior, whose inhabitants, until quite recently, were generally left alone. Then, around the region of the Caribbean, the Spanish and Portuguese were soon followed by the British and French, and by an influx of black African slave labor. The music of Latin America is a fascinating mix of these influences.

Mestizo *is the word for the mix of American Indian and Spanish colonial styles that make up much of Latin America's folk music. Here, two Colombians perform with flutes and gourd rattle or maraca. The flutes are* gaitas, *made from the stem of a cactus plant with mouthpieces fashioned from beeswax.*

MUSIC OF THE AMAZON

The Amazon Basin and neighboring Orinoco river comprise thousands of square miles of tropical rain forest. Portions of this huge territory are now being cleared (to the concern of environmentalists) for cattle raising and farming, but in remote enclaves of the Amazon Basin itself, and the surrounding Andean foothills and other highland areas, some tribal life still survives. These communities may have inherited practices and customs from the rest of the American Indian race; but other civilizations and cultures, either before or after the time of Columbus, have hardly impinged upon them.

So they offer an insight into a pre-literate lifestyle and into the role of music in societies which have in all probability remained unchanged for many thousands of years.

....

TRIBAL INSTRUMENTS Some Amazonian musical instruments, like those of tribal Africa, are ancient ancestors of today's more familiar types. Others, in terms of further development, represent a dead end. They are fascinating relics of a distant past.

As with nearly all tribal societies, percussion takes pride of place. There are scrapers of wood or bone; jingles made from animal hooves and claws, nutshells or kernels, strung together to be worn around the body; and rattles, using a gourd or calabash filled with stones or seeds. There are stamping sticks (heavy wooden posts or sticks for beating on the ground), and there are drums.

Many whistles and flutes are made from bone, including human bone. The urua, on the other hand, consists of two very long lengths of cane (one longer than the other), with vibrating reeds inside them, which some scholars describe as a kind of antique double-clarinet. There are so-called trumpets, fashioned either from wood, tree bark or bone. They have a flared end ('bell') made from animal horn or a kind of hardened wax.

Among curiosities found in the Amazon is the same bull-roarer that the Australian aborigines and natives of New Guinea spin round and round in the air, which is related, in principle, to the African buzz disk (see page 86). There is also the turtle or tortoise shell, exclusive to the Indians of Central and South America. It is another friction instrument (see also pages 100–101), its strange, squeaky noise produced by rubbing the moistened palm of the hand over the shell.

Two other points are worth making. One is that there are very few stringed instruments found among the Amazonian Indians (nor are there many among the pre-Columbian American Indians as a whole). The other is that musicologists see a certain resemblance between some of their bone flutes and other pipes and ancient specimens from China and Mongolia, so strengthening the belief that there was an Ice Age migration of Asiatic peoples to the Americas.

....

MUSIC AND RITUAL Music among the Amazonian Indians binds together the whole community. It is the essential accompaniment to all ritual and ceremony, and through song it preserves the lore and the laws of the tribe. A key figure in all this is the shaman priest, whose contact with the spirit world sustains

Amazonian Indian playing his bow and using teeth and mouth as a resonator and to modify the pitch of the vibrating string. The same kind of musical bows are found in tribal Africa (see page 85) and parts of the Far East.

Amazonian tribal dancers rehearsing outside their village, somewhere in the vast interior of Brazil.

the fortunes of the tribe. Such contact is made through music using a trance-like cantillation, punctuated by cries and snorts and shakings of a sacred rattle. The shaman may also intone syllables that only have meaning in this magical musical context.

Use of the voice takes other remarkable forms among the indigenous inhabitants of the Amazon and its surrounding lands. They imitate birds and other animals, to attract them while hunting, or to acquire some of their powers. In much of their other singing or chanting, they do not observe scales as we understand them, but are adept at carrying the voice through slurs and glissandos (sliding it up and down in pitch). A mark of true vocal prowess is to fill the lungs and sing or chant until all breath is exhausted, changing the voice in pitch, raising it from a whisper to a shout. Flute and drums may join the singers in a kind of melodic and rhythmic polyphony. There is also what scholars call heterophonic singing, which means that individuals or groups vary a melody, one against the other, as they sing.

One Amazonian dance celebrates initiation into adulthood, where candidates must face the frightening spectacle of a dancer, covered in lurid pigments. He comes running and leaping out of the jungle, a spirit of terror, accompanied by other dancers in the guise of wild animals.

THE INCAS

The Incas (Emperors) of Peru ruled over an empire that covered much of the Andes Mountains of South America. Despite the lack of such things as wheeled transportation, it seems to have been a well-ordered and prosperous society. Nobody is quite sure when this empire started (although it is thought to be during the twelfth century); but it was thriving right up to the moment when the Spanish conquistador Francisco Pizarro, greedy for its gold, destroyed it early in the sixteenth century.

Fortunately, some knowledge of Incan music has survived. In the case of their instruments, many were fashioned from clay or even more durable stone. These included pan pipes (*antaras*), other similar sets of three or four pipes molded together, and whistling pots. These latter are real instrumental curios, for water was used to force air out through a whistling head, similar in principle to the Greek and Roman hydraulus or water-operated organ. In general, musical instruments seem to have been highly prized by the Inca people, often accompanying their owners to the grave. Their color, size and their 'sex' (their supposed male or female qualities) gave status to those who played them. Trumpeters enjoyed high social standing (like their counterparts in Renaissance and baroque Europe), whether they played true metal trumpets, or the large conch shells found along the Pacific coast.

From the design of some wind instruments, musicologists conclude that the Incas used both pentatonic scales and scales with microtones, and preferred high notes to low ones. But the lack of any notated examples of their music means that musicologists have little idea how these factors actually shaped Inca melodies. It is known, however, that in their capital of Cuzco, festivals were held involving bands of up to one hundred players; and that mystical significance was given to the numbers four and eight. Very large individual drums had to have four players, or drums had to be assembled in sets of four or eight.

THE AZTECS

While the Incas ruled in South America, other civilizations flourished in Central America, dominant among them being the Aztec culture of Mexico. And just as the Inca empire was destroyed by Pizzaro, so other Spanish conquistadores, led by Hernando Cortez, put an end to Aztec society early in the sixteenth century. They left behind them monumental temples, sculptures, miniature paintings and a form of hieroglyphic script, from which a picture can be pieced together of what that society was like and how it was organized.

South American Indians with flute and pan pipes (jonkari).

Clearly, the Aztecs were a severe and fanatical people, with a religion that required human sacrifice on a massive scale. Music served this religion and was, therefore, taken very seriously. It was in the hands of a professional élite with a rigorous training behind them. They had to learn a very extensive repertory of music, based on a detailed and elaborate religious calendar. Musicians were a privileged group, though woe betide them if they sounded a wrong note or missed a beat in performance. Such errors carried the death penalty.

Surprisingly, perhaps, for people who attached such importance to music, the Aztecs had a quite limited range of instruments. They had a few wind instruments, some of which they may have inherited from more ancient times, including wooden or clay whistles and flutes, and tubular or shell-type trumpets. Otherwise, they concentrated on percussion, although most drums and idiophones were tuned to produce pitched notes. The teponaztli, for example, was a large slit-drum with two vibrating 'tongues,' each chiseled or filed down to a different length or thickness to produce two contrasting notes. These drums were held in awe, for they were thought to embody the gods, and the blood of sacrificial victims was poured into them. Some were carved with the images of bloodthirsty rites conducted to their baleful tattoo.

Two old Mexican Aztec instruments. Right: a clay rattle in the image of a mother and child. Below: a whistling pot. Clay and pottery musical instruments were a specialty of pre-Columbian America.

Because the Aztecs have not left any notated music, once again we can only guess at their actual melodies and rhythms. It is, however, worth noting that early Spanish settlers were moved by the snatches of Aztec music they heard. It apparently conveyed feelings or emotions they could appreciate, unlike much of the music of other American Indian races, whose idiom is quite alien to the European ear.

Despite living under threat from the Aztecs, some neighboring tribes and cultures managed to keep their own ways of life and their own styles of music. The Cuna Indians of Panama, for example, played ocarina-type wind instruments. Mostly made of earthenware, they are further examples of the widespread use of ceramics and stone among the musical cultures of pre-Columbian Central and South America.

LATIN AMERICAN MUSIC

The destruction of the Inca and Aztec empires was the end of one era. The rapid colonization of large areas of South and Central America by the Spanish and Portuguese was the beginning of another. The invaders brought with them their own music and their own instruments, notably stringed instruments – lutes, the Spanish vihuela and guitar – that had been so

A Quechuan Indian of Peru presenting another aspect of the mestizo *folk culture already mentioned on page 94. This kind of harp is a typical South American folk instrument. Note the two legs attached to its base, so that it may be swung right back and played in a near horizontal position.*

conspicuously absent from the music of the pre-Hispanic Indians. After the Spanish and the Portuguese came the British and the French, then the thousands of black African slaves imported to work the plantations of the Caribbean and elsewhere. Out of this mixture came a colorful folk music. This was to be the foundation of Latin American music as everyone knows it today; lazily seductive, or filled with the irresistible exotic color and gaiety of carnival time.

....

THE LATIN BEAT Many of the folk song and dance styles of Latin America are delightful. There are, for example, the hundreds of South American love songs, called *tonadas* (tunes or airs) in Spanish and *toadas* in Portuguese-speaking Brazil. There is also

Continued on page 104

South and Central America

The big division in the musical instruments of South and Central America is between pre-Columbian times and the much more recent, largely Europeanized post-Columbian period. During the earlier period, there were many clay and pottery instruments, but very few stringed instruments. Today's Latin American music is noted for its percussion.

WIND INSTRUMENTS

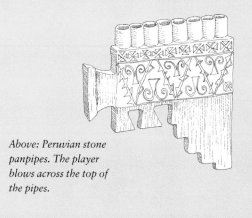

Above: Peruvian stone panpipes. The player blows across the top of the pipes.

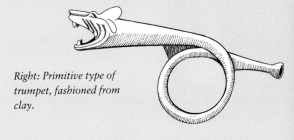

Right: Primitive type of trumpet, fashioned from clay.

PERCUSSION

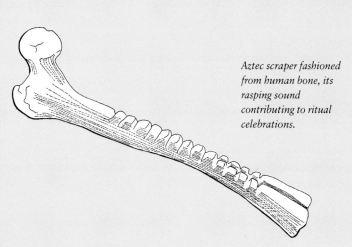

Aztec scraper fashioned from human bone, its rasping sound contributing to ritual celebrations.

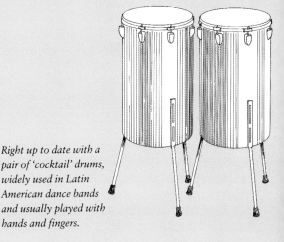

Right up to date with a pair of 'cocktail' drums, widely used in Latin American dance bands and usually played with hands and fingers.

Instruments are not drawn to scale

Cuban fiddle with cane body, one of the few traditional stringed instruments of the Americas.

Peruvian pipe player, keeping alive ancient musical traditions.

Below: Pre-Columbian America was also famous for its stone or clay whistling pots. This one comes from Peru.

Right: One of the most ancient of instruments: a wooden bull-roarer from Brazil. In fact, it sounds more like the voice of the wind as it spins round and round in the air.

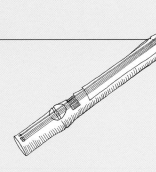

More panpipes, this time made from lengths of bamboo.

Above: One of the horn or conch shells widely used among Pre-Columbian Americans.

Simple Peruvian kettledrum of cloth or animal hide stretched across the top of a clay pot.

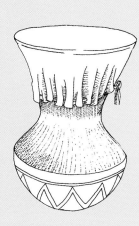

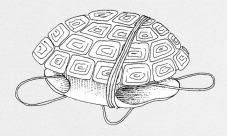

Fascinating example of a friction instrument: a waxed tortoise shell rubbed with a length of cord, producing a squeaking sound.

Rattle made from a gourd, probably containing dried seeds or beans and generously decorated with feathers.

The World Goes Latin

The music of Latin America, as the rest of the world knows it, is an exhilarating and intoxicating cocktail of the melodies and rhythms of black Africa and of colonial Spain, Portugal and France, with perhaps a dash of American Indian. Along with jazz, Latin American music has become an enduring and universal musical language that has conquered the world of popular song and dance.

The irrepressible Carmen Miranda from Brazil, the personification on film of Latin American song and dance's verve.

*I*n 1933, Fred Astaire and Ginger Rogers danced the 'Carioca' in the Hollywood musical *Flying Down to Rio*. It was the start of film's most famous dancing partnership, launched by the rhythms of Latin America. Carmen Miranda from Brazil gyrated her way to stardom to the same intoxicating rhythms.

Latin America's conquest of popular song and dance began with the tango, a folk dance from Argentina, whose name was probably taken from an old Spanish word, *tañer,* meaning to play an instrument. It was already popular in New York, London and Paris before World War I, and in the 1920s, it became a craze. The daring sexuality of the steps put to it – so easily reduced to comic parody – were very much in line with the new social emancipation of the era. There is, in fact, no definitive tango rhythm. It may remain close to the Cuban *habañera* or take on that characteristic syncopated beat at the end of each bar, ending perhaps with a strongly accented half-cadence, leaving the dance, so to speak, suspended in mid-air.

The more energetic rumba seems to have begun as a ritual dance in some Cuban religious cult. There was not much religion in evidence by the time it reached the dance halls and night clubs of America and Europe. Its jaunty beat was now reinforced by those Latin American specialties, the maracas and the hard-wood claves or resonating batons with their chinking syncopation. Later

variants include the mambo and the cha cha, whose insistent little three-beat phrase can cheekily re-vamp almost any tune.

The Brazilian samba, more relaxed than the rumba, has given rise to the even more langorous bossa nova, whose associated drowsy singing style has inspired such numbers as 'The Girl from Ipanema', who, as she ambles along the surf-flecked fringes of the famous Rio de Janeiro beach, 'looks straight ahead, not at me'. American songwriter Cole Porter's famous 'Begin the Beguine' cleverly parodies a similar dance rhythm.

The word conga means circle, suggesting ritualistic beginnings of this dance in its native Cuba. It has long been a favorite at European and American parties, where revelers form not a circle but a long snaky line, lurching forward with three steps and a side kick. There are also 'conga drums', played, like most Latin American drums, with hands and fingers. The pitch of the drum, as with some African percussion, can be instantly altered, in this case by putting pressure on the skin.

The Latin beat and melodic turns of phrase have appealed to many composers beyond the shores of Latin America itself. There are tangos by the Spanish composer Albéniz and by Walton, in his music to *Façade*. Latin American rhythms made a lasting impression on Darius Milhaud (1892-1974) after his time in Brazil, an example being his music to the ballet *Le Boeuf sur le Toit*. Australian Arthur Benjamin's *Jamaican Rumba* is one of the best pieces of light orchestral music. Another type of Caribbean dance inspired Frederick Delius's (1862-1934) 'La Calinda', an orchestral interlude from his opera *Koanga*, the name of an African chieftan sold into slavery. Among Americans, Gershwin contributed a 'Cuban' Overture and Morton Gould (born 1913) a 'Latin American' Symphony; while Copland went Mexican in *El Salón México*, and Bernstein added an exhilarating twist to the rumba in 'America' from his musical *West Side Story*.

Left: A colorful and acrobatic Cuban dance troupe.

Latin American music has inspired many composers outside the continent itself. Above: The Frenchman Darius Milhaud wrote much music with a Latin American flavor. Left: Two dancers sway to the tango from William Walton's music for *Façade*.

CALYPSO

Most of us today think of West Indian calypso singing as a form of entertainment – a clever and amusing way of making up fresh and topical words to a tune. In times past, this kind of song was taken more seriously.

The origins of calypso can be traced back to the griots of West Africa, those bards and disseminators of local news and gossip (see page 89). Their traditions were carried across the Atlantic by the black slaves who were put to work in different parts of the Americas. They resurfaced with most effect among the slaves of the Caribbean sugar plantations, whose only means of saying what they thought and felt was by singing songs with words that said one thing, but meant another. Their songs acted as a kind of musical grapevine, conveying news, gossip and opinion. As with many tribal communities, the singers sometimes also traded insults through their songs, as a way of resolving quarrels.

Some people think the word calypso comes from 'kaiso,' 'cariso' or 'kaliso,' themselves probable corruptions of an old French colonial word meaning 'festivity.' Others say it comes from the West African 'kaito,' meaning something like 'serves him right.' Most calypsos were originally sung in French Creole dialects, the singers often switching from one dialect to another to conceal further the true meaning of the words. In the nineteenth century, the British brought in a law banning calypso singing on both political and moral grounds, though it never worked.

During its 200-year history, calypso singing has produced some splendid characters, adopting such names as Attila the Hun and The Roaring Lion, who would often compete with each other in the art of clever and spontaneous wordplay. A more recent celebrity has been the singer known as The Mighty Sparrow.

Today's calypso style, shaped by such artistes as Harry Belafonte, has adopted easy-going 'soca' rhythms (from 'soul' and 'calypso'). But the calypso heritage, as songs of political and social intent, goes marching on in the music of reggae and rap.

Carnival time in Rio de Janeiro. Such events, originally religious festivals, but now given over almost entirely to merry-making, pulsate with the rhythms of Latin America.

the lively Argentinian dance called the *gato*, clearly Spanish in origins with its rapid footwork and guitar accompaniment. It is, however, the underlying rhythms of this wealth of song and dance that have traveled around the world. Syncopation is their hallmark; the accented or misplaced beat that lifts the music off the ground. They share this, of course, with early jazz, both being strongly influenced by the black and creole populations of both North and South America. However, the character of this Latin American music is made quite distinctive by its expressive use of percussion instruments: bongos (small hand-beaten drums), maracas (rattles traditionally made from gourds filled with dried seeds or coffee beans), and the tuneful marimba (a local type of xylophone).

Perhaps the most stately and aristocratic Latin American rhythm is that of the haba-

nera, which many people think of as Spanish, but in fact comes from Cuba, being named after its capital city of Havana. The tango, probably originating in Argentina, has a similar skipped beat. It is more famous today because in the early years of this century it joined the jazz-inspired Charleston as the dance sensation of the age. The way people danced the tango, locked in a suggestive embrace, also created a scandal. The Cuban rumba and mambo are much faster and clearly infected by the spirit of African dance, whereas the Brazilian samba and bossa nova are more relaxed, evoking images of white sand, blue sea, and gently waving palms.

. . . .

THE LATIN AMERICAN HERITAGE Latin American music joined hands with jazz to revolutionize the world of popular song and dance. Latin American countries have also produced some fine composers. Between them they form what may be called a Latin American nationalist school – composers dedicated to promoting their homelands through their music.

The doyen among them is Heitor Villa-Lobos (1887–1959) from Brazil. He composed the well-known set of pieces, *Bachianas Brasileiras,* cleverly combining in them his love of Bach and other baroque composers with Brazilian folk music. One piece is the charming 'The Little Train of the Caipira,' suggesting the sound and motion of a rustic little steam train puffing across the hot, empty Brazilian countryside. Another group of his pieces are the *Chôros* for a variety of instruments and voices, inspired by the traditional Brazilian *choro* or folk music bands.

Manuel Ponce (1882–1948) and Carlos Chavez (1899–1978) of Mexico studied indigenous American Indian music, which greatly influenced their own work. One of Chavez's pieces is *Xochipili,* named after the Aztec god of music, and features old Mexican Indian percussion instruments. Alberto Ginastera (born 1916) was inspired for many years by the music of his native Argentina, before turning to serialism (see pages 157–158) and other more abstract methods of composition. His ballet *Estancia,* for example, features the dances and songs of the gauchos, or cowboys, of the cattle-raising lands of the pampas.

Villa-Lobos and Ponce, it is worth adding, also wrote much music for the Spanish guitar. Indeed, between them they have probably produced a finer body of guitar music than has come out of Spain itself, the home of that instrument.

STEEL BANDS

One of the happiest sounds in the Caribbean, or wherever West Indian people gather together, is that of a steel band. It is like an orchestra of softly metallic xylophones. These steel or steel pan bands are also a fine example of do-it-yourself music-making. They originated in Trinidad about sixty years ago, among local black people who wanted something cheap and cheerful to play at Carnival time. At first, they used cookie tins and garbage can lids, to the annoyance of other local residents, who complained so much about the noise that for a time there was a ban on such ensembles. But

the so-called steel band enthusiasts were not so easily discouraged. They turned their attention from tins and trash cans to old oil drums, which form the basis of most steel bands today.

Turning the oil drums into pitched or semi-pitched percussion instruments is done in several stages. The bottom of the drum, with no tap hole in it, is the part that matters. This potential drumhead is first hammered into a concave shape, which improves its tone. Further indentations may then be hammered into the surface, each of which, if the job is skillfully done, can sound a note of different pitch. The length or height of the supporting drum cylinder, it should be added, determines the overall pitch of the instrument. Finally, the drum needs to be tempered by heating and cooling rapidly with cold water. The highest-pitched drums, usually also those with the largest range of pitched notes, are called ping-pongs, and in a band they play the melody. Lower-pitched drums are classed more conventionally as alto, tenor and bass.

The homemade ingenuity of steel or pan bands extends to the drum sticks. These have often been made by stretching a section of the inner tube of an old bicycle tire over a wooden stick.

The Western Tradition

7

The Flute Concert *by Adolph von Menzel, painted c. 1850.*

The Western Tradition

The Greeks and Romans are usually considered to be the founders of European architecture, literature, government and law – what we know as Western civilization. But, as discussed at length elsewhere in this book, their music – notably that of classical Greece – was still closely related to that of the ancient Middle East. Western or European music is thought to have its origins at about the time when the Roman Empire was breaking up and Christianity was taking its place, that is from about AD 300 to 800. It has a short history, therefore, when compared with the far more ancient musical traditions and heritages of Africa, India or China. On the other hand, in well under two thousand years, Western music, along with Western civilization as a whole, has expanded, changed and taken on radically new forms and styles at a rate unmatched by that of any other race or culture around the world.

Woodcut of Pope Gregory I, whose name is traditionally linked with the Gregorian chant, still sung in the Roman Catholic Church.

MEDIEVAL MUSIC

During the early Middle Ages, music had quite a limited role to play. The centers of early Christianity were the monasteries; and the only music regularly heard in them was chanted by monks, most of whom were not trained musicians, but men with other jobs to do in and around the monastery. This music, sung to the hymns, psalms and prayers of the church liturgy, was plainsong, or plainchant. It was a simple, gently meandering kind of melody, sung in unison and with no particular rhythm, since it stuck closely to the syllables and inflections of the words. Plainsong was derived partly from the ancient chants of the synagogue, and partly from the old Greek modes or scales (since some of the first Christian communities grew up in Greece and neighboring countries of the eastern Mediterranean, where St. Paul had preached). As far as is known, for hundreds of years, plainsong was the only kind of Western music, and to today's ears it has a distant, almost timeless sound. But, for all the apparent timelessness of plainsong, change was at hand. The catalyst was written or notated music.

NOTATION Long before the European Middle Ages, attempts had been made at writing music down, but none, as far as is known, was anything like as accurate or comprehensive as Western notation. The need for this came primarily from the Church,

One of the rose windows in Chartres Cathedral. The building of the great French Gothic cathedrals and churches coincided with the development of polyphony – the first great period in European music.

whose leaders, notably Pope Gregory I (*c.* 470-520), wished to lay down set forms of doctrine and worship as Christianity spread further and further afield. This meant writing down the words of the liturgy for use in churches and monasteries, and, where applicable, noting down also the plainsong melodies that went with them. The consequences of a proper system of notation, dating from about 1000, went far beyond the mere noting down of lines of music. No longer did monks and choristers simply learn melodies by rote and, in turn, pass them on to others; musicians and scholars now had a permanent record of the music at their disposal. This allowed them to study and reflect upon the music at their leisure, and also encouraged them to think of ways of changing and perhaps

Harmony of the Spheres

The scope of early medieval music may seem rather limited to us – most of it for small, all-male choirs, to be sung only in chapel or church. Nevertheless, scholars and theologians thought and wrote a great deal on the subject. Their ideas were based on the much older notions of a 'Harmony of the Spheres,' already discussed on page 13; the belief that there is a relationship, both scientific and mystical, between the mathematics of astronomy and the mathematics of pitched notes. The Roman scholar Anicius Boethius (c.AD 470–520) wrote a famous treatise, De Musica, which sums up these wonderful ideas. The study of music, he wrote, should progress from the proven mathematics of pitched sounds to a deeper appreciation of the way music echoes the organization of life on earth and in the heavens. Thus music lay at the heart of medieval scholarship. Through a true understanding of it, a wise and learned man may understand the workings of God. This idea, of reaching out to God through music, informed the work of musicians for centuries to come. Listening to medieval and Renaissance polyphonic church music, it is fascinating to think of the deeper ideas that may lie behind the notes.

improving it. No other musical culture has given itself this facility. Performing music brilliantly is one thing, shared by good musicians of every time and place. Being able to sit down and compose it, to create something original and personal, is what has made the progress and character of Western music unique. It is the difference between folk music, created and shared by a whole community or people, and what may be termed art music.

POLYPHONY The Greek and Latin words for the various musical changes that accompanied the spread of staff notation may be unfamiliar to most people; but the processes they describe are quite straightforward. A melisma was a group of notes sung to a single word or syllable, usually to emphasize an important moment in the liturgy. Tropes were new, sometimes newly composed, sections of text or melody inserted into the existing liturgy and plainsong. Most important of all was organum, which meant adding a whole new line of melody to the original plainsong. In strict organum, the notes of the new melody line were the same pitch interval apart from the first melodic line, note for note. In free organum, the pitch intervals between the two melodic lines sometimes varied, each following a more independent line of its own. Today, the idea of singing or playing two lines of music together may not seem anything very special or daring, but in the context of musical history, organum was a big breakthrough. It formed the start of a long and glorious era in Western music that goes under the heading of polyphony – the music of 'many sounds'.

During the eleventh and early twelfth centuries, one major center in the development of polyphony and of notation was the monastery of St. Martial, at Limoges, in France. Another was Winchester, in England, whose churchmen produced two volumes of notated settings of liturgical texts in the eleventh century known as the *Winchester Tropers*. The most important center, though, was Paris, whose university, recruiting such great scholars as Peter Abelard, was medieval Europe's foremost center of learning. Its prestige was further enhanced by the building of the great gothic cathedral of Notre Dame. Two masters of the choir school during the building of the cathedral were Léonin (Leoninus) and his successor Pérotin (Perotinus Magnus), whose careers spanned the period from about 1160 to 1240. As well as developing organum, they are credited with introducing rhythm into church music; that is, of introducing notes of

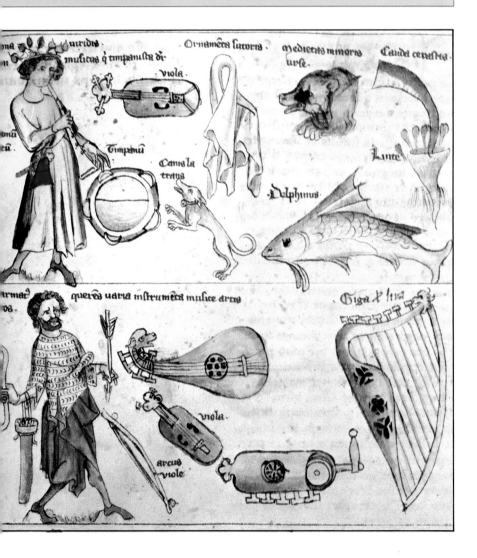

Two minstrels from a famous thirteenth-century Spanish manuscript, the Cantigas de Santa Maria. *Their instruments, left to right, are rebab and large lute, both of Moorish-Arabic origin.*

different duration and grouping them to create a sense of metrical flow to the music. Much of this pioneer work may, in fact, have been carried out in other cathedrals, churches and monasteries in and around Paris; but it is spoken of collectively as the Notre Dame School; Léonin and Pérotin are two of the first musicians now thought of as true composers – men who created original pieces of music.

. . . .

MINSTREL-KNIGHTS By the time of Léonin and Pérotin and the Notre Dame School, the course of European music was no longer in the hands of the Church alone, for there was a growing body of secular music. Among the various groups of performers were the goliards, itinerant students, some of whose riotous drinking songs were gathered into a manuscript called the *Carmina Burana* (the basis for the very popular twentieth-century choral work by the German composer Carl Orff). Jongleurs, as their French name suggests, were street entertainers, often jugglers and acrobats as well as singers and dancers. Then at a much more elevated level, both social and artistic, were the minstrel-knights. In different parts of France, they were called troubadours or trouvères. These two titles, in old Provençal and French respectively, mean 'seekers' or 'finders,' in the sense of finding or composing the verses and melodies of songs. Many troubadours and trouvères were true knights and noblemen, such as William IX, Duke of Aquitaine (1071–1127), and Richard Coeur de Lion (1157–99), French by birth,

later King of England, and a crusader knight. One center of the minstrel-knights' art was the court of Eleanor of Aquitaine at Poitiers. Their songs extolled courtly love and chivalry (the knight dedicating his life to some idealized lady), or they recalled distant and exotic lands, visited during the Crusades or fighting the Moors in Spain. In the German-speaking lands, such gifted noblemen were known as minnesingers ('singers of love'); in Britain there were other minstrels, who kept alive the art of the old Celtic bards, recalled today in the Welsh eisteddfods.

In all, the minstrel-knights' music is notable, not just because it marked the rise of secular art, but because much of it was homophonic (a single sound) as distinct from polyphonic. This led to a new concept of music, based both on melody and a growing interest in instruments, since many troubadours, minnesingers and such, accompanied themselves on harps or early kinds of fiddle.

. . . .

ARS NOVA The fabled world of the knight errant and of courtly love faded and died with such brutal happenings as the Albigensian Crusade, which destroyed a happy but heretical sect in southern France. Other events had an even more unsettling or disastrous effect on medieval Christendom: the Black Death, which decimated populations during the fourteenth century; the squalid circumstance of two rival popes, one in Rome, the other in Avignon; and the Hundred Years' War, the long power struggle among the English

Facing page: Page from a fourteenth-century Dutch manuscript about astrology, but also featuring many instruments. The top figure is holding a shawm or early oboe and touching a tambourine. Also included, clockwise, are an early fiddle (called viola), harp, hurdy-gurdy (or 'wheel-fiddle'), lute and another fiddle with bow.

Right: Manuscript of the celebrated Sumer is icumen in. *By the thirteenth century, notation was well advanced, with stave lines and clefs, and the music clearly divided into bars or measures. Note also the alternative sets of words, secular and sacred.*

and French nobility. But from this age of turmoil sprang new impulses in music and the arts. Philippe de Vitry, a fourteenth-century French churchman and scholar, wrote of them as the Ars Nova or New Art of his age.

A piece of music which breathes this new spirit is *Sumer is icumen in*, attributed to John of Fornsete, a monk of Reading Abbey, whence it is also known as the *Reading Rota*. Rota means a round, a type of composition in which the melody is taken up by different singers or instrumentalists in turn and follows itself round and round. It is a clever type of poly-

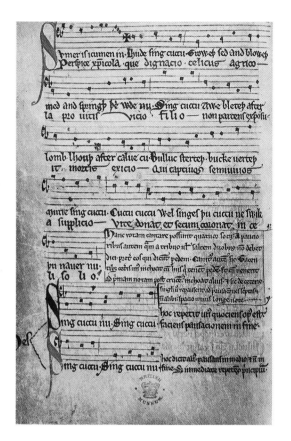

phony or musical counterpoint (meaning 'note against note'). The melody of *Sumer is icumen in* has a delightful freshness and rhythmic swing, appropriate to a song welcoming the spring. Significantly, the piece at one time had two sets of words, one secular (as quoted above), the other liturgical, pointing to a blending of the sacred and the secular in music and the other arts. Another example of this fruitful mixing of religious and secular ideas and styles in the music of the Ars Nova is the melody of a popular French folk song, *L'Homme Armé* (The Armed Man), used again in hundreds of pieces of church music.

FLEMINGS AND BURGUNDIANS Many of the finest musicians of this period came from the old provinces of Flanders and Burgundy, now comprising much of eastern France and Belgium; at no other time in history have musicians been given more honor and respect. As scholars and churchmen, as well as composers, they were men of high status. Some traveled widely and were welcomed everywhere, no matter what wars or other disturbances were taking place.

Guillaume de Machaut (c.1300–77) was a canon at Rheims Cathedral and was also a diplomat who served, among others, the kings of Navarre and Cyprus. He composed many secular vocal ballades, virelai and rondeaux,

A FEAST TO REMEMBER

During the fifteenth century, the court of Duke Philip the Good of Burgundy rivaled that of France, or anywhere else in Europe, for its pageantry and music. As proof of this, in 1454, Duke Philip staged the Banquet of the Oath of the Pheasant. Ostensibly, its purpose was to launch a new crusade against the Turks, who had recently captured the ancient Christian citadel of Constantinople (Istanbul). It was a spectacular occasion.

In the tapestry-hung banqueting hall, Philip's guests were greeted by some amazing sights. Among other marvels, there was a model church, large enough to house a bell, four choristers and an organ; there was also an enormous pie, concealing, according to one chronicler, thirty or so musicians 'playing on divers instruments.' (Could this be the origin of the ditty about 'Four and twenty blackbirds

baked in a pie'?) Throughout the feasting, these singers and musicians accompanied an equally amazing pageant. Two trumpeters, mounted back to back on a horse draped in orange silks, sounded fanfares. A boy seated on a magnificent white stag sang a song, joined by a second unseen vocalist who pretended to be the voice of the stag. Finally, in came an elephant with a castle on its back, imprisoning another singer dressed as Mother Church and lamenting the fall of Constantinople.

The same chronicler does not mention any musicians by name. But it is likely that the song sung by the boy and the stag (Je ne vis oncques la pareilles) was by Binchois, while the closing lament was by Dufay – two of the finest composers of their age. By the way, the crusade came to nothing.

Left: Fourteenth-century misericord, the underside of a wooden choir stall, in Chichester Cathedral in England. The carved figures are playing harp and recorder.

Below: Fifteenth-century Flemish tapestry of a lady playing a positive (non-portable) organ. Her companion pumps the bellows. A fabled unicorn is featured among the animals.

including one very striking piece with the words 'Ma fin est mon commencement' (My end is my beginning), in which the notes of the melody are repeated backwards, in obedience to the meaning of the words. Machaut is best remembered, though, for his *Messe de Notre Dame*, the earliest surviving setting of the full Catholic Mass. The Englishman John Dunstable (*c.*1390–1453), astrologer and mathematician as well as composer, probably traveled to Flanders and Burgundy, where his settings of parts of the Mass and his motets were much admired. One of the composers he influenced was Guillaume Dufay (*c.*1400–74), a priest whose busy career in France and Italy was matched by the variety of his sacred and secular music. Dunstable also influenced the Flemish composer Gilles Binchois (*c.*1400–60), who served at the court of Burgundy, the richest and most illustrious of its age, noted for its lavish ceremonies and entertainments. Then there was Johannes Ockeghem (*c.*1420–97), chaplain to the French king, who composed some of the most cleverly thought-out polyphonic music of the age. Ockeghem also taught the Flemish-born Josquin des Prés, or Després (*c.*1440–1521). He worked for many years in Milan and then in Rome, before returning to the French royal household. The richness and variety of Josquin's compositions, sacred and secular, lead into the next major period of European history and art: the Renaissance.

Music and the Mass

The close historical links between Western music and the Church has given us hundreds of settings of the Mass (Latin Missa), the principle service of the Roman Catholic Church (known in other churches as the Eucharist or Holy Communion). Through the early Middle Ages, different parts of the service were often rendered in plainsong, but over the centuries, those parts of the liturgy of the Mass regularly set to music became established as follows: Kyrie Eleison (Lord have mercy); Gloria (Glory be to God); Credo (I believe);

Sanctus and Benedictus (Holy and Blessed), and Agnus Dei (Lamb of God). There is also the Catholic Requiem Mass, a service for the dead, which has inspired fewer, but generally very fine, musical settings. It includes these sections: Requiem Aeternam (Rest Eternal); Dies Irae (Day of Wrath); Lux Aeterna (Light Eternal), and Libera Me (Deliver Me). They are all in Latin (Greek in the case of Kyrie Eleison), now replaced by vernacular versions of the liturgy for everyday use.

From the end of the Middle Ages, music became more secular. But up to the present

day, composers (some avowed unbelievers) have continued to write great settings of the Mass or Requiem Mass. Bach's B minor Mass, Beethoven's Missa Solemnis and Verdi's Requiem are three outstanding examples.

The titles of Mass or Requiem have also been used by some composers in a much more personal way. Brahms set to music passages from the Lutheran Bible in his Ein Deutsches Requiem; and Delius's A Mass of Life was inspired by the German philosopher Nietzsche's book Also Sprach Zarathustra, which has nothing to do with Christianity.

THE RENAISSANCE

*R*enaissance means 're-birth.' Strictly speaking, it refers to the re-birth or re-discovery of the art and ideas of classical Greece and Rome that had been largely forgotten or suppressed by the Church as pagan throughout the long period of the Middle Ages. In a much broader context, the Renaissance period, from about 1400 to 1600, saw a major shift in ideas and attitudes, away from religion and toward humanism. The Church remained a very powerful institution, and many great Renaissance works of art were dedicated to it. But its teaching and authority were seriously challenged both from within (by the events of the Reformation), and by men of scholarship and science. The Renaissance was a time of invention and discovery, of looking at the world and its ways in a new light. It was the time of Leonardo da Vinci, Michelangelo, Shakespeare, Copernicus, Galileo, Columbus and Magellan. Politically, too, the Renaissance brought significant changes, not just in national boundaries, but in attitudes. France, England, Spain and Portugal, became powerful sovereign states; and writers, artists and musicians began also to think of themselves and their work in nationalist terms.

POLYPHONY'S GOLDEN AGE The biggest religious event of the Renaissance period was the Reformation. Like most political and religious movements, its consequences went far beyond the original intentions of those who started it. Its chief driving force was Martin Luther, a German priest who, initially, was offended by what he saw as widespread abuse and corruption among the clergy and wished to correct it. After long years of appalling bloodshed, it ended by dividing most of Europe between the Catholic and Protestant churches. There was also a Counter-Reformation, organized by the Catholic Church which, recognizing that there had been corruption within its confines, introduced many reforms on its own account. Many composers were inspired by its spiritual zeal, writing devotional choral music of great polyphonic beauty for their church. Roland (or Orlando) de Lassus (1532–94), another in the long line of composers of Flemish birth, spent some time in Rome, then settled at the royal court in Munich, in that part of the German-speaking lands that remained loyal to the Catholic Church. Among his hundreds of works are his *Penitential Psalms*. In Rome

itself, the fountainhead of the Catholic faith, Giovanni Pierluigi da Palestrina (*c.*1525–94) composed his celebrated *Missa Papae Marcelli* (Mass for Pope Marcellus), which was taken as a model of the new purity and clarity both in terms of music and words that the Counter-Reformation demanded of church music.

One of Palestrina's colleagues was the Spanish-born Tomás Luis da Victoria (*c.*1548–1611). Spain was the most devout Catholic country in Europe, home of the Spanish Inquisition, which aimed at stamping out all traces of heresy in the country; the Society of Jesus (the Jesuits) was founded by a Spaniard. Victoria's church music fully expresses this intense spiritual devotion. In Tudor England, Thomas Tallis (*c.*1505–85) and William Byrd (*c.*1542–1623) had to tread very carefully as the Catholic and the newly established Anglican churches struggled for ascendancy through the reigns of Henry VIII,

Facing page: sixteenth-century Italian porcelain, depicting monks at the organ. The man on the right is probably operating a slider, a device to admit air to a particular group of pipes. The organ keyboard encouraged the development of polyphony and counterpoint.

Above: Giovanni Pierluigi da Palestrina, honored by his peers as 'the Prince of Music' for his masses, motets and other examples of polyphonic vocal church music.

The Court of Maximilian

Maximilian I, who was connected with Philip the Good of Burgundy through marriage, was crowned Emperor of the Holy Roman Empire in 1493. This oddly named chunk of central Europe included present-day Germany and Austria and a large part of Italy. From Maximilian's time, it grew into the far more important Hapsburg Empire, which survived until the end of World War I. Maximilian, like his Burgundian forerunner, wished to make a big impression as a lover of the arts. Among the eminent musicians he attracted to his courts at Innsbruck and Vienna were the Flemish-born composers Jacob Obrecht (c.1451–1505) and Heinrich Isaac (c.1450–1517), the Swiss-born composer Ludwig Senfl

(c.1490–1543), and the celebrated scholar Heinrich Glarean, whose musical theories prepared the way for the change from the medieval modes to the new diatonic system of major and minor scales and keys.

Maximilian himself is an important figure in the history of the arts and music. He took a keen interest in musical instruments, and the many woodcuts and other illustrations he commissioned (from the German Renaissance artist Albrecht Dürer among others) show much about the instruments of his time, how they were made and how they were played. As a man of the Renaissance, he helped to establish the tradition of aristocratic patronage of the arts, which has meant so much to

European art. And as the first important Hapsburg emperor, he drew the German-speaking peoples into the mainstream of European music, paving the way for the long period of German musical ascendancy, from Schütz and J.S. Bach all the way through to Wagner and Richard Strauss. An institution owing its existence to his patronage is the world-famous Vienna Boys Choir

Below: A woodcut from The Triumph of Maximilian I (1526).

Thomas Tallis (left) and William Byrd, the two most illustrious names in English Tudor music. The two men also worked closely together, as organists at the Chapel Royal and in the relatively new business of music printing, in which they were granted a monopoly by Queen Elizabeth I.

Queen Mary and Elizabeth I. Despite the dangerous politics of those years, Tallis and Byrd wrote equally fine polyphonic choral music for each church, as the occasion required. Indeed, Tallis's motet, *Spem in alium*, is one of the richest-sounding of all choral works, with forty separate parts.

....

MADRIGALS AND SONGS The madrigal is a landmark in the story of secular music and belongs almost exclusively to Renaissance music. It is a type of vocal polyphony performed by a small group of singers, but, with a few exceptions, is very different in style and mood from the sacred music of the age. The singing of madrigals went with the fine clothes, furnishings and other trappings of wealth and leisure that were a mark of Renaissance prosperity among the nobility and the new merchant classes. And as music for entertainment, they expressed (like the writings of Cervantes and Shakespeare's plays) the pleasures and pains of temporal life, the delights of good food and wine, the beauties of nature, the joys and anguish of love.

The form originated in Italy, in the grand palaces and homes of the Venetian Republic and other city-states. It flourished in the hands of such composers as Adriaan Willaert (*c.*1490–1562) and Giaches de Wert (*c.*1535–96), two of the many Flemish-born musicians who found fame and fortune in more southern climes; Willaert's pupil, Cipriano de Rore (1516–65); Luca Marenzio

(*c.*1553–99); and the strange and brooding (he arranged the murder of his wife and her lover) Prince Carlo Gesualdo (*c.*1560–1613), who invested his madrigals with amazingly advanced and expressive harmonies.

The popularity of madrigals spread across Western Europe, aided by the relatively new invention of printing, which could deal with notated music as well as words. A collection of existing pieces, their words translated into English, was published in London in 1588 (the year of the Spanish Armada) with the title *Musica Transalpina* (Music from across the Alps); and soon after that came a flood of new madrigals by native composers. Examples by, among others, Thomas Morley (1557–1602), organist at the old St. Paul's Cathedral, London, John Wilbye (1574–1638), Thomas Weelkes (*c.*1575–1623) and Orlando Gibbons (1583–1625), contributed to Tudor England's golden age of music and literature.

John Dowland (1563–1626) was another illustrious English composer of the late Renaissance, but he specialized in solo songs, as distinct from madrigals, sung with lute accompaniment (just as the medieval troubadours and other minstrels had accompanied themselves with harp or fiddle). In fact, Dowland was best known in his own time as a lutenist, being invited to play for, among other European monarchs, the famous Danish king Christian IV and, back in his native land, for the English king James I.

INSTRUMENTAL MUSIC The stringed lute, at which Dowland excelled, was just one of many instruments that came to prominence during the Renaissance. The lute itself, with its many variants, bowed stringed instruments, woodwind recorders and oboes, brass trumpets and horns, had all been in existence, in one form or another, for hundreds or thousands of years. But major advances in technology, from printing to firearms, brought with them big advances and improvements to the design and construction of musical instruments. In addition, their availability went hand in hand with the growing domestic ease and prosperity of the time. People who could afford them collected groups, or consorts, of the same family of instruments, say, stringed viols, or woodwind recorders, which they proudly displayed in their homes. There were also regals and other conveniently small models of organ; and, newest of all on

Continued on page 120

Ancient and Folk Instruments

The folk instruments of Europe provide some strong cultural contrasts. Many from eastern and southern Europe are of middle eastern origin; while those from northern and western Europe belong to the old Nordic and Celtic races. There are also such interesting hybrids as the serpent, once popular in both military and church bands.

Percussion

The 'rommelpot' or friction drum, shown right, is not really a drum at all. The inserted stick rubs against the membrane, making it vibrate.

Wind Instruments

Ivory hunting horn decorated with silver, very different from the more familiar coiled metal horns.

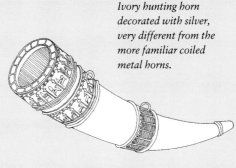

Stringed Instruments

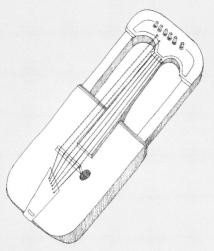

Old Welsh crwth, classed as a lyre, but technically more like a fiddle and played with a bow.

Hurdy gurdy, a semi-mechanical instrument, with a rotating wheel instead of a bow, and a set of keys to 'stop' the strings and play different notes.

Instruments are not drawn to scale

Spanish tambourine with metal jingles, an instrument inherited from the ancient Middle East.

Tabor, a drum once widely used by soldiers, jongleurs and other entertainers.

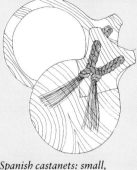

Spanish castanets: small, hand-held ivory or wooden clappers, much used in Flamenco song and dance.

Below: Single-reed Welsh pibcorn or hornpipe. Compare it with the example on page 77.

Above: Traditional craftsmanship is still employed in the making of this Swiss Alphorn.

Ancient Viking bronze lur, variously described as a type of trumpet or horn.

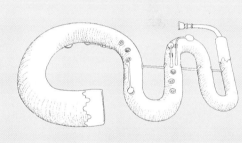

The aptly named serpent, a curious cross between brass and woodwind, once popular in both military and church bands.

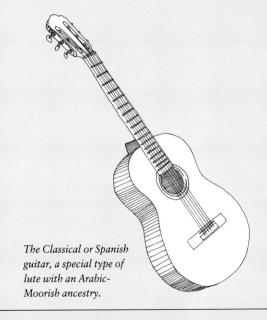

The Classical or Spanish guitar, a special type of lute with an Arabic-Moorish ancestry.

Left: The 'Brian Boru' harp, named after the tenth-century Irish king. Old Celtic harps like this were usually supported between the knees and held against the chest.

Norwegian Hardanger fiddle, very like a violin but with four extra 'sympathetic' strings, hence the eight tuning pegs.

the scene, stringed keyboard instruments, virginals and harpsichords.

These keyboard instruments – organs (from small household models to large church organs), virginals and harpsichords – are of special interest in more ways than one. They were technically the most advanced and sophisticated instruments of the Renaissance period. Also, just one performer, one pair of hands, could reproduce a piece of music complete with melody, rhythm, harmony and counterpoint. This concentration of all the essential elements of music on a single keyboard was to prove almost as important for the future development of Western music as notation had been five or six hundred years before. For example, it speeded up the change from the use of the old medieval modes to the new harmonic system of major and minor keys and scales that was to revolutionize music in the years to come.

Antonio de Cabezón (1510–66) was blind from childhood, yet was an outstanding performer and composer of Renaissance keyboard music, also exercising a good deal of influence through his position as court organist to the powerful Philip II of Spain. At about the same time, Tallis and Byrd in England were composing music for the virginals and harpsichord; and the so-called *Fitzwilliam Virginal Book* (now in the Fitzwilliam Museum, Cambridge, England) is perhaps the finest collection of early keyboard pieces. Two great organist-composers, coming right at the end of the Renaissance period, were Girolamo Frescobaldi (1583–1643) in Rome, and Jan Pieterszoon Sweelinck (1562–1621) in Amsterdam. The latter inaugurated a north European school or style of organ music that looked forward a hundred years to the masterworks of J.S. Bach.

MUSIC OF THE BAROQUE

The word 'baroque' comes from an old Spanish expression meaning 'rough pearl;' that is, something odd, almost grotesque. Indeed, it was used as a term of abuse by those people at the time who did not like the new, exuberant kind of art and architecture that grew out of the styles of the high or late Renaissance, during the early part of the seventeenth century. Today, baroque art is considered to be grand and opulent, full of confidence and well-being. The mighty basilica of St. Peter's, Rome, with its gorgeous high altar, Louis XIV's huge Palace of Versailles, with its surrounding fountains, lakes

and parks, and the paintings of Rubens, are all manifestations of it.

In music, one of the key figures in the transition from the Renaissance period into the baroque period of the seventeenth century was the Italian Claudio Monteverdi (1567–1643). He wrote some of the finest, most expressive of all madrigals, which, historically, at least, belong to Renaissance music. On the other hand, much of his sacred choral music, such as the celebrated *Vespers* of 1610, has the rich, soaring qualities associated with the spirit of baroque music. Above all, Monteverdi was the man who set baroque opera on its course as the most colorful and extravagant of all stage and musical entertainments.

OPERA'S BEGINNINGS Opera, combining drama and spectacle with music, had its antecedents in the miracle or morality plays of the Middle Ages, usually performed in or close to churches and cathedrals, and in courtly pageants and masques. But the history of opera as we know it, is reckoned to have begun with a group of Italian noblemen and scholars (including Vincenzo Galilei, father of the astronomer Galileo Galilei) living in Florence toward the end of the sixteenth century. They called themselves the Camerata, meeting informally in each other's homes, to discuss and perform classical Greek drama – a reminder of what 'renaissance' originally

Left: Portrait thought to be of the young Monteverdi. The first great composer of opera, initially at the court of Mantua and then in Venice, Monteverdi survived the plague in Venice and lived until his seventy-sixth year, a venerable age in his day.

Facing page: A seventeenth-century Dutch portrait of a woman and virginal; one finger lightly depresses a key. Note the elaborate decoration on both the inside and exterior of the instrument.

meant. They believed that this should be declaimed in a sing-song manner, called a recitative or recital. From these early and very tentative beginnings flowered the whole concept of setting words to music in a new kind of musico-dramatic entertainment, or *dramma per musica*, as the first operas were called.

Since the members of the Camerata were interested primarily in ancient Greek drama, it was natural that the subjects for these early *dramma per musica* were mostly inspired by legends and stories from Greek mythology or history. The legend of Orpheus and Eurydice was particularly popular, perhaps because Orpheus, with his lyre, was a musician. It was the basis for the Florentine composer Jacopo Peri's *Euridice*, first performed in 1600, to celebrate the wedding of the French king Henri IV to Maria de Medici (the Medicis of Florence were one of the most powerful Italian families of the late Renaissance). Seven years later, Monteverdi turned to the same

legend when he composed *La favola d'Orfeo* for the Gonzaga family at the court of Mantua. The singing and the use of accompanying instruments were far more dramatic than anything previously seen and heard. The fanfare-like prelude or overture is itself most arresting, one of the earliest pieces of purely orchestral music. Monteverdi later became director of music at St. Mark's Basilica, Venice, where he composed much church music. Venice was the first city to open commercial opera houses, so Monteverdi also had the chance to write more dramatic stage works: a remarkable dramatic cantata called *Il Combattimento di Tancredi e Clorinda*, with such innovative stage effects as galloping horses when the two warriors charge at each other, and several more full-scale operas, including *Il Ritorno d'Ulisse in Patria*, about the legendary Greek hero Ulysses. With such works, opera was well and truly established as the most exciting new art form of the age.

Period print of the splendid Byzantine front of St. Mark's Basilica, Venice. Venice was the long-time home of Vivaldi and an important center of baroque instrumental music (see overleaf).

Jean-Baptiste Lully, Italian by birth, but founder of the school of French opéra-ballet.

OPERAS AND BALLETS Baroque opera was big business. Alessandro Scarlatti (1660–1725) composed over a hundred operas, which indicates the demand for them; and other composers of the time were just as prolific. Poets and playrights, such as Apostolo Zeno (1668–1750) and, after him, Pietro Metastasio (1698–1782), specialized in creating libretti, the plots and words of the *opera seria*, the serious operas, which continued to be based on stories from classical myth and history. The singers in these elaborately worked out and also very formalized operas, were the superstars of their day, especially the castrati, castrated men who therefore remained singing like boys or women. In addition, a whole new industry centered around the creation of spectacular stage effects, such as storms at sea, gods appearing from the clouds, and palaces burning down (no wonder so many opera houses did actually burn down).

Another type of opera, rather different from the Italian *opera seria*, was created at the French court of Louis XIV, the 'Sun King,' most powerful monarch of his age, installed in his Palace of Versailles. He loved dancing, and his lavish stage entertainments were a combination of singing and dancing, known in their various forms as opéra-ballet. Louis' court composer, Jean-Baptiste Lully (1632–87), collaborated with the two most eminent French playwrights of the time, Corneille and Molière, in the production of some of these opéra-ballets. The special style of speaking in the French theater encouraged Lully also to give special attention to the dramatic delivery of the words. This aspect of French opéra-ballet, of words and music dramatically blended, was brought to perfection, after Lully's death, by Jean-Philippe Rameau (1683–1764). *Castor et Pollux*, another story from classical mythology, is Rameau's most famous stage work.

In England, such a frivolous diversion as opera was strictly banned during the Puritan regime of Oliver Cromwell, which probably helps to explain why Henry Purcell (1659–95) subsequently composed only one true opera which is set to music throughout: *Dido and Aeneas*. The work, however, is a masterpiece; and its famous and moving aria, or song, 'Dido's Lament,' is a landmark in operatic history. Purcell did, however, write a good deal of other music for the stage, including that for *The Faery Queen* (an adaptation of Shakespeare's *A Midsummer Night's Dream*) and *King Arthur* by John Dryden.

Continued on page 128

Tapestry of Louis XIV and members of his court. He once danced the part of 'The Sun King', a title that also expresses the splendor of his reign.

Keyboard Instruments

The keyboard, through different stages of its development, is perhaps the most striking and the most successful marriage between Western technology and music. Probably more music, certainly more music of great stature, has been written for the keyboard, in its various applications, than for any other group of instruments.

For many people, organs and churches are inseparable, but in fact the history of the organ has far wider horizons. The Greek and Roman hydraulus, which used water pressure to feed air into a set of pipes, dates back to about 200 B.C. Large and cumbersome instruments, with huge sets of bellows and heavy, stiff keys, were installed in some medieval churches and cathedrals, but during the Renaissance period, much smaller models – regals, positive and portative organs – were favorite household instruments among the rich and educated classes.

Some of the finest instruments of Bach's time, built in Germany by Andreas and Gottfried Silbermann, were recognizably similar to modern ones, apart from their often beautiful baroque decoration. In the nineteenth century, one of the most successful organ builders was Aristide Cavaillé-Col in Paris, and some of his grandest models were installed in town halls. France, it is worth noting, has a tradition of organ music second only to Germany, which organist-composers from Franck, Charles Widor (1844-1937) and Louis Vierne (1878-1937) to Messiaen and Maurice Duruflé (1902-86) have kept alive to the present day.

The history of stringed keyboard instruments is less venerable. Virginals (possibly taking their name from the Latin *virga*, which means 'rod'), spinets and harpsichords date from the fifteenth century. In England,

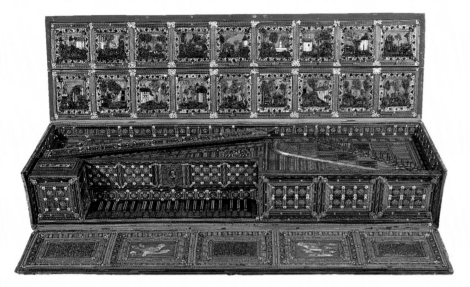

Facing page:
The beautiful
baroque decoration,
by Grinling Gibbons,
on the organ of
St. James's Church,
Piccadilly, London.
Handel and Bach
played similar
instruments.

Left: Sixteenth-
century Italian
spinet, extravagantly
decorated in enamel
and glass.

Byrd, John Bull (*c.*1562-1628) and
Giles Farnaby (*c.*1565-1640) were
among the first important stringed
keyboard player-composers; and
in Antwerp Hans Ruckers, at the
end of the sixteenth century, was
the first notable harpsichord
maker. The action and tone of
baroque harpsichords varied
considerably, leading to the quite
different styles of keyboard music
of Bach in Germany, Couperin in
France and Domenico Scarlatti in
Italy and Spain.

In about 1710, meanwhile, the
Italian instrument-maker
Bartolommeo Cristofori had
invented a new mechanism, with
hammers that struck the strings
instead of plectrums that plucked
them. This was his *gravicembalo
col piano e forte*, or 'soft-loud'
harpsichord, offering the potential
for a greater dynamic range than
any existing keyboard instrument.
Gottfried Silbermann also made
some of these new 'piano-fortes';
and from the end of the eighteenth
century, pianos improved rapidly,
with tighter strings, stronger
frames, more efficient actions and
better pedal effects for softening
or sustaining the string sound.

They also now came in various
shapes and sizes, leading to the
space-saving, vertically strung
upright model alongside the more
traditional horizontally strung
grand piano. The piano music of
Beethoven, Schubert, Schumann,

Chopin, Brahms, Debussy and
Ravel in turn, together with the
instruments of Clementi and
Broadwood in London, Pleyel and
Erard in Paris, Bösendorfer in
Vienna, Blüthner in Leipzig,
Bechstein in Berlin and Steinway
in New York, all mark the advance
of what was soon the world's most
popular instrument.

The keyboard itself has
spawned numerous other
instruments along the way, such as
harmoniums, piano accordions
and the celesta. Its own special
discipline of pitched notes, on
which so much of Western music
is based, still has its place among
today's synthesizers and other
electronic hardware.

Below: Handsome,
two-manual
harpsichord, made
by Hans Ruckers'
son Jan, dated 1634.

125

Instruments of the Orchestra

The instruments of the modern orchestra are a refinement of many of the other types featured in this book. Their organization into strings, woodwind, brass and percussion provides an excellent balance between chordophones, aerophones, membranophones and idiophones. Note that only the principal instruments are shown here.

THE MODERN ORCHESTRA

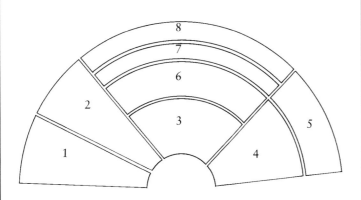

The diagram above shows the usual, though by no means invariable, seating plan for the modern symphony orchestra. The string section, for instance, is sometimes rearranged so that the cellos are in the center (3), second violins at 4 and violas at 2.

1 *First violins*
2 *Second violins*
3 *Violas*
4 *Cellos*
5 *Double basses*
6 *Woodwind (principal instruments; flutes, clarinets, oboes, bassoons)*
7 *Brass (principal instruments; trumpets, trombones, tubas, horns)*
8 *Percussion*

STRINGS

Violins form the most numerous group in an orchestra. The viola is slightly larger and deeper-toned.

WOODWIND

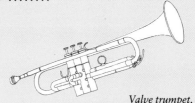

Oboe, with double-reed. The oboe d'amore and curiously-named cor anglais (English horn) are deeper-toned versions of it.

BRASS

Valve trumpet, popular also in jazz, dance and military bands.

PERCUSSION

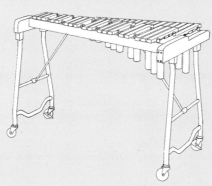

Modern xylophone, with tubular resonators beneath each bar.

Double-headed bass drum, which usually stands on its side.

Instruments are not drawn to scale

The cello, more than twice the size of the violin, rests between the player's legs, with a supporting spike at its base.

The double bass, largest and deepest-toned member of the string section.

Concert harp, introduced into the orchestra during the nineteenth century.

Bassoon, also with double-reed. The double bassoon plays deeper notes.

Modern metal transverse or side-blown flute. The piccolo is a smaller, higher-pitched version.

Clarinet, with single reed. The bass clarinet is larger, with a curved, flared metal 'bell.'

Modern valve horn. The player can insert a hand into the 'bell' to modify the tone or adjust the pitch.

Slide-valve trombone. A few modern trombones have piston valves instead of the traditional slide valve.

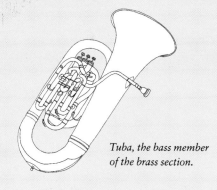

Tuba, the bass member of the brass section.

Tubular bells, usually struck with small hammers.

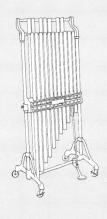

Modern kettledrum or timpani, with pedal tuning.

Side drum with traditional wooden sticks.

ORCHESTRAL AND CHAMBER MUSIC

Throughout the seventeenth and into the eighteenth centuries, there was also a great proliferation of instrumental music. Violins were among the new instruments of the time, stringed instruments played with a bow, like viols, but brighter and richer in tone, and more versatile. With their deeper-toned relatives, violas and cellos, they inspired the development of the concerto grosso, or great concerto, a style of composition in which a large body of strings (a tutti or ripieno) and a smaller group of soloists (a concertino or concertante) created contrasts of volume and tone that sounded very effective in the splendid interiors of baroque palaces and churches. This was music for the big occasion. But there was also a growing demand for music at home, by the many amateur musicians among the nobility, merchants and clergy. For them, composers wrote trio sonatas (usually for three stringed instruments, plus an accompanying, or continuo, harpsichord or small organ). The concerto grosso and similar works on the one hand, and the trio sonata on the other supply, the foundations of the orchestra and of chamber music, and these became the cornerstones of Western music in the years to come.

Italian composers led the field in this new instrumental music. Alessandro Stradella (c.1638–82) wrote many pieces with contrasting tutti and concertino effects that are embryonic examples of the concerto grosso. Incidentally, he seems to have led a rather scandalous life and was murdered. The first true master of the concerto grosso was Arcangelo Corelli (1653–1713), also one of the first great teachers of the violin. Corelli was employed for much of his life by the rich and powerful Cardinal Ottoboni in Rome, and he was a fastidious and self-critical craftsman (unusual at a time when most composers were prepared to dash off pieces of music at a moment's notice). His concerti grossi provided a model for nearly every other composer of the baroque period, because of the fine balance achieved between tutti and concertino passages and his refined but expressive writing for stringed instruments. His trio sonatas show the same elegance and attention to detail. Giuseppe Torelli (1658–1709), working mainly in Bologna, was another early master of the concerto grosso form.

Perhaps the best-known Italian composer of the baroque era is Antonio Vivaldi (1678–1741). Working mainly in Venice, he taught at a famous girls' school and orphanage, where he directed one of the best instrumental ensembles of his time. He composed hundreds of concerti grossi and other concerto-like pieces including the very well-known group called *The Four Seasons*, noted for their descriptive evocations of the seasons, from freezing winter to summer's sultry heat. Vivaldi also wrote at least forty operas and a good deal more choral and vocal music. His output was truly prodigious, like that of so many of his contemporaries. They wrote pieces very quickly and on demand, which were often played just once and then discarded. Palaces, churches and libraries throughout Europe are still full of the manuscripts of forgotten seventeenth- and eighteenth-century pieces of music, gathering dust, waiting to be rediscovered.

KEYBOARD SUITES While the Italians excelled at stringed instruments, French composers made a name for themselves at the keyboard, writing for organs and harpsichords that were making big strides technically and were also as beautiful to look at as the furniture and clocks of the period. Indeed, before turning his attention to opéra-ballet, Rameau wrote many pieces for the harpsichord (as well as an important book on harmony). Louis Nicolas Clérambault (1676–1749) was a leading organist in Paris and at the Versailles court, writing much music both for organ and harpsichord. But the foremost French composer of baroque keyboard music was François Couperin (1668–1733), known as 'Couperin le Grand,' to distinguish him from other members of his large musical family. As Louis XIV's court organist and harpsichordist, he wrote sets of keyboard *ordres*, or suites – sequences of pieces, mostly based on dance styles favored by the court, such as the minuet, bourrée, gavotte and courante. He gave many of these pieces fanciful titles, such as *Les Petites Moulins à Vent* (The Little Windmills) and *Les Abeilles* (The Bees), suggested by the music's charming and decorative

Sixteenth-century gilded and painted Italian harpsichord. The placing of the strings, running the length of the instrument, can clearly be seen. This one has a single keyboard or manual. Some harpsichords have two or even three manuals.

character. Couperin also wrote *L'art de Toucher le Clavecin*, a manual on keyboard technique, which is valuable to music historians and scholars for the information it gives about the conventions of keyboard playing in his time, not always indicated in the written music.

BACH AND HANDEL For hundreds of years, Italy and France had generated most of the new ideas in music, and attracted or produced many of the greatest musicians. With Johann Sebastian Bach (1685–1750) and George Frideric Handel (1685–1759), that situation changed. They were born in the same year and within a hundred miles of each other (though they never met), and between them they crowned with fresh splendors every important form and style of music as it had developed through the Renaissance and baroque periods. From that point of view, they came at the end of a long musical era. The two musicians were also both from Germany; and starting with them, composers from the German-speaking lands produced much of the greatest music for the next two centuries.

Bach, like Couperin in France, was born into what amounted to a family dynasty of musicians. Indeed, in parts of Germany, the word 'Bach' was for generations synonymous with 'musician.' Johann Sebastian himself was a devoted family man (twenty children by two marriages), providing for them all by salaried court and church appointments. He was, perhaps above all else, a superb organist,

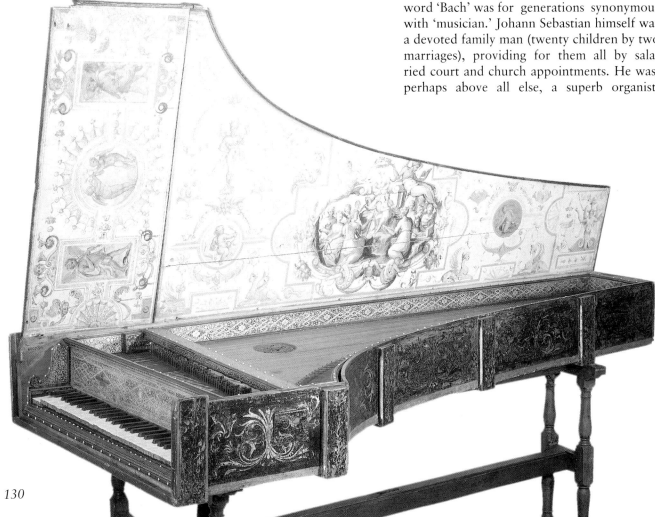

Portrait of Johann Sebastian Bach by an unknown artist, probably dating from his years as cantor or music director at St. Thomas's church and school, Leipzig.

belonging to the tradition of north German organist-composers going back to the time of Sweelinck. As a young man, he walked nearly two hundred miles to listen to Dietrich Buxtehude (1637–1707), another great practitioner in this tradition. His organ chorales, preludes and fugues are the finest ever written in the polyphonic style. The same can be said of the keyboard works for harpsichord. He even introduced counterpoint into many of his pieces for solo violin and cello, which are basically single-note melodic instruments. For various instrumental and orchestral ensembles, Bach composed suites (the 'Air on the G string' comes from one of these), and the *Brandenburg Concertos*, which brought a new richness and variety to the concerto grosso form. Bach adhered mainly to the Lutheran Protestant Church and, indeed, his longest appointment was as music director to the church and school of St. Thomas in Leipzig. It was there that he composed much of his

church choral music: a great collection of cantatas (Cantata no. 147 contains the melody known in English as 'Jesu, Joy of Man's Desiring'); the most celebrated of all settings of the Passion, the St. John and the St. Matthew Passions, in a style he inherited principally from the late Renaissance German composer Heinrich Schütz (1585–1672); and one mighty setting of the Catholic Mass.

Handel, by comparison, was more a man of the world, traveling first to Italy (where he met Corelli and Alessandro Scarlatti), returning briefly to Germany to a court appointment, and then setting off again for the great bustling city of London, affluent capital of a rapidly expanding empire, where he finally settled and adopted British nationality. There he succeeded for many years in the tough, sometimes rough commercial world of the theater, composing the grandest of operas such as *Julius Caesar, Berenice* and *Atalanta* in the opera seria style (the one major musical form

Continued on page 134

The Orchestra

A large orchestra tuning up before a concert is one of the most thrilling sounds in music – a minute or so of tense anticipation before the evening's program. Such ensembles did not spring into existence overnight, however. They have evolved over several centuries, to a large extent carrying the evolution of Western music with them.

Above: Detail from Edgar Degas' painting, In the Orchestra Pit. *Bassoon and flute hustle with a phalanx of strings, an unlikely arrangement today.*

The word orchestra comes from the Greek and originally described the area in front of the stage of a classical Greek theater, where the chorus sang and danced. The story of the orchestra in Western music also has theatrical origins. Monteverdi's imaginative use of instruments in his operas has already been mentioned (see pages 121 and 122), and thus the beginnings of the orchestra as we know it were closely linked with the beginnings of opera.

Early orchestras were very much scratch ensembles, composed of whatever instruments and players were available at the time. They usually included viols, hautboys (oboes), trumpets, drums and perhaps an organ. Even in Bach's time, there was still a good deal of 'open-endedness' about the size and composition of orchestras, and Bach himself made numerous arrangements of his own and other composers' instrumental pieces (for example, Vivaldi's concertos) without changing the basic character of them.

The new classical forms of the symphony and concerto in the latter part of the eighteenth century required the tighter organization we associate with a concert orchestra: the familiar grouping of the instruments into 'families' of strings, woodwind, brass and percussion. Orchestras

Right: The English Chamber Orchestra, of about the same size and composition as an eighteenth-century classical ensemble.

themselves were maintained by many royal and princely courts, their strength usually being between thirty and forty players. They were often directed by the composer, playing a 'continuo' part on a keyboard instrument or from his place at the head of the violin section.

The nineteenth century saw the orchestra grow and blossom like a great flower. It increased both in size – from about thirty-five members to seventy plus – and in the variety of instruments. Double-bassoon, bass clarinet, tuba, more percussion, and concert harp were regular additions to orchestral scores. There were also technical improvements to many instruments, such as valves added to horns and trumpets to give them a greater range of notes, and new fingering systems for the woodwind, making them easier to manipulate. The old court orchestras had now almost disappeared, and new commercially managed ones took their place in the rapidly growing

towns and cities of the Industrial Revolution. Conductors were needed to rehearse and direct performances of increasingly difficult music .

Mendelssohn was a pioneer conductor, in charge of the Leipzig Gewandhaus Orchestra, one of the first commercial orchestras. This scene was the background to the careers of Berlioz, Wagner, Tchaikovsky, Rimsky-Korsakov and the other great orchestrators of the period.

Orchestras grew to their largest extent around the turn of the century. Mahler, Richard Strauss and their contemporaries frequently wrote for an orchestra of well over a hundred players, calling for such special effects as tubular bells, large gongs and wind machine (which does not produce wind, but simulates its sound). Since then, composers have begun to reduce their orchestral needs or have written for unconventional groupings, thus again breaking up the basic foundation of the classical orchestra.

....
Above: The London Philharmonic Orchestra, strings each side of the rostrum, woodwind, brass and percussion arranged behind.
....

....
Above: A large orchestral work in score: the opening bars of Mahler's Sixth Symphony.
....

Bach's Forty-Eight
Preludes and Fugues

One of the greatest sets of keyboard pieces is Bach's two books, each of twenty-four preludes and fugues, known collectively as Das Wohltemperierte Clavier, or more simply as 'The Forty-Eight.' As well as being marvelous pieces of music, they also have a very interesting technical background. In Bach's time, there was much debate about how stringed keyboard instruments should best be tuned. If tuned to strictly acoustic rules, based on one leading note with all the others tuned exactly to it, they were to all intents and purposes limited to pieces of music in a few keys only. However, if the tuning was adjusted (making some notes very slightly lower or higher in pitch than was strictly allowed), a harpsichord or clavichord could sound just as good in whatever key a piece of music was written. In both sets of Das Wohltemperierte Clavier (or 'The Well- or Equally Tuned Keyboard'), Bach wrote a prelude and fugue in each of the twelve major and twelve minor keys. By so doing, he was in effect proclaiming what could be played if the newer system of tuning was adopted.

Seen in an even broader musical perspective, these pieces also demonstrate the final triumph of the diatonic system of major and minor keys and scales, with all their harmonic implications, over the much older and more inflexible system of modes.

that Bach did not touch). His much-loved 'Largo,' an arrangement of an aria from the opera *Serse*, is an example of the new expressiveness and dignity he brought to an already quite venerable operatic tradition. When the fashion for that kind of opera at last began to wane, Handel turned to oratorio, a form of dramatic but unacted choral music, usually with a religious theme, that began in Rome at about the same time as opera. (Giacomo Carissimi (1605–74) and Alessandro Scarlatti were earlier composers of oratorios.) Handel's *Messiah*, with its rousing 'Hallelujah Chorus,' is the best-loved of all works in this form. Indeed, at an early performance of *Messiah*, the English king, George II, and the whole audience, stood in tribute to this wonderfully uplifting chorus, a tradition occasionally observed to this day. Handel also wrote splendidly for baroque orchestras; his famous *Water Music* and *Music for the Royal Fireworks* are stirring compositions prompted by events in the life of Georgian London and the royal court.

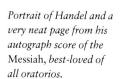

Portrait of Handel and a very neat page from his autograph score of the Messiah, *best-loved of all oratorios.*

THE CLASSICAL STYLE

*T*he eighteenth century is known as The Age of Reason, inspired by the ideas and opinions of Voltaire, Jean-Jacques Rousseau and other philosophers and political thinkers. The spirit of reason and tolerance they engendered did not do much to improve the lot of the poor and oppressed, but for the nobility, the wealthy and the educated few, life could be very pleasant and civilized. The style of art that went with this happy mood was called rococo, less grand and florid than baroque art, more soft and delicate, given over to sheer pleasure. Its musical equivalent was the *style galant* ('courtly style'), conveyed in some of the prettily ornamental keyboard pieces of Couperin and his French contemporaries. In a sense, it toned down the grandeurs of Bach and Handel, making way for the brand new classical style.

SYMPHONIES AND SONATAS The word 'classical' refers back to the architecture of classical Greece and Rome, with its columns and pediments and its sense of geometrical order, which appealed to eighteenth-century taste. As the century progressed, music more and more expressed this same sense of order. Sinfonias or symphonies, originally types of overture played at the beginning of an opera or other theatrical piece, became smart new pieces of orchestral music with well-balanced and contrasted fast and slow sections. Keyboard sonatas followed the same pattern. Most impressive of all was an entirely new way of constructing a single piece of music, basically in three linked sections – exposition, development and recapitulation – called sonata form (as distinct from a sonata as such). With sonata form, composers could concentrate more ideas into a single piece of music, or 'movement,' than had ever before been possible.

The classical idea of order, balance and well-considered contrast was equally apparent in the new instrumentation of the period. The rather diffuse assembly of baroque orchestras, suitable enough for the rich, polyphonic nature of much of the music, was rationalized and tightened up to match the orderly character of the new sinfonias, symphonies and concertos. The arrangement of the modern orchestra into the instrumental divisions of strings, woodwind, brass and percussion, dates from this time. There was also the arrival on the scene of a stringed keyboard instrument with a new type of

Carl Philipp Emanuel Bach, court musician to Frederick the Great, then successor to the famous Georg Philipp Telemann as director of church music in Hamburg. He is best remembered as a pioneer of the classical symphony and sonata, and for the fire and passion of some of the music he composed.

mechanism that hit instead of plucked the strings and allowed for greater precision and far greater contrasts in dynamics between soft and loud than the harpsichord, hence its Italian name, the pianoforte (the soft-loud).

Two of J.S. Bach's sons were prominent composers of this new classical music, writing in styles very different from their father. Carl Philipp Emanuel Bach (1714–88) was employed for many years at the court of Frederick the Great of Prussia, at Potsdam, near Berlin, while his younger brother, Johann Christian (1735–82), found work in London. Other composers of symphonies and similar works included Johann Stamitz (1717–57), director of one of the best orchestras of his day, at the Rhineland court of Mannheim; his son Carl (1745–1801); and Johann Christian Cannabich (1731–98), who succeeded Johann Stamitz as concert-master at Mannheim. Giuseppe Tartini (1692–1770) advanced violin technique in various ways, such as the improvement to the bow that he introduced, and was also a pioneer in the field of the instrumental sonata. Alessandro Scarlatti's son Domenico (1685–1757) similarly pioneered new keyboard forms and techniques in hundreds of delightful harpsichord sonatas. However, just as Bach and Handel summed up the music of the baroque age, so two more composers, above all others, are associated with bringing classical music to perfection. They are Franz-Joseph Haydn (1732–1809) and Wolfgang Amadeus Mozart (1756–91).

Continued on page 138

The Conductor

Many people fantasize about standing in front of the members of a large orchestra and getting them to play at the wave of a stick. The reality of conducting demands far more than that: a vast knowledge of all aspects of music, many years of experience and training, and a strong-personality – part-showman, part-scholar, part-teacher.

The conductor of the orchestra, an imposing, autocratic figure always in the limelight, is the most glamorous person in the concert world. Yet, until the last century, he did not exist. Previously, composers had usually directed performances of their music themselves, sometimes playing the harpsichord and sometimes leading the orchestra from the front row of the violins. Lully, however, followed the French practice of banging time on the floor with a large rod. One day, he hit his foot and subsequently died from the wound.

But from the time of Beethoven, orchestral music became increasingly complex and difficult, requiring someone to rehearse new pieces and direct their performance from a central and commanding position. There are accounts of Beethoven himself trying to direct or conduct some of his own works, sadly impaired by his deafness. Much more successful in this new role was a contemporary, the composer Weber. Another German composer, Ludwig Spohr, was probably the first to conduct with a lightweight stick or baton, while Mendelssohn, in charge of the Leipzig Gewandhaus Orchestra, was the first great composer-conductor. Berlioz and Wagner, by all accounts, were also talented conductors, but Tchaikovsky hated it and used to hold his head with one hand, afraid it might fall

Above: The nineteenth-century French caricaturist Gustave Doré's impression of Berlioz conducting.

Right: Arturo Toscanini, perhaps the most famed of all conductors, famed also for his adherence to every detail of a score.

off from all his exertions!

Meanwhile, others began to make conducting their chief claim to fame. François Habaneck first conducted all of Beethoven's symphonies in Paris. The eccentric Louis Jullien wielded a jeweled baton, handed to him at the start of each concert on a silver platter. Hans von Bülow worked closely first with Wagner and then with Brahms, directing the first performances of some of their greatest works. By the end of the nineteenth century, Mahler (who first made his name as a conductor), Hans Richter and Artur Nikisch had raised the status of the position to the high level it enjoys today.

Most conductors start their careers as orchestral players, and to do their job properly, they need a detailed knowledge of every instrument in the orchestra. Their first duty, of course, is to beat or indicate time, and keep everybody playing or singing together. Beyond that, a conductor has personal ideas about how a piece of music should be interpreted, as does a pianist, violinist or any other musician. Some do all their work in rehearsal, going over a composition bar by bar and leaving nothing to chance. Others prefer to leave some surprises in store for the actual performance.

Some conductors are very demonstrative, while others are quite sparing in their gestures. Some have a reputation as tyrants; others can gently coax a beautiful performance from an orchestra. Many conductors specialize, for example in opera or concert music, or build their reputations on the music of a particular composer, period or style. It is endlessly fascinating to compare the personalities, as well as the performances, of such masters of the rostrum as Arturo Toscanini, Wilhelm Furtwängler, Sir Thomas Beecham, Pierre Monteux, Felix Weingartner, Sir John Barbirolli, Otto Klemperer, Herbert von Karajan and Carlo Maria Giulini.

Above: Sir George Solti discusses a technical point in rehearsal with the London Philharmonic Orchestra.

Below: The Austrian Karl Böhm, noted especially for his work in opera.

Romantically-inclined portrait of Haydn, dated 1791, the year of his first triumphant visit to England.

HAYDN AND MOZART Early in his career, Haydn was fortunate in securing employment with the Austro-Hungarian Prince Nicholas Esterházy – though he had to work very hard indeed, rehearsing the court orchestra and choir, and composing, often at short notice, operas, church music and any other pieces that the Prince might require. The hundreds of pieces he wrote for the baryton (a bass viol) are due entirely to his master's passion for this otherwise quite obscure stringed instrument. The important thing was that at the Esterházy court, he had security, and an excellent orchestra at his disposal. So it was that over the years, Haydn – sometimes called 'the father of the symphony' (he composed 108 symphonies) – was able to work out the best forms and orchestration for it. He developed the symphony from the early kind of orchestral sinfonia or overture to the classic four-movement form: a fairly fast opening movement (perhaps with a stately introduction inherited from the overture), a slower second movement, a minuet with a central 'trio' section (inherited from the earlier dance suite), and a lively finale. When he was famous, Haydn traveled to Paris, then to London, writing his last and finest symphonies for those two cities. Some of them soon acquired nicknames, arising from a particular feature of the music (*e.g.* 'The Bear,' 'The Surprise,' 'The Clock,' 'The Military'), helping to set a fashion for attributing names to otherwise abstract pieces of music.

Haydn was also a pioneer of the string quartet; the perfect chamber music for the talented amateur musicians of the time to play in the ease and comfort of their homes. Haydn's string quartets, even more than his symphonies, are full of good humor, as though he and the music know they are among old friends. One of them, String Quartet Opus 76 no. 3 in C major, includes variations on the theme known as the 'Emperor's Hymn,' which has since become the German national anthem.

While Haydn is best known for his mastery of the classical symphony, string quartet, trio (keyboard, violin, cello) and sonata, toward the end of his long and mostly happy life, he returned to older musical forms, composing several big settings of the Mass and two oratorios, *Die Schöpfung* (The Creation) and *Die Jahreszeiten* (The Seasons). The opening of *Die Schöpfung* is an extraordinary piece of orchestral writing depicting Chaos before the biblical account of Creation begins. Elsewhere in these late choral masterpieces, Haydn's same robust good humor keeps breaking through.

Born twenty-four years after Haydn, Mozart was a child prodigy, paraded, along with his little sister, by their shrewd father Leopold before the aristocracy of Europe, for whom he played the harpsichord and wrote charming little pieces of music in the *style galant*. Later in life, though, he did not have Haydn's good fortune, for he failed to secure a decent court appointment. Of one minor post he wrote bitterly of the salary, 'too much for what I am asked to do, too little for what I could do'. However, whatever his circumstances, they made no difference to the quality of his music. In every form and style he touched – symphonies, piano concertos, wind serenades, string quartets and quintets, keyboard and other instrumental sonatas – Mozart combined a flawless technique with a beauty of sound and a growing depth of expression, sometimes real passion, that no one else could match. This sense of passion, held in check by a perfect control of classical form, is evident in such works as the Symphony no. 40 in G minor, the String quintet in the same key, and the Piano Concerto no. 20 in D minor. The Piano Concerto no. 24 in C minor looks forward to the dramatic power and strength of Beethoven (and was a work Beethoven himself much admired). By contrast, two other works which Mozart wrote for Anton Stadler, first great virtuoso of the clarinet, the *Clarinet Quintet* and the *Clarinet Concerto*, both in A major, are warm and lyrical in mood.

Some would say that Mozart was first and foremost an operatic composer. Opera, in fact, was the one medium in which he did have some real success. He was aware of the reforming ideas of Christoph Willibald Gluck (1714–87), who declared that *opera seria* had grown too worn and formalized, and that opera should be made much more truly dramatic. And he quickly assimilated the newer, racy *opera buffa* (comic opera) style created by Giovanni Pergolesi (1710–36) and others earlier in the century. The result was such an opera as *Le Nozze di Figaro* (The Marriage of Figaro). After the robust and bustling overture, the curtain goes up on the character in the title measuring out the space for his marriage bed. Never before had an opera been so realistic and down-to-earth; nor had an opera so openly dared to challenge the existing social order; nor had laughter and sorrow been so marvelously juxtaposed in a single work. It is based on a political play that had already got its author, Pierre Beaumarchais, into trouble in France. *Don Giovanni* (Don Juan) is an equally masterful interweaving of the comic and the dramatic, never before realized in the musical theater. *Die Zauberflöte* (The Magic Flute) shows how easily Mozart could switch from Italian opera to the totally different style of Viennese, German-speaking *singspiel* or pantomime, and, alongside all the clowning, raise the music to moments of lofty idealism. In these ways, Mozart was a truly revolutionary artist. *Die Zauberflöte* was Mozart's last opera, but not quite his last work. He was feverishly working on a Requiem Mass, to a special and rather mysterious commission, almost up to the moment he died. It was completed by his pupil, Franz Süssmayr, so that his widowed Constanze could collect the commission.

The Mozart family, painted in the winter of 1780. Left to right: father Leopold, Wolfgang (aged 25) and his sister Maria Anna (Nannerl), their hands charmingly crossed on the keyboard. Behind them is a portrait of Wolfgang's recently deceased mother.

Continued on page 143

139

The Changing Face of Ballet

For some people, ballet conjures up a picture of prettily-clad ballerinas. This does not accord with ballet as it has developed through this century, for it is now an art form that is able to convey almost any situation or emotion in the most daring terms. A modern ballet dancer must be as strong and fit as any international athlete.

Above: The rococo charm of eighteenth-century French court ballet, featuring the ill-fated Queen Marie Antoinette.

Ballet was an offspring of the stately court dances of Renaissance times. Its first important center was the court of Louis XIV at Versailles, where new dance steps were devised (choreographed) and new music written for them by court composer Lully. Because of its origins in France, French is still the principal language of ballet, and the word itself is a gallicized form of the Italian word *ballo*, which means a dance or ball.

In the eighteenth century, Jean-Georges Noverre jettisoned many of the old courtly formalities, thus paving the way for such creations as *Don Juan*, with music by Gluck. This was one of the first 'action ballets,' portraying a dramatic story by dance alone, and this in turn heralded the period of nineteenth-century romantic ballet with its naturalistic settings and its love of make-believe and the supernatural.

Some romantic ballets still formed a part of opera, but others, like the earlier *Don Juan*, existed in their own right. *La Sylphide* (not to be confused with *Les Sylphides*, using music by Chopin) was first danced by the Italian-born Marie Taglioni, the epitome of the romantic ballerina, wraith-like and fleet of foot. *Giselle*, with music by Adolphe Adam (1803-56), was another romantic scenario of love and the super-natural. Léo Delibes (1836-91) composed splendid scores for two more famous French ballets, *Coppélia* and *Sylvia*.

Meanwhile, in imperial Russia, the French choreographer and ballet master Marius Petipa founded the school of Russian classical ballet symbolized by the now-familiar tutu or short frilly skirt. This gave the ballerinas increased freedom of movement and thus the chance to display more intricate steps. *Swan Lake*, *The Sleeping Beauty* and *The Nutcracker* are the finest fruits of this school, their music by Tchaikovsky being as well known and as popular in the concert hall as in the theater.

The greatest figure in the history of ballet, however, was the Russian Sergei Diaghilev, not a dancer himself, but an impresario who took his ballet company to Paris in 1909. No one else has ever surrounded themselves with so much talent. The list of those who worked for him at some time includes the composers Stravinsky, Debussy, Ravel, Falla, Prokofiev and Poulenc; the dancers and choreographers Mikhail Fokine, Leonide Massine, Georges Balanchine, Anna Pavlova, Vaslav Nijinsky and Tamara Karsavina; and the artists Pablo Picasso, Henri Matisse and Leon Bakst. Diaghilev's Ballet thus revolutionized dance. Productions like *The Rite of Spring* (see also page 156) stripped ballet of whatever prettified image it still retained and propelled it into the twentieth century.

American dancer Isadora Duncan, almost the same age as Diaghilev, also promoted the freedom of expression that characterizes ballet today, ranging from the most abstract creations to the energetic routines that are found in many stage and screen musicals. The center of gravity in the world of ballet has also shifted in this century, moving away from France and Russia to Britain and the U.S., with the work of such dancers and choreographers as

Marie Rambert, Dame Ninette de Valois, Martha Graham, Robert Helpmann, Dame Margot Fonteyn, John Cranko, Kenneth MacMillan and Jerome Robbins and George Balanchine.

....
Nineteenth- century ballerinas among the opulent surroundings of the Paris Opéra.
....

....
Top left: Cartoon of Diaghilev by Alexandre Benois, another of those artists who worked closely with the great impresario.
....

....
Right: A vivid moment in a recent production of Stravinsky's The Rite of Spring, *offering the strongest contrast to the scene above.*
....

....
Facing page, bottom: Bakst's costume designs for the first (1912) production of Ravel's ballet Daphnis et Chloé *(see also page 156).*
....

BEETHOVEN AND REVOLUTION By the time Mozart died, the political and social ideas long debated by the philosophers were translated into revolution. In 1776, the American colonists issued their Declaration of Independence, with its call for a new kind of free and democratic society. In 1789, the French Revolution called for 'Liberty, Equality, Brotherhood.' Ludwig van Beethoven (1770–1827) was nineteen in that year. He applauded the Revolution and at first welcomed Napoleon Bonaparte (almost his exact contemporary) as the symbol of a new and better order. He originally dedicated his Third Symphony to him. But when Napoleon crowned himself Emperor of the French, Beethoven saw it as a betrayal of the Revolution's ideals and angrily scratched out the dedication on the title page of the manuscript score, leaving it simply as his *Eroica* or 'Heroic' Symphony. Beethoven himself certainly tried to live by his ideals, asserting his independence and rather scorning the old aristocracy of Vienna; though because of his genius and his magnetic if uncouth personality, he still attracted them. He wanted his music to have a universal appeal, not just please a privileged minority; and he believed it should speak for generations yet unborn. He was indeed a new kind of artist, standing for his revolutionary age.

Beethoven gradually went deaf, the worst possible thing that could happen to a musician. What direct effect this may have had on his music is debatable, but the fact that he triumphed over his affliction speaks volumes for the power of his mind and spirit. He inherited the classical forms of symphony, concerto, sonata and string quartet. But from his first published works (he only attached opus or publication numbers to compositions that satisfied his own demanding standards), there is a feeling of a tremendous new force at work in the music, exploring, expanding, pushing it in new directions, using the whole vocabulary of music to achieve a new depth of thought and expression. This sense of constant growth and change runs through individual works and, on a much broader plane, through his entire output. In the process, he filled classical forms to bursting point.

His nine symphonies are as central to music as the plays of Shakespeare are to literature and the theater. That he composed only nine may be due partly to the fact that in the turmoil of the Napoleonic Wars, most of the old court orchestras were disbanded, and it was difficult for a composer to organize his own concerts. But this small number, compared with Haydn's output, signifies also the importance Beethoven attached to his symphonies and the enormous effort he put into them. (The evidence of his sketch books, in which he jotted down ideas and revised them many times over, attests to the huge effort he put into the act of composition.) Certainly, no group of works before Beethoven's symphonies had possessed so much individuality and variety. The Symphony no. 5 opens abruptly with the famous four-note motto theme, which runs through the entire work, changing symphonic form in the process. The Symphony no. 6, the *Pastoral*, is the first symphony with a romantic 'programme.' It also has five movements instead of the usual four, with the last three linked together. Wagner called the Symphony no. 7 'the Apotheothis of the Dance,' because of the unequaled rhythmic drive that propels each of its movements, after a majestic slow introduction. One of Beethoven's novel ideas was to replace the classical minuet with a much more dynamic piece called a scherzo. The scherzo in Symphony no. 9 is a tremendous movement, with explosive drum beats that drew spontaneous applause at the first performance. Here Beethoven also broke the classical symphony mold by bringing in voices to sing the final 'Ode to Joy.'

Beethoven was a brilliant pianist before he went deaf. The Fourth and Fifth ('Emperor') piano concertos are just as epoch-making as the symphonies. Among the thirty-two piano sonatas, the so-called 'Moonlight,' the 'Waldstein,' 'Appassionata' and the immense 'Hammerklavier' sonatas, pushed the instruments of the time almost beyond their limits. The 'Diabelli' Variations is another monumental piano work. The seventeen string quartets include the last music he composed, music so visionary that some people still find it baffling today.

Beethoven did not have Mozart's flair for the theater. He struggled, on and off, for years with his opera *Fidelio*, a story, very close to his heart, of love and justice triumphing over tyranny. The power and conviction of the music vindicates all his efforts. These included the composition of three *Leonora* overtures for different productions. The way these overtures build upon each other also demonstrates why people often speak of Beethoven as a great 'musical architect.' When Beethoven died, much of this stupendous body of music was hardly understood. Yet thousands of Viennese attended his funeral.

Facing page: Portrait of Beethoven by an unknown artist, but probably a good likeness of the composer around his thirtieth year, when he first began to have trouble with his hearing.

A musical evening with Schubert in Vienna. The mild-mannered composer, with dog, waits by the piano. He had friends, but very little success.

THE ROMANTICS

Beethoven can be seen as the turning point between the classical, orderly eighteenth century and the romantic, revolutionary nineteenth century. His brooding image, certainly, was never far from the thoughts of the romantic composers. The romantics saw themselves as solitary figures, pursuing their own visions, expressing themselves in their own way, working out their own destinies. Whereas the classical artist was primarily concerned with form and style, what the romantic artist wanted to express came first; form and style must bend to his will. In keeping with the turbulent political spirit of the nineteenth century, the romantic movement was about individualism above all else. Composers' styles became increasingly personal and distinctive from this time on.

The romantics loved nature, seeing in mountains, oceans, rivers and cataracts, wind and storm, some sort of reflection of themselves. They were also much attracted to literature: to Shakespeare, Dante, Byron; to the fantastical stories of the German writer E.T.A. Hoffmann; to the legendary figure of Faust, torn between heaven and hell, as enshrined in Goethe's dramatic masterpiece. This affinity with nature and literature is most apparent in song. With the romantic movement, song-writing, primarily German art-song or *Lied*, attained the highest levels of art.

THE VOICE AND THE PIANO The first and perhaps the greatest master of *Lied* was Franz Schubert (1797–1828). In his brief life, he composed some masterly symphonies (including the famous Eighth, the 'Unfinished'), string quartets and other instrumental works; but it is with his *Lieder* that romantic music really takes wing. Some have sublime melodies; but their most telling feature is their accompaniments. Schubert used the piano to set the scene or mood of a song, and to point up every shade of meaning in the words. In *Gretchen am Spinnrade*, there is the monotonous turn of the spinning wheel, until suddenly it stops at the most dramatic point in the song. In *Der Erlkönig* (a poem by Goethe), there is a relentless pounding, as the specter of Death pursues the father and his sick child on horseback. Greatest are the two linked groups of songs, or song-cycles, *Die Schöne Müllerin* and *Die Winterreise*, dealing with unrequited love, despair and madness. Schubert is popularly imagined as a carefree youth. The bitterness and grief of many of these songs do not bear out such a picture.

Robert Schumann (1810–56) was

another master of *Lieder*. *Frauenliebe und Leben* (Woman's Love and Life) and *Dichterliebe* (Poet's Love) are his two best-known song-cycles. But his literary inclinations spilled over into his instrumental compositions, especially his piano works. Schumann was a music critic and publisher as well as composer, and lurking behind many of his groups of piano pieces are all kinds of fascinating literary ciphers and other allusions. His pieces titled *Carnaval* are based on the notes (in German nomenclature) A, S, C, H, which made up the name of a small town where he had a girlfriend, and which occur also in his own name. The *Davidsbündlertanze* celebrate an imaginary 'League of David,' conceived by Schumann in his newspaper columns to fight the 'Philistines' of music.

So fond were the romantics of finding some literary or pictorial allusion in music, that, if it was not there in the first place, they often made one up. Such was the case with Beethoven's so-called 'Moonlight' Sonata. So, too, did some of Frédéric Chopin's (1810–49) piano pieces, such as the 'Raindrop' prelude and 'Winter Wind' study (étude). Chopin was very much a romantic, composing almost exclusively for the piano in forms he either invented or adapted for himself; nocturnes, preludes, études (studies), ballades, waltzes, and other groups of pieces. The music is alternately passionate and impulsive or romantically dreamy in mood. But he was a fastidious craftsman, fretting over every note until a piece was polished to perfection, and notions of rain or wind probably never entered his head. Schumann, incidentally, in his capacity as a critic, was one of the first to praise and publicize Chopin's music ('Hats off, gentlemen, a genius!').

....

PROGRAM MUSIC By Chopin's time, the piano was already a bigger, stronger instrument than in Beethoven's day. Nobody made more of this than Franz Liszt (1811–86), a romantic figure if ever there was one, a young Adonis, and a phenomenal pianist, who carried virtuosity to its limits. Women swooned when he started to play. His real importance in music, however, lies elsewhere. Like many of the other romantic composers, Liszt, too, was much attracted to literature and the idea of conveying feelings and images in music. Composers had been doing this, off and on, for centuries; but Liszt gave the idea a special name and so a special significance: he called it program music. Following in the footsteps of Beethoven with his 'Pastoral'

THE WALTZ

The waltz, with its lilting three beats to the bar, is the Western world's best-loved dance. It probably grew out of an older type of German and Austrian peasant dance called the ländler *rather than from the more courtly minuet, and such examples as Weber's well-known* Invitation to the Dance *and Schubert's sets of waltzes indicate that it was already popular early in the nineteenth century. It reached the glittering height of its popularity later in the century, thanks largely to the magnificent waltzes composed in Vienna by the Johann Strausses, father and son. The latter was the composer of* The Blue Danube, Tales from the Vienna Woods *and the particularly grand* Emperor Waltz. *These, in fact, are not single tunes but sequences of melodies, with a return to the opening theme – the full concert waltz.*

Many other composers have been inspired by the waltz. Among them are Chopin, Brahms, Tchaikovsky, Sibelius (Valse Triste), Ravel *(La Valse and Valses nobles et sentimentales) and Richard Strauss (no relation to the Viennese Strauss family), who included opulent examples in his opera* Der Rosenkavalier, *often played as a concert suite. Across the Atlantic, George and Ira Gershwin affectionately and cleverly poked fun at the waltz with their Oom pah pah by Strauss!. Other dances, from the tango to rock 'n' roll, have created a sensation, but the world goes waltzing on.*

and 'Choral' symphonies, Liszt composed two of the finest purely programatic symphonies – The Faust Symphony and the Dante Symphony – inspired by the legend of the former and the poetry of the latter. However, he also went further still, creating a new kind of programatic composition, called a 'symphonic poem,' very like a painting in sound framed within a single movement. Numbered among the thirteen he composed are *Les Préludes, Tasso* and The *Battle of the Huns.* Liszt, it is worth adding, also made hundreds of piano transcriptions of other composers' orchestral works and operas, including the Beethoven symphonies, so introducing great music to the thousands of music-lovers who might otherwise have little or no chance of hearing it.

Other composers were masters of different forms of program music. Felix Mendelssohn (1809–47) drew magical effects from the orchestra in his overture to Shakespeare's *A Midsummer Night's Dream* (written when he was only seventeen). He suggested the sea surging around great rock columns in his overture *The Hebrides* ('Fingal's Cave'), inspired by a tour of the Western Isles of Scotland. The Frenchman Hector Berlioz (1803–69) was the most imaginative and daring of all in the fields of romantic orchestration and program music. For him, each instrument had a tonal quality, as important as colors to an artist, and these he blended in orchestral works that blaze with sound. His *Symphonie fantastique* (Fantastic Symphony) evokes the dreams and nightmares of a love-crazed man (the composer himself, who was desperately in love with an actress at the time). It ends with a wild and abandoned 'Witches' Sabbath.' Two more of Berlioz's works with the same vivid orchestration are the Symphony *Harold en Italie* and his overture *Le Corsair*, the musical portrait of a swashbuckling pirate, both inspired by Byron's poetry. Berlioz also wrote music for huge bands and choruses, for the kind of big public occasions that were a part of life in post-revolutionary France.

....

GRAND OPERA Opera was the most exciting prospect for romantic composers who wanted to combine music with literature. Berlioz clearly thought so, to judge by the time and effort he devoted to his most ambitious work, his great two-part opera *Les Troyens* (The Trojans), based on legends of the Trojan Wars. But even Berlioz's vision of what opera could aspire to was soon overtaken by the work of Richard Wagner (1813–83). Wagner's own life reads like some extravagent novel – political exile, turgid love affairs, constant escape from debtors, an extraordinary relationship with the half-mad King Ludwig of Bavaria. Through it all, he nourished the idea of elevating opera to a new and supreme art form; drama, philosophy and music rolled into one. Beethoven, he believed, had been moving toward such an ideal, but he, Wagner, would accomplish it. At the heart of his thinking was the concept of 'through-composed' opera; a

OPERETTA

Operetta, or 'Little Opera,' dates from about the middle of the nineteenth century, meeting the needs of the new urban bourgeoisie or middle class for a lighthearted and mildly satirical type of stage entertainment, with tuneful songs and dances. One of its first masters was Jacques Offenbach (1819-80), German by birth, but settled in Paris for most of his life. La Belle Hélène and Orpheus in the Underworld (with its famous French 'can-can' dance) are the best known of his operettas today. His other famous stage work, The Tales of Hoffmann, is closer to 'opéra-comique,' a more serious and dramatic style of French opera, and not necessarily comic at all.

Offenbach's sparkling example was quickly taken up in Vienna where it joined the existing singspiel tradition of spoken dialogue interspersed with songs and arias.

Johann Strauss II's (1825–99) masterpiece, Die Fledermaus (The Bat), including one of his famous waltzes, is perhaps the finest operetta of them all. It set the pattern for a Viennese style that continued well into the twentieth century, with such charming pieces as Franz Lehár's (1870–1948) The Merry Widow and Emmerich Kálmán's (1882–1953) The Gypsy Princess. In England, too, the partnership of W.S. Gilbert and Arthur Sullivan (1842-1900) produced The Pirates of Penzance, Patience, Iolanthe, The Mikado, The Gondoliers and other perennial favorites, which gently poked fun at current fashions and institutions. Edward German (1862–1936) struck a more sentimental note with Merrie England.

Operetta has spawned many other types of musical theater. Victor Herbert (1859–1924) took operetta to the United States and played an important part in the genesis of the American stage and screen musical (see pages 198-199). Back in England, at around the time of World War I, operetta led to such immensely successful musical comedies as Frederic Norton's Chu Chin Chow; then to the stage shows and revues of Ivor Novello (1893–1951) – The Dancing Years, Perchance to Dream, King's Rhapsody – and Noël Coward's (1899–1973) This Year of Grace, Bitter Sweet and Conversation Piece.

work that dispensed with recitative, aria, and the other existing ingredients of opera, in favor of a continuous unfolding of music and drama, and a total unity between them. He had a few precedents to go on. Mozart had 'through-composed' sections of some of his operas, and Beethoven and Berlioz had sometimes used motto themes to bring an extra sense of unity to their compositions. Wagner also acknowledged his debt to Carl Maria von Weber (1786–1826), a younger contemporary of Beethoven, who had helped to create a new type of German romantic opera with *Der Freischütz*, so providing Wagner with his starting point.

In terms of dramatic scope and sweep of the music, each of Wagner's early operas – *Der Fliegende Holländer* (The Flying Dutchman), *Tannhäuser* and *Lohengrin* – shows a big advance on the one before. Meanwhile, a colossal project was gestating in Wagner's mind; four individual operas, or music-dramas, bound together into one huge cycle. This was *Der Ring des Nibelungen* (The Ring of the Nibelungs), finally completed in 1874 after twenty-five years of work. The story of 'The Ring' is based on Norse and Teutonic mythology, in accordance with Wagner's belief that mythologies are expressions of our collective unconscious, and have a universal relevance and appeal. It is a saga of power, corruption and final redemption and its interpretation is a big subject. The British playwright and socialist George Bernard Shaw, who was also a music critic, thought it was an allegory about the collapse of capitalism; Adolf Hitler thought it was a vindication of Nazi racism. Musically, it is constructed from an elaborate system of repeated *Leitmotiven* (leading motives, or musical symbols) – the famous 'Ride of the Valkyries' is based on one of these – woven into an ever-richer tapestry of harmony and orchestration. There is plenty of glorious singing, but it is the orchestra that sustains the work from beginning to end.

The influence of 'The Ring' cycle, and of Wagner's other mature music-dramas – *Tristan und Isolde*, *Die Meistersinger von Nürnberg* (a paean of praise to German history and art) and *Parsifal* – not just on music, but on the whole of art and literature, was immense. Many other writers and composers were completely spellbound by his work and ideas, although it has to be said that equally as many hated them. Despite such massive works, Wagner himself did not monopolize the world of nineteenth-century opera.

In Italy, Giuseppe Verdi (1813–1901)

Continued on page 150

BAYREUTH FESTIVAL

No other composer, perhaps no other artist in any field of work, cherished such huge ambitions as Richard Wagner. Not only did he create the revolutionary opera-cycle of The Ring (not forgetting his other great music-dramas), but he decided that The Ring itself should have a special theater built for its performance. To this end, he selected a hillside site in the small Bavarian town of Bayreuth, and with help from his royal patron King Ludwig II of Bavaria, eventually raised the money to build the theater, largely to his own designs. Wagner's most original idea was to have the orchestra concealed from the auditorium and placed partly beneath the stage, to create a better blend of sound between orchestra and singers and at the same time draw the audience closer in to the action.

Wagner laid the foundation stone for his new Festspielhaus, or Festival Theater, in 1872, and it was opened four years later with the first complete production of The Ring. His last music-drama, Parsifal, was composed specially for the new theater. After the composer's death in 1883, the idea of turning Bayreuth into a regular festival for his works was realized by his widow Cosima (Liszt's daughter), who presided over the enterprise for some years before handing over to her son Siegfried. In this way, Wagner's children and grandchildren remained closely connected with the festival almost up to the present day.

Hitler tried to turn the theater into a Nazi shrine, and it was damaged during World War II. But soon after the war, production of Wagner's operas and music-dramas was resumed, and the Bayreuth Festival remains one of the great annual events in the musical calendar, with people coming to it from all over the world.

Above: The Wagner Theater, Bayreuth.

The Changing Face of Opera

Opera has never had a shortage of fervent enemies and critics, ever ready to mock the often absurd nature of some of its conventions and its improbable plots. But through all changes of taste and fashion, this unique blend of music and drama is as popular now as it has ever been. Today, modern composers are creating musical dramas that are far removed from the operas of the eighteenth and nineteenth centuries.

Doctor Samuel Johnson, living in London at the same time as Handel, called opera 'an exotic and irrational entertainment'. It should be realized that baroque operas, of which he was speaking, usually did have highly improbable or impossible plots, and were extravagantly staged. Right from the start, opera had inspired extremely elaborate stage sets and costumes; for example, one set for a production of Antonio Cesti's *Il pomo d'oro* in 1666 was of an enormous mouth of hell revealing in the distance the flames themselves. Other productions had palaces crashing in flames or destroyed by earthquakes, shipwrecks, monsters rising from the sea and gods descending from the clouds. (The latter related to the *deus ex machina* of theater and opera – a god who arrived providentially to sort out some complicated situation.) A whole new industry, employing painters, carpenters and engineers, grew up to meet the needs of opera. With so much emphasis on fire and smoke, together with all the candles needed for lighting, it is small wonder that many opera houses and theaters burned down.

This taste for the spectacular continued through the nineteenth century and the period of romantic grand opera, most notably in Paris. The famous Paris Opéra, completed in 1875 and still

Scene from Haydn's L'Incontro improvviso (The Unexpected Meeting), *staged in the Esterházy Palace in about 1775, with the composer directing the performance.*

one of the city's best-known landmarks, was designed by Charles Garnier, with a huge stage and backstage area designed to accommodate elaborate scenarios and all the accompanying machinery. Among those who composed operas specially to meet the Parisian demand for spectacle were Gaspare Spontini (1774-1851) and Jakob or Giacomo Meyerbeer (1791-1864). Meyerbeer's *L'Africaine*, an opera about the explorer Vasco da Gama, called for a set showing a cross section of the decks of a large galleon, one of the most ambitious ever conceived. Rossini's *William Tell*, with its storms and mountains, was also composed for the Paris Opéra, and Wagner added a bacchanale in the Venusberg mountain to *Tannhäuser* for a Paris production – to satisfy the French love of ballet in opera.

During this century, there has been a reaction against this extreme theatricality. Stage and costume designers, in line with developments in painting and sculpture, have created more abstract sets, with greater use of lighting and less scenery and props. Producers and directors have also tried new interpretations of operatic classics. A striking and controversial example of this trend

was Patrice Chéreau's centenary production of Wagner's 'Ring' cycle at Bayreuth, in which the opening set was a hydroelectric dam instead of the watery depths of the Rhine. Another was Jonathan Miller's handling of Verdi's *Rigoletto*, moving the action from Renaissance Italy to New York's Mafia underworld. Opera producers now have the power and prestige once given only to the star singers. At one time, the prima donnas (leading ladies) would claim that the audience had come only to listen to them and would take little notice of anybody else. Today's operagoers, however, are as much interested in the production as the singing.

....
Above: One of the very realistic scenes designed by Max Bruckner for the first production of Wagner's 'Ring' at Bayreuth in 1876.
....

....
Below left: The very different 'pop art' set for a recent production of Mozart's Cosi fan tutte *by the Philadelphia Opera.*
....

....
Right: Enrico Caruso, most celebrated of all operatic tenors, playing Don José in Bizet's Carmen.
....

VERISMO OPERA

Verismo, *meaning 'truth' or 'realism,' describes a fashion in Italian opera for stories that gave audiences a true 'slice of life.' Instead of opulent settings and grand or heroic themes, verismo opera focuses on some of the grimmer or at any rate more prosaic aspects of life. Puccini was very much a part of this school or movement. La Bohème, for all its apparent glamor, centers around a group of penniless students living very frugally in a chilly Paris garret. La Fanciulla del West (The Girl of the Golden West) transports us to a log cabin in the Wild West. Puccini's one-act opera Il Tabarro (The Cloak) is a story of murder on board a river barge. Other popular examples of Italian* verismo *opera are Pietro Mascagni's (1863–1945) Cavalleria Rusticana (Rustic Chivalry), portraying life and death in a Sicilian village, and Ruggiero Leoncavallo's (1858–1919) I Pagliacci (Clowns), exposing the real-life dramas of a troupe of traveling players. The last two are both one-acters, and are often billed together, nicknamed 'Cav and Pag.'*

Of course, operas with down-to-earth scenarios have not been confined to one country and one short period of time. Mozart's The Marriage of Figaro, Beethoven's Fidelio, Berg's two operas Wozzeck and Lulu, and Britten's Peter Grimes are all equally 'verismo' in their own ways.

Title page of the first edition of the words and music to Aida. Verdi's opera, set in ancient Egypt, is often associated with the opening of the Suez Canal in 1869, though it was not specifically commissioned for that event.

inherited a rich tradition that reached back to Monteverdi and opera's very beginnings. Verdi's immediate predecessors were Gioacchino Rossini (1792–1868), Gaetano Donizetti (1797–1848) and Vincenzo Bellini (1801–35), masters, in their different ways, of *bel canto*, of concentrating, above all, on the qualities of the voice. Through his exceptionally long working life, Verdi built upon this style, all the while heightening the drama of his operas vocally and orchestrally. Verdi was a practical man of the theater, not given to theorizing like Wagner. Yet from the first of his truly mature operas, *Rigoletto* (the dramatic story of a hunchbacked court jester), to his last two Shakesperian adaptations, *Otello* and *Falstaff*, he achieved his own version of 'through-composed' music-drama.

His successor, Giacomo Puccini (1858–1924), blended soaring melody with brilliant orchestration. His characters do not brood upon their thoughts and feelings like Wagner's; they pour them out like good Italians (whatever nationality, in their operatic context, they are supposed to be). At least three of Puccini's operas, *La Bohème*, *Tosca* and *Madame Butterfly*, must be included

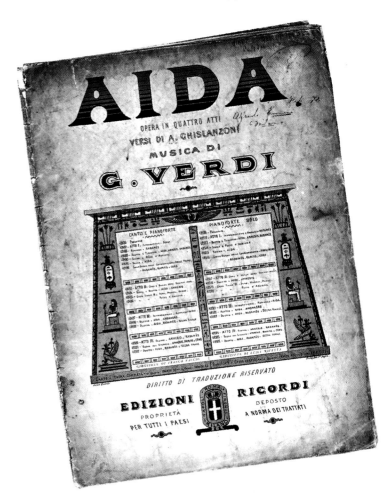

among everybody's all-time favorites.

. . . .

ROMANTIC SYMPHONISTS Johannes Brahms (1833–97) was Wagner's great German rival. Such rivalry was largely foisted upon the two composers by the controversy that divided much of the musical world during the latter part of the nineteenth century. On one hand, Liszt and Wagner were champions of the avante-garde, "the music of the future," as they themselves called it. Brahms, by contrast, was seen as the defender of traditional artistic values. As a young man, Brahms was befriended by Schumann who, in

his own symphonies, concertos and chamber works, had shown how romantic ideas could be reconciled with established forms. After Schumann's death, Brahms remained a close friend of his widow Clara, who was herself a highly gifted musician; and with her encouragement and support, he continued working along the same lines, blending the classical with the romantic. His four symphonies and other large concert works have the strength of Beethoven, tempered by a rich, warm lyricism. The same combination of symphonic thought and a more romantic lyrical vein applies to Brahms's far greater output of chamber and instrumental works, and to his many fine *Lieder*.

Brahms, in his turn, befriended the Bohemian-Czech Antonín Dvořák (1841–1904). Dvořák was associated with one of the so-called nationalist schools of music, discussed in more detail on pages 152–153, but he learned from Brahms how to graft his own

musical idiom onto symphonic forms. Dvořák's best-known work is his '*New World*' symphony, inspired by his visit to America. It is, however, not so typical of his generally warm, sunny, Bohemian style as some of his other symphonies, his delightful *Slavonic Dances* and his instrumental compositions.

In Russia, where other composers were forming themselves into a strongly nationalist school, Peter Tchaikovsky (1840–93) kept closer in touch with the mainstream of European music and literature. Dante and Shakespeare appealed to him almost as much as did Alexander Pushkin and other Russian writers; and he also found a way of adapting the symphonic form to his own style. Tchaikovsky had a wonderful gift for orchestration. He was also a very emotional man, and sometimes found it hard to reconcile these features of his art and temperament with the discipline of symphonic writing. Despite this, his Symphony no. 6, completed not long before his suicide, is a masterly blend of vivid orchestral writing, extreme contrasts of mood, and a highly original use of symphonic

Above: Peter Tchaikovsky, perhaps the most popular of all composers because of the romantic passion and drama of his music and its masterful orchestration.

Above left: Johannes Brahms was born in Hamburg, but, like Haydn, Mozart and Beethoven before him, he settled in Vienna, where he lived an outwardly uneventful bachelor existence.

Continued on page 154

151

Nationalism

Some of the best-loved music has been inspired by composers' feelings of patriotism and love for their homeland. Such music is part of the much broader nationalist movement that threw Europe into political and artistic upheaval during the nineteenth century and is still active today, in Europe and many other parts of the world.

The Napoleonic Wars at the beginning of the nineteenth century shook the old order of royal dynasties which had controlled most of Europe for centuries. Moves toward political independence sprang up across the continent, and soon musical 'flags' were being unfurled all over Europe. Chopin spent most of his

Left: Bedrich Smetana of Bohemia, more intensely nationalist than his compatriot Dvorák.

Below: Design for the Polovtsi camp, from Borodin's Prince Igor. *The 'Polovtsian Dances' are a well-known episode from this popular opera.*

life in France, but he was born in Poland, and he expressed Polish desires for national sovereignty in his stirring polonaises and more reflective mazurkas. Verdi, through his operas, was associated with the 'Risorgimento', the movement for Italian political unity. Wagner extolled German history and folklore, as the confederation of German kingdoms and principalities moved toward political unity under Bismarck.

In Bohemia and neighboring Moravia, there was a movement to break away from the German-speaking Habsburg Empire and set up an independent nation – the future Czechoslovakia. This fired Bedrich Smetana (1824-84) to compose his folk-opera *The Bartered Bride* and his cycle of patriotic symphonic poems called *Ma Vlast* (My Country). Early in this century, Leos Janácek (1854-1928) was on hand to celebrate Czech independence with his remarkable collection of operas and such strong orchestral works as his Sinfonietta.

Right at the end of the nineteenth century, Jean Sibelius (1865-1957) in Finland gave voice to national aspirations in his tone-poem *Finlandia* and his pieces inspired by Finland's folk epic, *Kalevala*. Sibelius went on to write seven symphonies, which convey in a much more original way the spirit and atmosphere of his country and carry his name well into the twentieth century.

Elsewhere in Europe, there was a desire simply to create an indigenous musical school, free

from the domination of German, Italian or French culture. The remarkable group known as 'The Five' or 'The Mighty Handful' in Russia all started as amateurs, yet three of them emerged as great composers. These were Modest Mussorgsky (1839-81) and Alexander Borodin (1834-87), with their grand and vivid historical operas *Boris Godunov* and *Prince Igor*, respectively, and Nikolai Rimsky-Korsakov (1844-1908) with his vividly orchestrated *Sheherazade* and other concert works and operas. Tchaikovsky, as already mentioned, stood somewhat apart from 'The Five', being academically trained and thus rather closer to the mainstream of European music. Sergei Rachmaninov (1873-1943), on the other hand, remained profoundly Russian in mood in his symphonies and concertos long after he had left his homeland to settle in the United States.

Manuel de Falla (1876-1946) from Andalusia in Spain drew on the rich and colorful native music of flamenco, with its Moorish echoes. The thrilling 'Ritual Fire Dance' from his ballet *El Amor Brujo* (Love, the Magician) shows how effectively he tapped this source. His two compatriots, Isaac Albéniz (1860-1909) and Enrique Granados (1867-1916), were closer to the musical idioms of their native Catalonia in their many piano pieces.

At the start of this century, Edward Elgar (1857-1934) was hailed as the greatest English composer since Purcell and as the herald of an English musical renaissance. His *Enigma Variations* and other big concert works are indeed fine compositions, though still much influenced by German music. Ralph Vaughan Williams (1872-1958) came closer to being a nationalist composer, through his studies of English folk music and of Tudor church music.

Folk song and dance was also an inspiration for Edvard Grieg (1843-1907) in Norway. Critics sometimes speak a little disparagingly of him as a 'miniaturist', because – apart from a youthful symphony and the very popular Piano Concerto – he did not write any large-scale works. But he composed with great skill and refinement and almost single-handedly put his country firmly on the musical map.

Left: Modest Mussorgsky, composer of Boris Godunov, *another great opera that celebrates Russian history.*

Below: Jean Sibelius, whose evocation of Finland, its legends and landscapes, runs through so much of his music.

form. Tchaikovsky hinted that the work had an autobiographical program. At his brother's suggestion, however, he settled for the word 'Pathetic' as the symphony's subtitle. In this context, it means 'passionate,' 'full of feeling.' Just before the start of the nineteenth century, Beethoven had applied it to one of his piano sonatas; Tchaikovsky found it just as appropriate right at the century's end.

Gustav Mahler, better known in his lifetime as a great conductor, notably of the Vienna Opera, than as a composer of emotionally supercharged symphonies and song-cycles.

THE TWENTIETH CENTURY

Western music did not change over-night, as the bells rang in a new year and the start of a new century. Germany and Austria still seemed the dominant musical nations, and the influence of Wagner, especially, loomed large in the massively proportioned symphonies of Anton Bruckner (1824–96), and then in the music of Gustav Mahler (1860–1911). It was Mahler who carried both the symphony and the song-cycle with orchestra to the limits of size, complexity and personal expression. His Symphony no. 8 is known as 'The Symphony of a Thousand' because of the huge orchestra and chorus it requires. Richard Strauss (1864–1949), in his dazzlingly orchestrated symphonic poems (*Till Eulenspiegel, Don Quixote*, Also *Sprach Zarathustra, Ein Heldenleben*) and his early operas (*Salome, Elektra, Der Rosenkavalier*), was hailed as Wagner's heir and successor. But for all their technical mastery, these composers were bringing the long and rich tradition of German symphonic and romantic music to a close. Several key works, meanwhile, composed in the early years of the new century, proved to be the real milestones for the future course of music.

MUSICAL IMPRESSIONISM One of these was *La Mer* by Claude Debussy (1862–1918). It opens with a very soft roll on the drums, a held note on double basses and open chords from two harps as the first glimmer of dawn spreads over the cold, gray, empty sea. The light increases, the sun rises over the waters, a breeze fans the waves, the ocean comes alive to another day. *La Mer* is written for a large orchestra, and it is romantic program music of a kind. But the orchestration itself, the harmonies, the cross-rhythms, are quite subtle, different from anything heard before. The music does not have the orchestral weight of Mahler or Strauss; but the intricate scoring makes it just as difficult to perform.

Through the nineteenth century, France had produced some outstanding composers. Berlioz and Chopin (half French and domiciled in France for most of his life) have been discussed. Charles Gounod (1813–93) at one time enjoyed great fame and popularity with his opera *Faust* and other operas and instrumental pieces. Georges Bizet's (1838–75) *Carmen* is one of the most colorful, tuneful and popular of all operas. Camille Saint-Saëns (1835–1921) wrote elegant and stylish operas, symphonies and concertos, besides his delightful *Le Carnaval des Animaux* (The Carnival of the Animals). César Franck's (1822–90) *Symphonic Variations* for piano and orchestra and his Symphony in D minor, with its Wagnerian chromatic harmonies, are concert favorites. Gabriel Fauré (1845–1924) composed one of the best-loved settings of the *Requiem Mass*, quite worthy to be counted with those of Mozart and Verdi, while being very different in mood from them both. The work of these composers, though, had been overshadowed by the German-speaking giants of the century, Beethoven, Schubert, Mendelssohn, Schumann, Wagner, Brahms. With Debussy, the situation changed. He was too original to be overshadowed by anyone. Indeed, with him, and his compatriot Maurice Ravel (1875–1937), French music took a decisive step into the twentieth century.

People often speak of Debussy and Ravel – especially the former – as musical impressionists, whose sound compositions were

Design for a ballet set to Debussy's Prélude à l'Après-midi d'un faun, *very much in the art nouveau style fashionable at the time.*

parallels to the canvas compositions of the impressionist painters. Indeed, the titles of some of their compositions do suggest this. Apart from *La Mer*, there are, for example, *Jardins sous la pluie* (Gardens in the Rain), *Nuages* (Clouds), *Jeux d'eau* (Fountains), and *Brouillards* (Mists). But they were, perhaps, even closer in spirit to the symbolist poets, whose aim was to suggest atmosphere and sensation, rather than straight pictorial imagery. In their orchestral works, and their many more piano pieces and songs, Debussy and Ravel evoke scenes or moods from antiquity, from distant and exotic lands, Spain (a favorite subject with many French composers), the macabre, and the worlds of fairytale and childhood. Their idioms have points in common and points of difference. Debussy used whole-tone scales (closer in some respects to the old medieval modes or certain oriental scales) and suggested rhythms and timbres of the Javanese gamelan bands he once heard in Paris. He used chords as a means of expression in themselves, ignoring every academic rule in the book. Ravel, on the other hand, developed a very sharp, clear harmonic   style, and was

Leon Bakst's stage design for the first production of the ballet Daphnis et Chloé, *set in mythical Greece, which inspired Ravel's most ravishing score.*

quite strongly influenced by the new music of jazz. Taken together, theirs was a whole new world of harmony, rhythm and form; a new world, also, of sometimes ravishing, sometimes mysterious sound.

STRAVINSKY AND BARTOK   A second key work of the early twentieth century was the ballet *The Rite of Spring* by Igor Stravinsky (1882–1971), which came as much more of a shock to the musical world than did *La Mer*. The first performance, in Paris in 1913, ended in a riot. A ballet about the ending of winter in ancient Russia, *The Rite of Spring* has ice beginning to crack, the earth once more stirring with life, and the people giving fearful thanks in pagan dancing and sacrifice. This time, the score opens somewhat weirdly on the highest notes of a bassoon; then it hits the ear with music of unprecedented dissonance and rhythmic force. The music, in fact, is also full of melody, taken from Russian song and dance. This was the way forward for Stravinsky, a re-creation of Russian folk music and the music of the Orthodox Church; making something excitingly new from something old. People sometimes speak of Stravinsky as a musical chameleon because he often changed his musical style, in accordance with the wider changes of twentieth-century art and music. But the special nuances of traditional Russian music run through nearly everything he wrote, however much he may have appeared a cosmopolitan figure, living first in France and Switzerland and then in the United States.

Béla Bartók (1881–1945) felt even closer to the folk music of other parts of eastern Europe and used it to become one of the most original composers of this century. He traveled around his homeland of Hungary, and neighboring countries, taking note of age-old songs and dances, before this heritage of folk music should be forgotten. The drone of a shepherd's bagpipes and wild or plaintive Magyar tunes, sung and danced to an old fiddle or dulcimer, stirred his imagination and breathed life into his own music. One of Bartók's most powerful group of works are his six string quartets. The way he transformed this long-established classical form into music of a sometimes quite primeval force is truly amazing. It certainly shook those early listeners who imagined folk music as something quaint and pretty. Other works, just as great as the string quartets, are for more unusual combinations of instruments, such as the Music for Strings, Percussion and Celesta, and the Sonata for Two Pianos and Percussion.

Above: Béla Bartók, who used folk song and dance as the basis for some of this century's most original and compelling music.

TWELVE-TONE MUSIC   Schoenberg's *Pierrot Lunaire* (which, like *The Rite of Spring*, was composed in 1912) was the most perplexing piece of music to be composed at that time. It isn't another large orchestral work, but a song-cycle, with a small accompanying group of instruments, inspired by morbid, nightmarish poems, delivered in a voice that hovers strangely between speech and song. Arnold Schoenberg (1874–1951) was moving rapidly toward the most radical change music had known for centuries. This was concerned with tonality and the system of major and minor keys on which Western music had been based since the Renaissance. The use of these keys, and the way composers modulated harmonically from one key to

Left: Portrait of Igor Stravinsky in his thirties, while he was living in France and changing his style from that of the rich and complex early ballet scores to his more austere neo classical period.

The Folk
Music Revival

Throughout this book are many references to folk music. In the sphere of European music, Haydn, Beethoven, Liszt, Smetana, Dvořák and Grieg sometimes quoted folk tunes, or made arrangements of folk songs. But the real revival began with composers who made a special study of folk song and dance. In Hungary, Béla Bartók was joined by his friend and colleague Zoltán Kodály (1882–1967). There were also Leoš Janácek and Bohuslav Martinů (1890–1959) in Czechoslovakia; Karol Szymanowski (1882–1937) in Poland, and Marie-Joseph Canteloube (1879–1957), with his very popular arrangements of Songs of the Auvergne, in France. In Spain, Felipe Pedrell's researches into old Iberian music inspired Falla, Granados, Albéniz, Joaquin Turina (1882–1949) and Joaquin Rodrigo (born 1902). Thanks to this revival, flamenco song and dance flourishes as never before.

The folk music revival has also been strong in the British Isles. Here the pioneer was Cecil Sharp, with his collections of British folk songs and his creation of the English Folk Dance Society.

Vaughan Williams, Gustav Holst and Percy Grainger were three of the composers drawn into his orbit. Another big figure in this British revival was the Scottish singer Ewan MacColl. With his American wife Peggy Seeger, he turned from the countryside to some of the hundreds of songs of old industrial Britain, such as The Ballad of John Axon, recounting the tragic death of a railroadman.

MacColl and his colleagues remained as faithful as they could to these folk song traditions. However, a blurring of musical categories and styles has today resulted in the music of such groups as the Anglo-Irish The Pogues, who mix folk tunes and rock. Purists might object; but, after all, the life-blood of true folk music is constant change and renewal.

Mention of Peggy Seeger prompts a few words about the equally lively American folk music revival, led by such figures as the father-and-son team of John and Alan Lomax.

Above: Folk dancers at a festival in Kalocsa, Romania.

another, was becoming increasingly fluid and complex. Wagner had already taken harmonic modulation, or chromaticism, to such a point that it was almost outside the tonal compass of any particular key. This was atonality. Others, including Mahler, had taken atonality still further. Now Schoenberg, with *Pierrot Lunaire*, was poised to take a very daring and courageous step beyond atonal music. He abandoned the existing harmonic system altogether and put in its place a new kind of scale, or note-row, using all twelve notes of the chromatic scale (from one octave to the next) in varying sequences, as the basis for individual compositions. This was twelve-tone, or dodecaphonic, music and was the reconstruction of music according to an entirely new set of rules.

At first, Schoenberg's compositions in this style met with total incomprehension and ridicule; but, as with all true pioneers and trail-blazers, he attracted a few devoted disciples. Among these was Anton Webern (1883–1945), who produced music of extreme economy and concentration, in which each note carries the weightiest significance. In his music he extended the organization of notes to include not only pitch, but also their rhythmic, dynamic and timbral qualities – known as serialism, a technique more fully developed by many American composers (see page 201). Alban Berg (1885–1935), in his opera *Wozzeck* and his Violin Concerto, was able to bring drama and emotion to the discipline of twelve-tone and serial composition.

Schoenberg soon won other converts. One of these was the Italian Luigi Dallapiccola (1904–75). Like Berg, Dallapiccola could harness twelve-tone or serial techniques to expressive ends, in such works as his opera *Il Prigioniero* (The Prisoner), dealing with the themes of liberty and justice.

MUSIC AND POLITICS Back in Tudor England, Tallis and Byrd, in their lives and in their work, had to contend with bitter, sometimes bloody, religious dispute. The Napoleonic Wars made life difficult for Beethoven. But no other century has been so shattered by politics and war, nor so affected the lives of composers and other artists, as the present one.

Dmitri Shostakovich (1906–75) and Sergei Prokofiev (1891–1953) well illustrate the problems that have faced artists caught up in the politics of this century. They grew up in Russia at the time of the Bolshevik Revolution and became the Soviet Union's two leading

The two giants of Soviet music, Dmitri Shostakovich (below) and Sergei Prokofiev (left). Both managed to come to terms with the demands and constraints of Soviet ideology.

composers. In this situation, it was their political duty to write music that praised the state, had mass appeal and inspired patriotism in time of war. They managed, through the perilous years of Stalin's dictatorship and the horrors of World War II, to fulfill these obligations and to gain worldwide recognition and praise.

Shostakovich is best known for his fifteen symphonies. Some of these are very emotional and Russian, in the tradition of Tchaikovsky. Others are more bitter or sardonic, as though he were mocking the Soviet bureaucracy he had to deal with, even Stalin himself. It is worth noting also that a number of his works are based on the notes that make up the initials of his name, somewhat after the manner or fancy of earlier composers, notably Schumann. In Shostakovich's case, however, this was a way of asserting his individuality in a society that tried to impose conformity on all walks of life. Prokofiev never really conformed either, thanks to his brilliant versatility. Whether he was writing symphonies, concertos, string quartets and sonatas, film music and ballet scores, or such charming pieces as his music for the tale of *Peter and the Wolf*, his musical personality shines through.

While Shostakovich and Prokofiev struggled to come to terms with the Marxist-Leninist politics of their country, a number of German and Austrian composers were

neighboring Hungary when the Nazis threatened to invade his country.

Even in what the Nazis contemptuously called 'the decadent democracies,' composers and other artists could not escape from the tribulations of their time. The British composer Michael Tippett (born 1905) went to prison during World War II as a pacifist and a conscientious objector. His beliefs inspired his oratorio *A Child of our Time*, appealing for reconciliation amid the horrors of war. The terrible events of these years are reflected in other major musical works, too. For example, Schoenberg, by then living and working in the United States, wrote his oratorio-like *A Survivor from Warsaw* in 1947, about the Nazi

Scene from a Philadelphia Opera Company production of Britten's Peter Grimes, *the tragic story of a fisherman set on the English Suffolk coast, where the composer made his home.*

compelled to leave their homelands after the Nazis came to power. Schoenberg and Kurt Weill (1900–50), the latter having written some very clever satirical operas, had little choice in the matter, since both were victims of Nazi anti-Semitism. But others, including such major figures as Paul Hindemith (1895–1963), were equally unacceptable to the Nazis and had no alternative but to pack their bags and find a home elsewhere. Béla Bartók, too, left

persecution of the Jews. And some fifteen years later, Benjamin Britten (1913–76), also a pacifist, wrote his *War Requiem*, setting to music verses by the British poet Wilfred Owen, who had been killed in World War I.

....

ELECTRONIC SOUNDS This century's technological explosion has had just as great an effect on the arts as its politics and war. A mere seventy-five years ago, radio, television, computers and space exploration were all still in the future; today, they are a routine part of life. Some composers have not been much affected by these enormous changes to the quality and character of our lives; they have continued to work with traditional instruments, and in traditional forms, proving that these still have much to offer. Britten composed such gripping operas as *Peter Grimes* and *Billy Budd*. Francis Poulenc (1899–1963) gave a new polish to Gallic charm and wit in his many songs, or *mélodies*, and instrumental pieces. The Polish composer Krzysztof Penderecki (born 1933) has used instruments and voices to create such effects as microtonality – chords or sequences of notes with pitch intervals less than those in the normal major and minor scales. Meanwhile, other composers have responded more directly to the new technologies, just as their Renaissance predecessors wrote for the technically-advanced keyboard instruments of their time. For them, the space age should and will have its own music.

Soon after World War I, the first semi-electric instruments were produced; pianos and violins were wired up to modify their sounds. Then came the use of electronics – valves and oscillators – to create the sounds themselves. With these, the way was open for the electronic synthesizer and a whole new world of aural experience. Edgard Varèse (1883–1965) was one of the first to explore it, in such pieces as *Amériques* (New Worlds), composed in 1922, which features the wail of sirens and other sounds of the new technologically-based urban life. Olivier Messiaen (born 1908) in France, like Debussy before him, has been attracted to oriental rhythms and timbres. He has also studied and analyzed bird songs, and the result is one of the most original and immediately recognizable musical voices of our age. He has added to many of his works a part for an early electronic instrument, the ondes-martenot (Martenot waves), which produces acoustically pure, ethereal tones. Messiaen conveys a mood of spiritual ecstacy with the ondes-martenot in his giant *Turangalîla* Symphony, with its allusions to Hindu mythology.

Pierre Boulez (born 1925) from France, Karlheinz Stockhausen (born 1928) from Germany and Luciano Berio (born 1925) from Italy really carried music into the electronic age. They experimented first with tape recorders, taking everyday sounds, such as snatches of conversation, a passing train or a car, and slowing them down, speeding them up, re-recording them, cutting and re-splicing the tapes, so creating the aural equivalent of those collages of scraps of clothing, old newspapers, and so on, that Picasso and the Cubists had produced some years before. This *musique concrète*, as they called it, was divorcing music entirely from centuries of pitched notes and measured rhythms.

Then they moved on to synthesizers and computers, and to composing work of a more serious character. Boulez also studied mathematics, and he has applied the same rigorous principles to his music, combining electronics with twelve-tone methods of composition. He is constantly revising his work, like a mathematician who sees new possibilities in an equation. Stockhausen appears a more romantic figure, closer in spirit to his teacher Messiaen, with his interest in metaphysics, religion and mysticism. One of his key works is *Stimmung* ('moods' or 'tunings'), in which a small group of singers chant mantras and other mystical words into microphones. Their voices are electronically mixed, creating acoustical effects comparable with the shifting patterns of light in a kaleidoscope.

Benjamin Britten at work in his study. Besides his prolific output as a composer, he also helped to found the Aldeburgh Festival in Suffolk, devoted to the music of many composers besides his own.

Renaissance and Baroque

The Renaissance saw a rapid growth of both secular and instrumental music. There were madrigals to be sung, and much music for the keyboard (organ, virginals and harpsichords), viols, lutes, oboes (hautboys), rackets (related to bassoons), trombones (sackbuts) and trumpets. The succeeding Baroque period brought added richness and variety to instrumental music and saw the rise of opera and oratorio. Much great religious and choral music continued to be written.

TOMASO ALBINONI
(1671–1750)
CONCERTOS
12 *concerti a cinque* (opus 9) for violin and strings (the well-known Adagio in G minor for organ and strings is spurious).

THOMAS AUGUSTINE ARNE
(1710–78)
OPERA
Masque, *Alfred* (including 'Rule, Britannia!').

Eighteenth-century engraving showing a concert in the time of Bach.

JOHANN SEBASTIAN BACH
(1685–1750)
CHORAL AND VOCAL
St. John Passion (BWV245);
St. Matthew Passion (BWV244);
Mass in B minor (BWV232);
Christmas Oratorio (BWV248);
Magnificat in D (BWV243);
church cantatas, no.140 (*Wachet auf*) and no.147 (*Herz und Mund und Tat und Leben*, includes 'Jesu, Joy of Man's Desiring'); Secular Cantata no.208 (*Was mir behagt*, includes 'Sheep may safely graze').
ORCHESTRAL AND CHAMBER
Brandenburg concertos nos 1–6 (BWV1046–51).
SUITES nos 1–4 (BWV1066–9) (No 3 in D includes 'Air on the G string').
CONCERTO
in D minor for two violins and strings (BWV1043).
INSTRUMENTAL
KEYBOARD Forty-eight preludes and fugues (*Das Wohltemperierte Klavier*, BWV846–93); Goldberg Variations (BWV988); Italian Concerto (BWV971).
ORGAN *Orgelbüchlein* (Little Organ Book) (BWV599–644); Fantasia and Fugue in G minor (BWV542); Prelude and Fugue in E minor (BWV548) ('Wedge Fugue'); Toccata and Fugue in D minor (BWV565).
MISCELLANEOUS three partitas for unaccompanied violin (BWV1002, 1004, 1006); six suites for unaccompanied cello (BWV1007–12); *Das Musikalische Opfer* (The Musical Offering) (BWV1079), and *Die Kunst der Fuge* (The Art of Fugue) (BWV1080), both for various instruments.

Note: BWV stands for *Bach Werke-Verzeichnis* (Index of Bach's works). The numbering refers to categories of works rather than chronological order.

DIETRICH BUXTEHUDE
(1637–1707)
INSTRUMENTAL
ORGAN Passacaglia in D minor (WV161); Prelude and Fugue in F sharp minor (WV146).

WILLIAM BYRD
(1543–1623)
VOCAL
Cantiones Sacrae (Sacred Songs).
INSTRUMENTAL
KEYBOARD Contributions to *Parthenia* (Maidenhood), a book of English keyboard music.

ARCANGELO CORELLI
(1653–1713)
CHAMBER
12 concerti grossi (opus 6) (including the so-called 'Christmas Concerto').

FRANÇOIS COUPERIN
(1668–1733)
INSTRUMENTAL
KEYBOARD *Pièces de Clavecin* comprising four books of *ordres* (suites).

JOHN DOWLAND

(1563–1626)

CHAMBER
Lachrimae for viols and lute.
VOCAL
Awake, Sweet Love; Flow My Tears; In Darkness Let Me Dwell.

GIROLAMO FRESCOBALDI

(1583–1643)

INSTRUMENTAL
ORGAN *Fiori musicali* (opus 12).

GIOVANNI GABRIELE

(1557–1612)

INSTRUMENTAL
Sacrae Symphoniae.

ORLANDO GIBBONS

(1583–1625)

VOCAL
The Silver Swan and other madrigals.
INSTRUMENTAL
KEYBOARD Contribution to *Parthenia* (see also Byrd).

Portrait of Handel.

GEORGE FRIDERIC HANDEL

(1685–1759)

OPERAS
Giulio Cesare; Ariodante; Berenice; Serse (includes 'Largo').
CHORAL WORKS
ORATORIOS *Acis and Galatea; Israel in Egypt; Messiah* (includes 'Hallelujah Chorus'); *Judas Maccabaeus. Chandos Anthems.*
CHAMBER AND ORCHESTRAL
Water Music; Music for the Royal Fireworks.
INSTRUMENTAL
KEYBOARD Harpsichord suite no. 5 in E (includes air and variations 'The Harmonious Blacksmith').

ROLAND DE LASSUS

(c. 1532–94)

CHORAL
Penitential Psalms.

JEAN-BAPTISTE LULLY

(1632–87)

BALLET
Incidental music to Molière's *Le Bourgeois Gentilhomme.*

CLAUDIO MONTEVERDI

(1567–1643)

OPERAS
La Favola d'Orfeo (The Fable of Orpheus); *Il Ritorno d'Ulisse in Patria* (The Return of Ulysses to his Homeland); *L'Incoronazione di Poppea* (The Coronation of Poppaea).
CHORAL
Vespers.
VOCAL
MADRIGALS 9 books including *madrigali guerrieri e amorosi* (madrigals of war and love).

THOMAS MORLEY

(1557–1603)

VOCAL
MADRIGALS
Arise, Awake and *Hard by a Crystal Fountain* (from the collection *The Triumphs of Oriana*). SONG *It was a Lover and his Lass* (from Shakespeare's *As You Like It*).

JOHANN PACHELBEL

(1653–1706)

CHAMBER
Canon and Gigue in D (in many arrangements).

GIOVANNI PIERLUIGI DA PALESTRINA

(c. 1525–94)

CHORAL AND VOCAL
Missa Papae Marcelli (Mass for Pope Marcellus) for six voices; *Lamentations* for four voices.

GIOVANNI BATTISTA PERGOLESI

(1710–36)

OPERA
Intermezzo *La Serva padrona* (The Maid as Mistress)
CHORAL
Stabat Mater.

ALESSANDRO SCARLATTI

(1660–1725)

OPERA
Mitridate Eupatore.

DOMENICO SCARLATTI

(1685–1757)

INSTRUMENTAL
KEYBOARD Harpsichord sonatas (or *esercizi*), including no. 30, known as 'Cat's Fugue.'

HEINRICH SCHÜTZ

(1585–1672)

CHORAL
Die Sieben Worte Jesu Christi am Kreuz (The Seven Words of Christ on the Cross) for five voices and instruments.

THOMAS TALLIS

(c.1505–85)

CHORAL AND VOCAL
Forty-part motet, *Spem in alium; Lamentations of Jeremiah* for five voices.

GEORG PHILIPP TELEMANN

(1681–1767)

INSTRUMENTAL
Tafelmusik (Table Music) of suites.

TOMAS LUIS DE VICTORIA

(c.1548–1611)

VOCAL
MOTETS *Jesu, dulcis memoria; O magnum mysterium.*
CHORAL
Requiem Mass.

ANTONIO VIVALDI

(1678–1741)

CONCERTOS
Four violin concertos, *Le Quattro Stagione* (The Four Seasons); twelve concertos, *L'Estro armonico* (Harmonious Inspiration).
CHORAL
ORATORIO *Juditha Triumphans.*

Classical Composers

The symphony, concerto, string quartet and sonata emerge as new forms in orchestral and instrumental music. The orchestra itself is reorganized, with clear divisions between strings, woodwind, brass and percussion. The piano supersedes the harpsichord. Opera is transformed by Gluck and Mozart. Beethoven adheres to classical forms, but opens the door to romanticism. Schubert does likewise through song.

CARL PHILIPP EMANUEL BACH

(1714–88)
CONCERTOS
for flute and strings in D minor (also arranged as harpsichord concerto).

JOHANN CHRISTIAN BACH

(1735–82)
ORCHESTRAL
Sinfonia Concertante in A major.

LUDWIG VAN BEETHOVEN

(1770–1827)
ORCHESTRAL
SYMPHONIES no. 1 in C, opus 21; no. 2 in D, opus 36; no. 3 in E flat, opus 55 (*Eroica*); no. 4 in B flat, opus 60; no. 5 in C minor, opus 67; no. 6 in F, opus 68 (*Pastoral*); no. 7 in A, opus 92; no. 8 in F, opus 93; no. 9 in D minor, opus 125 ('Choral').
OVERTURES *Coriolan*, opus 62; *Leonora no. 3*, opus 72a; *Fidelio*, opus 72b; *Egmont*, opus 84.
CONCERTOS
PIANO no. 1 in C, opus 15; no. 2 in B flat, opus 19; no. 3 in C minor, opus 37; no. 4 in G, opus 58; no. 5 in E flat, opus 73 ('Emperor').
VIOLIN in D, opus 61.
CHORAL
MASS in D, opus 123 (*Missa Solemnis*).
OPERAS
Fidelio, opus 72.
CHAMBER
STRING QUARTETS three quartets, opus 59 ('Rassumovsky'); in F minor, opus 95; *Gross Fuge*, opus 133.
PIANO TRIOS in D, opus 70 no. 1 ('Ghost'); in B flat, opus 97 ('Archduke').

Christoph Willibald Gluck, one of the greatest eighteenth-century composers of opera.

INSTRUMENTAL
VIOLIN Sonata in A, opus 47 ('Kreutzer').
PIANO Sonatas; no. 14 in C sharp minor, opus 27 no. 2 ('Moonlight'); no. 21 in C, opus 53 ('Waldstein'); no. 23 in F minor, opus 57 (*Appassionata*); no. 29 in B flat, opus 106 ('Hammerklavier').
'Diabelli' Variations, opus 120.

WILLIAM BOYCE

(1710–79)
ORCHESTRAL
8 symphonies.

LUIGI CHERUBINI

(1760–1842)
OPERAS
Médée; Anacréon.

MUZIO CLEMENTI

(1752–1832)
INSTRUMENTAL
PIANO Sonata, 'Didone abbandonata' (Dido Abandoned); Studies *Gradus ad Parnassum* (Steps to Parnassus).

CHRISTOPH WILLIBALD GLUCK

(1714–87)
OPERAS
Orfeo ed Euridice; Alceste; Iphigenie en Tauride.
BALLET *Don Juan.*

JOSEPH HAYDN

(1732–1809)
ORCHESTRAL
SYMPHONIES no. 45 in F sharp minor ('Farewell'); no. 82 in C ('Bear'); no. 83 in G minor ('Hen'); no. 88 in G; no. 92 in G ('Oxford'); no. 94 in G ('Surprise'); no. 96 in D ('Miracle'); no. 99 in E flat; no. 100 in G ('Military'); no. 101 in D ('Clock'); no. 102 in B flat; no. 103 in E flat ('Drumroll'); no. 104 in D ('London').
CHORAL
ORATORIOS *Die Schöpfung* (The Creation); *Die Jahreszeiten* (The Seasons).
MASS in D minor ('Nelson').
CHAMBER
STRING QUARTETS in D, opus 64 no. 5 ('Lark'); in D minor, opus 76 no. 2 ('Fifths'); in C major, opus 76 no. 3 ('Emperor').

JOHANN NEPOMUK HUMMEL

(1778–1837)
CONCERTOS
PIANO in A minor.
TRUMPET in E flat.

Above: An eighteenth-century chamber concert, from an engraving by Duclos.

Below: Medallion portrait of Mozart.

WOLFGANG AMADEUS MOZART

....

(1756–91)

OPERAS

Idomeneo (K366); *Die Entführung aus dem Serail* (The Abduction from the Harem) (K384); *Le Nozze di Figaro* (The Marriage of Figaro) (K492); *Don Giovanni* (K527); *Cosi fan tutte* (K588); *Die Zauberflöte* (The Magic Flute) (K620).

ORCHESTRAL

SYMPHONIES no. 29 in A (K201); no. 31 in D (K297, 'Paris'); no. 35 in D (K385, 'Haffner'); no. 36 in C (K425, 'Linz'); no. 38 in D (K504, 'Prague'); no. 39 in E flat (K543); no. 40 in G minor (K550); no. 41 in C (K551, 'Jupiter').

CONCERTOS

PIANO no. 20 in D minor (K466); no. 21 in C (K467); no. 23 in A (K488); no. 24 in C minor (K491); no. 25 in C (K503); no. 27 in B flat (K595).
CLARINET in A (K622).

CHORAL

Exsultate, Jubilate (K165).
REQUIEM MASS in D minor (K626).

CHAMBER

Eine Kleine Nachtmusik (A Little Serenade) (K525).
WIND SERENADES in B flat (K361); in E flat (K375); in C minor (K388).
PIANO QUARTETS in G minor (K478); in E flat (K493).
PIANO AND WIND QUINTET in E flat (K452).
CLARINET QUINTET in A (K581).
STRING QUINTETS in C (K515); in G minor (K516); in D (K593); in E flat (K614).
STRING QUARTETS in G (K387); in D minor (K421); in E flat (K428); in B flat (K458, 'Hunt'); in A (K464); in C (K465, 'Dissonance').

Note: The K number stands for Ludwig Köchel, who catalogued Mozart's works in their probable order of composition.

FRANZ SCHUBERT

....

(1797–1828)

ORCHESTRAL

Incidental music to *Rosamunde*.
SYMPHONIES no. 4 in C minor ('Tragic'); no. 5 in B flat; no. 8 in B minor ('Unfinished'); no. 9 in C major ('Great').

CHAMBER

PIANO QUINTET in A major ('Die Forelle' or 'Trout') (D667).
STRING QUARTET in D minor ('Der Tod und das Mädchen' or 'Death and the Maiden') (D810).
STRING QUINTET in C major (D956).
OCTET in F major (D803).

INSTRUMENTAL

PIANO Sonata in C major for four hands ('Grand Duo') (D813); Sonata in B flat (D960); *Marches militaires* for two pianos; *Impromptus; Moments musicaux*.

VOCAL

SONGS *Gretchen am Spinnrade* (Gretchen at the Spinning Wheel); *Erlkönig* (The Erl King); *An die Musik* (To Music); *Heidenroslein* (Wild Rose); *Die Forelle* (The Trout); *Der Tod und das Mädchen* (Death and the Maiden); *Die Sterne* (The Stars); *Horch, horch, die Lerch* (Hark, hark, the Lark).
SONG-CYCLES *Die Schöne Müllerin* (The Fair Maid of the Mill); *Winterreise* (Winter Journey); *Schwanengesang* (Swan Song); *Der Hirt auf dem Felsen* (The Shepherd on the Rock), with clarinet obbligato.

Note: D numbers stand for Otto Deutsch, who catalogued Schubert's works.

Romantic Composers

Romantic music, in general, is concerned with personal expression rather than with form. Hence a great diversity of individual styles and sources of inspiration; though very fine symphonies, concertos and other works in established forms continue to be written. Rich orchestration and harmonies and piano virtuosity are hallmarks of romantic music; while opera reaches its grandest proportions.

Johannes Brahms. His work can be seen to represent the more classical aspect of romanticism.

HECTOR BERLIOZ

(1803–69)

SYMPHONIES
Symphonie Fantastique (Fantastic Symphony); *Harold en Italie*.
OVERTURES *Les Francs-Juges; Le Corsaire; Le Carnaval Romain*.

CHORAL
REQUIEM *Grand Messe des Morts*;
Dramatic Symphony
Roméo et Juliette; La Damnation de Faust; L'Enfance du Christ (The Childhood of Christ).
ORCHESTRAL SONG-CYCLE *Les Nuits d'été* (Summer Nights).
OPERAS
Les Troyens; Béatrice et Bénédict.

GEORGES BIZET

(1838–75)
OPERAS
Les Pêcheurs de perles (The Pearl Fishers); *Carmen*.
ORCHESTRAL
Incidental music to *L'Arlésienne*;
Symphony in C.
INSTRUMENTAL
PIANO duet, *Jeux d'enfants* (Children's Games) (later orchestrated as *Petite Suite d'Orchestre*).

ALEXANDER BORODIN

(1833–87)
OPERA
Prince Igor (completed by Rimsky-Korsakov and Glazunov).
ORCHESTRAL
SYMPHONY no. 2 in B minor.
TONE-POEM *In the Steppes of Central Asia*.
CHAMBER
STRING QUARTET No. 2 in D.

JOHANNES BRAHMS

(1833–97)
ORCHESTRAL
Variations on the St. Anthony Chorale (opus 56).
SYMPHONIES no. 1 in C minor (opus 68); no. 2 in D major (opus 73); no. 3 in F major (opus 90); no. 4 in E minor (opus 98).
OVERTURES *Academic Festival; Tragic*.
CONCERTOS
PIANO no. 1 in D minor (opus 15); no. 2 in B flat (opus 83).
VIOLIN in D (opus 77).
VIOLIN AND CELLO in A minor (opus 102).
CHORAL
Ein Deutsches Requiem (A German Requiem) (opus 45).
CHAMBER
PIANO QUINTET in F minor (opus 34).
CLARINET QUINTET in B minor (opus 115).
STRING QUARTETS in C minor and A minor (opus 51, nos 1 and 2).
HORN TRIO in E flat (opus 40).
INSTRUMENTAL
CELLO Sonata in E minor (opus 38).
VIOLIN Sonatas, in G major (opus 78), in A major (opus 100), in D minor (opus 108).
PIANO Variations and Fugue on a Theme of Handel (opus 24); rhapsodies; intermezzos.

ANTON BRUCKNER

(1824–96)
ORCHESTRAL
SYMPHONIES no. 3 in D minor; no. 4 in E flat ('Romantic');
no. 5 in B flat; no. 6 in A major; no. 7 in E major;
no. 8 in C minor; no. 9 in D minor.
CHORAL
Te Deum.

EMMANUEL CHABRIER

(1841–94)
ORCHESTRAL
Rhapsody *España; Joyeuse Marche*.

FRÉDÉRIC CHOPIN

(1810–49)
CONCERTOS
PIANO no. 1 in E minor; no. 2 in F minor.
INSTRUMENTAL
PIANO Sonatas, no. 2 in B flat minor, no. 3 in B minor; Ballades; Scherzos; *Etudes* (Studies); Nocturnes; Preludes; Waltzes; Polonaises; Mazurkas; Impromptus.

LÉO DELIBES

(1836–91)
BALLETS
Coppélia; Sylvia.
ORCHESTRAL
Incidental music to *Le Roi s'amuse.*

GAETANO DONIZETTI

(1797–1848)
OPERAS
Anna Bolena (Anne Boleyn); *Lucia di Lammermoor; Don Pasquale.*

ANTONIN DVORAK

(1841–1904)
ORCHESTRAL
SYMPHONIES no. 5 in F major; no. 6 in D major; no. 7 in D minor; no. 8 in G major; no. 9 in E minor ('From the New World').
OVERTURE *Carnaval.*
MISCELLANEOUS Slavonic Dances; Scherzo Capriccioso.
CELLO CONCERTO in B minor.
INSTRUMENTAL
Serenade for Strings; Serenade in D minor for Wind.
CHAMBER MUSIC
PIANO QUINTET in A major.
STRING QUARTET in F major ('American').
PIANO TRIO in E minor ('Dumka').

GABRIEL FAURÉ

(1845–1924)
CHORAL
Requiem Mass.
INSTRUMENTAL
PIANO duet, *Dolly Suite* (later orchestrated).
VOCAL
SONG *Après un rêve* (After a Dream).
SONG-CYCLE *La Bonne Chanson.*

CÉSAR FRANCK

(1822–90)
ORCHESTRAL
SYMPHONY in D minor.
Symphonic Variations.
Symphonic Poem *Le Chasseur maudit* (The Accursed Huntsman).

MIKHAIL GLINKA

(1804–57)
OPERAS
A Life for the Tsar (Ivan Susanin); Ruslan and Ludmila.

CHARLES GOUNOD

(1818–93)
OPERA
Faust.
CHAMBER
Petite Symphonie in B flat for Wind.

EDVARD GRIEG

(1843–1907)
ORCHESTRAL
PIANO CONCERTO in A minor.
Incidental music to *Peer Gynt.* Lyric Suite; Four Norwegian Dances; Holberg Suite.

FRANZ LISZT

(1811–86)
ORCHESTRAL
SYMPHONIES *Faust; Dante.*
SYMPHONIC POEMS *Les Preludes; Mazeppa; Hamlet.*
MISCELLANEOUS *Totentanz* (Dance of Death) for piano and orchestra; *Mephistowalzer* (Mephisto Waltzes).
CONCERTOS
PIANO no. 1 in E flat; no. 2 in A major.
INSTRUMENTAL
PIANO Sonata in B minor; *Années de Pèlerinages* (Years of Pilgrimage), including *Dante* Sonata; *Liebesträume* (Dreams of Love); Hungarian Rhapsodies.

JULES MASSENET

(1842–1912)
OPERAS
Manon; Le Cid.
CHORAL
ORATORIO *La Vierge* (including 'Last Sleep of the Virgin').

FELIX MENDELSSOHN

(1809–47)
ORCHESTRAL
SYMPHONIES no. 3 in A minor ('Scotch'); no. 4 in A major ('Italian') Overture and incidental music, to *A Midsummer Night's Dream* (including 'Wedding March').
OVERTURES *Ruy Blas; The Hebrides* (Fingal's Cave).
CONCERTOS
PIANO no. 1 in G minor; no. 2 in D minor.
VIOLIN in E minor.
CHAMBER
OCTET in E flat for strings.
INSTRUMENTAL
PIANO *Lieder Ohne Worte* (Songs Without Words), including no. 34 in C ('Bee's Wedding' or 'Spinning Song'), no. 30 in A ('Spring Song').

MODEST MUSSORGSKY

(1839–81)
OPERA
Boris Godunov.
ORCHESTRAL
Night on the Bare Mountain.
INSTRUMENTAL
PIANO *Pictures at an Exhibition* (orchestrated by Ravel and others).
VOCAL
SONGS *The Nursery; Songs and Dances of Death; Song of the Flea.*

Franz Liszt: composer, teacher and virtuoso pianist.

Giuseppe Verdi, the greatest figure in Italian music of the nineteenth century.

GIACOMO PUCCINI

(1858–1924)
OPERAS
Manon Lescaut; La Bohème; Tosca; Madama Butterfly; Gianni Schicchi (from Il Trittico); Turandot.

NICHOLAI RIMSKY-KORSAKOV

(1844–1908)
OPERAS
The Legend of Tsar Saltan (including 'Flight of the Bumblebee'); The Golden Cockerel.
ORCHESTRAL
Symphonic Suite, Sheherazade; Spanish Caprice; Russian Easter Festival Overture.

GIOACCHINO ROSSINI

(1792–1868)
OPERAS
La Scala di seta (The Silken Ladder); L'Italiana in Algeri (The Italian Girl in Algiers); Il Barbiere di Siviglia (The Barber of Seville); La Cenerentola (Cinderella); La Gazza Ladra (The Thieving Magpie); Semiramide; Guillaume Tell (William Tell).

CAMILLE SAINT-SAËNS

(1835–1921)
ORCHESTRAL
SYMPHONY no. 3 in C minor ('Organ Symphony'); Carnaval des Animaux (Carnival of the Animals), for two pianos and orchestra.
SYMPHONIC POEMS Le Rouet d'Omphale (Omphale's Spinning Wheel); Danse Macabre.
CONCERTOS
PIANO no. 2 in G minor.

ROBERT SCHUMANN

(1810–56)
ORCHESTRAL
SYMPHONIES no. 1 in B flat ('Spring'); no. 2 in C; no. 3 in E flat ('Rhenish'); no. 4 in D minor.
OVERTURE Manfred.
CONCERTO
PIANO in A minor.
CHAMBER
PIANO QUINTET in E flat.
INSTRUMENTAL
PIANO Papillons (Butterflies); Davidsbundlertänze (Dances of the League of David); Carnaval; Kinderszenen (Scenes from Childhood); Kreisleriana; Waldszenen (Woodland Scenes).
VOCAL
SONG-CYCLES Liederkreis; Frauenliebe und Leben (A Woman's Love and Life); Dichterliebe (Poet's Love).

BEDRICH SMETANA

(1824–84)
OPERA
The Bartered Bride.
ORCHESTRAL
Cycle of symphonic poems, Má Vlast (My Country).

PETER TCHAIKOVSKY

(1840–93)
ORCHESTRAL
SYMPHONIES no. 4 in F minor; no. 5 in E minor; no. 6 in B minor (Pathetic).
Symphonic fantasies Francesca da Rimini; Manfred.
MISCELLANEOUS Overture 1812. Fantasy Overture Romeo and Juliet; Variations on a Rococo Theme for Cello and Orchestra; Serenade for Strings.
CONCERTOS
PIANO no. 1 in B flat minor.
VIOLIN in D.
BALLETS
Swan Lake; The Sleeping Beauty; The Nutcracker.
OPERAS
Eugene Onegin; The Queen of Spades.

GIUSEPPE VERDI

(1813–1901)
OPERAS
Nabucco; Macbeth; Rigoletto; Il Trovatore (The Troubadour); La Traviata (The Woman Gone Astray); Simone Boccanegra; Un Ballo in Maschera (A Masked Ball); La Forza del Destino (The Force of Destiny); Don Carlos; Aida; Otello; Falstaff.
CHORAL
Requiem Mass.

RICHARD WAGNER

(1813–83)
OPERAS AND MUSIC DRAMAS
Der Fliegende Holländer (The Flying Dutchman); Tannhäuser; Lohengrin; Tristan und Isolde; Die Meistersinger von Nürnberg (The Mastersingers of Nuremberg); Der Ring des Nibelungen (The Ring of the Nibelungs) – Das Rheingold (The Rhinegold), Die Walküre (The Valkyries), Siegfried, Götterdämmerung (Twilight of the Gods); Parsifal.
ORCHESTRAL
A Faust Overture; Siegfried Idyll.

CARL MARIA VON WEBER

(1786–1826)
OPERA
Der Freischütz.
ORCHESTRAL
OVERTURES to Oberon and Euryanthe.
CONCERTOS
CLARINET no. 1 in F minor, no. 2 in E flat.
INSTRUMENTAL
PIANO Rondo Brillante, Invitation to the Dance (later orchestrated).

HUGO WOLF

(1860–1903)
VOCAL
SONG-CYCLES Mörike Lieder; Spanisches Liederbuch (Spanish Song Book); Italienisches Liederbuch (Italian Song Book).
CHAMBER
Italian Serenade for strings.

The Twentieth Century

The shattering events of our century and rapid advances in technology have fragmented music. There have been the great innovators (Debussy, Stravinsky, Bartók, Schoenberg, Boulez); the traditionalists (Richard Strauss, Elgar, Rachmaninov, Shostakovich); and the many other composers somewhere in between. Some have embraced electronics; some have worked with existing instruments and forms. Politics, too, looms large in the music of this turbulent age.

Béla Bartók, one of the leading nationalists and modernists of the earlier twentieth century.

BÉLA BARTÓK

(1881–1945)
OPERA
Duke Bluebeard's Castle.
BALLET
The Miraculous Mandarin.
ORCHESTRAL
Music for Strings, Percussion and Celesta.
CONCERTOS
Violin concerto no. 2; Piano concerto no. 3; Concerto for Orchestra.
CHAMBER
6 String quartets.
Sonata for two pianos and percussion.
INSTRUMENTAL
PIANO *Allegro barbaro; Mikrokosmos.*

ALBAN BERG

(1885–1935)
OPERA
Wozzeck.
CONCERTO
Violin.
ORCHESTRAL
Lyric Suite.

PIERRE BOULEZ

(born 1925)
ORCHESTRAL
Pli selon pli (Fold upon Fold), for soprano and orchestra.
CHAMBER
Le Marteau sans maître (The Hammer without a Master), for contralto and instrumental ensemble.

BENJAMIN BRITTEN

(1913–76)
OPERAS
Peter Grimes; Billy Budd; The Turn of the Screw.
BALLET
The Prince of the Pagodas.
ORCHESTRAL
Variations on a Theme of Frank Bridge; Young Person's Guide to the Orchestra.
VOCAL
Les Illuminations, for voice and strings; Serenade for Tenor, Horn and Strings.
CHORAL
War Requiem.

CLAUDE DEBUSSY

(1862–1918)
OPERA
Pelléas et Mélisande.
BALLET
Jeux.
ORCHESTRAL
Prélude à l'Après-midi d'un faune (Prelude to the Afternoon of a Fawn); three Nocturnes, *Nuages, Fêtes, Sirènes; La Mer;* Images, *Gigues, Ibéria, Rondes de Printemps.*
CHAMBER
STRING QUARTET in G minor.
INSTRUMENTAL
PIANO *Suite Bergamasque* (including 'Clair de lune'); *Estampes; Images,* Books I and II; Preludes, Books I and II (including 'La fille aux cheveux de lin'); Twelve Studies; *En Blanc et Noir* (for two pianos).
VOCAL
SONGS *Ariettes oubliées; Chansons de Bilitis.*

FREDERICK DELIUS

(1862–1934)
ORCHESTRAL
Brigg Fair: an English Rhapsody;
Intermezzo from
A Village Romeo and Juliet;
On Hearing the First Cuckoo in Spring.

EDWARD ELGAR

(1857–1934)
ORCHESTRAL
SYMPHONIES no. 1 in A flat;
no. 2 in E flat.
OVERTURE *Cockaigne.*
MISCELLANEOUS *Pomp and Circumstance*
Marches; *Enigma Variations.*
CHORAL
ORATORIO *The Dream of Gerontius.*
CONCERTOS
VIOLIN in B minor.
CELLO in E minor.

MANUEL DE FALLA

(1876–1946)
BALLETS
El amor brujo (Love, the Magician);
The Three-Cornered Hat.
ORCHESTRAL
Nights in the Gardens of Spain, for
piano and orchestra.
VOCAL
Seven Popular Spanish Songs.

ENRIQUE GRANADOS

(1867–1916)
INSTRUMENTAL
PIANO *Goyescas* (including 'The Maiden
and the Nightingale').

HANS WERNER HENZE

(born 1926)
OPERA
We Come to the River.
CHORAL
ORATORIO *Das Floss der Medusa* (The
Raft of the Medusa).

PAUL HINDEMITH

(1895–1963)
ORCHESTRAL
SYMPHONY *Mathis der Maler.*
Symphonic Metamorphosis of Themes
by Weber.

GUSTAV HOLST

(1874–1934)
ORCHESTRAL
SUITES *The Planets; The Perfect Fool.*

LEO JANÁCEK

(1854–1928)
OPERAS
*Jenúfa; Káta Kabanová; The
Makropoulos Affair.*
CHORAL
Glagolitic Mass.
ORCHESTRAL
Sinfonietta.
STRING QUARTET no. 2 ('Intimate
Letters').

ZOLTÁN KODÁLY

(1882–1967)
ORCHESTRAL
Háry János Suite.
Peacock Variations.

WITOLD LUTOSLAWSKI

(born 1913)
ORCHESTRAL
Concerto for Orchestra; *Venetian
Games.*

GUSTAV MAHLER

(1860–1911)
ORCHESTRAL
SYMPHONIES no. 2 in C minor
('Resurrection'); no. 4 in G major; no. 5
in C sharp minor; no. 6 in A minor; no.
8 in E flat ('Symphony of a Thousand');
no. 9 in D.
SONG-CYCLES *Kindertotenlieder; Das
Lied von der Erde* (The Song of the
Earth).

PETER MAXWELL DAVIES

(born 1934)
ORCHESTRAL
Foxtrot for orchestra,
St. Thomas Wake.
VOCAL
Eight Songs for a Mad King.

OLIVIER MESSIAEN

(born 1908)
ORCHESTRAL
Turangalila Symphony; *Oiseaux
exotiques.*
INSTRUMENTAL
PIANO *Vingt Regards sur l'Enfant Jésus;
Catalogue d'Oiseaux.*
Organ *L'Ascension; La Nativité du
Seigneur.*
CHAMBER
Quatuor pour la fin du temps.

CARL NIELSEN

(1865–1931)
ORCHESTRAL
SYMPHONIES no. 2 ('The Four
Temperaments'); no. 3 ('Sinfonia
Espansiva'); no. 4 ('The
Inextinguishable').
CHAMBER
Wind Quintet.

KRZYSZTOF PENDERECKI

(born 1933)
OPERA
The Devils of Loudon.
CHORAL
ORATORIO *St. Luke Passion.*

FRANCIS POULENC

(1899–1963)
BALLET
Les Biches.
CONCERTO
for two pianos and orchestra.
INSTRUMENTAL
PIANO *Mouvements perpétuels.*

SERGEI PROKOFIEV

(1891–1953)
ORCHESTRAL
SYMPHONIES no. 1 ('Classical'); no. 5 in
B flat; no. 7 in C sharp minor.
CONCERTOS
PIANO no. 1 in D flat; no. 3 in C. VIOLIN
no. 1 in D.
BALLET
Romeo and Juliet.
INSTRUMENTAL
PIANO Sonatas: no. 6, in A minor; no. 7
in B flat; no. 8 in B flat.

SERGEI RACHMANINOV

(1873–1943)
ORCHESTRAL
SYMPHONIES no. 2 in E minor; no. 3 in A
minor. Symphonic Dances.
CONCERTOS
PIANO no. 2 in C minor; no. 3 in D
minor. Rhapsody on a Theme of
Paganini for piano and orchestra.

MAURICE RAVEL

(1875–1937)
OPERAS
*L'Heure espagnole; L'Enfant et les
Sortilèges.*
BALLET
Daphnis et Chloé.
ORCHESTRAL
Rhapsodie Espagnole; Ma Mère l'Oye
(Mother Goose).

Maurice Ravel, who together with Claude Debussy was a leader of musical impressionism.

CONCERTOS
PIANO in G; for the Left Hand.
CHAMBER
STRING QUARTET in F.
Introduction and Allegro for harp, string quartet, flute, clarinet.
INSTRUMENTAL
PIANO *Pavane pour une infante defunte* (orchestrated); *Jeux d'eau*; Sonatine; *Miroirs* (part-orchestrated); *Gaspard de la Nuit; Valses Nobles et Sentimentales* (orchestrated); *Le Tombeau de Couperin* (part-orchestrated).

ARNOLD SCHOENBERG
(1874–1951)
OPERA
Moses und Aaron.
ORCHESTRAL
Gurrelieder (Songs of Gurra) for voices and orchestra; *Verklärte Nacht* (Transfigured Night) for strings; *Erwartung* (Expectation) for soprano and orchestra.
VOCAL
SONG-CYCLE *Pierrot Lunaire.*

ALEXANDER SCRIABIN
(1872–1915)
ORCHESTRAL
SYMPHONIC POEM *Prometheus, The Poem of Fire.*

INSTRUMENTAL
PIANO Sonata no. 9 ('Black Mass').

DMITRI SHOSTAKOVICH
(1906–75)
ORCHESTRAL
SYMPHONIES no.1 in F minor; no. 5 in D minor; no. 7 in C major ('Leningrad'); no. 10 in E minor; no. 15 in A major.
CONCERTOS
CELLO no.1 in E flat; PIANO no. 2 in F.
CHAMBER
STRING QUARTETS no. 8 in C minor; no. 11 in F minor.
INSTRUMENTAL
PIANO 24 Preludes.

JEAN SIBELIUS
(1865–1957)
ORCHESTRAL
SYMPHONIES no. 1 in E minor; no. 2 in D; no. 3 in C; no. 4 in A minor; no. 5 in E flat; no. 6 in D minor; no. 7 in C.
MISCELLANEOUS *Finlandia; En Saga; The Swan of Tuonela; Tapiola; Valse Triste.*
CONCERTO
VIOLIN in D minor.

KARLHEINZ STOCKHAUSEN
(born 1928)

Gesang der Jünglinge for taped voices; *Hymnen* for taped voices; *Kontakte,* for piano, percussion and tape; *Stimmung,* for amplified voices; *Zyklus* for solo percussion.

RICHARD STRAUSS
(1864–1949)
OPERAS
Salome; Elektra; Der Rosenkavalier.
ORCHESTRAL
SYMPHONIC POEMS *Don Juan; Till Eulenspiegel; Don Quixote; Ein Heldenleben* (A Hero's Life).
CONCERTOS
HORN nos. 1 and 2, both in E flat.
VOCAL
Four Last Songs.

IGOR STRAVINSKY
(1882–1971)
BALLETS
The Firebird; Petrushka; The Rite of Spring; Les Noces (The Wedding); *Pulcinella; Agon.*
OPERAS AND OTHER STAGE WORKS
Oedipus Rex; The Rake's Progress; The Soldier's Tale.
ORCHESTRAL
SYMPHONIES Symphony of Psalms; Symphony in C; Symphony in Three Movements.
CONCERTOS
VIOLIN 'Dumbarton Oaks.'

MICHAEL TIPPETT
(born 1905)
OPERAS
The Midsummer Marriage; King Priam.
CHORAL
ORATORIO *A Child of our Time.*
ORCHESTRAL
Concerto for Double String Orchestra.

RALPH VAUGHAN WILLIAMS
(1872–1958)
ORCHESTRAL
SYMPHONIES no. 5 in D; no. 6 in E minor; no. 7 (*Sinfonia Antartica*).
OVERTURE *The Wasps.*
MISCELLANEOUS Fantasia on a Theme of Thomas Tallis; Fantasia on *Greensleeves; The Lark Ascending* for violin and orchestra.

WILLIAM WALTON
(1902–1983)
ORCHESTRAL
Symphony no. 1; *Façade* suite.
OVERTURES *Portsmouth Point; Scapino.*

Music in North America

8

The Count Basie band, with solo trumpet spot. Basie, at the piano, is on the left.

Music in North America

Antonin Dvořák called his Ninth Symphony, composed mainly in the United States, *From the New World*. For Europeans, this 'New World' was discovered by Christopher Columbus in 1492; but it had its own people and cultures going back thousands of years into pre-history. In South and Central America, there were the Incas, Aztecs and other pre-Columbian peoples; in North America – the United States and Canada – there were the American Indians. They migrated from Asia some time during the last Ice Age (about 15,000 or more years ago), when ice and land connected the Asian and American continents across the Bering Sea. As they spread southward and eastward, from the arctic to the prairies and beyond, they split into many tribes, each with their own languages and customs. But nearly all shared animistic beliefs. For them, the world was alive with the spirits of mountains, rivers, lakes and forests, of eagles, bears, buffaloes, snakes, fishes and every other living thing.

North American Indians performing their buffalo dance, another striking example of the kind of mimetic ritual song and dance discussed in the chapter on African music.

AMERICAN INDIAN MUSIC

*M*ost American Indians were nomadic people. They kept no systematic record of many aspects of their culture, and knowledge of their music is scant. Much of it was inspired by their animism, and the narration of epic myths and legends about the creation of the world and of life. Their singing was probably monophonic, that is, restricted to a single line of melody, with perhaps some drone-like harmonies. Like most tribal societies, rhythm probably meant more to them. Song and dance – which seems to have been almost exclusively the preserve of the men – was often accompanied by drums, rattles and rasps, perhaps also by simple types of whistle and flute.

The Pueblo Indians of the arid southwestern deserts had rainmaking dances involving the handling of live rattlesnakes. They also performed a graceful Eagle Dance, emulating the flight of the great birds that were to become one of America's national emblems. There was also the famous Sun Dance of the Plains Indians, the Crows, Dakotas and Cheyennes. This, in fact, was a collective name for a variety of dances whose purpose, for those who took part, was to atone for some sin, or honor some pledge made to the spirits in time of sickness or other misfortune. Sun Dances often went on for days on end. Dancers sometimes skewered themselves to a length of rope attached to a pole, pulling on the rope until they ripped themselves free. This ability to endure self-torture provides another example of the hypnotic power of music over mind and body.

The Eskimos, isolated in their arctic lands, developed a remarkable kind of 'mouth music', creating very complex rhythms with grunts, whistles, snorts and hisses. They also engaged in songs of abuse and ridicule as a way of settling disputes, no doubt because life for them was tough enough already without fighting among themselves.

THE COLONIAL SPIRIT

*A*merican Indian music died with the rest of the Indian way of life, as first the covered wagons and then the railroads carried white settlers and fortune hunters deeper and deeper into their lands. What might be seen and heard today, by tourists on some reservation, can only be a faint echo, a pale shadow, of this tradition.

During the seventeenth and eighteenth

centuries, the new Americans, initially the French and the British, had to create their music in much the same spirit as they pushed into the North American interior, waged war against the Indians, prospected and cleared the land, plowed the fields, cut down trees and built their first log cabins. For most, their only contact with music was in church or chapel, or at some open-air prayer meeting, with its lusty hymn singing. If they were Puritans, following in the footsteps of the Pilgrim Fathers, they may not have had any music at all. Daniel Boone and Davy Crockett are the heroes of this period of American history, rather than any composer or, indeed, any other artist.

Music, though, was important among particular groups of people. German-speaking Moravians, from what is now a part of Czechoslovakia, were among the other groups of European immigrants who arrived in North America during the seventeenth and eighteenth centuries. They belonged to the old Hussite religious sect, similar in many ways to the Lutheran Church, and most settled in

Benjamin Franklin, American statesman and administrator, scientist and writer, who also invented the glass harmonica, for which Mozart wrote some pieces of music.

Pennsylvania. Their schools, their whole way of life, won the admiration of such eminent first-generation Americans as Benjamin Franklin and George Washington himself. Many of them were also excellent and industrious musicians. Johann Friedrich Peter (1746–1813) wrote a splendid group of church anthems. David Moritz Michael (1751–1827) founded an orchestra and choir, directed the first American performance of Haydn's oratorio *The Creation*, and composed anthems, psalm settings and instrumental suites.

There was also, in the first half of the nineteenth century, Anthony Philip Heinrich (1781–1861). He was from Bohemia, and he entered enthusiastically into the frontier spirit of his adopted land, trudging hundreds of miles across Pennsylvania, then down the course of the Ohio River into Kentucky. He was a prolific composer, too, and his compositions rejoice in such titles as *The Dawning of Music in Kentucky, or the Pleasures of Harmony in the Solitudes of Nature* (a collection of songs and instrumental pieces), and the orchestral *The War of the Elements and the Thundering of Niagara*. These splendid titles convey both the poetic and the sturdy character of his music. At the time he wrote these pieces, a hearing would probably have come a poor second to the fact that he reveled musically in the places and moods of the vast new continent of promise and hope he had made his home.

The Moravians and Heinrich, however, were still European immigrants. One of the first native-born American composers whom Americans themselves remember with pride was William Billings (1746-1800). He was almost entirely self-taught and made known his own self-reliant, pioneering outlook in such statements as 'Nature is the best dictator.' In his part-songs, he cheerfully disregards harmonic conventions and his 'fuguing pieces' are highly idiosyncratic exercises in counterpoint.

In their various ways, men like Heinrich and Billings were doing in music what Grandma Moses and other so-called American 'primitives' were doing in their paintings and drawings. They were creating a kind of folk art, now much admired and valued by Americans themselves. But in their own lifetime, they made very little impact on the wider musical and cultural scene.

AMERICANS IN EUROPE

*L*ouis Gottschalk (1829–69) was a much more cosmopolitan man in outlook. At least he was in his own estimation. For when he went to Europe to further his studies, the Paris Conservatoire turned him down, simply because he was an American! An episode like that underlines the cultural isolation that American composers had to break down. Happily for Gottschalk, he met Chopin and Berlioz, and with help and encouragement from them proved himself a gifted pianist-composer, both in Europe and back home. *The Dying Poet* is the epitome of romantic sentimentality. Later in the century, Edward MacDowell (1860–1908) did study in Paris and Frankfurt, was befriended by Liszt, and composed attractive romantic concertos, symphonic poems and piano pieces. After him came John Philip Sousa (1854–1933), bandmaster and composer, who raised military music to new heights of excellence. He and his band made a big impression in Europe in the early years of this century, playing his own splendid marches.

Gottschalk, MacDowell and Sousa began to put their country on the world musical map, and to implant in people's minds the idea of an American brand of music. Gottschalk, from New Orleans, featured local, catchy Creole songs and dances in some of his pieces. MacDowell composed an *Indian Suite* and *New England Idyls*. Sousa's marches match such patriotic titles as *The Stars and Stripes*, *The Washington Post* and *The Liberty Bell*, with a typically American kind of gusto and swagger. These examples, though, still did not

The Shakers were an early American religious community who expressed their fervor in impromptu movement and dance, hence their name.

The waterfront of New Orleans in the late nineteenth century, with bales of cotton and Mississippi riverboats. The city, founded largely by the French, was the birthplace of jazz.

add up to anything that could honestly be called an American musical school or style; a musical idiom grown out of the deeper experience of American life.

For white Americans at the start of the century, that music was soon to come from the most unexpected, and for some of them, the most unwelcome quarter.

THE DEVELOPMENT OF JAZZ

*N*obody is quite sure how jazz got its name. It may have come from the French word *jaser*, meaning to 'chat' or 'gossip,' which well suited the impromptu, very informal character of early jazz. Its origins, though, are well documented. They go back to the African slave trade of the seventeenth and eighteenth centuries, when victims were shipped by their thousands across the Atlantic to work on the Caribbean sugar plantations, or on the cotton plantations of America's southern colonies. The songs of Stephen Foster (1826–64) – 'Oh! Susanna,' 'Camptown Races,' 'My Old Kentucky Home' – conjure up a rosy picture of plantation life in the old American South. But however true or false this musical impression may have been, it was not destined to last. The main issue of the Civil War of 1861–65 was slavery, and in 1862 President Abraham Lincoln officially abolished the practice. This was a fine political gesture; but by the end of the war, most of the estates

Continued on page 180

THE SPIRITUAL

The American spiritual has a rich history. The word is short for 'spiritual song,' and spirituals are quite different in content and style from established church hymns and psalms. What are known as 'white spirituals' describe the kind of nonconformist types of worship and singing practiced by many of the early settlers during the eighteenth and nineteenth centuries. These were the days of 'camp meeting spirituals,' of the lusty open-air singing that Charles Ives heard as a boy and which made such a lasting impression on his own music.

For most of us, though, the spiritual is much more associated with black people ('Negro spirituals' as they used to be called). This was the revivalist hymn singing of the black slaves on the plantations, based on their African heritage of responsorial song – there was one lead singer to whom the rest of the congregation responded, line by line. Outsiders who listened in on such gatherings described the spontaneous excitement of it all, everybody singing and shouting much as the spirit moved them. In the latter part of the nineteenth century, more practiced black

singers and choirs, such as the famous Fisk Jubilee Singers, began to collect and arrange the old spirituals – for example, Old Ship of Zion, Roll Jordan Roll and Nobody Knows the Trouble I Seen – creating a big new audience for the music in the U.S. and Europe. In this century, such internationally acclaimed artists as the bass Paul Robeson have kept alive the tunes and words of many black spirituals, though without the feverish excitement and passion that must have seized the old-time singers.

Military Music

The field of battle, and everything connected with it, may not seem a propitious arena for music. But the body of military music is large and varied, and its influence on music as a whole has been striking, ranging from Mozart to jazz. In fact, an impetus to the rise of New Orleans jazz is said to have been a ready supply of surplus army instruments.

'A good march,' declared American bandmaster John Philip Sousa, 'should make a man with a wooden leg want to step out.' His own marches are as good as his word. Another famous one of the same vintage is British bandmaster Kenneth Alford's *Colonel Bogey* (used in the film *Bridge on the River Kwai*).

Military music has always had a functional role. We think of it today as music to stir a soldier's pride and encourage a sense of *esprit de corps*, but going right back in history, the beating of drums, blasts on the loudest wind instruments and shrieks and cries were intended both to fire the blood and strike fear into the enemy. The Celtic *carnyx*, a type of bronze trumpet often displaying the head of a braying horse, the circular Roman trumpet, or *cornu*, and the horn-like Viking *lur* fulfilled the same roles.

The growing size of armies and increasing complexity of military maneuvers called for other instruments. Side drums and fifes (small, high-pitched flutes) accompanied armies on the march, drum rolls called them to order, and trumpet and bugle calls sounded such commands as 'advance' and 'retreat' amidst the noise and confusion of battle.

With the rise of Britain, France and Prussia as great military powers, the status of military music rose, too, and regimental bands grew larger and more professional. They appeared in resplendent uniforms, and music was written specially for them. The *Prince of Denmark's March* (known also as the 'Trumpet Voluntary') by Jeremiah Clarke (*c.*1670-1707) is one early example, and Johann Strauss I's *Radetzky March* another. Rouget de L'Isle's stirring *La Marseillaise*, composed in 1792, soon became

the national anthem of revolutionary France and then rallied Napoleon's armies. The Civil War produced more fine marches , among them *Marching Through Georgia*, *The Yellow Rose of Texas* and *The Battle Hymn of the Republic* (originally sung to the words *John Brown's Body*). American military bands and instruments were also one of the starting points for jazz.

Much concert music and opera rejoices in martial sounds. There is the bright clash of Turkish janissary (infantry) percussion in both Haydn's 'Military' Symphony' and the finale of Beethoven's 'Choral' Symphony. Mozart ends Act I of *The Marriage of Figaro* with a march and trumpet calls as Cherubino is sent off to the wars. Verdi's triumphal march in *Aida* is on a grander scale. There are concert marches by Schubert (*Marches Militaires*), Emmanuel Chabrier (1841-94), Elgar (*Pomp and Circumstance*) and Holst; and Sibelius's *Karelia* suite has a joyful, march-like opening movement. Handel, Beethoven, Chopin and Wagner also included in their works some great funeral marches, modeled on the solemn tread of the ceremonial slow march.

Composers have often parodied military music. Berlioz did so with the 'March to the Scaffold' in his *Symphonie Fantastique*, and so did Mahler in several of his songs and symphonies, Shostakovich in some of symphonies, Berg in his opera *Wozzeck* (which is set in a barracks), Stravinsky in *The Soldier's Tale*, and Gounod with his humorous 'Funeral March of a Marionette'.

....

Facing page, left: Flute player and drummer from the time of the English Civil War (1642–9).

....

....

Facing page, bottom: An Austrian military band dressed in traditional regalia.

....

....

Above right: The sousaphone, a type of tuba designed to be played on the march, was named after the American composer J.P. Sousa.

....

....

Below: A Fourth of July parade, with the band in period uniforms.

....

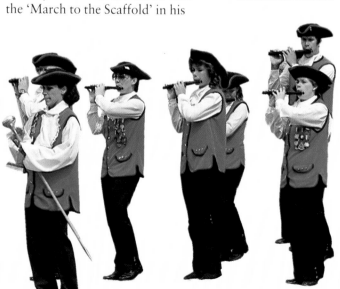

Facing page: Ma Rainey, born Gertrude Pridgett, 'Mother of the Blues'. She sang with, among others, Louis Armstrong, and made many early recordings. She was also active in the Baptist Church.

Below: Trumpeter Louis 'Satchmo' Armstrong was born in New Orleans. He also sang in his own inimitable way and appeared in films. His nickname is a contraction of 'Satchelmouth', on account of his broad, toothy grin.

and plantations of the defeated southern Confederacy were financially ruined, and the old black slave population suffered most of all. Thousands of their number drifted into the neighboring towns of Memphis, Atlanta, and especially to the port of New Orleans, which handled much of the cotton trade with the outside world.

The one thing that sustained them was their music. As people of African descent, they had a tradition of rhythm as natural to them as breathing, and an age-old custom of communal song and dance. They sang work songs together, and fervent religious songs or spirituals, inspired by the evangelical kind of faith grafted onto their way of life by their white masters. In the towns and cities of the American South, this music developed a stronger urban character. In New Orleans, more cosmopolitan and easy-going than most

other towns, it mingled with the part-Spanish, part-French, part-black, Creole songs and dances. It absorbed something, too, from the military music of the Civil War. The resulting mix of styles formed the seeds of jazz.

....

RAGS AND STOMPS By professional standards, this music was often pretty crude. Many of those who played it could not write their own name, let alone read music. They acquired instruments as and when they could – even old washboards were used as rhythm instruments – and taught themselves to play. They devised brash and jaunty pieces called rags and stomps, noted for their syncopations, their tendency to sidestep the basic rhythmic beat, which gave them their jazzy appeal. They played at open-air revivalist meetings, in funeral processions, on river pleasure steamboats, in saloons and brothels. It was all the same to them.

The first really talented jazz musicians emerged during the very first years of the twentieth century. One of these players was Scott Joplin (1868–1917) with his classic composition *Maple Leaf Rag*. Joplin's fairly genteel syncopations still had one eye on polite society, however, and his self-styled 'ragtime' was soon overtaken by more hot-blooded spirits. Among these were Edward 'Kid' Ory with his trombone, Joe 'King' Oliver with his Creole Jazz Band, pianist Ferdinand 'Jelly Roll' Morton (who later made some historic recordings with his Red Hot Peppers band), cornet player Freddie Keppard and the brilliant young trumpeter Louis Armstrong. By the time World War I ended, the sheer vitality of their music had set it well apart from any other in the world. Their rags and stomps – *King Porter Stomp, Kansas City Stomp, Ory's Creole Trombone, Muskrat Ramble, Twelfth Street Rag* – were the bright, extrovert face of early jazz. But there was another side to this new music, much more deeply felt, and in the long run much more important to the future development of jazz. This was the blues.

....

THE VOICE OF THE BLUES The blues were a sung lament. In addition to the age-old themes of faithlessness in love, sickness and death, the blues dwelt upon vicissitudes more directly concerning black Americans at the time: long, hot days of backbreaking work; the urge to move on as a way of escape, often by 'jumping' railroad trains (very few could ever afford the fare); the grim penal farms, where the wretched inmates were dressed in striped convict overalls, shackled together, taken to

and from work in cages, guarded by dogs. There were blues about the plight of those living in shacks near the Mississippi when it burst its banks. There were even blues sung about the dreaded boll weevil, which ravaged the cotton crops.

The earliest kinds of blues were true folk music; their words, their tunes and rhythms shared and modified by hundreds of singers. Many of these early performers, like Homer and the epic poets of the ancient world, were blind or in some other way unfit for normal work, wandering from homestead to village to town across the hot plains of the old South. They often sang to a harmonica, banjo or guitar, their voices mostly cracked and broken by years of hard living and booze; but the cruelties, injustices and deprivations they voiced gave their singing an elemental force and conviction.

Among those who stood out from this remarkable band of minstrels were Huddie Ledbetter, known as Leadbelly, who served time in a chain gang; Blind Lemon Jefferson, and 'Peg Leg' Howell, whose *Rock and Gravel Blues* invites us, 'Honey, let's go down to the river and sit down. If the blues overtakes us, jump overboard and drown.' Two of the greatest blues singers, in fact, were women: Gertrude 'Ma' Rainey and Bessie Smith ('Empress of the Blues'), whose voices had the strength and carrying power of any man's. Ma Rainey's *Bo-Weevil Blues* and Bessie Smith's *Empty Bed Blues* are two classic numbers preserved on record. There was also the pianist and bandleader W.C. Handy (1873-1958), who gave the music definitive form in

Continued on page 184

THE FORM OF THE BLUES

The classic form of the blues has twelve bars of music. These are subdivided by chord changes corresponding to the lines of the song. This form, both so strict and basically so simple, has provided for some of natural and flattened notes is what gives the blues and much other jazz its distinctive harmonic ambiguity. Singers can exploit this easily, and so can some instrumentalists, if they are skilled enough. It is the score to Milhaud's ballet La Création du Monde; the second movement of Gershwin's Concerto in F and the main theme of An American in Paris.

the most inspired jazz singing and improvised playing.

The chord changes within the twelve-bar framework concern the famous 'blue notes' referred to in the main body of the text. These involve flattening or diminishing (taking down by half a tone) the third and seventh notes of a major scale (for example, E natural to E flat and B natural to B flat in the case of C major). The switching or drifting between the not so easy on the piano, with its rigidly tuned pitched notes. This is why many blues and boogie pianists prefer a 'honky-tonk' instrument that is slightly out of tune to a perfectly tuned concert grand. It suggests this ambiguity for them.

There are some striking examples of 'blue notes' in jazz-inspired concert works: the first movement of Ravel's Piano Concerto in G and Concerto for the Left Hand; parts of

Above: Delapidated chapel house in Yazoo City, Mississippi, the kind of place familiar to the old blues singers. 'May God Bless This House' is the slogan above the boarded-up windows.

Mechanical Instruments

The player-piano, which was developed mainly in the U.S., was one of the most advanced forms of mechanical music-making ever devised. The astonishing ingenuity of many mechanical instruments, and the flights of fancy they inspired, are a large part of their fascination and charm. Today, surviving examples of many of these complex instruments have become rare and expensive collectors' items.

Right: A nineteenth-century clockwork Polyphon, made in Leipzig. It plays a selection of disks.

The bizarre Tipu's Tiger, made for the Sultan of Mysore in about 1790. The animal mauls a British merchant, to the growls and moans of a mechanical organ.

Organs, pianos and other keyboard instruments have complicated mechanisms, but they cannot make a sound without somebody to play them. Mechanical instruments, on the other hand, operate more or less automatically. They reached their most sophisticated form at the close of the nineteenth century with the player-piano, or pianola in the case of the best-known brand. Perforated rolls of paper were driven pneumatically play to the notes. Similar mechanical devices, using compressed air or steam, operated fairground organs or calliopes. For all their ingenuity, player-pianos, pianolas and mechanical organs lost out to the phonograph, the gramophone and then the loudspeaker, bringing several centuries of interesting work in this field to an end.

The earlier mechanical instruments were worked by a revolving drum or cylinder with pegs or pins. In music boxes, developed mainly in Germany and Switzerland during the eighteenth and ninteenth centuries, these revolving cylinders, with their arrangements of pins, struck or plucked small bells or a row of tuned metal prongs. Some were turned by hand and others by clockwork. Later models, anticipating phonographs had detachable revolving disks, offering customers a variety of tunes.

Revolving drums or barrels, with other arrangements of pegs, played bell chimes or carillons or activated sets of organ pipes, hence the name 'barrel organs'. Eighty or ninety years ago, these barrel organs and mechanically operated pianos (often mistakenly called barrel organs also) were a familiar sound and sight in city streets, hooting or rattling out popular tunes of the day at the turn of a handle.

Musical boxes, barrel organs, model birds in cages, doll-like figures playing trumpets or drums, even growling tigers and bears, all belong to the exotic, sometimes bizarre realm of mechanical instruments. Just occasionally, they have brushed with greatness. Mozart wrote some fine pieces for a type of mechanical organ. In 1813, Beethoven wrote his 'Battle Symphony' ('Wellington's Victory, or the Battle of Victoria') for the panharmonicon, a type of mechanical 'orchestrion' with wind and percussion effects, built by his friend Johann Maelzel. In the event, however, the piece was performed 'live' at a concert. The clockwork-like second movement of Beethoven's Eighth Symphony, incidentally, is probably a humorous allusion to another of Maelzel's devices, a type of ticking chronometer or metronome.

Returning to player-pianos and pianolas, a number of great composers and pianists in the early years of this century, among whom were Debussy, Rachmaninov and Ignaz Paderewski, 'cut' piano rolls for mechanical reproduction. It can be quite eerie, watching piano keys, activated from within, respond as though to the touch of some ghostly, unseen player's hand.

*Above: An American
Wurlitzer juke box,
or automatic record
player, of art deco
design. The Wurlitzer
Company also made
player-pianos and
electric organs.*

such classics as *St. Louis Blues*, thereby earning for himself the title of 'Father of the Blues.' Like most such epithets, however, this one was not literally true.

....

FROM BLUES TO BOOGIE One of the most distinctive musical features of the blues were the so-called blue notes, which created an ambiguous effect between major and minor tonalities, and influenced both melody and harmony. As jazz men traveled further afield, during and just after World War I, up the Mississippi to Kansas City and St. Louis, and on to the great industrial centers of Chicago, Detroit and New York, so these blue notes pervaded jazz as a whole. At the same time, things were happening to the blues themselves. They were speeded up and galvanized into boogie, whose insistent rhythms and short melodic motifs echoed the thud and clatter of

the railroad trains and the haunting two-toned wail of the locomotive sirens that rang in the ears of so many migrant black people.

Boogie was primarily piano music, not vocal. Its essence lay in the strongly accented and constantly repeated (ostinato) chords and rhythms of the pianist's left hand. Jimmy Yancey, born in Chicago, hub of the nation's railroad network, is credited with inventing boogie, at least in the sense that he gave it an identity of its own. That would have been around 1925. Clarence Smith, known as 'Pine Top' because he was so tall, developed a special left-hand boogie style. Albert Ammons, Meade 'Lux' Lewis, composer of *Honky Tonk Train Blues*, and Charlie 'Cow Cow' Davenport, were three more boogie pioneers. Seldom, if ever, had music delivered such a punch. Said another boogie pianist of the period, 'When you listen to what I'm playing, you got to see in your mind all them gals out

Dancing the Charleston in the lobby of a New York theater, to promote the film of F. Scott Fitzgerald's Tender is the Night, *a novel about society highlife in the 1920s, when the dance was all the rage.*

there swinging their butts and getting' men excited. Otherwise, you ain't got the music rightly understood.' He put it all in a nutshell. Boogie was brash, provocative, electrifying, hammered out in dance halls, saloons and poolrooms, in the shadow of skyscrapers, or down by the huge Chicago stockyards. And like it or not, it was now the music that really spoke for America.

....
JAZZ CONQUERS ALL A good many white Americans did not like it at first. There was still racial segregation in their country: blacks mostly lived in urban ghettos. With a few exceptions, they were second-class citizens. For a good many whites, their music carried the stigma of crime and violence, especially during the Prohibition years, when gangsters like Al Capone controlled the illicit liquor trade. Jazz musicians, usually through no fault of their own, lived dangerous lives. Pine Top Smith was killed in a Chicago shootout. Their tough lifestyle drove many of them to drink and drugs. Jazz was widely condemned as crude, uncivilized and immoral, and attempts were made to get it banned from respectable society. But its attractions were too strong. The popular dances of World War I and after, both in America and in Europe, were nearly all jazz-inspired. People in fashionable New York, London and Paris, who would not have been caught dead in Basin Street, New Orleans' old red light district, happily danced to the jazzy, syncopated music of the Charleston and the Black Bottom.

Some of the greatest composers of the age were fascinated by the music before even the name 'jazz' was coined for it. The English composer Frederick Delius (1862–1934) was enchanted by the black American songs and spirituals that he heard during his stay in Florida, and their harmonies run through many of his compositions. Debussy (see also pages 154 and 156), too, wrote several pieces in the style of the Cakewalk, another early jazz-like dance. Ravel's (see also pages 154 and 156) two piano concertos and his *Bolero* revel in the use of blue notes. A movement in his Violin Sonata is actually named 'Blues.' Similarly, Kurt Weill (1900–50) and Ernst Krenek (born 1900) in Germany, and William Walton (1902–83) and Constant Lambert (1905–51) in England, made effective use of jazz rhythms and tunes. Stravinsky (see also page 156) wrote *Ragtime* and *Piano Rag Music*, as well as his *Ebony Concerto* for jazz clarinetist Woody Herman.

Most significant for the future course of jazz, white musicians began to play it, and, from the 1920s on, to change something of its character. Leon 'Bix' Beiderbecke played the cornet, and his impeccable phrasing, his masterly understanding and use of harmony, and a warm, clear tone suggested a smoothing away, a toning down, of the rougher edges to the music. One of those who hired Beiderbecke to play was band leader Paul Whiteman. He added violins to his band (something almost unheard of among the old jazz pioneers), made detailed band arrangements, and even conducted with a baton. The music became softer, sweeter, smoother still, like the glossy brilliantine hair-dressing so fashionable at that time. Jazz turned into swing and became respectable.

....
SWING TIME The swing era of the 1930s and 1940s coincided with the heyday of radio. Many swing bands earned far more from

Leon 'Bix' Beiderbecke, one of the first great white jazzmen, whose alcoholism and early death mirrored the world of F. Scott Fitzgerald's novels.

THE BIG BAND SOUND

The big swing and dance bands never reached symphonic proportions. But some of them could pack a very big punch in decibels – without any electronic aids. Their basic line-up (with many variations and additions) consisted of four or five saxophones and clarinet (the reed section), three or four each of trumpets and trombones (the brass), plus a battery of drums, guitar, string bass and piano (rhythm section). Some of the early bands of the 1920s, such as the Paul Whiteman and Fletcher Henderson bands, featured a sousaphone instead of a string bass, its oom-pah accompaniment forever linked with the straw boaters, and bootleg hooch of the Prohibition era.

Through the 1930s and 1940s, the big American bands, of the Dorsey Brothers, Benny Goodman, Artie Shaw, Woody Herman, Harry James, Glenn Miller, Count Basie and Duke Ellington, were unquestionably the best. But British dance bands, such as those of Harry Roy, Bert Ambrose and Geraldo, formed an impressive group, producing, by turns, a slick chirpiness and a creamy blandness, in contrast to the solid strength of their American counterparts. British-born Ray Noble had a foot in both musical camps, leading excellent bands first at home then in the U.S., and composing such well-known 'standards' of the swing era as The Very Thought of You,

Goodnight, Sweetheart and Love is the Sweetest Thing.

In the 1950s, the rise of rock 'n' roll and the tough economics of the business led to the demise of most of the big bands. A few stalwarts carried on, among them British bandleader Ted Heath, who maintained the highest standards into the 1970s. There are still many enthusiasts for the 'big band sound,' with bands faithfully and lovingly re-creating the music of such past masters as Count Basie and Glenn Miller.

Above: The Big Band Sound as played by the Dorsey Brothers: a scene from the film The Fabulous Dorseys.

broadcasting than from live performances. Even during the worst years of the Depression, most of them prospered for, along with the movies they were forms of escapism from the anxieties of real life. The syncopations of swing – the slurs and off-beats – became the common currency of popular music. There was even a craze for 'swinging the classics.' Weber, Schubert, Chopin, Verdi, Tchaikovsky and Rimsky-Korsakov, among others, were given the treatment (they, incidentally, were all romantic rather than strictly classical composers). In the circumstances, swing could easily become slack, self-indulgent, harnessed to a weary formula. The best swing bands, however, were highly professional, as drilled and disciplined as any symphony orchestra, their music sharp and alive.

The men who led them were household names by the time of World War II. Benny Goodman, 'The King of Swing,' created a sensation when he appeared with his band on the hallowed platform of New York's Carnegie Hall. He was equally happy making music of superb bounce and precision with his quartet of selected soloists, and with Hungarian composer Béla Bartók (see also page 156), from whom he commissioned *Contrasts* for clarinet (his own instrument), violin and piano. Clarinetist Woody (Woodrow) Herman, who worked with Stravinsky, as mentioned earlier, formed a succession of brilliant bands known as the 'Herman Herds,' and introduced one of the all-time swing classics, *At the Woodchopper's Ball*. Artie Shaw was yet another marvelous clarinet player. Like Goodman, he also formed a 'chamber group' called The Gramercy Five. The brothers Tommy and Jimmy Dorsey (*I'm Getting Sentimental Over You, The Sunny Side of the Street*) both led their own swing bands. Trombonist Glenn Miller rose to the height of fame on the strength of such numbers as *Moonlight Serenade* and *In the Mood*. When the United States entered World War II, Miller formed an American army band. In 1944, he took off on a flight to Paris and was never seen again. Stan Kenton created another swing classic with *Intermission Riff*, though he went on to do much more experimental work.

BASIE AND ELLINGTON Most bandleaders were white Americans. By the 1930s, there were excellent white jazz musicians in Europe also, notably Belgian gipsy guitarist Django Reinhardt and French violinist Stephane Grappelli, who formed the nucleus of the famous Quintet of the Hot Club of France.

Benny Goodman, most celebrated of all jazz clarinetists, was just as happy playing Mozart and Bartók as big band swing.

Above: Duke Ellington directing his band in a recording session, hence the casual clothes. Veteran Ellington saxophonist Johnny Hodges is seated on the right.

Right: Canadian-born jazz pianist Oscar Peterson, happiest playing in small groups, whose cool and sophisticated fingerwork and harmonies owe much to Art Tatum.

Such Sweet Thunder. Purists argue that improvisation is the soul of jazz and that composition is therefore alien to its spirit. In fact, Ellington usually allowed for some improvisation among his brilliant team of soloists (for example, Johnny Hodges and Paul Gonsalves); for all his sophistication and musical polish, he never lost the spirit of jazz.

There were many other marvelous and innovative black musicians. Coleman Hawkins, Ben Webster and Lester Young headed the ranks of the saxophonists, who composed the 'front line' of nearly every big jazz and swing band. Pianists created their own bouncy swing styles. Thomas 'Fats' Waller was a master of the 'stride piano,' with its strong left-hand beat. He was also a delightful entertainer, clowning his way through renditions of *My Very Good Friend the Milkman*, *Ain't Misbehavin'* and other favorites, sometimes diverting attention away from his immaculate pianism. Earl 'Fatha' Hines and the almost blind Art Tatum had as much technique and dexterity as any concert pianist – inspiring in their turn two fine pianists of a younger generation, Erroll Garner and Oscar Peterson. Lionel Hampton, working closely with Goodman, brought a similar virtuosity to the vibraphone. There was also vocalist Billie Holiday, whose career throws

The great majority of jazz and swing musicians, though, continued to be black artists. They included two more bandleaders, William 'Count' Basie and Edward 'Duke' Ellington; and it is interesting to compare them with the others. Both Basie and Ellington led their bands from the piano keyboard instead of 'up front' – a return to the kind of direction used by J.S. Bach, Haydn and other composers in the days before conductors waved a stick (see also page 136). Basie ('The Atomic Mr. Basie') could draw from his players a sense of power and drive that was perhaps never quite equaled by anyone else.

Ellington goes down in history as much as a composer and arranger as a pianist and bandleader, with such classics as *Take the 'A' Train*, *Mood Indigo*, *Caravan*, *Sophisticated Lady*, *Satin Doll* and several more extended suites, including *Black, Brown and Beige* and

into sharp relief the deep racial prejudice that still existed in much of the United States until well after World War II. She sang with the best bands and was everywhere acclaimed. But off stage, she was often segregated from her white colleagues in trains, buses, restaurants and hotels, because she was black. Her later recordings bear stark witness to the suffering in her life.

TRAD, MAINSTREAM AND PROGRESSIVE

By the end of the 1940s, there was a feeling among lovers and students of jazz that the true spirit of the music had nevertheless been lost to the commercialization of swing. Some looked back nostalgically to its early days in and around New Orleans, and worshipped such old-timers as trumpet player Bunk Johnson and clarinetists George Lewis and Sidney Bechet, whose careers went all the way back to the springtime of jazz. These were the traditionalists; their revivalist jazz was known as 'trad,' or 'Dixieland' after Dixie, the old name for the southern states. Others applauded the way Count Basie and Duke Ellington had energized swing and so kept the jazz spirit alive. Such music was too good to be brushed aside by passing fashions and changes in popular entertainment. It was dubbed 'mainstream;' more up-to-date than 'trad,' more accessible than the music of the new 'progressives.'

Use of the word 'progressive' to describe the new developments in jazz in the 1940s and 1950s carried political and social connotations. Many black Americans still regarded jazz as their own special kind of music. They certainly resented the commercial exploitation of swing very largely by white entrepreneurs. They looked sadly at such a personality as Louis Armstrong, as someone who, in their opinion, had sold out to show business. They wanted to explore new forms and styles of jazz that would still speak for themselves as black people, and show them as capable of technical innovation and creative imagination as any white artist.

Such music came into being in an almost clandestine way, mainly in New York City during the 1940s, among jazzmen meeting privately in off-beat night spots or in their own homes. The music acquired the name 'bebop,' which was soon shortened to 'bop,' on account of the frenetic little musical phrases that fragmented the old stylized harmonies and structures of traditional jazz and swing and which propelled the music into a new harmonic and rhythmic stratosphere.

Continued on page 192

SONGSTERS OF SWING

Before the days of radio and amplified sound, vocal power was what counted in a singer. Ma Rainey and Bessie Smith in the realm of jazz, and Al Jolson in vaudeville, could bawl out a song. In the swing band era, the microphone changed all that. Vocalists now sang quietly, almost as softly as a mother crooning to her child, and aptly, they were described as 'crooners.' They caressed the microphone and sang as though they were murmuring in someone's ear, in a dreamy vocal style that fitted in well with the sweet tone of the bands.

Two of the biggest names in American show business, Bing Crosby and Frank Sinatra, began their careers this way. Sinatra sang with Tommy Dorsey's band, modeling his early vocal style on Dorsey's own sweetly sentimental trombone playing. From the late 1920s to the present day, Rudy Vallee, Dick Haymes, Jo Stafford, Dinah Shore, Perry Como, Doris Day (before she became a movie star), Tony Bennett and Mel Tormé, among many others, have kept alive this tradition of popular song. Some jazz men have had an appealing singing style, notably trombonist Jack Teagarden and pianist Nat King Cole, with his velvety tone. Al Bowlly in Britain, and Frenchmen Jean Sablon and Charles Trenet, also ranked high among the swing and dance band vocalists.

They could sing with verve and gusto too. Crosby, 'the old groaner' as he was affectionately called, loved the springy rhythms of 'Dixieland,' which he delivered to perfection in some of his early, briskly taken numbers.

Ella Fitzgerald, one of the most versatile jazz vocalists, equally at home singing 'scat' (wordless improvising) or popular ballads.

Film Music

Virtually every film produced since the end of the 1920s has had accompanying music. Much of it has been routine and indifferent, sometimes downright abominable. But when a musical soundtrack is good, it is like a breath of life to a film. Good, bad or indifferent, film music has an extremely full and interesting history.

Above: Singer Peggy Lee dubbing her voice to the image of two Siamese cats in the Walt Disney cartoon film The Lady and the Tramp.

Right: Bernard Herrmann's score for Alfred Hitchcock's Psycho *caught the mood of psychopathic terror.*

In 1908, Saint-Saëns (see page 154) wrote some music for a very early silent film, *L'Assassinat du Duc de Guide.* There were other examples of music being specially written to accompany the silents, but it was *The Jazz Singer* of 1927 – with singing star Al Jolson's prophetic words 'You ain't heard nothing yet!' - that really ushered in the era of film music. Thenceforth, films had a synchronized sound track.

The aim of film music, just like that of the incidental music that Beethoven, Schubert, Mendelssohn, Bizet, Grieg and others wrote for the theater, is to heighten the drama. Writing film music is also a very exacting task, because the composer must synchronize his score to the film with stopwatch precision. Technique as much as inspiration is needed.

Many films from the 1930s through to the 1950s had a virtually continuous musical sound track; and in Hollywood, especially, studio composers and arrangers had to turn out film scores almost by the yard. Their work rate, their unblushing musical plagiarisms (notably of Debussy and Ravel) were comparable to those of Vivaldi and others back in the hectic days of baroque opera. Against this inevitably mediocre norm, the scores of Sergei Prokofiev (*Lieutenant Kije, Alexander Nevsky*), of British composers Arthur Bliss (*Things To Come*), Walton (*The First of the Few, Henry V, Hamlet, Richard III*), Vaughan Williams (*Scott of the Antarctic*), Britten (*Night Mail*), and of Americans Virgil Thomson (*The Plow That Broke The Plains*)

and Copland (*Of Mice and Men, The Heiress*), brought a new prestige to the realm of film music.

Prokofiev, Walton and other composers of their caliber wrote their film scores to special commissions. They are not primarily remembered for their film music. But others became specialists in this very demanding sphere of work and raised standards from within the industry. Four of the best composers who worked in Hollywood were Erich Korngold (*The Sea Hawk, The Private Lives of Elizabeth and Essex*), Max Steiner (*Gone With The Wind*), Miklos Rozsa (*Spellbound, Ben Hur*) and Bernard Herrmann (*Citizen Kane, Psycho*).

By the 1960s, the nature of film music was changing, to become much more selective. One cleverly conceived piece of music, often a song, could almost serve an entire film. British-born band leader and composer John Barry set the pace with his themes to several of the immensely stylish James Bond films. In the U.S., Henry Mancini, working with veteran lyricist Johnny Mercer, produced 'Moon River' for the film *Breakfast at Tiffany's* and the title songs for *Charade* and *Days of Wine and Roses*. 'Raindrops Keep Fallin' on My Head,' inserted into *Butch Cassidy and the Sundance Kid,* was a huge success for composer Burt Bacharach. French composer Michel Legrand wrote 'The Windmills of Your Mind' for *The Thomas Crown Affair*. One of today's most successful film composers is Carl Davis (*The French Lieutenant's Woman, The Rainbow*), who has written much work also for television and live theater.

Songs of such outstanding quality as 'The Windmills of Your Mind' have passed into the common currency of popular music. Sometimes the process has worked the other way also, with concert music finding a new audience through its use in the

cinema. Even today, over forty years after *Brief Encounter* (the original version) was made, many people cannot listen to Rachmaninov's Second Piano Concerto without thinking of the film. *Elvira Madigan* introduced millions to the tender beauty of the slow movement from Mozart's Piano Concerto no. 21 in C major (K467). The 'Adagietto' from Mahler's Fifth Symphony might have been specially written for *Death in Venice*, so surely does it encapsulate the mood of the film.

....
Above: A moment from the enchanting The Wizard of Oz, *starring Judy Garland, a film owing much to the songs of Harold Arlen and Yip Harburg.*
....

....
Below: Disney's first animated cartoon classic, Snow White and the Seven Dwarfs, *with songs by Larry Morey and Frank Churchill.*
....

The Jazz Saxophone

The saxophone was invented by the Belgian instrument-maker Adolphe Sax around 1840. Technically, it is a hybrid, with vibrating reed and stopped holes like a woodwind, but made of metal, with a conical bore and flared 'bell' more like a brass instrument. Sax hoped his new instrument would be taken up by military bands, but it has not been widely used by them. Composers from Bizet onward have sometimes written for the saxophone, though it has not found a regular place in symphony orchestras either.

The saxophone found its true home in the swing and dance bands of the 1930s and 1940s. In its varying sizes and ranges of pitched notes – soprano, alto, tenor, baritone – it comprised the 'front-line' instrumental chorus in most bands. No doubt Sax would have been astonished to see a row of saxophones in such a setting.

Many of the greatest jazz musicians have also chosen the saxophone as their instrument. In poor hands, it can sound sleazy. But its inventor would surely have been amazed at the variety of expressive tone, from silky seduction to snorting aggression, extracted from it by such jazz masters as Lester Young, Coleman Hawkins, Ben Webster, Benny Carter, Charlie Parker, Johnny Hodges, Paul Gonsalves, Stan Getz, Gerry Mulligan, John Coltrane and Ornette Coleman. More great jazz has probably been played on the saxophone than on any other instrument.

Trumpeter and composer Dizzy (John Birks) Gillespie was one of its guiding spirits. The very words to his best-known piece, *Salt Peanuts*, obsessively repeated, encapsulate the jumpy energy of vintage bop. 'Dizzy' was a good description too, of his breathtaking style, raising trumpet virtuosity to hitherto undreamt of heights. Moreover, Gillespie was not jealous of his technique, like many jazzmen; he shared his ideas with colleagues, encouraging them and helping them to raise their own sights. The other giant of bop, and friend of Gillespie, was saxophonist Charlie Parker (known to every other jazz musician as 'Bird'), spinning out harmonic and rhythmic patterns which, for all their complexity, he made sound almost childishly easy. Sadly, while Dizzy Gillespie's career continued well into the 1970s, Bird succumbed to drink and drugs and had burned himself out by the time he died in 1955, aged only thirty-five.

Other big names associated with the evolution of bop are drummer Kenny Clarke (who had a hand in the writing of *Salt Peanuts*), guitarist Charlie Christian, pianist, composer and arranger Mary Lou Williams (one of the few prominent women of jazz,

Two masters of the saxophone, Charlie Parker (left) and Johnny Hodges, their contrasting personalities reflecting also the very wide range of jazz saxophone styles.

Milt Jackson, a cool performer on the vibraphone (vibes) compared with the exuberant Lionel Hampton. For more than twenty years, he played with the Modern Jazz Quartet (MJQ).

besides the vocalists), saxophonist Cannonball (Julian) Adderley and Miles Davis.

Trumpeter Davis began with the intricacies of bop before finding a more personal, reflective style, at the same time helping to circulate the term 'cool jazz' – though this had been used among jazz musicians long before the 1950s. Davis also contributed to the development of 'modal jazz,' which describes a style of improvised playing based on scales or other sequences of notes rather than on the chord sequences that most jazzmen had followed up to then. Through the 1950s and 1960s, pianists Bud Powell and Thelonius Monk, bass player Charles Mingus, saxophonists John Coltrane and Ornette Coleman, pianist John Lewis and the Modern Jazz Quartet (MJQ), carried these ideas into ever more esoteric musical realms.

All this was music for the intellectual. Its admirers gathered in cafés and night spots, sometimes in concert halls, listening as intently, applauding as discreetly, as to a piece of twelve-tone music by Webern. Jazz had indeed come a long, long way since 1900 and the days of such a legendary and heroic figure as Buddy Bolden of New Orleans, who, so it was claimed, could be heard fourteen miles away on a clear night, blasting on his horn.

ROCK AROUND THE CLOCK

. . . .

*I*n 1956, meanwhile, Bill Haley and the Comets recorded *Rock Around the Clock* for the film *The Blackboard Jungle*. Another musical revolution was afoot. The piece was founded on blues and boogie, and to this extent it was not especially original. What was new was the instrumentation: electric guitars and drums. Both literally and figuratively, the music was given a new voltage. This was rock 'n' roll. The solid, four-square beat of rock 'n' roll – in contrast to the smooth syncopations of swing – was already familiar to fans of jazz vocalist Louis Jordan, through such snappy or comic songs as *Choo Choo Ch'Boogie* and *Ain't Nobody Here but Us Chickens*. Even the term rock 'n' roll had been around for some time among black Americans. But it hit the world's headlines with Bill Haley, Chuck Berry *(Roll Over, Beethoven)*, Little Richard *(Good Golly, Miss Molly)*, and Elvis Presley, greatest rock 'n' roller of them all. Presley was white, but he was born and brought up in Mississippi and Tennessee, and strong childhood doses of both black rhythm and blues and revivalist ('Bible Belt') hymn singing galvanized his own rock 'n' roll style, sending shivers of excitement through tens of thousands of pubescent girls. Through the late 1950s, he hit the charts with such up-tempo numbers as *Blue Suede Shoes*, *Hound Dog* and *Jailhouse Rock*, and went on to become one of the greatest popular cult figures of all time.

The musical aspects of this revolution were striking enough. It was the end of swing and the big bands as the prime force in popular music. Those who still played and sang in the old swing style catered to an aging public. It brought electronics squarely into the arena

A youthful Elvis Presley, not yet a superstar. His simple clothes and large acoustic guitar are closer to the hillbilly types opposite than to the brash new world of rock 'n' roll and pop.

of popular music too. But the advent of rock 'n' roll signaled social and political changes far beyond the music itself. It was widely condemned as immoral and socially disruptive. So, in their time, had been the waltz, the tango, and boogie. What lay at the root of public outcry this time was the so-called generation gap; the new spending power and the social emancipation enjoyed by many young people in America and elsewhere that came with economic recovery from World War II. Rock 'n' roll focused attention on this. It was the music of the young. It identified its supporters by age rather than class. Elvis Presley dictated not only the musical tastes of the young, but their clothes and hairstyles, their language, their whole way of life. Politicians, church leaders, schoolteachers and others in authority felt threatened or outraged, and blamed it on what British conductor Sir Malcolm Sargent haughtily dismissed as 'roll and rock.'

Rock 'n' roll was the last big development in popular music to come directly out of the United States. The last chapter of this book looks at how it fanned out into the worldwide arena of pop music.

IVES THE REVOLUTIONARY

Since the day Gottschalk was shamefully turned down by the Paris Conservatoire because of his nationality, American academic and concert music had taken giant strides forward. European conductors – Arthur Nikisch, Gustav Mahler, Felix Weingartner, Leopold Stowkowski, Arturo Toscanini, Sir Thomas Beecham – gladly accepted invitations to lead the big American orchestras: the New York Philharmonic, the Philadelphia and the Boston Symphony. European and other international singers – Nellie Melba, Enrico Caruso, Feodor Chaliapin, Kirsten Flagstad, Lauritz Melchior – were the stars of New York's prestigious Metropolitan Opera. What very few Americans realized until long after was that in the early years of this century they could boast a great composer of their own. His name Charles Ives (1874–1954).

Ives was a rugged individualist in the old colonial tradition of William Billings, who worked in the insurance business and only wrote music in his spare time. Ives loved his native New England countryside and way of life and the stirring events in American history that had taken place there. He also loved the open-air prayer meetings and hymn singing, the village dances and military parades, and he liked jazz, too, when he got to hear it. All this he packed into his own music in what at first hearing sometimes sounds like a glorious jumble. The really amazing thing is that Ives, working almost entirely on his own, came up with many of the same advanced ideas about atonality and polytonality as Stravinsky, Bartók and Schoenberg in Europe, and at much the same time. Indeed, as he sharply pointed out to people who said he must have been influenced by those composers, nearly all his major compositions predate theirs. The element of chance in musical performance, of allowing the performers some choice in the manner or order in which they play the music, was something else Ives thought of first.

Thus his music is as American as Thanksgiving Day and apple pie, while also astonishingly original and audacious. *Central Park in the Dark* is one of his best-known orchestral pieces, an impression of New York City suggesting the park as a strange island of darkness and stillness in the midst of all the bustle, cacophony and bright lights of Manhattan. Like Heinrich, Billings and other free spirits of the past, Ives seems often to have composed for the sheer joy (or hell) of it, and to have cared little about the practicalities of performance. His massive *Concorde* piano sonata, inspired by the work of four New England writers (Ralph Waldo Emerson, Nathaniel Hawthorne, Louisa May Alcott and Henry David Thoreau) was considered virtually unplayable for years. A performance in 1939, nearly twenty-five years after its composition, finally helped to wake people up to his genius. Soon after World War II, he was awarded a Pulitzer Prize for his Third Symphony. Scornful of conventional society to the end of his days, he gave the prize money away, declaring, 'Prizes are for boys. I'm grown up.'

....

MUSICAL STARS AND STRIPES Other American composers since Ives have proudly paraded the traditions of their native country in their music. Henry Cowell (1897–1965), an early admirer of Ives' sturdy independence and iconoclasm, came up with some remarkable ideas of his own, such as 'tone clusters,' chords consisting of several adjacent notes, sometimes played on the piano with the palm of the hand or forearm. Still taking his lead from Ives, Cowell also made a study of the old colonial music, which he revived in his 'Hymns and Fuguing Tunes.' Roy Harris (1898–1979) studied in Europe, but remained faithful to the

COUNTRY AND WESTERN

Country and Western is a broad-based style of popular (as distinct from pop) music with fans all over the world. Its roots lie in various North American folk music traditions. Strongest style is the so-called 'hillbilly' music in and around the Appalachian Mountains, whose songs and dances, especially 'square dances,' were brought by the early settlers from England, Scotland and France. The old hillbilly musicians were a resourceful bunch, making a lot out of a little on fiddle, banjo, guitar, mouth organ, and corrugated washboards played with thimbles worn on their thumbs. In the 1950s, this style of music gave rise to a craze for 'skiffle,' a kind of home-spun music-making, given a lively transatlantic twist by Britisher Lonnie Donegan.

Moving west of the Mississippi, cowboys built up a repertory of song that had its latter-day imitators in a rash of 'singing cowboy' movie stars, headed by Roy Rogers, Gene Autry and Tex Ritter.

Then there was the religious revival movement that swept across the old South, from Georgia to Texas, with its vigorous hymn singing, colored by the rhythms and vocal styles of the local black population. Rock 'n' roll superstar Elvis Presley owed a lot to this kind of music, as well as the many singers of 'gospel' and 'soul.'

The borderline between Country and Western and the American folk music revival (see also page 158) has sometimes been a hazy one. Balladeer Burl Ives was an accomplished performer who gave a new polish to many old songs. Fellow American Woody Guthrie was a student of folk music who acted as a spur to Bob Dylan, Pete Seeger, Johnny Cash and Joan Baez, many of whose ballads through the 1960s sounded a strong political note.

The world center for today's thriving Country and Western scene is Nashville, Tennessee. The music is crisp and sentimental by turns, somewhat sanitized by the sound of electric guitars, a long way from the banjos and booze of roistering days gone by.

A Country and Western get-together in Virginia, banjo and guitar flanking the singer, wearing farmyard gear.

colonial roots of American music in many of his own works. His Third Symphony seems to evoke the old frontier spirit and wide open spaces of the prairie, while his Sixth Symphony is subtitled 'Gettysburg Address,' after Lincoln's famous Civil War speech.

Above: George Gershwin working at the piano. He died, aged 39, from a brain tumor, soon after completing his opera Porgy and Bess.

RHAPSODY IN BLUE Jazz was the life-blood of George Gershwin's (1898–1937) music. His social and musical background was entirely different from those of Ives, Cowell and Harris. He was a first-generation American, whose family were Russian Jewish immigrants (named Gershovitz). His meteoric rise from humble pianist in 'Tin Pan Alley,' New York's old music-publishing district, to one of the world's most gifted and successful song-writers, is a model American success story. But money and fame were not everything for Gershwin; he also wanted to become a 'serious' composer, and jumped at the chance when Paul Whiteman asked him to write a piece of 'symphonic jazz.' The result was *Rhapsody in Blue*, conceived originally for jazz band and piano, then orchestrated to bring it closer to the sound of concert music. Critics have pointed out its technical weaknesses, notably the way it is a number of ideas mainly strung together instead of being worked into true symphonic form. But from the clarinet's first exciting wail, the music itself remains as fresh and exhilarating as ever, with a big, blues-inspired theme that would have done Tchaikovsky or Rachmaninov proud had they been born on Manhattan Island instead of in

The American stage and screen star Sammy Davis, Jr., as Sportin' Life in the film version of Gershwin's opera Porgy and Bess.

Aaron Copland, like Gershwin, was born in Brooklyn, New York. Copland was more academic than Gershwin, but did just as much to popularize American concert music.

Russia. It was rapturously applauded at its première in New York in 1924, a concert piece as truly American as the Statue of Liberty. Gershwin wrote other concert works, including a symphonic poem, *An American in Paris*, and an opera with an all-black cast, *Porgy and Bess*, the latter containing some of his most deeply felt music, including such lovely songs or duets as 'Summertime' and 'Bess, you is my woman now.'

COPLAND AND BERNSTEIN Aaron Copland (1900–1990) went to Europe for a period of study and looked all set for an academic life. His first compositions certainly were academically tough and difficult pieces. The German-American conductor Walter Damrosch said of his early and dissonant Symphony for Organ, 'If he can write like that at twenty-three, in five years he'll be ready to

Continued on page 200

The Musical Comedy

The stage and screen musical belongs to America. Composers from other countries have tried their hand at it, but, with the exception of Andrew Lloyd Webber, usually with only moderate success. Until recently, the verve of the true musical – as distinct from musical theater as a whole – has thrived only in New York and in Hollywood.

Above: Fred Astaire and Ginger Rogers, the greatest dance team in the history of the movies, seen here in The Barkleys of Broadway.

Right: The most famous moment in the story of the screen musical: Gene Kelly performs the title song in Singin' in the Rain.

through American and popular music, much as the bright lights of Broadway itself cut a strip down Manhattan Island.

The titles, and the composers and lyricists, of some of the great American musicals are household names: *Showboat* (Jerome Kern and Oscar Hammerstein); *Strike Up the Band, Funny Face, Girl Crazy* (George and Ira Gershwin); *On Your Toes, Babes in Arms, Pal Joey* (Richard Rodgers and Lorenz Hart); *Oklahoma, South Pacific, The King and I, The Sound of Music* (Rodgers and Hammerstein); *Anything Goes, Kiss Me Kate* (Cole Porter); *Annie Get Your Gun* (Irving Berlin);

'Give my regards to Broadway' sang composer-impresario George M. Cohan in 1903. Cohan's song is better known today than the show it came from, *Little Johnny Jones*. But that show, and the famous series of *Ziegfeld Follies* that began four years later, heralded the rise of the American musical (short for 'musical play'). This grew principally from nineteenth-century operetta, notably the Viennese type of Johann Strauss II, Franz Lehar and Oscar Straus.

Soon after the World War I, under the stimulus of the new 'jazz age,' it took off, becoming a powerhouse of song, dance and spectacle that no other country (and no other city outside New York) could equal. For forty years, the musical ran like a vein of gold

Guys and Dolls (Frank Loesser); *My Fair Lady* (Alan Jay Lerner and Frederick Loewe); *West Side Story* (Leonard Bernstein and Stephen Sondheim). These were all initially Broadway hits. Many of them became Hollywood films, though in the process they were often

much changed (original songs cut out, new ones added), spreading the credits among other songwriters and lyricists. Other equally famous musicals originated as films: *Top Hat, Holiday Inn, Easter Parade* (Irving Berlin); *Cover Girl* (Jerome Kern); *The Wizard of Oz* (Harold Arlen); *Singin' In the Rain* (Nacio Brown); *High Society* (Cole Porter); *A Star is Born* (Harold Arlen and Ira Gershwin); *Gigi* (Lerner and Loewe).

Changing fashions and the decline of the Broadway theater saw a decline also of the 'blockbuster' musical. A low-key, sophisticated style emerged with the 1960s, anticipated by the musicals of German composer Kurt Weill (*Lady in the Dark, One Touch of Venus*) after he had left Nazi Germany for America. Stephen Sondheim, with *Company* and *A Little Night Music*, and Marvin Hamlisch, with *A Chorus Line*, have continued in this style.

Even more enduring in many cases than the shows themselves are the hundreds of individual songs. These are the great 'standards,' the work of an élite band of songwriters who marvelously rejuvenated the same popular sentiments over and over

again. They are songs that continue to inspire the best vocalists and jazz musicians: Jerome Kern's 'Ole Man River,' 'Smoke Gets in Your Eyes' and 'All the Things You Are;' George and Ira Gershwin's 'Somebody Loves Me,' 'Lady Be Good,' 'The Man I Love,' 'Embraceable You' and 'Love Walked In;' Irving Berlin's 'Always,' 'Blue Skies,' 'White Christmas' and 'There's No Business Like Show Business;' Cole Porter's 'Begin the Beguine,' 'Night and Day,' 'Just One of Those Things' and 'I've Got You Under My Skin;' Rodgers and Hart's 'Mountain Greenery,' 'My Heart Stood Still' and 'There's a Small Hotel;' Walter Donaldson's 'Making Whoopee;' Harry Warren and Mack Gordon's 'Chatanooga Choo-Choo;' Harry Warren and Al Dubin's 'Lullaby of Broadway' and 'September in the Rain;' Hoagy Carmichael's 'Star Dust;' Hoagy Carmichael and Johnny Mercer's 'Skylark;' Harold Arlen and Yip Harburg's 'It's Only a Paper Moon' and 'Over the Rainbow;' Harold Arlen and Johnny Mercer's 'The Second Time Around;' Sammy Cahn and Jimmy Van Heusen's 'That Old Black Magic;' Kurt Weill's 'September Song.'

....
Above: A balletic sequence in West Side Story, *an updating of the Romeo and Juliet story transposed to Manhattan.*
....

....
Below: Irving Berlin at the piano. In fact, the great songwriter could only play in one key.
....

Samuel Barber, whose generally melodic, traditional musical style places him among America's more conservative composers.

commit murder!' Then Copland had a change of heart. He felt that music should serve a social purpose, that it should entertain and enlighten audiences and not scare them off. It is worth noting that this conviction was similar to official Soviet policy at the time, though Prokofiev and Shostakovich had it imposed on them, while Copland in the U.S. reached it in his own way. Like Gershwin, he also recognized in the vitality of jazz a force in American music that he could use in his de-sire to build a bridge between 'popular' and 'serious' music. His jazz-inspired Piano Concerto was composed two years after *Rhapsody in Blue*, and he followed it some years later with a Clarinet Concerto in the same jazz-based idiom. Copland tapped other sources of indigenous American music: Mexican song and dance in *El Salón México*; a light-hearted cowboy square dance in *Rodeo*; an evocation of the land and history of the old Wild West in his ballet *Billy the Kid*; and an even finer recreation of old American colonial life in the ballet *Appalachian Spring*. These works transport us all the way across the American continent, from the sunny banks of the Rio Grande to the thickly wooded slopes of the Blue Ridge Mountains. Cleverly crafted, beautifully scored, they may have a touch of musical tourism about them, but they express Copland's love of America just as strongly as the bracing 'frontier spirit' of Ives.

Composer-conductor Leonard Bernstein (1918–90) delighted in the bustle and energy of America's big cities and especially of New York, where he spent much of his life. His use of jazz and Latin American rhythms made *On The Town* and *West Side Story* two of the most thrilling and highly praised American stage and screen musicals. Elements of jazz and other popular music styles also feature in some of Bernstein's other works, such as his Second Symphony, *The Age of Anxiety*, and his most unusual and controversial treatment of the Mass ('a theater piece for singers, players and dancers'), written for the opening of the John F. Kennedy Center for the Performing Arts in Washington, DC.

Copland and Bernstein, both men of winning personalities, have been great musical popularizers, not only through their own compositions, but also through their writing and broadcasting.

MORE DISTINGUISHED AMERICANS

Other American composers of this time have kept closer to the main-stream of European or Western music. Indeed, many of them, like Copland, crossed the Atlantic to study in Europe, notably with the celebrated French teacher Nadia Boulanger. Walter Piston (1894–1976) was a distinguished academic who wrote an important textbook on harmony. His compositions – symphonies, concertos and much chamber music – are solidly in the European symphonic tradition. Samuel Barber (1910–81) is best known for his *Adagio for Strings* (arranged from a string quartet), an alternately grave and passionate piece that sounds very like a cross between Tchaikovsky and Mahler. Barber wrote much more substantial works, including operas and choral pieces (he himself was a good singer), in the same generally late-romantic style.

Gian Carlo Menotti (born 1911), a close friend of Barber, was born in Italy, but studied in the United States and has lived and worked there for much of his life. Opera has been his specialty, in the generally tuneful and unashamedly dramatic Italian tradition. Virgil Thomson (1896–1989) is also best known for his operas, notably the one with the intriguing title *Four Saints in Three Acts*. This has a libretto by the American poet Gertrude Stein. She spent much of her life in France, and Thomson's music is influenced by Debussy and other French composers; at its best, his work has echoes of both France and America.

....

CAGE AND THE AMERICAN AVANT-GARDE John Cage (born 1912) has been influenced by many ideas outside music itself, including Zen Buddhism. The title of 'composer' hardly describes him; he is a philosopher, mystic, sage, and a man with a roguish sense of humor, who has stood many of our most cherished notions about music on their heads. Like Varèse (see page 161), Cage has been as interested in sound for its own sake as in what we understand as music, and he has spent his whole life deliberately avoiding every established musical idea or practice. His studies with Schoenberg drew him into serialism. His 'prepared piano' (modifying the sound of the strings by placing objects on or between them) and his interest in electro-acoustics are all part of his search for new aural experiences beyond the recognized boundaries of music. *Imaginary Landscapes* are some of the fruits of this work. These are musical explorations combining radio or electronic effects with his interest in aleatory devices – allowing for some element of choice among performers, even random chance. His most extraordinary concept – it cannot be called a composition – is called *4 min 33 sec.* For this period of time, a pianist sits at a piano without playing a note. In other words, it is silence we are invited to share, plus any extraneous sounds (perhaps the dropping of the proverbial pin) that might intrude upon our consciousness.

The eccentricities of men like Cage do not fit into any category or class, but many people see him as the doyen of America's musical avant-garde. These include Roger Sessions (1896–1985) and his pupil Milton

John Cage signing autographs during a visit to London. Today, his views on music are as iconoclastic as ever.

Babbitt (born 1916), who between them have extended serial techniques to include rhythm and dynamics as well as pitched notes. Babbitt has also done much work with synthesizers. Elliott Carter (born 1908) is known especially for what he has called 'metrical modulation,' creating an interplay between different rhythms – something we can also encounter in African drumming. Harry Partch (1901–74), like Cage, rejected all notions of established scales and keys and invented several new instruments, such as his 'bamboo marimba,' in his pursuit of a new world of sound.

Jazz and Swing

The story of jazz and swing covers almost a century, from the rags, stomps and blues of New Orleans, through the swing era, to the progressive styles of bebop and beyond. Titles listed under each musician may refer to a particular number or to a recorded album.

NEW ORLEANS/TRADITIONAL

HENRY 'RED' ALLEN (1908–67)
Trumpet *I ain't got Nobody, Feelin' Good*

LOUIS ARMSTRONG (1900–71)
Trumpet *Tiger Rag, Cornet Chop Suey, Potato Head Blues, Satch Plays Fats*

SIDNEY BECHET (1897–1959)
Soprano sax, clarinet *Wild Cat Blues, Jazzin' Babies Blues*

LEON 'BIX' BEIDERBECKE (1903–31)
Cornet, piano *Dardanella, In a Mist* (piano), *The Bix Beiderbecke Legend*

HUMPHREY LYTTELTON (born 1921)
Trumpet, bandleader *Bad Penny Blues, Beano Boogie*

FERDINAND 'JELLY ROLL' MORTON (1890–1941)
Piano, bandleader *The Pearls, Dead Man Blues, Sidewalk Blues, Grandpa's Spells, Wolverine Blues*

JOE 'KING' OLIVER (1885–1938)
Cornet, bandleader *Canal Street Blues, Working Man Blues, New Orleans Stomp, High Society Rag*

EDWARD 'KID' ORY (1886–1973)
Trombone, bandleader *Ory's Creole Trombone, Muskrat Ramble*

ORAN 'HOT LIPS' PAGE (1908–54)
Trumpet *Skull Duggery, The Sheik of Araby*

GERTRUDE 'MA' RAINEY (1886–1939)
Singer *Bo-Weevil Blues, Moonshine Blues*

BESSIE SMITH (1895–1937)
Singer *Downhearted Blues, Backwater Blues*

MAINSTREAM AND SWING

WILLIAM 'COUNT' BASIE (1904–84)
Pianist, bandleader *One O'Clock Jump, L'il Darlin'* (Neal Hefti) *April in Paris, Basie in Birdland*

BUNNY BERIGAN (1908–42)
Trumpet, bandleader *I can't get started with you*

EDDIE CONDON (1905–73)
Guitar, bandleader *Jam Session Coast to Coast*

BLOSSOM DEARIE (born 1926)
Singer/songwriter *My New Celebrity Is You*

TOMMY DORSEY (1905–56)
Trombone, bandleader *I'm Getting Sentimental Over You, On the Sunny Side of the Street* (Sy Oliver)

EDWARD 'DUKE' ELLINGTON (1899–1974)
Piano, bandleader, composer *Take the 'A' Train* (Billy Strayhorn), *Mood Indigo, It Don't Mean a Thing, Sophisticated Lady, Cotton Tail, Black Brown and Beige, Such Sweet Thunder*

ELLA FITZGERALD (born 1918)
Singer *A Tisket, A Tasket, Manhattan, How High the Moon*

ERROLL GARNER (1921–77)
Piano *Misty, Concert by the Sea*

BENNY GOODMAN (1909–86)
Clarinet, bandleader *After You've Gone, Airmail Special, Carnegie Hall Concert*

LIONEL HAMPTON (born 1909)
Vibes, drums *Lionel Hampton's Jazz Giants*

COLEMAN HAWKINS (1904–69)
Tenor sax *Body and Soul, Duke Ellington Meets Coleman Hawkins*

WOODY HERMAN (born 1913)
Clarinet, bandleader *Woodchopper's Ball, At Carnegie Hall, Encore: 1963*

EARL 'FATHA' HINES (1903–83)
Piano, bandleader *Blues in Thirds, Earl Hines Plays Duke Ellington*

BILLIE HOLIDAY (1915–59)
Singer *Did I Remember? No Regrets, Billie's Blues, Lover Man*

LENA HORNE (born 1917)
Singer/Actress *Stormy Weather, Lady and Her Music.*

HARRY JAMES (1916–83)
Trumpet, bandleader *Strictly Instrumental, Ridin' High, Carnival of Venice*

STAN KENTON (1912–79)
Bandleader *Eager Beaver, Intermission Riff*

GENE KRUPA (1909–73)
Drums, bandleader *Drummin' Man, Manhattan Transfer*

GLENN MILLER (1904–44)
Trombone, bandleader *Moonlight Serenade, String of Pearls, Pennsylvania 6–5000, In the Mood, Tuxedo Junction*

ANITA O'DAY (born 1919)
Singer *Anita Sings the Most, Wave*

DJANGO REINHARDT (1910–53)
Guitar *Lady Be Good, Limehouse Blues* (with the Quintette du Hot Club de France)

ARTIE SHAW (born 1910)
Clarinet, bandleader *Begin the Beguine, Frenesi, Summit Ridge Drive*

GEORGE SHEARING (born 1919)
Piano *Lullaby of Birdland*

ART TATUM (1909–56)
Piano *Tea for Two, Sweet Lorraine, Get Happy, Body and Soul*

JACK TEAGARDEN (1905–64)
Trombone, singer *Knockin' a Jug, Jack Hits the Road*

SARAH VAUGHAN (1924–90)
Singer *Moonlight in Vermont, Misty*

THOMAS 'FATS' WALLER (1904–43)
Piano, singer *Ain't Misbehavin', Honeysuckle Rose, Alligator Crawl, Your Feets' Too Big*

BEN WEBSTER (1909–73)
Tenor sax *Blue Skies, My Funny Valentine, No Fool, No Fun*

LESTER YOUNG ('PREZ') (1909–59)
Tenor sax *These Foolish Things, Lady Be Good*

Bebop and After
. . . .
JULIAN 'CANNONBALL' ADDERLEY (1928–75)
Alto sax *Somethin' Else*

CARLA BLEY (born 1938)
Piano, synthesizer, composer *Escalator Over the Hill, Tropic Appetites*

DAVE BRUBECK (born 1920)
Piano *Take Five* (Paul Desmond), *Two Generations of Brubeck*

ORNETTE COLEMAN (born 1930)
Alto and tenor sax, trumpet, violin *Jazz Abstractions, At the Golden Circle*

JOHN COLTRANE (1926–67)
Tenor and soprano sax *Giant Steps, Ascension*

CHICK COREA (born 1941)
Piano/electric keyboards *La Fiesta, Return to Forever*

JOHN DANKWORTH (born 1927)
Alto sax, bandleader, composer *What the Dickens, Zodiac Variations*

MILES DAVIS (born 1926)
Trumpet *Miles Ahead, Milestones, Bitches Brew*

BILL EVANS (1928–80)
Piano, composer *Undercurrent, Conversations with Myself*

GIL EVANS (1912–88)
Piano, composer *Sketches of Spain* (with Miles Davis) *Svengali*

John Coltrane, probably the most imitated jazz saxophonist ever.

STAN GETZ (born 1927)
Tenor sax *Stan Getz Meets Gerry Mulligan, The Dolphin*

DIZZY GILLESPIE (born 1917)
Trumpet *Night in Tunisia, Groovin' High, Salt Peanuts, Live at the Spotlite*

MILT JACKSON (born 1923)
Vibes *Milt Jackson and the Modern Jazz Quartet*

WYNTON MARSALIS (born 1961)
Trumpet *Think of One, Hot House Flowers*

CHARLES MINGUS (1922–79)
Bass, piano, composer *Black Saint and the Sinner Lady*

THELONIUS MONK (1917–82)
Piano, composer *Round Midnight, Solo Monk*

WES MONTGOMERY (1925–68)
Guitar *The Incredible Jazz Guitar of Wes Montgomery*

GERRY MULLIGAN (born 1927)
Baritone sax, composer *Walkin' Shoes, Venus de Milo*

CHARLIE PARKER ('BIRD') (1920–55)
Alto sax *Scrapple from the Apple, Anthropology, Ornithology, Groovin' High*

OSCAR PETERSON (born 1925)
Piano *Canadian Suite, Affinity*

BUD POWELL (1924–66)
Piano *Hallucinations, The Glass Enclosure*

SONNY ROLLINS (born 1930)
Tenor sax *Doxy, Valse Hot, Blue 7*

HORACE SILVER (born 1928)
Piano *Opus de Funk, Doodlin', Sister Sadie*

CECIL TAYLOR (born 1933)
Piano, composer *Unit Structures, Live at Bologna*

MARY LOU WILLIAMS (1910–81)
Piano, composer *Zodiac Suite, Trumpet No End*

TEDDY WILSON (1912–86)
Piano *Between the Devil and the Deep Blue Sea*

American Composers

Some American composers (MacDowell, Piston, Barber, Virgil Thomson) have remained fairly close to the styles and forms of European music. Others (Ives, Gershwin, Copland, Bernstein) have a much stronger American identity, compounded of folk music and jazz. Yet others (Ives again, Cage, Steve Reich, Philip Glass) are, or have been, in the vanguard of this century's music.

JOHN ADAMS

(born 1947)
OPERAS
Nixon in China; The Death of Klinghoffer.
INSTRUMENTAL
Shaker Loops, for strings; Light over War, for brass and synthesizer.

MILTON BABBITT

(born 1916)
Philomel for soprano, recorded soprano and tape.

SAMUEL BARBER

(born 1910)
VOCAL AND INSTRUMENTAL
Dover Beach, for baritone and strings; Knoxville, Summer of 1915, for soprano and orchestra; Adagio for Strings.

LEONARD BERNSTEIN

(1918–90)
ORCHESTRAL
SYMPHONIES no. 1 (Jeremiah Symphony); no. 2 (The Age of Anxiety).
OVERTURE Candide.
CHORAL
Chichester Psalms; Mass.
MUSICALS
On The Town; West Side Story.

MARC BLITZSTEIN

(1905–64)
ORCHESTRAL
Airborne Symphony.
OPERA-MUSICAL
The Cradle Will Rock.

JOHN CAGE

(born 1912)
INSTRUMENTAL
Amores for two prepared pianos and percussion.
PIANO Music of Changes.

ELLIOTT CARTER

(born 1908)
ORCHESTRAL
Variations.
VOCAL
A Mirror on Which to Dwell, for soprano and instrumental ensemble.

AARON COPLAND

(1900–90)
BALLETS
Billy the Kid; Rodeo; Appalachian Spring.
ORCHESTRAL
Dance Symphony; Symphony no. 3 (includes 'Fanfare for the Common Man'); El Salón México; Quiet City; A Lincoln Portrait, for speaker and orchestra.
CONCERTOS
Piano; Clarinet

HENRY COWELL

(1897–1965)
ORCHESTRAL
Saturday Night at the Firehouse; Hymns and Fuguing Tunes.
CHAMBER
Pulse, for five percussion players.

GEORGE GERSHWIN

(1898–1937)
OPERA
Porgy and Bess.
ORCHESTRAL
An American in Paris.
CONCERTOS
PIANO in F; Rhapsody in Blue, for piano and orchestra.
VOCAL
Songs: 'Strike Up the Band,' 'Swanee,' 'I Got Rhythm,' 'Fascinatin' Rhythm,' 'Lady Be Good,' 'A Foggy Day,' 'The Man I Love,' 'Love Walked In,' 'I'll Build a Stairway to Paradise,' 'S'Wonderful,' 'Embraceable You,' 'Nice Work If You Can Get It,' 'Liza,' 'Somebody Loves Me,' and many more.

PHILIP GLASS

(born 1937)
OPERAS
Einstein on the Beach; Akhnaten.

LOUIS MOREAU GOTTSCHALK

(1829–69)
INSTRUMENTAL
PIANO The Dying Poet, a meditation; caprice, Minuit à Seville.

HOWARD HANSON

(1896–1981)
ORCHESTRAL
SYMPHONY no. 2 ('Romantic').

ROY HARRIS

(1898–1979)
ORCHESTRAL
SYMPHONIES nos. 3 and 5.

Leonard Bernstein at work. His wide-ranging output includes West Side Story *and the* Chichester Psalms.

*C*HARLES IVES

(1874–1954)
ORCHESTRAL
Symphony no. 3 ('The Camp Meeting'); *Holidays Symphony; Three Places in New England; The Unanswered Question; Central Park in the Dark;* Variations on 'America.'
INSTRUMENTAL
Piano Sonata no. 2 *(Concord Sonata),* with parts also for viola and flute.

*E*DWARD MACDOWELL

(1860–1908)
CONCERTOS
PIANO nos. 1 and 2.
INSTRUMENTAL
PIANO *Ten Woodland Sketches* (including 'To a Wild Rose').

*G*IAN-CARLO MENOTTI

(born 1911)
OPERAS
Amelia Goes to the Ball; The Medium; The Telephone; Amahl and the Night Visitors.

*W*ALTER PISTON

(1894–1976)
BALLET
The Incredible Flutist.
ORCHESTRAL
Concerto for Orchestra.

*S*TEVE REICH

(born 1936) *Desert Music,* for amplified chorus and orchestra. *Different Trains,* for string quartet and tapes.

*T*ERRY RILEY

(born 1935)
Poppy Nogood and the Phantom Band, for soprano, saxophone and electronics; *A Rainbow in Curved Air,* for electric keyboards.

*C*ARL RUGGLES

(1876–1971)
ORCHESTRAL
Suntreader.

*W*ILLIAM SCHUMAN

(born 1910)
ORCHESTRAL
Symphony no.3; *American Festival Overture.*

*R*OGER SESSIONS

(1896–1985)
ORCHESTRAL
Concerto for Orchestra.

*V*IRGIL THOMSON

(1896–1989)
OPERA
Four Saints in Three Acts.
ORCHESTRAL
Symphony no. 2.

Finale: World Music Today

9

Finale: World Music Today

This book began by quoting some recent compositions or happenings that have brought together musical styles and ideas from around the world. In the course of the text, a global journey has been made, traveling back thousands of years, tracing some of the myriad threads that make up the pattern of world music. That journey is nearly over, and the traveler who has come almost full circle, back to the starting point, will be better able to understand music today.

As the century closes, one thing that characterizes world music is a proliferation of styles, categories and labels, created largely by commercial marketing. In reality, many overlap or are synonymous, or simply change meaning as tastes change. It seems that as music moves toward some sort of universality, there is an almost schizophrenic need to reduce it into smaller and smaller pieces.

Mick Jagger and Keith Richard of The Rolling Stones. The electric guitar thrust suggestively out in front of Jagger personifies the tough, uncompromising age of rock music.

POP AND ROCK

The development of Western popular song and dance ended on page 194 with the rock 'n' roll of Chuck Berry and Elvis Presley. The rock 'n' roll revolution, and the huge social ramifications that went with the music – the dress, behavior, attitudes – was just a start. The Beatles quickly followed the Elvis Presley cult into the 1960s. The famous four (George Harrison, Paul McCartney, John Lennon and Ringo Starr) were British, a landmark in itself after half a century or more of American domination of popular and dance music. They were a scruffy bunch before their new manager, Brian Epstein, spruced them up and set the tone for Britain's 'swinging sixties.' The marketing job done on them, the projection of their image, eclipsed even the Presley phenomenon. Epstein's clever cosmetic job was not, of course, enough on its own to explain their staggering success. Musically, the fact that they were Europeans distanced them a little from the blues and boogie roots of rock 'n' roll. Their rhythms ('the Mersey Beat'), initially at any rate, had a more solidly insistent sound. They also had, in Lennon and McCartney, a song-writing duo that took their music far beyond the confines of rock 'n' roll. *Yesterday*, *Michelle* and *Penny Lane* are true songs and ballads now well on their way to immortality. The Who (including Pete Townshend, Roger Daltry and Keith Moon) and The Rolling Stones (led by Mick Jagger and Keith Richard) were different again. The Rolling Stones, especially, added to this heavier kind of beat an arrogant, aggressive, and overtly sexual image. They were into drugs, and their concerts did not just generate hysteria, but sometimes violence, too. They were a symbol of the alienation of a whole generation from the rest of society. 'Pop' had already replaced 'popular' as the term to distinguish the new music of the young. 'Rock' superseded 'rock 'n' roll,' something – in the opinion of its detractors, at any rate – as unyielding as its name.

. . . .

SPLINTERS OF ROCK The evolution of rock music during the 1960s and beyond is a barometer of today's urban society, with all its enormous social pressures, conflicts, problems and changes. Rock, perhaps more than any other kind of music, is also a whole way of life. It draws into its orbit clothes, customs, food, drink, drugs, religion, politics, exploding technology, and a rampant commercialism.These elements have all been present in some of the huge rock and pop festivals of the last thirty years. These would, of course, have been impossible without the resources of modern PA systems, able to broadcast live music to a hundred thousand or more people gathered together in the open air. Some of these mega-events, such as Monterey, California, and Woodstock in upstate New York, were organized primarily for the music, and were generally peaceful and happy occasions. Others, undermined by drugs, turned violent. Still others have been harnessed to some political or social end, such as the Live Aid marathons, staged almost simultaneously in Britain and America on behalf of famine relief, or the concert celebrating the release from prison of the black African leader Nelson Mandela. Sometimes, the music seems quite buried beneath everything else that is going on in its name.

The pop music scene, worldwide, is like a chemical change involving thousands of 'free radicals' – atomic particles that constantly join up, break apart and re-group. Personalities arrive overnight, they team up, they scatter, they survive or they disappear again into oblivion. Terms and styles, like folk, rhythm and blues, soul, gospel, funk rock, funk reggae, jazz funk mean different things to different people from one month to the next. It is a state of never-ending flux. Nevertheless, behind all the ballyhoo, beneath all the froth, rock music has settled into world culture. The now legendary Elvis Presley, The Beatles, The Rolling Stones, the huge success of the

THE DISC JOCKEY

The disk jockey is a phenomenon of popular and pop music. Nobody knows who first coined the name; but it is a good one for the man or woman who rides the airwaves on a pile of records. The role of the disk jockey, DJ or Deejay, goes all the way back to the early 1930s when the great economic Depression had just hit America. Theaters and movies were feeling the pinch, but radio, bringing entertainment into people's homes, thrived. Across the nation, thousands of radio stations, large and small, filled the air with soap operas and programs of recorded popular music, compèred by disk jockeys. At first, this new breed of broadcaster was attacked by musicians and record companies, who feared that radio would rob them of live audiences and sales. But in reality, the DJs stimulated interest in the music, and the records they promoted climbed high in the sales charts. In the 1950s, DJ Alan Freed secured a place in history with his early enthusiasm for rock 'n' roll, so doing much to usher in the whole new world of pop music.The commercial power the DJs wielded, the bribes they took from the recording companies to plug their products ('payola'), also landed many of them in serious trouble.

Today's DJs have come a long way from passively placing one record after another on a 78rpm turntable. Many now use equipment more like the flight deck of Concorde. To electronic knowhow, they must add showmanship and a shrewd commercial sense. Radio stations, discos, hospitals and luxury liners all want DJs, from the most suave and anodyne to the most frenetic dispensers of rap and hip-hop. Pop and popular music could hardly survive without them.

American Stevie Wonder (Steveland Judkins), blind from birth, has successfully bridged the gap between 'pop' and popular music. He has also been politically active, successfully campaigning to have Martin Luther King's birthday adopted as an American national holiday.

American Motown record company promoting such stars as Diana Ross and Stevie Wonder, the creative brilliance of composer, arranger and guitarist Frank Zappa, and the wizardry of guitarists Jimi Hendrix and Eric Clapton, permeate the fabric of this century.

Rock music, then, is an extraordinarily volatile means of expression. One of the problems is simply trying to keep track of all its off-shoots, or its splinters, and give them some viability. Hard rock and heavy metal, jazz rock and progressive rock, acid rock, punk and funk, glam rock, teenybopper pop, are just some of the labels attached to this or that style or scenario. Distinctions between these categories are frequently blurred, as new mutations come and go. A few categories or styles, though, have made their mark, and between them give some idea of the wide diversity of rock music as a whole.

....

HEAVY METAL Heavy metal, with its roots going back to the 1960s, suggests the yard, brawn and sweat, ton-up bikes, leather gear, studs and chains. Over the years, its groups have built on this image: Led Zeppelin, Deep Purple, Iron Maiden, Megadeth, Whitesnake, Motorhead. Their liberties with spelling, as much as their imagery, point also to a rough, sardonic humor. The music demands a pounding beat, guitars fed through a fearsome amplification, ready to bludgeon the unsuspecting listener to the floor. One of the

notable things about heavy metal – living right up to its name – is its solid durability. Other rock styles and crazes have come and gone, but for over twenty years now, the same electrophonically hard-driven sounds of heavy metal have grabbed a large slice of each rising generation. Anthrax, a menacing enough title in anyone's book, is one of the latest heavy metal groups.

....

ACID ROCK Acid means LSD, the drug first associated, outside strictly medical circles, with the hippie cult of San Francisco and elsewhere along the West Coast. Acid and other hallucinogenic drugs can raise or open the mind to a new level of awareness. They may also induce a distorted mental state of near madness. Acid rock, employing all the resources of electronic music, plus the flashing colors of stroboscopic lights, seeks to recreate the experience of a 'trip.' The Pink Floyd, Tangerine Dream, The Grateful Dead, The Velvet Underground, The Jefferson Airplane and Quicksilver Messenger are among the groups who have projected aspects of this psychedelic realm. Their music can also be extremely loud, intended simply to numb the senses; or it can explore strange and fascinating sound patterns, bringing it close to much progressive rock and to the work of such composers as Stockhausen.

In recent years, acid house parties, private or clandestine affairs because of their use of drugs, have spawned new dance styles to go with the music: acid, garage, new beat, techno and ambient.

....

PUNK ROCK Punk rock began in America, among thousands of teenagers stimulated by the new sounds of The Beatles and The Rolling Stones. They were mostly amateur groups, whose records, when they made them at all, rarely became hits. Punk then crossed the Atlantic to Britain, and its image drastically changed. In the eyes of its critics, it came much closer to the dictionary definition of punk as something rotten, dirty, and worthless. Punk rockers gave voice to the deep urban disillusion that followed the euphoric 'swinging sixties.' Their dress, their outrageous, brightly-colored hairstyles, their four-letter words, were meant to give offence. 'You don't hate us as much as we hate you,' they shouted at the rest of the world. The Sex Pistols were punk's leading British group. Their music was hard rock stripped down to a few essentials. Their songs had such titles as *Pretty Vacant* and *Rip Off*. Music before punk

Tina Turner, the American singer, whose dynamic energy and glamor have made her one of today's superstars of pop.

British group The Sex Pistols, including Johnny Rotten and Sid Vicious, looking untypically cheerful for punk rockers.

had seldom been called to serve such nihilism. At least punk can be said to have enlarged the vocabulary of music, for better or for worse.

....

GLAM AND GLITTER ROCK Where heavy metal scorns finesse, and punk was out to give offence, glam and glitter, as their names suggest, go more for good old-fashioned show-business razzmatazz. Their personnel take infinite time and trouble over their appearance and stage persona. They have not,

by any means, all aimed to create the same image. Elton John and Stevie Wonder may sometimes look eccentric in an entertaining way, quite like circus clowns. Others, such as David Bowie, Prince and Boy George, in their skin-tight pants and sequins, dyed and elaborately styled hair, and heavy make-up, project a sexual ambiguity that has a long history in the *demi-monde* of Paris's Left Bank, London's Soho, or Berlin in the days of the Weimar Republic. With so much attention given to the image, it is perhaps not surprising that the actual music can be quite conventional, even vapid. It might include songs closer to old-time sentimental ballads than incitements to mayhem, or mark a return to the good old days of rock 'n' roll in the aptly named persons of Gary Glitter and Alvin Stardust.

The American superstar Madonna (Madonna Louise Ciccone) is one of the late twentieth-century's more glam artists. A former university and ballet student, through the 1980s she climbed steadily in the American and European charts, primarily as a singer. With the arrival of the 1990s, she has advanced into a whole new scenario of erotic song and dance. Indeed, her stage show, *Like a Prayer*, now on video, is an exploration of the very thin dividing line between religious and sexual hysteria. This kind of eroticism has long

Continued on page 214

211

Recording

Until the very end of the nineteenth century, there was only live music (except for such novelties as the music box and the barrel organ). Today, it is almost impossible to imagine music without the recording industry – indeed, some works are almost impossible to perform live. Musicians, from symphonic conductors to pop stars, often put more thought and effort into recordings than into live performances.

'Mary had a little lamb, its fleece was white as snow.' These were the first words that American inventor Thomas Edison recited into his original phonograph in 1877. 'Gott in Himmel,' cried his German assistant when the phonograph played them back, 'it have spoke!' So began the history of recorded sound. Emile Berliner's gramophone came ten years later. Instead of Edison's cylinders, this used disks, which were easier to handle and to duplicate. Edison had made the great technical breakthrough, but Berliner pointed the way forward.

From the beginning, the story of recorded sound has been one of continual and often dramatic technical advance. In the 1920s, acoustical recording (registering sound impulses directly onto a surface) was superseded by electrical recording (converting sounds into electrical impulses before recording them), with much improved sound quality. In the late 1940s, disks with only a few minutes' playing time per side gave way to long-playing (LP) records, with commensurate improvements in the range and clarity of sound.

*Above and right :
Two examples of
early acoustic
recording, the horn
transmitting sounds
directly onto the
recording surface.*

Stereophonic sound recording soon followed, and then the entirely new technology of recording on magnetic tape. This had a dual advantage, as it not only led to the taped cassette, but also facilitated the recording process, allowing performances to be edited to a wellnigh perfect standard. In the 1980s came the compact disk (CD), digitally recorded and with a laser beam to scan the disk. This offers as much as an hour of music and the best sound reproduction yet.

Music was integral to the story of recorded sound almost from the start. Brahms recorded a piano rendering of one of his Hungarian Dances (though you would hardly recognize it unless you were told), and Bartók seized the opportunity to record folk songs on the phonograph. Among the first to record commercially were British music-hall artistes Marie Lloyd and George Robey, quickly followed by opera stars Enrico Caruso, Nellie Melba and Feodor Chaliapin. In those early days, the voice came across much better than instruments, though in 1913 His Master's Voice (HMV) issued Beethoven's Fifth Symphony on eight single-sided disks.

Electric recording and the swing era arrived almost simultaneously, cross-fertilizing each other. The biggest names in swing and dance-band music – Paul Whiteman, 'Fats' Waller, Tommy Dorsey, Benny Goodman, Glenn Miller and Bing Crosby – owed much of their fame to the phonograph, and tailored their music to it. Multi-track recording later revolutionized pop and rock music by permitting different instruments or voices to be recorded over each other. In the field of concert music, Herbert von Karajan headed a generation of conductors who were as much wizards of recording technology as of the baton. Many orchestras and individuals depend on recording contracts to stay in business.

The already immense library of recorded music provides a valuable archive going back nearly a century. We no longer have to guess at how a piece of music was performed; we can hear great composers – Elgar, Stravinsky, Britten – directing their own, and can listen to people like 'Jelly Roll' Morton reminiscing about the styles and origins of jazz.

Right: Vintage 78 rpm recording of the swing era. For many years, His Master's Voice (HMV), with its accompanying emblem, was the most famous name in the British record industry. The same emblem was used by RCA in the United States.

Above: Recording engineer at the controls of a modern multi-track recording and mixing console.

been used by artists, writers and composers, but only for the delectation of an intellectual élite. Madonna has given it to everybody, making 'glam and glitter,' or any other designation of rock, quite inadequate to describe her work.

....

AFRO-AMERICA: REGGAE Heavy metal, acid rock, punk, glam and glitter, are primarily the music of American and European whites. Much as they created jazz, the rumba, the samba, a century or more ago, in the last thirty or forty years, America's blacks and hispanics have forged new styles of rock and pop which are distinctively their own. And just as black

Americans of an earlier generation felt cheated of their jazz when whites commercialized it and turned it into swing, so blacks in the Caribbean, especially on the island of Jamaica, have resented the colonial erosion of their African cultural roots. This inspired the part-religious, part-political Rastafarian movement, focusing the attention of black people on their African homeland and specifically on Ethiopia as their equivalent of the Jewish Zion, or 'promised land.' Connected with this is reggae music, a colorful blend of other local styles, Christian revivalist hymn singing, magical cult drum music, ska (a type of calypso singing), rock, and rudie ('rude boy' or 'street-wise') blues. Its chief rhythmic feature is a type of accented beat, distinguishing it from other types of rock music.

The world beyond Jamaica and the Caribbean woke up to reggae in the 1960s, thanks largely to Jamaican-born Bob Marley and his group, originally called the Wailin' Wailers. This prime reggae style is now widely known as rasta reggae. Funk reggae, as performed by Peter Tosh (who first played with Bob Marley) and Jimmy Cliff, is colored by what people often call 'soul.' The pop reggae (or 'spouge') of Toots and the Maytals, includes elements of calypso and even the old-style 'Mersey Beat' of The Beatles.

....

AFRO-AMERICA: RAP AND HIP-HOP Whereas reggae began in what the tourist guides would call an 'island paradise,' its younger urban cousins, rap and hip-hop, have come out of New York City, out of the black ghettos of Harlem (long ago stripped of whatever glamour it might once have enjoyed) and the even grimmer tenements and vacant lots of the Bronx just across the Harlem River. Along with the street gangs and the drugs, it was here that the phenomenon of graffiti art first blossomed, carrying – on walls, on trains and buses – the enigmatic scrawl of an urban sub-culture. Rap and hip-hop are like a vocal equivalent of this graffiti, a rapid-fire delivery of words, sometimes so fast you can hardly distinguish them, to a background of records, tapes or live rock. Afrika Bambaata, Grand Master Flash and Trouble Funk are masters of it. The verses may be funny, surreal or, like these from another master of the quick-fire recitation, Brother D, much more serious:

The Ku Klux Klan is on the loose
Training their kids in machine-gun use.
The story might give you stomach cramps
Like America's got concentration camps.'

Bob Marley from Jamaica, resplendent in dreadlocks, symbolizing the Rastafarian movement and its reggae music. Marley, the first star of reggae, died from cancer in 1981.

Open-air rock concert in Budapest. Around the world, the scene is much the same; a vast and eager crowd, the players up on stage backed by an array of percussion and electronic hardware.

Indeed, black American rap and hip-hop have now taken a strong political turn. The group Public Enemy are called 'the guerillas of rap' and are associated with the black American movement for a Republic of New Africa. But the same graffiti, the same semi-private language and rhythms, the same hip-hop street and disco dances ('itch,' 'rubberlegs,' 'lego-mania') have also spoken for London's Brixton and Notting Hill, and for other big towns and cities around the world where blacks live out an urban culture of their own.

....

RED ROCK AND AFTER   In the spirit of *glasnost*, rock and pop music today permeate life from the ruins of the Berlin Wall to Vladivostok. But long before the events of recent years, pop music had been steadily undermining the authority of stony-faced politicians in Moscow, Warsaw, Prague and Budapest. While Stalin still ruled, Soviet and East European youth eagerly took to rock 'n' roll as a way out of the cultural isolation they felt from the rest of the world. Bill Haley, Elvis Presley and The Beatles had as passionate a following in Leningrad and Moscow as anywhere else. The authorities may have fulminated against this 'ape culture' and 'social poison' (sentiments, it must be said, shared by many people in the West); but by the end of the 1960s, there were reckoned to be 200 or more rock groups in Moscow alone, bearing such names as Hairy Glass, Purple Catastrophe and Nasty Dogs. Communist leaders bowed before the inevitable. Dean Reed, a liberal expatriate American looking very like such contemporary British singing stars as Engelbert Humperdinck, was a semi-official Soviet pop idol of the 1970s. Elton John and other Western pop stars also visited the Iron Curtain countries.

Even before President Mikhail Gorbachev's arrival in 1985 and the era of *glasnost*, Soviet bloc rock musicians, such as the Czech group The Plastic People of the Universe, and the Soviet Russian group Time Machine, were already a part of the international pop scene. The Polish group Lady Pank and Soviet star Boris Grebenschikov have since toured the United States or released records in the West. Another Soviet rock star, Alla Pugacheva, has sold over 150 million records and tapes, at home and abroad, putting her in the same commercial super league as Elvis Presley, The Beatles and Michael Jackson.

....

VARIEGATED JAZZ   Back in the 1960s and 1970s, jazz went through one of its periodic crises of identity. Rock had taken over from swing as the popular or vernacular music of the Western world, leaving post-bop jazz, with

Miles Davis, a seminal jazz figure for forty years, carrying his style forward from the bop and cool sounds of the 1940s and 1950s to the rock-orientated music of more recent times.

all its intricacies, feeling rather stranded. Could it make some chameleon-like adjustments to the ever more volatile musical scene around it? Yes, it could and it has. In the late 1960s, Miles Davis, who went from bop to 'cool' jazz, proceeded once more to adapt his style to rock rhythms and the electronic hardware of the times. Three brilliant electronic keyboard/pianist-composers – Herbie Hancock, Keith Jarrett and Chick Corea – worked with Davis in this field. Since then, a new generation of jazz musicians, of many nations and races, has straddled the diverse musical worlds of rock, Latin American, reggae, funk (a vaguely-defined style derived from blues) and the concert hall.

Wynton Marsalis, born in New Orleans, the cradle of jazz, has stepped easily from jazz itself to the concert hall with award-winning recordings of trumpet concertos by Leopold Mozart, Haydn and Hummel. American Carla Bley is a true jazz composer with such works as her recent jazz-operatic setting of *Under the Volcano*, Malcolm Lowry's compelling novel about alcoholism. Moving from America to Europe, London-born saxophonist Courtney Pine identifies with Britain's large black population through his love of calypso and reggae. Joe Zawinul from Vienna has followed in the footsteps of Bartók and Kodaly, by working Hungarian Magyar and gypsy folk music into some of his synthesizer-based jazz. German trombonist-composer Albert Mangelsdorff, though now in his sixties, continues to be a focus of attention in European jazz.

Moving even further afield, Turkish percussionist Okay Temiz brings to his music something of the brash exuberance of his country's old janissary bands. Similarly, Trilok Gurtu from Bombay has introduced Indian tabla drums to jazz, and black South Africans Dudu Pukwana (saxophone), Mongezi Feza (cornet), Abdullah Ibrahim, (piano), Louis Moholo (drums) and Hugh Masekela (trumpet and flugelhorn) have their jazz roots in black township and *kwela* music (see also page 230).

POST-MODERNISM

At the time of writing, Stockhausen is working on a whole sequence, or cycle, of operas under the collective title of *Licht* (Light); a project which promises to carry electro-acoustic techniques, plus effects of light and color (reminiscent of much rock music), into new realms of space-age sound. Meanwhile, other composers are, in a sense, pausing for breath after years of headlong advance, starting back with Schoenberg and moving up to the present with such figures as Boulez, Berio, and Stockhausen himself. They are spoken of as today's post-modernists. On the face of it, this is a self-contradictory term, but it is one used to describe a general reaction against this century's avant-garde, and it marks the return to some of music's more traditional

qualities of drama and emotion, excitement and charm. This does not necessarily mean that the post-modernists are reactionary or old-fashioned. But they share the attitude that musical thinking and technology have advanced too far too fast through much of this century, leaving most music lovers bewildered by it all. Audiences, they believe, must be won back to the cause of new music.

....

A NEW GALLERY OF COMPOSERS Back in the 1950s, when Boulez was just emerging as the new hero of the modernist avant-garde, Polish composer Witold Lutoslawski (born 1913) wrote his *Concerto for Orchestra*. This is a thrilling piece of orchestral writing, like the very best in film music; and it is music like this, clever, but conventionally scored and not too technically advanced, that many post-modernists admire. While Lutoslawski's younger compatriot, Penderecki (see page 161), has been highly original and rather more advanced in some of his music, his opera *The Devils of Loudon* is a riveting piece of theater about religious hysteria. The Hungarian György Ligeti (born 1923) might also be considered avant-garde in some respects; but he, too, has enjoyed wide popularity with such works as his opera *Le Grand Macabre*, with its weird symbolism. Like Ligeti, the German composer Hans Werner Henze (born 1926) is is considered to be part of today's musical avant-garde, but he has tempered his work with a love of the theater. By combining this love with strong political ideals, he has created such dramatic stage works as *Elegy for Young Lovers*, *The Bassarids* (based on a play by Euripides), and the opera-oratorio *Das Floss der Medusa* (The Raft of the Medusa), inspired by the famous painting by Géricault and the grim story behind it.

Today's British composers are following Britten and Tippett with music that is often original and distinctive, while also having a strong dramatic appeal. The following are perhaps the most popular works among this genre. One of Peter Maxwell Davies' (born 1934) works is *Eight Songs for a Mad King*, a tragi-comic musical portrait of the deranged mind of the English king George III, who suffered from a rare mental disease. Another of Davies' dramatic works is his chamber opera *The Martyrdom of St. Magnus*, inspired by his love of the wild beauty of Scotland's Orkney Islands, where he has lived for many years. Harrison Birtwistle's (born 1934) orchestral *The Triumph of Time* is based, like

The German composer Karlheinz Stockhausen, using electronics to create a whole new world of sound, and one of today's great musical luminaries.

much of Tippett's music, on philosophical thoughts about man's place in the scheme of things, and his earlier one-act opera *Punch and Judy* spotlights the violence inherent in the popular old puppet show. Nicholas Maw (born 1935) has been called a 'modern romantic,' a composer who still sees plenty of possibilities in traditional instruments and forms. His opera *The Rising of the Moon* is one of his most successful works to date.

Other post-modernist composers include the Finnish Aulis Sallinen (born 1935), who has written works following in the footsteps of his great compatriot Sibelius, evoking the legend and landscape of his northern homeland. In neighboring Estonia, Arvo Pärt (born 1935) began as a serialist composer, but has since become interested in reworking old musical forms and styles, such as polyphony and plainsong. In Soviet Russia, too, Alfred Schnitke (born 1934) has been influenced by serial techniques and electronic music, but has

WOMEN COMPOSERS

With such works as the ominously titled opera The Black Spider, Judith Weir (born 1954) has joined this century's growing ranks of women composers.

In the Middle Ages, a German abbess, Hildegarde of Bingen (1098–1179), was one of the foremost scholars, mystics, poets and composers of her time. After her, for nearly a thousand years, a male-dominated society made it next to impossible for women to shine as creative artists. As far as music is concerned, only with the nineteenth century were women able to assert themselves again. Still in Germany, there was Clara Schumann (1819–96), who might have won far more recognition as a composer in her own right, as well as pianist, had she not had to live in the shadow of her late husband Robert's fame and reputation. In France, Cécile Chaminade (1857–1944) wrote operas, ballets and concert works, though she is now remembered only by a few graceful 'salon' piano pieces.

At the beginning of this century came the Englishwoman Ethel Smyth (1858–1944), who combined her gifts as a composer with her work as a militant suffragette in the cause of women's rights. In England and in Germany, she made a big name for herself with her powerful opera The Wreckers. Following her indefatigable example, Britain has produced more eminent women composers: Elisabeth Lutyens (born 1906), who has written much film and radio music; Elizabeth Maconchy (born 1907), and her daughter Nicola LeFanu (born 1947); Thea Musgrave (born 1928) from Scotland; and now Judith Weir, also from Scotland.

In France, Germaine Tailleferre (1892–1983) was a member of the celebrated group known as 'Les Six', that included Poulenc and Honneger; while Nadia Boulanger's (1887–1979) great talents as a teacher of other famous composers has tended to eclipse her own creative achievements.

Among Americans, there are Amy Marcy Beach (1867–1944), Ruth Crawford Seeger (1901–53) and Pauline Oliviers (born 1932); also jazz composer Carla Bley (born 1938).

Below: Scene from Judith Weir's opera The Vanishing Bridegroom, *produced here by Scottish Opera.*

added much of the emotional weight of a composer like Shostakovich to his own music.

THE MINIMALISTS One prominent group of post-modernist musicians is known as minimalists. Their style, or school, of minimalism takes its name from their technique of using a minimum amount of musical material to construct a whole piece of music, in much the same way as some abstract artists use a few basic colored shapes, curves or lines to create eye-catching patterns or designs. Their working principle is repetition; taking one or two basic motifs – a brief melodic phrase or chord sequence – and repeating it many times over. At the same time, the sequence is gradually changed by a note here, a rhythmic accent there, so that the music evolves like a shifting aural kaleidoscope. This idea of change growing from repetition is by no means new in itself. It can be heard in all sorts of music; African tribal drumming, Javanese gamelan music, Indian ragas, bell ringing, the opening C major prelude from Bach's *Forty-Eight Preludes and Fugues*, numerous passages in Sibelius's works, Eric Satie's well-known *Gymnopédies*. What makes the work of today's minimalists so distinctive is their concentration on a linear approach to music, the technique of following a single line of development, in contrast to the fuller harmonic and melodic forms we are used to. Their sound patterns can be very pleasing, gentle and quite hypnotic; they can also be vigorous and more closely related to jazz and rock. The music often stops dead, as though the evolving patterns have endless permutations and so must stop somewhere.

The leading minimalist exponents so far have been Americans. Terry Riley (born 1935) is a saxophonist as well as composer, featuring that instrument in some of his pieces. His California background, with its fringe religious cults and surrealist atmosphere, may lie behind the dream-like titles to some of these; *Poppy Nogood and the Phantom Band* and *Rainbow in Curved Air*. Steve Reich (born 1936) has shown that minimalist techniques can be used with serious intent. *Passing Trains* is a remarkable piece for string quartet and prerecorded sounds, contrasting his train journeys across wartime America as a little Jewish boy with the transportation of other Jews to Nazi death camps. Philip Glass (born 1937), who made a study of Indian music, has created several operas based entirely on minimalist ideas, including *Akhnaten* and *Einstein on the Beach*. John Adams (born

A scene from Philip Glass's minimalist opera Akhnaten, *based on the life of the Egyptian pharaoh who tried to change the course of history and religion.*

1947) has written a very popular opera, *Nixon in China*. The same composer's *Shaker Loops* refers to the old American religious community (illustrated on page 176), with their hymn singing, movement and dance.

AROUND THE WORLD TODAY

The Laplander with his reindeer, the Indian peasant farmer plodding across the rice paddies with his water buffalo, the Australian aborigine still gazing into the distance of the great outback, can all hear the same pop music through their transistor radios. A star conductor, pianist or singer can be seen or heard in London one day, two days later in Los Angeles, a week after that in Tokyo or Tel-Aviv. Such is the blanket coverage of Western-style music today. Indeed, what is called Western music is now an international lingua franca, belonging to virtually every nation, race and creed. Happily, the world has not yet been reduced to one common musical coinage, however golden that coinage may be. Many of the cultures, regions and countries looked at in earlier sections of this book have kept at least a part of their own musical identity and are giving back as much as they have taken from the wider musical scene.

Bio-Music

More than two thousand years ago, Plato, Aristotle, Confucius and other sages believed that music had unique powers over mind and body, for good or ill. Today, there is a growing use for music as a therapy, in the treatment of certain nervous or mental disorders, or as an aid to some kinds of surgery and childbirth.

Bio-music is taking music as a therapy into a whole new region of research. It does not have much to do with such things as rhythm, pitch, melody and so on, as we usually understand them.

Instead, it is concerned with the patterns – of line and color as well as sound – already familiar enough in medicine, that register such bodily functions or conditions as electrical impulses of the brain, heartbeat, respiration and tissue temperature, and which can be used to reveal and diagnose disease. Publicists for bio-music claim that such patterns can do much more than reveal physical ailments. They make the interesting point that many mental and emotional states are hard to describe or explain because of the imperfect state of

ordinary language. However, the audio-visual means just referred to are a new way of communicating these conditions, rapidly and accurately. By processing and feeding them back to the person who generated them, or to other people, troublesome physical, mental or emotional conditions can be corrected. Bio-music certainly gives a whole new meaning to 'body language.' Could it open up a vast new field of communication between us? Could it be the music of the future? We must wait and see.

Electronic Music

For thousands of years, the acoustic principles of musical instruments remained the same, though the mechanics employed have become far more sophisticated. This century, however, electronics have opened up a whole new world of aural experience. Increasingly, electronic music and sound effects are a part of our everyday lives.

Earlier in the book, the important distinction was made between electrically aided instruments and true electronic ones – those that generate their own sounds. A remarkable start in this field was made in 1906 when the American Thaddeus Cahill unveiled his telharmonium. This did generate and amplify its own sounds, but it was also extremely heavy and bulky, and once its novelty wore off, it was soon discarded.

A more eminent American inventor, Lee De Forest, then introduced the valve oscillator as the best way to create purely electronic sounds. A number of new instruments were based on this. The theremin, named after its inventor Leon Theremin, had an antenna electrically sensitive to movement of the player's hands; the trautonium (Friedrich Trautwein) was dependent on contact between a wire and a rod; and the Ondes-martenot or

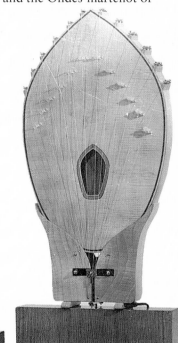

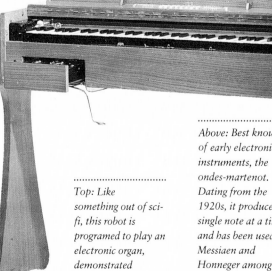

Top: Like something out of sci-fi, this robot is programed to play an electronic organ, demonstrated recently in Tokyo.

Above: Best known of early electronic instruments, the ondes-martenot. Dating from the 1920s, it produces a single note at a time, and has been used by Messiaen and Honneger among other composers.

'Martenot waves' (Maurice Martenot) employed a keyboard. Two others were the partiturophone (Jörg Mager), whose simulated bell tones were used in a 1930s production of Wagner's *Parsifal*, and the popular Hammond electric organ (Lorens Hammond).

Soon after World War II, a French radio engineer, Pierre Schaeffer, began experimenting with gramophone recordings, doctoring their sounds by speeding them up, slowing them down, playing them in reverse and transferring these effects from one disk to another (*musique concréte*). Others did the same kind of thing with the newly perfected and much more versatile tape recorder. Although this experimental line of research opened up fascinating new sonic horizons and possibilities, it was not strictly speaking electronic sound production, since the sources of the sounds were recorded in the first place.

The next and biggest step forward in true electronic music came in the 1960s with the synthesizer, the product of many brilliant minds, and especially of Robert Moog and Donald Buchla, both Americans. Based on the laws of harmonics this could separate sounds into their fundamental tones and synthesize or build them up again into an almost infinite sonic range, imitating existing instruments or creating entirely new effects.

Synthesizer terminology – or jargon – leads us to the heart of electronic music. Electro-acoustic wave forms or patterns include 'sine' waves (pure sounds, free from all harmonics), 'sawtooth' and 'square' waves. There is 'white noise,' an indiscriminate hiss of sound from many wavelengths. 'Mixers' and 'filters' combine sounds or filter out (suppress) some frequencies, thus modifying the tone or timbre of a sound. An 'envelope' is the 'shape' of a sound, its initial 'attack,' 'growth' and 'decay.'

Many of this century's composers have contributed to a greater or lesser degree to the development of electronic music. Varèse, Messiaen, Cage, Boulez, Stockhausen, Berio, Babbitt and Reich have already been mentioned. Three further big names in this realm of sound are the Franco-Greek Iannis Xenakis (born 1922), who has pioneered the use of computers to program a synthesizer, and two more Americans, La Monte Young (born 1935), who attaches to his work such graphic directions as 'build a fire in front of the audience,' and Frank Zappa (born 1940), who has worked mainly with progressive rock groups.

Above: The multi-keyboards of a modern synthesizer.

Below: New technologies need new systems of notation: page of a score for solo oboe and computer by the American David Rosenboom. It also allows for indeterminacy (leaving choices open to the performer).

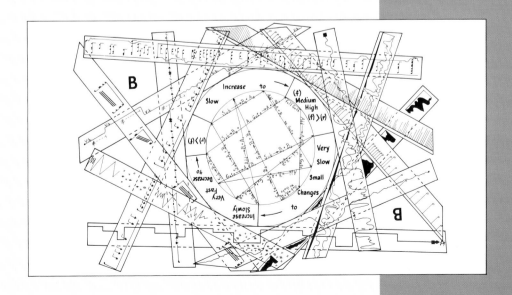

....
THE MIDDLE EAST The politics of oil, the running sore of Arab-Israeli relations, Islamic fundamentalism, paramilitary terrorism; this is the embattled scenario across North Africa and the Middle East today. But music, like life, goes on. The biggest style in popular music through much of the Arab community is Algerian *rai*, traditional Arabic song and dance revamped by rock rhythms and electrophonic sounds. In Algeria itself, *rai* was banned on radio and television until a few years ago, because of its associations with sex, drugs and alcohol – all anathema to devout Muslims. However, this did not much hinder its spreading popularity, locally and in Europe, especially in France, with its old but still culturally close colonial links with the region. Today, such stars of *rai* as Cheb Khaled, Safy Boutella, Chaba Fadela, Cheb Sahraoui, Bellemou Messaoud and Cheb Zahouania, mean big business north and south of the Mediterranean.

Egypt and other more liberal-minded Arab nations have reached a fairly happy accommodation with Western pop music, as Arabic melodies and singing styles join hands with dance band rhythms and the swoop of orchestral violins. It may sound a bit of a hodgepodge to outsiders, but this broadly popular (as distinct from pop) Arabic music, coming out of almost every radio and movie

Above: Cheb Khaled at the microphone. Born in Oran, Algeria, he has been hailed as the 'King of Rai', and is a hero for today's North African youth.

Right: Ravi Shankar, most famous Indian musician around the world (see page 224). He is playing the sitar. In the foreground, a tabla drum and a vina.

theater from Cairo to Casablanca, easily grows on the ear.

The modern state of Israel, set down in the very heart of the Arabic-Islamic Middle East, tells a very different musical story. Its own pop, *sabra* music, has trodden a sometimes uneasy path between the more Arabic-orientated *rai* and the Greek *rembetika* style. But in the process, it has created such stars as Ofra Haza, Zohar Argov (both originally from Yemen) and Eli Luzon. The ethnic mix of *sabra* is, in fact, just a microcosm of the remarkable story of Israeli music.

Long before Israel was founded in 1948, Jews had been arriving and settling in Palestine. They brought with them songs and dances from Russia, Poland, Hungary and other parts of central Europe, as well as Yiddish music (part-Hebrew, part-German), and the ancient cantillation of the synagogue. Their growing national consciousness also focused attention on the long line of great Jewish composers, songwriters, conductors and instrumentalists, who had contributed so much to music around the world:

Mendelssohn, Mahler, Schoenberg, Gershwin, Irving Berlin, Ernest Bloch (composer of *Shelomo*, *Baal Shem* and other specifically Jewish works), Bruno Walter, Jascha Heifetz, Isaac Stern, Arthur Rubinstein, Solomon, and Yehudi Menuhin, to name but a few. One result of this was the founding of the Palestine Symphony Orchestra in 1936; an audacious move for a group of people who still had no official homeland. It became the Israel Philharmonic Orchestra, one of the world's finest, attracting to it more outstanding Jewish musicians, conductors Leonard Bernstein and Daniel Barenboim among them. Such is the extraordinary concentration and variety of musical talent packed into Israel today, winning friends all over the world, no matter what people may think of its government and politics.

....

INDIA During the period of British rule, through the nineteenth century and well into the twentieth, Indian classical music fell upon hard times. It lost the support of many of the country's old rulers, the princes or maharajas,

while the British ignored it altogether. But as Indians began to agitate for political independence, they recognized that this classical music was a precious part of their heritage. Poet and musician Rabindranath Tagore took a lead in its revival. With independence in 1947, All India Radio (AIR) became a major patron of music, very like the BBC in Britain and ORTF in France, supported by other institutions such as the National Academy of Music and Dance in New Delhi.

The two leading figures in this modern renaissance of classical Indian music are the brothers Ravi and Uday Shankar. Virtuoso sitar player Ravi Shankar was for some years director of music for Indian radio and founder-director of a new music school in Bombay. He has also been a magnificent

A modern group of Indian drummers and dancers, keeping alive a thousand or more years of traditional Hindu song and dance.

ambassador for Indian music abroad, creating a worldwide audience for ragas and other Indian classical forms, and forging links with Western symphonic and pop music. Today, Ravi Shankar has been joined by such young virtuosi as sarod player Amjad Ali Khan, who draws a big audience whenever he appears.

Uday Shankar, meanwhile, was working with the celebrated Russian ballerina Anna Pavlova. As a result, he adapted some forms of Indian classical dance to the styles of modern Western ballet. Ballet itself has been enriched by some of the more venerable traditions of Indian dance.

India's huge rural population has helped to keep alive thousands of age-old folk songs and dances. But alongside this ancient folk music, a new, urbanized folk and popular music has grown up since independence. India's film industry has much to do with this. Indian movie fans like plenty of music with their films, mainly in the form of *filmi git* (film song), songs in a familiar idiom, but glamorized with a Western-style dance band or orchestral backing. This musical hybrid of native song and imported styles can be heard everywhere today, from the teeming city streets to the village water hole. Other current manifestations of Indian music include the much-praised devotional singing of Nusrat Fateh Alik Khan, who has a large following, and Sheila Chandra, a star of 'Indipop.'

JAPAN The Japanese people have a great gift for absorbing foreign ideas and technologies, taking them over, and selling them back to the rest of the world. In terms of automobiles and electronics, such household names as Suzuki, Hitachi, Mitsubishi, Sony and Nissan, are proof enough. Much the same thing has happened with Western music. Although the influence of Portuguese missionaries and their music, in the sixteenth century, was short-lived (see page 52), there was a great revival of Japanese interest in foreign arts and crafts, including music, toward the end of the nineteenth century (at about the time when the American Lieutenant Pinkerton marries the geisha girl Cio-Cio-San in Puccini's opera *Madame Butterfly*). By the end of the century, European and American musicians were already in demand for concerts and recitals. However, the rise of militant Japanese nationalism, the invasion of Manchuria and China, and then World War II, brought this expanding cultural scene to a temporary halt. Since then, Japan has embraced Western musical culture with the same tenacious enthusiasm as Western technology; witness its craze some years back for Elvis Presley look-alike competitions!

Japan's contribution, worldwide, to Western concert music has been much more substantial. The Yamaha company has added its name to the roll-call of such illustrious European and American piano manufacturers as Steinway, Bechstein, Blüthner, Broadwood and Pleyel. Schoolchildren in many countries are learning music by the Suzuki method, based on the belief of the Japanese teacher and violinist Shinichi Suzuki that children should be introduced to music, and to playing a musical instrument, at the same time as they learn to read and write. Japanese dance companies are also in the forefront of contemporary ballet, adapting the swift and sudden movements of their old martial arts to modern dance routines.

Turning to individuals, the importance of composer Toru Takemitsu (born 1930) was acknowledged right at the start of this book. Takemitsu has won many friends and admirers around the world for the way he has cleverly adapted the sound of such traditional Japanese instruments as the koto to Western-style composition. Among executive musicians, conductor Seigi Ozawa and pianist Mitsuko Uchida are two of the biggest names.

Neighboring Korea is also represented in concert halls around the world, and on recordings of symphonic music, most notably by the violinist Kyung-Wha Chung.

....

CHINA   Recent Chinese history has taken quite a different path from that of Japan. In 1949, the People's Republic of China was created, and under the direction of Chairman Mao Tse-tung, policy toward the arts was much the same as then prevailed in the Soviet Union. In line with Marxist ideology, art and music were used as political instruments, to disseminate ideas and encourage a sense of corporate purpose among the mass of the people. An All China Association of Music Workers was set up, which condemned most individual composers and other musicians as élitist, while harnessing classical and folk music to these political ends. For example, the famous Peking Opera (see page 50) became the vehicle for such new stage pieces as *The Red Lantern*, extolling revolutionary principles. The Cultural Revolution of the 1960s intensified this political ethos. Since then, however, there has been a gradual relaxation of cultural policies, though China remains musically very conservative, compared with Japan. Performances of Western concert music do take place, but only of established classics; the authorities are still likely to frown upon any music later than Brahms and Tchaikovsky. A few individual composers and other artists are just beginning to show their heads again. Meanwhile, artists such as the Chinese pianist Fou t'song pursue their careers abroad.

East meets West in the clearest possible way with this picture of a modern Chinese workshop turning out violins and other Western-type instruments. At present, official Chinese policy remains very conservative toward Western music.

Right: King Sunny Ade, one of the biggest stars of Nigerian juju – guitars, drums and vocals married to the old music of the Yoruba people of West Africa.

Below: The exotic Papa Wemba, star of African rumba-rock, noted especially for his sometimes rather melancholy vocals. His mother was a mourner or 'wailer' at funerals.

AFRICA Well within living memory, Africa has endured sometimes brutal disruption and civil war marking the end of colonial rule, the bestiality of despots like Idi Amin and Jean Bokassa, the worst famines in modern times, and the heavy burden of apartheid. Yet today, the continent positively hums and bubbles with music, as the jazz and Latin American idioms that once flowed from it have returned and been regenerated afresh.

As already noted, West Africa supplied the Americas with most of their black slave labor; and the history of the region's 'highlife' music, with its mix of local black rhythms and European military marches and dances (courtesy of the Portuguese, French and British around the Gulf of Guinea) has been uncannily like that of early jazz in and around New Orleans. When Louis Armstrong toured West Africa back in the 1950s and met the Ghanaian 'highlife' trumpeter E.T. Mensah (known everywhere locally as 'ET'), he said he felt as though he had returned home. The older types of 'highlife' instrumentation – pianos, harmoniums, concertinas and banjos – have now been elbowed aside by the ubiquitous electric guitar, and the old-style dances replaced by offshoots of rock. Nana Ampadu's African Brothers Band and Mohammed Malcolm Ben's African Feeling are two of the new-style 'highlife' guitar bands. There is also 'palm-wine' music (named after a local type of beer), maringa (rhythmically akin to a rumba) and Nigerian juju. This latter, quite unconnected with the older meaning of juju as a charm or fetish, combines Yoruba rhythms, tunes and instruments with a pleasantly relaxed guitar style. Established juju stars

Ebenezer Obey and King Sunny Ade have more recently been joined by Segun Adewale with his updated 'Yoruba Pop' or 'Yopop.' Fellow Nigerian singer-composer Fela Kuti takes a more serious political line in some of his 'Afro-beat' songs to much press comment at home and abroad.

In West Africa, the tradition of griot lives on. Senegal, historically a stronghold of this tradition (see page 89) has now fostered such stars as Toure Kunda and Youssou N'Dour. During the 1980s, Youssou N'Dour worked with Paul Simon on his album *Graceland*, spent some valuable time performing and recording in Paris, and is now a big name internationally. From neighboring Mali, reaching into the heart of the Sahara Desert, comes a whole crop of other interesting vocalists; Salif Keita, Kasse Mady, Nahama Doumbia, Ali Farka Toure and Boubacar Traoré. Sometimes, they resurrect the old griot themes of local life and gossip, occasionally merging them with the form and harmonies of the blues.

Around the southern end of the Gulf of Guinea, in Kinshasa, capital of Zaire, the popular music of the 1970s and 1980s has been the guitar and rumba-based harmonies and rhythms of *soukous* (from the French verb *secouer*, 'to shake'). Colorful vocalists Papa Wemba and M'Bilia Bel have carried the sounds of *soukous* far and wide. Now comes *moutouashi* (meaning something like 'take him' or 'grab her'), closer to traditional African dance of the old Congo Basin. It has helped to turn singer Tshala Muana into another of Zaire's rising stars, with her own following, especially in Paris, as well as throughout West Africa. Zimbabwe, too, has produced some rising international stars, including singer Thomas Mapfumo and Stella Chiweshe, the 'Queen of Mbira,' *mbira* being another name for the ancient African *sansas*, or 'thumb pianos' described on page 85.

Youssou N'Dour from Senegal, one of the biggest names in today's African musical scene. His mother was a local singer, and he claims griot (minstrel) ancestry.

Continued on page 230

Reviving the Past

Until the nineteenth century, music was regarded very much as a thing of the moment. It was written, played and, except in a few cases, quickly forgotten. Today, however, reviving the music of the past – not just the music itself, but its authentic period performance – is a huge area of interest and often impassioned debate.

Forty or fifty years ago, music before Bach and Handel was a closed book for most people, and even the music of those two composers was limited to a handful of arrangements. Today, the operas of Rameau and Monteverdi are box-office sell-outs. The masses and motets of Lassus and Palestrina, the songs of the troubadours, and Gregorian chant are all regularly performed, broadcast and recorded. And many of today's music-lovers frown on the artist who plays Bach on a piano instead of a harpsichord. The revival of old music, together with its so-called authentic performance, is now big business.

Mendelssohn led the way as long ago as 1829, with a performance of Bach's *St. Matthew Passion*, the first for nearly a hundred years. The modern revival of old music, however, really dates from earlier in this century. Its pioneers included the Swiss musicologists Arnold and Carl Dolmetsch, who restored and played viols, lutes, recorders and other Renaissance instruments; the Polish harpsichordist Wanda Landowska; the counter-tenor Alfred Deller, who revived the sound (or something fairly close to it) of the old castrati singers, and Karl Haas and his London Baroque Ensemble. Outstanding among the younger generation was David Munrow, founder-director of the Early Music Consort, who

Above: A baroque-type trombone of the Orchestra of the Age of Enlightenment. The 'bell' has much less flare than its modern counterpart.

Right: Members of the same orchestra, playing period instruments.

Left: The English
guitarist and lutenist
Julian Bream, who
pioneered the revival
of Renaissance lute
music. He is pictured
here with a fine
example of the
instrument.

did much to popularize early music in the 1950s and 1960s. Tragically, he committed suicide in 1976.

Today, the list of artists and ensembles in this field of operations is formidable indeed: Christopher Hogwood and his Academy of Ancient Music; harpsichordist Trevor Pinnock and the English Concert; Roger Norrington and his own London Baroque Ensemble; John Eliot Gardiner with the English Baroque Soloists; Raymond Leppard, conductor, harpsichordist and authority on Monteverdi; Julian Bream, lutenist; Anthony Rooley (also a lutenist) with the Consort of Musicke; Nikolaus Harnoncourt with the Concentus Musicus of Vienna; Dutch harpsichordist and organist Gustav Leonhardt; Musica Antiqua of Cologne; the Orchestra of the Age of Enlightenment, and Gothic Voices.

The interests of these individuals and groups range over the whole field of old music. There is the use of 'period' instruments, such as valveless or 'natural' horns, violins with gut strings and played with softer bows, early types of bassoon and clarinet, old kettledrums using animal hides and so on. There is also the sometimes vexatious question of how the music of exactly this or that period should be played or sung. Baroque keyboard music, for example, had conventions requiring performers to add decorative little phrases to the notes that were actually printed on the page. The 'authentic' singing of baroque opera, or the 'bel canto' style of Italian opera, demand the same painstaking specialist knowledge and skills.

Above: Another member of the Orchestra of the Age of Enlightenment, this time with a period horn. Instead of valves, it has crooks (detachable parts), which alter its playing length and its tuning.

In South Africa for the past forty years, people's lives have been dominated by apartheid, which has created a special culture in the black African townships. These are tough, sometimes violent places, with their own internal hierarchy and morality, dominated by, among others, the notorious sheeben queens, mistresses of the drinking clubs and brothels. At the same time, black South African music has flowed steadily outward into the world pop scene. The most publicized example of this was American pop star Paul Simon's (formerly of Simon and Garfunkel fame) collaboration, in 1986, with the black South African group Ladysmith Black Mambazo over the creation of the award-winning LP *Graceland*. The next year, Simon appeared in London with Miriam Makeba, a South African performer now firmly established on the international pop stage. Mahlathini and the Mahotella Queens is another popular South African vocal group.

The modern beat of Brazil; the old Latin American rhythms given the pleasantly relaxed treatment of today's saudade *style by Gilberto Gil and friends.*

Within South Africa itself, the black townships have generated their own attractive street music, widely known as *kwela*. This is a Zulu word meaning 'rise up' or 'win,' though it has had very little to do with political action. *Kwela* music has taken jazz and given it a local twist. It was originally played on types of whistle and flute, skilled performers gliding up and down the scales and exploiting their instruments' natural harmonics to create a special kind of blues. Today, though, in the black townships around Johannesburg and elsewhere, we are more likely to hear electric guitars and organs giving out a kind of jive rock, known locally as *simanje-manje*.

....

LATIN AMERICA The massive political and economic problems facing much of present-day South and Central America – the military juntas, oppressive but ineffectual, the corruption, galloping inflation, exploding populations and yawning gaps between rich and

Global galaxy of instruments at a Havana jazz festival; violins and woodwind, percussion and electronic and, out in front, a large Afro-Caribbean hourglass drum.

poor – cannot wipe the perennial smile from its music, nor wrong-foot its captivating beat. Caribbean reggae and rap have been absorbed into the big city cultures of North America and Europe, but the whole vast Latin American region, from Chile to the Gulf of Mexico, is alive with other local styles. There is the *parang* folk music of Trinidad, played by small troupes of 'serenaders' around Christmas and Easter, going from village to village and house to house; the *jonkanoo* masquerades, a bit like the old mummers of medieval Europe; and the song and dance of the Kumina, Shango and other Caribbean religious cults. Much of this music is strictly for local consumption. Other styles, old, new, changing all the time, have their following in more distant and often colder climes.

Brazil, giant of South America, traditional home of the *samba* and the *bossa nova*, has now come up with *lambada*, a sexually demonstrative style of dancing which may still leave something to the imagination, but not much. *Saudade*, more relaxed, more nostalgic and reflective in mood, causes less heavy breathing in all senses of the word. Margareth Menezes and Gilberto Gil are two big stars of these newer Brazilian popular styles. Brazilian Latin jazzman Egerto Gismonti has cleverly worked Amazonian Indian forest calls and flute music into some of his compositions.

Merenge is the name for a fairly broad spectrum of popular music with a basic rumba beat which can be heard in and around Venezuela and the Caribbean. But the region is better known today for other more quickly identifiable styles. *Salsa*, as far as its name goes, can be traced back to the 1940s and specifically to Cuba, applying the indigenous rumba beat to local swing bands. *Salsa* then moved on to the 'Latin jazz' of some American big bands. Today, Columbia rather than Cuba has given back to *salsa* music more of a true pan-Caribbean sound; and the Fruko y su Tesos band and Joe Arroyo are two of its best ambassadors around the world. *Zouk*, originating in the old French islands of Martinique and Guadeloupe, is closer to mainstream pop, mainly vocal with electric guitar and keyboard backing, and Kassav are currently its biggest star group.

A CLOSING HOMILY

A hundred years ago, going to the opera, a concert, even a local dance, was a big event for most people, something to look forward to weeks or months in advance, something to remember perhaps for the rest of their days. And the music rang in their ears. Today, we have music at the press of a button, the turn of a switch, music fed to us in public places whether we want it or not. We also have music neatly and insidiously packaged for our convenience – 'classical,' 'easy listening,' 'country and western,' 'soul,' 'trad jazz,' 'rhythm and blues,' 'rock,' and so on. The dangers are obvious; over-indulgence, indiscriminate or blinkered listening, until all the gold of music is turned to dross. Sometimes, the best antidote is the one that has always been music's true companion and friend – the gift of silence.

Music Worldwide

Popular and pop music is now a global business. In recent years there has also been a revival of worldwide musical traditions; many of these forms have been employed by musicians working in non-traditional contexts, forming fascinating cross-cultural mixes. The following list encompasses both these developments. The styles and artists range from the most outrageous to the most tuneful and anodyne. There is, of course, much overlapping between categories; some types, styles and artists may be known also by alternative classifications. Note that the composition of many pop groups frequently changes. Note also that, as with jazz, the titles given here may refer to particular numbers or to albums.

AFRICAN JAZZ-ROCK/ HIGHLIFE/TOWNSHIP/KWELA/ FOLK AND TRADITIONAL

KING SUNNY ADE
Nigerian singer/guitarist *Ju Ju King, Synchro System*

SEGUN ADEWALE
Nigerian singer/composer *Ojo Je*

M'BILIA BEL
Zairean singer *Boya Ye*

STELLA CHIWESHE
Zimbabwean mbira player/singer *Ndizvozvo*

MANU DIBANGO
Cameroon instrumentalist/composer *Soul Makossa, Electric Africa*

NAHAWA DOUMBIA
Malian singer *Didadi, Nyama Toutou*

SALIF KEITA
Malian singer *Soro, Nous pas Bouger*

OUSMANE KOUYATE
Guinean singer *Domba*

FELA KUTI
Singer/composer from Niger *Fela Kuti and The Africa 70*

LADYSMITH BLACK MAMBAZO
South African singer *Shaka Zulu, Rain, rain beautiful rain*

KASSE MADY
Malian singer *Fode*

MIRIAM MAKEBA
South African singer *Click Song, Pata Pata*

KANTE MANFILA
Guinean electric guitarist *Mobereya*

SAM MANGWANA
Zairian singer *Aladji*

ZEKE MANYIKA
South African singer *Runaway Freedom Train (R.F.T.)*

HUGH MASEKELA
South African trumpeter *African Breeze, Wimoweh*

YOUSSOU N'DOUR
Senegalese singer *The Lion, Immigrées, Rubber Band Man*

EBENEZER OBEY
Nigerian singer *Juju Jubilee, On the Rock*

KOFFI OLOMIDE
Zairean instrumentalist *Les Prisonniers Dorment*

DUDU PUKWANA
South African alto saxophonist *In the Townships*

PAPA WEMBA
Zairian singer *Bokulaka*

COUNTRY AND WESTERN/ FOLK/SKIFFLE

JOAN BAEZ
American singer *The Best of Joan Baez, We Shall Overcome*

GLEN CAMPBELL
American singer/guitarist *By the Time I get to Phoenix, Rhinestone Cowboy, Galveston*

JOHNNY CASH
American singer/guitarist *I Walk the Line, Folsom Prison Blues, Riders in the Sky*

LONNIE DONEGAN
British singer/guitarist *Rock Island Line, Battle of New Orleans, Cumberland Gap*

EVERLY BROTHERS
American duo *Bye Bye Love, Wake Up Little Suzie*

TENNESSEE ERNIE FORD
American singer *Mule Train, Sixteen Tons*

CRYSTAL GALE
American singer *Don't It Make My Brown Eyes Blue*

EWEN MacCOLL
British singer *Bundook Ballads, Steam Whistle Ballads*

ROY ORBISON
American singer/songwriter *Running Scared, Blue Bayou, Oh Pretty Woman*

DOLLY PARTON
American singer/songwriter *Joshua, Coat of Many Colors, Here You Come Again*

THE POGUES
Irish group *Dark Streets of London, Dirty Old Town, Rum, Sodomy and the Lash*

JIM REEVES
American singer *Mexican Joe, Yonder Comes a Sucker, He'll Have To Go*

TEX RITTER
American singer *High Noon, High, Wide and Handsome*

PETE SEEGER
American singer/guitarist *If I Had a Hammer, Guantanamera, Where Have All the Flowers Gone?*

Heavy Metal

AC/DC
Australian group *Highway to Hell*

BLACK SABBATH
British group *Paranoid, Black Sabbath*

THE DAMNED
British group *New Rose, Neat Neat Neat*

DEEP PURPLE
British group *Black Night, Fireball, Demon's Eye*

IRON MAIDEN
British group *Running Free, Sanctuary, The Number of the Beast*

KISS
American group *I Was Made for Loving You, Lick It Up*

Bass guitarist from Kiss, glam-rock supremos and masters of outrage.

LED ZEPPELIN
British group *Whole Lotta Love, Stairway to Heaven*

MEGADETH
British group *Wake Up Dead*

MOTORHEAD
British group *Ace of Spades, Overkill, No Sleep till Hammersmith*

IGGY POP (JAMES OSTERBERG)
American singer *The Idiot, Lust for Life*

SAXON
British group *Denim and Leather, The Eagle Has Landed*

THE SCORPIONS
German group *Love at First Sting*

THIN LIZZY
Irish group *Jailbreak, Killer on the Loose*

UFO
British group *Lights Out, Obsessions, Strangers in the Night*

URIAH HEEP
British group *Look at Yourself, Still 'Eavy, Still Proud*

WHITESNAKE
British group *Come and Get It, Snakebite*

Indian Classical/Popular/Folk and Traditional

BATISH FAMILY
North Indian Folk and Classical Music

SHEILA GHANDRA
Singer *Nada Brahma, Roots and Wings.*

HARISPRASAD CHAURASIA
Bamboo flute *Raga Chanrakauns – Raga Lalit*

JNAN PRAKASH GHOSH
Drums of India

AMJAD ALI KHAN
Sarod player *Raga Shree*

ORISSA
Eternal India

RAVI SHANKAR
Sitar player *Morning and Evening Ragas, Pancha Nadai Pallavi, West Meets East* (with Yehudi Menuhin)

Latin American Samba and Bossa Nova/Lambada/Soca/Salsa/Zouk

JOE ARROYO
Colombian singer *Fire in my Mind, Rebellion*

GILBERTO GIL
Brazilian bandleader *Palco, Toda Menina Baina*

ASTRUD GILBERTO
Brazilian singer *The Girl from Ipanema, One Note Samba*

EGBERTO GISMONTI
Brazilian pianist/guitarist/ singer *Danca Das Cabecas, Sol Do Meio Dia*

KASSAV
Antilles group *Zouk is the Only Medicine We Have, Majestic Zouk*

NARA LEAO
Brazilian singer *The Girl from Ipanema, Desafinado*

TANIA MARIA
Brazilian singer *The Lady from Brazil*

MARGARETH MENEZES
Brazilian singer *Tenda Do Amor*

SILVIO RODRIGUEZ
Cuban singer *Dias y Flores, Oh Melancolia*

The Middle East and North African Rai/Sabra/Folk and Traditional

TAOS AMROUCHE
Algerian singer *Chants de l'Atlas, Chants Berbères*

KOL AVIV
Israeli singer *Songs and Dances from Israel*

OFRA HAZA
Israeli singer *Desert Wind, Yemenite Songs*

CHEB KHALED
Algerian singer *Kutché, Ya Taleb* (with Chaba Zahouania)

OKAY TEMIZ
Turkish instrumentalist *Oriental Wind*

RECOMMENDED LISTENING

APANESE JAZZ-ROCK/
TRADITIONAL
....
TOSHIKO AKIYOSHI
Pianist/composer *Sumi-e, Insights*

ANDRAS ADORJAN
Lyrical Melodies of Japan

IPPU DO
Lunatic Menu

MAKOTO OZONE
Pianist/composer *Makoto Ozone, After*

YOSUKE YAMASHITA
Pianist/composer *Clay, Banslikana*

EGGAE/RAP/HIP HOP
....
AFRIKA BAMBAATAA
American singer *Renegades of Funk, Planet Rock*

BLACK UHURU
American – Jamaican group
What is Life?, Party Next Door

GRANDMASTER FLASH
American singer *Adventures of Grandmaster Flash, The Message*

BOB MARLEY (AND THE WAILERS)
Jamaican singer *One Love, Kinky Reggae, Small Axe, Rebel Music*

TOOTS AND THE MAYTALS
Jamaican group *Al Capone, Stick It Up Mister*

RHYTHM AND BLUES/
GOSPEL/SOUL
....
JAMES BROWN
American singer/songwriter *Please, Please, Please, Try Me*

CAPTAIN BEEFHEART (DON VAN VLIET)
American singer *Unconditionally Guaranteed*

RAY CHARLES
American singer *Georgia on my Mind, Come Rain or Come Shine, Your Cheatin' Heart*

FATS DOMINO
American singer *Blueberry Hill, Blue Monday*

BOB DYLAN
American singer/guitarist/ songwriter *The Times They Are A-Changing, Mr. Tambourine Man, Blowin' in the Wind, Highway 61 Revisited*

ARETHA FRANKLIN
American singer *Respect, Chain of Fools, Spanish Harlem*

JOHN LEE HOOKER
American singer *Boogie Chillun, I'm in the Mood*

B.B. KING
American guitarist/singer *Woke Up This Morning, The Thrill is Gone*

GLADYS KNIGHT
American singer *Help Me Make It Through the Night*

MIDDLE-OF-THE-ROAD
(MOR)/EASY LISTENING
....
CHARLES AZNAVOUR
French singer/composer *Amour Toujours, The Old Fashioned Way*

BURT BACHARACH
American songwriter *I Say a Little Prayer, Twenty-four Hours from Tulsa, I'll Never Fall In Love Again, Raindrops Keep Fallin' on my Head, What's New Pussycat?*

JOHN BARRY
British songwriter *From Russia With Love, Goldfinger, Thunderball, You Only Live Twice, Born Free, Midnight Cowboy*

SHIRLEY BASSEY
British singer *Kiss Me Honey Honey Kiss Me, I Who Have Nothing, Big Spender*

HARRY BELAFONTE
American singer *Island in the Sun, Coconut Woman*

TONY BENNETT
American singer *I Left My Heart in San Francisco*

BUCKS FIZZ
British group *Land of Make Believe*

KATE BUSH
British singer/songwriter *Wuthering Heights, Strange Phenomena*

HOAGY CARMICHAEL
American pianist, songwriter *Stardust, Skylark, The Nearness of You*

THE CARPENTERS
American duo *Close to You, Please Mr. Postman*

NAT 'KING' COLE
American singer/pianist *Nature Boy, Stay as Sweet as You Are, Sweet Lorraine, Unforgettable*

PERRY COMO
American singer *Catch a Falling Star, Magic Moments*

BING CROSBY
American singer *Where the Blue of the Night, White Christmas, How Deep is the Ocean, Swinging on a Star*

VIC DAMONE
American singer *On the Street Where You Live, Arrivederci Roma*

BOBBY DARIN
American singer/songwriter *Queen of the Hop, Mack the Knife*

DORIS DAY
American singer *Love Me or Leave Me, It's Magic, Que Sera Sera*

NEIL DIAMOND
American singer/songwriter *Cherry Cherry, You Don't Bring Me Flowers Anymore*

DURAN DURAN
British group *Planet Earth, A View to a Kill*

JUDY GARLAND (FRANCES GUMM)
American singer/actress *Over the Rainbow, Trolley Song, You Made Me Love You, The Man that Got Away*

JACK JONES
American singer *A Song for You, Bread Winners, Harbor*

TOM JONES
British singer *It's Not Unusual, Delilah*

EARTHA KITT
American singer *Just an Old Fashioned Girl, Let's Do It*

FRANKIE LAINE
American singer *Rawhide, Jezebel, High Noon*

PEGGY LEE
American singer/songwriter *Manana, Mr. Wonderful, Lover, Fever*

LULU (MARIE LAWRIE)
British singer *I'm a Tiger, Boom bang-a-bang*

HENRI MANCINI
American songwriter/ composer *Moon River, Days of Wine and Roses, The Pink Panther*

MANHATTAN TRANSFER
American group *Tuxedo Junction, On a Little Street in Singapore*

B. B. King.

DEAN MARTIN
American singer *Everybody Loves Somebody, Gentle on my Mind, That's Amore*

JOHNNY MATHIS
American singer *Too Much Too Little Too Late*

GUY MITCHELL
American singer *My Truly Truly Fair, She Wears Red Feathers, Pittsburgh Pennsylvania*

MATT MONRO
British singer *Portrait of my Love*

NANA MOUSKOURI
Greek singer *White Rose of Athens, Bridge Over Troubled Water, Never on Sunday*

GILBERT O'SULLIVAN
Irish singer/songwriter *Alone Again, Clair, Ooh Wakka Doo Wakka Day*

ELAINE PAIGE
British singer *Don't Cry For Me Argentina*

LES PAUL AND MARY FORD
American duo *How High the Moon*

EDITH PIAF
French singer *Non, je ne regrette rien, Milord, La Vie en Rose*

JOHNNIE RAY
American singer *Cry, The Little White Cloud that Cried*

OTIS REDDING
American singer/songwriter *Pain in my Heart, Try a Little Tenderness, I Can't Turn You Loose, Hard to Handle*

CLIFF RICHARD
British singer *Living Doll, The Young Ones, Bachelor Boy*

DIANA ROSS
American singer *Reach Out and Touch, Ain't No Mountain High Enough, Remember Me*

THE SEEKERS
Australian group *Georgy Girl, I'll Never Find Another You*

(PAUL) SIMON AND (ART) GARFUNKEL
American duo *Bridge Over Troubled Water, Mrs. Robinson*

NINA SIMONE (EUNICE WAYMON)
American singer/songwriter *Mr Bojangles, My Baby Just Cares for Me*

FRANK SINATRA
American singer/actor *She's Funny That Way, Nancy with the Laughing Face, I Couldn't Sleep a Wink Last Night, Come Fly With Me, My Funny Valentine, Old Devil Moon, You Make Me Feel So Young, Makin' Whoopee*

NANCY SINATRA
American singer *These Boots Are Made For Walking*

MEMPHIS SLIM
American singer/pianist *Cold Blooded Woman, Pigalle Love*

JO STAFFORD
American singer *You Belong to Me, Fools Rush In*

CAT STEVENS (STEVEN GEORGIOU)
British singer *Hard Headed Woman*

ROD STEWART
British singer *Maggie May, Sailing*

BARBRA STREISAND
American singer/actress *Don't Rain on my Parade, On a Clear Day*

THE SUPREMES
American group *Baby Love, Back in my Arms Again*

MEL TORMÉ
American singer *Baubles, Bangles and Beads, Mountain Greenery*

DIONNE WARWICK
American singer *This Girl's In Love*

MUDDY WATERS (McKINLEY MORGANFIELD)
American singer *Mud in your Ear*

ANDY WILLIAMS
American singer *Can't Take my Eyes off You, Killing Me Softly*

JIMMY WITHERSPOON
American singer *Ain't Nobody's Business, Skid Row Blues*

STEVIE WONDER
American singer/songwriter *You Are the Sunshine of my Life, Yester-me, Yester-you, Yesterday*

ROCK/ACID/HARD/ PROGRESSIVE

DAVID BOWIE
British singer *Aladdin Sane, The Rubber Band, Love You Till Tuesday*

ERIC CLAPTON
British guitarist/composer *Layla, I Shot the Sheriff, Lay Down Sally*

CREAM (GINGER BAKER, JACK BRUCE, ERIC CLAPTON)
British group *I Feel Free, Strange Brew, Badge*

THE DOORS
American group *Light My Fire, Riders on the Storm*

BRIAN ENO
British electric keyboards player/composer *Here Come the Warm Jets, Taking Tiger Mountain*

DAVID ESSEX
British singer/actor *A Winter's Tale, Silver Dream Machine*

GENESIS
British group *Duke, Abacab, Genesis*

GARY GLITTER (PAUL GADD)
British singer *I'm the Leader of the Gang, Always Yours*

GRATEFUL DEAD
American group *Dark Star, Workingman's Dead, American Beauty*

JIMI HENDRIX
American guitarist *Hey Joe, Purple Haze, Voodoo Chile, Are You Experienced? Electric Ladyland*

MICHAEL JACKSON
American singer *Got To Be There, Rockin' Robin, Off the Wall, Thriller*

JEFFERSON AIRPLANE
American group *White Rabbit, Somebody to Love*

ELTON JOHN (REGINALD DWIGHT)
British singer/pianist/composer *Your Song, Rocket Man, Daniel, Goodbye Yellow Brick Road, Captain Fantastic, Crocodile Rock, Don't Go Breaking My Heart*

JANIS JOPLIN
American singer *Janis Joplin in Concert*

MADONNA (MADONNA CICCONE)
American singer/dancer/songwriter *Holiday, Borderline, Crazy for You, Like a Virgin, Like a Prayer*

MANFRED MANN
South African keyboards player *5-4-3-2-1, Do Wah Diddy Diddy, Pretty Flamingo*

MEATLOAF (MARVIN ADAY)
American singer *Bat out of Hell, Paradise by the Dashboard Light*

PINK FLOYD
British group *Dark Side of the Moon, The Wall, Another Brick in the Wall*

POLICE
Anglo-American group *Ghost in the Machine*

PRINCE (PRINCE NELSON)
American singer *Little Red Corvette, Delirious, Lovesexy, Purple Rain*

SUZI QUATRO
American singer *Can the Can, Devil Gate Drive*

QUEEN
British group *Sheer Heart Attack, Seven Seas of Rhye, Killer Queen, A Night at the Opera*

THE ROLLING STONES (MICK JAGGER, KEITH RICHARD, BILL WYMAN, CHARLIE WATTS, BRIAN JONES)
British group *Satisfaction, Get Off My Cloud, Paint It Black, Honky Tonk Women, The Last Time, Jumping Jack Flash, Ruby Tuesday, Brown Sugar, Miss You*

ROXY MUSIC
British group *Virginia Plain, Pyjamarama, Love is the Drug*

THE SEARCHERS
British group *Sweets for my Sweet, Needles and Pins*

THE SHADOWS
British group *Apache, Kon-Tiki, Wonderful Land*

SOFT MACHINE
British group *Alive and Well and Living in Paris*

SPANDAU BALLET
British group *To Cut a Long Story Short, Musclebound, Glow*

STATUS QUO
British group *Piledriver, Picturesque Matchstickable*

TALKING HEADS
American group *Remain in Light, Stop Making Sense*

TANGERINE DREAM
German group *Alpha Centauri, Underwater Sunlight*

TINA TURNER (ANNIE BULLOCK)
American singer *What's Love Got To Do With It, We Don't Need Another Hero, Steamy Windows*

UB40
British group *I Got You Babe, Don't Break My Heart, Red Red Wine*

VELVET UNDERGROUND
American group *I'm Waiting for the Man, Venus in Furs*

RICK WAKEMAN
British keyboards player/composer *No Earthly Connection*

THE WHO (ROGER DALTREY, PETE TOWNSHEND, JOHN ENTWHISTLE, KEITH MOON)
British group *My Generation, Happy Jack, Pinball Wizard*

WINGS (PAUL AND LINDA McCARTNEY AND DENNY LAINE)
British group *Band on the Run, Venus and Mars*

THE YARDBIRDS
British group *For Your Love, Heartfull of Soul, Evil Hearted You*

FRANK ZAPPA
American singer/songwriter/electric keyboards *Hot Rats, Tinsel Town Rebellion*

ROCK 'N' ROLL/BEAT

THE BEATLES (JOHN LENNON, PAUL McCARTNEY, GEORGE HARRISON, RINGO STARR)
British group *She Loves You, I Want to Hold Your Hand, Hard Day's Night, Michelle, Penny Lane, Yesterday*

CHUCK BERRY
American singer/guitarist *Roll Over Beethoven, My Ding-a-Ling, Maybellene, Sweet Little Sixteen*

BO DIDDLEY
American singer/guitarist *Road Runner, I'm a Man*

GERRY AND THE PACEMAKERS
British group *Ferry Cross the Mersey, I Like It*

BILL HALEY AND THE COMETS
American group *Rock Around the Clock, Shake, Rattle and Roll, See You Later Alligator*

THE HOLLIES
British group *Here I Go Again, I'm Alive*

BUDDY HOLLY
American singer/guitarist *That'll Be The Day, Rave On*

JERRY LEE LEWIS
American singer/pianist *Whole Lotta Shakin' Goin' On, Great Balls of Fire, High School Confidential*

LITTLE RICHARD (RICHARD PENNIMAN)
American singer/pianist *Tutti Frutti, Good Golly Miss Molly*

ELVIS PRESLEY
American singer/guitarist *Hound Dog, Love Me Tender, It's Now or Never, Return to Sender, King Creole, Blue Suede Shoes, Jailhouse Rock, Are You Lonesome Tonight?*

SHAKIN' STEVENS (MICHAEL BARRATT)
British singer *Hot Dog, This Ole House, Green Door*

GENE VINCENT (EUGENE CRADDOCK)
American singer *Be-bop-a-Lula*

Biographies

The following listing includes biographies of major composers and performers mentioned throughout this book.

Louis Armstrong

LOUIS ARMSTRONG
(1900–71)

Like 'Jelly Roll' Morton (see below), Louis Armstrong was born in New Orleans and played a vital role in the first great period of jazz, playing his trumpet in the Kid Ory, 'King' Oliver and Fletcher Henderson bands, in New Orleans, Chicago and New York respectively. While many of his colleagues died or otherwise fell by the wayside, 'Satchmo' (short for 'Satchel Mouth') went from strength to strength, for many years leading his own All Stars band, adding gravel-voiced singing to his superb trumpet playing and also making many film appearances. He died a superstar.

JOHANN SEBASTIAN BACH
(1685–1750)

Bach belonged to a dynasty of German musicians, and his own life refutes the popular notion of the Bohemian artist. Sober and hard-working, he was born in Eisenach, learned music from relatives and other local musicians, and succeeded to the posts of organist at Arnstadt, Mühlhausen and the court of Saxe-Weimar, *kapellmeister* at the court of Anhalt-Cöthen, and finally cantor at St. Thomas's Church and School in Leipzig, where he remained until his death. He married twice (Maria Barbara, and upon her death Anna Magdalena), raising a large family, some of whom (notably C.P.E. and J.C. Bach) became celebrated musicians in their turn.

BÉLA BARTÓK
(1881-1945)

Hungarian-born Béla Bartók turned his back on a career as a virtuoso pianist-composer to study Hungarian and Romanian folk music. With his colleague and friend Zoltán Kodály, he traveled around Transylvania (home of vampire legends) noting down, and sometimes recording on a phonograph, hundreds of local songs and dances. His experiences transformed his own music, making him one of the most innovative and controversial composers of his age. Bartók remained in Hungary until 1940, when he emigrated to the U.S. in protest against his country's links with Nazi Germany. By then suffering from leukemia, with very little money and too proud to live off charity, his last years in New York were sad and lonely ones. He did, however, receive commissions for new works from, among others, the Koussevitsky Foundation, violinist Yehudi Menuhin and jazz clarinettist Benny Goodman. News of Bartók's tragic death kindled wider interest in his music.

Paul McCartney

THE BEATLES

Pop music's most celebrated group began life in Liverpool as the 'Silver Beatles,' not much different from other rock 'n' rollers of the time, until Brian Epstein, another Liverpudlian, began to manage them in 1961. With Ringo Starr on drums joining John Lennon, Paul McCartney and George Harrison, Epstein transformed their image and so set the cultural pattern for much of the decade. 'Beatlemania' attended everything they did and everywhere they went, including a sensational American tour in 1964. They finally broke up in 1970, the two most talented members, songwriters Lennon and McCartney, following new careers of their own. By then, The Beatles were already a part of twentieth-century history and legend.

SIR THOMAS BEECHAM
(1879–1961)

Beecham inherited a fortune from his industrialist father and used it to back numerous musical enterprises, notably the foundation of the London Philharmonic and Royal Philharmonic orchestras. As a conductor, Beecham was noted for his wit, elegance and flair, also for his championing of Mozart, French and Russian music, and, above all, the work of his friend Delius.

LUDWIG VAN BEETHOVEN
(1770–1827)

Beethoven was born in the Rhineland town of Bonn, and despite his drunken father and mediocre teachers, soon showed exceptional talent. Encouraged by Haydn, he settled in Vienna, where he remained for the rest of his life. The Viennese aristocrats were fascinated by his rough manner and tough, swarthy appearance, as well as his brilliance as a pianist, and he never lacked either for patrons or for lady admirers, including the enigmatic 'Immortal Beloved.' But growing deafness (first confessed in the so-called Heiligenstadt Testament of 1802), and the upsets of the Napoleonic Wars turned Beethoven increasingly in upon himself and made him very difficult to deal with. A drawn-out family dispute over the custody of his nephew Karl was another unhappy chapter in his life. When Beethoven died, worn out by his creative efforts and unsettled mode of life, he was already famous, and thousands attended his funeral.

IRVING BERLIN
(1888–1989)

Irving Berlin was a small, fragile-looking man, who lived to see his hundredth birthday. He was a Russian-Jewish migrant to America, where he changed his name from Israel Baline to Irving Berlin, due to a printing error on the title page of his first published song. He started as a song-plugger in New York's Tin Pan Alley, playing everything from memory, since he couldn't read music. The song that established him, in 1911, was *Alexander's Ragtime Band,* cashing in on the contemporary craze for early ragtime jazz. Berlin went on to write over 800 popular songs (both words and music in most cases), ranging from *God Bless America* to *There's No Business Like Show Business* and *White Christmas. Annie Get Your Gun* is one of his many stage and screen musicals.

Hector Berlioz

*H*ECTOR BERLIOZ

(1803–69)

The romantic drama and color of his music echoes much of Berlioz's own life. He rebelled against medical studies and led a Bohemian life in Paris as a young music student and composer. He also fell madly in love with an Irish actress, Harriet Smithson, whom he pursued, married and was then estranged from. Through the rest of his life, and despite help from such eminent people as Liszt, Berlioz grew increasingly embittered trying to get his music performed; he did, however, score some success as a talented conductor in London, Russia and elsewhere. He wrote some highly entertaining memoirs, which should, perhaps, be read with a pinch of salt.

*L*EONARD BERNSTEIN

(1918–90)

The flamboyant Leonard Bernstein straddled the worlds of show business and concert music. Educated at Harvard University and the Curtis Institute, Philadelphia, he pursued a dual career. As a conductor, he directed most of the world's top orchestras, noted for his interpretations of Mahler, but taking in a very broad repertory, from Cherubini operas to Britten. As a composer he was most successful with his scores for the stage and screen musicals *On The Town* and *West Side Story,* but, as time allowed, he also produced a number of larger-scale symphonic and choral works. He was also an excellent writer and broadcaster.

*P*IERRE BOULEZ

(born 1925)

Once the *enfant terrible* of modern music, Boulez studied engineering and mathematics before switching to music at the Paris Conservatoire, where Messiaen was one of his teachers. After World War II, he joined Stockhausen, Bruno Maderna and others at Darmstadt, experimenting with electronic music, and starting to compose the often rigorously intellectual works that perplexed so many people. He has also shone as a conductor. He was chief conductor of the BBC Symphony and New York Philharmonic orchestras, and directed the centenary production of Wagner's 'Ring' at Bayreuth. More recently, he has run the *Institut de Recherche et de Coordination Acoustique/Musique* (IRCAM), a new center for electronic and other experimental studies, back in Paris.

*J*OHANNES BRAHMS

(1833–97)

Born in a Hamburg dockside tenement, Brahms first scratched a living playing in local theaters and brothels. A meeting with the great Hungarian violinist Joseph Joachim led to an even more important meeting with Schumann, who gave him much encouragement and help. Brahms eventually settled in Vienna, leading an outwardly uneventful if somewhat eccentric bachelor life, though being drawn reluctantly into the controversy surrounding the ideas and music of Liszt and Wagner. One of his few enduring friendships was with Schumann's widow Clara.

*B*ENJAMIN BRITTEN

(1913–76)

Britten was born on St. Cecilia's Day (the patron saint of music), at Lowestoft on the Suffolk coast of England. By his early twenties he was already attracting attention as a composer. With his life-long companion, the tenor Peter Pears, he went to the U.S. in 1939, but returned home in the middle of World War II, courageously declaring his pacifism (along with his compatriot Michael Tippett). At the end of the war, his opera *Peter Grimes* really established his name, and from that time on, he was one of the few English composers to enjoy as much fame abroad as at home. Britten also established the Aldeburgh Festival, close to his East Anglian birthplace, where he performed the works of many of his contemporaries as well as his own. His homosexuality was no serious impediment to his career, as it had been for Tchaikovsky in the nineteenth century.

HANS VON BÜLOW
. . . .
(1830–94)
The German conductor Hans von Bülow was put in the humiliating position of directing the premières of *Tristan und Isolde* and *Die Meistersinger von Nürnberg* while his wife Cosima was having a blatant affair with their composer, Wagner, whom she subsequently married. Being cuckolded by Wagner has tended to overshadow the rest of Bülow's career. He was perhaps the first virtuoso conductor, tackling some of the most difficult new music of his time and raising the caliber of orchestral playing and discipline. He was also a very fine pianist, giving the first performance of Tchaikovsky's famous Piano Concerto no 1. The work is dedicated to Bülow.

MARIA CALLAS
. . . .
(1923–77)
Maria Callas was born in New York of Greek parents (the family name was Kalogeropoulos), but she studied music and made her singing debut in Athens. Her big break came when she stepped in for another singer in Bellini's *I Puritani,* revealing a superb gift for dramatic Italian *bel canto* soprano singing. This became her specialty, raising her to the peak of operatic fame. She worked also as a producer and teacher.

ENRICO CARUSO
. . . .
(1873–1921)
Photographs of Caruso in the U.S., in fur-lined coat, spats and puffing at a cigar, give him the look of an old-style gangster. In fact, like Al Capone, the world's most famous operatic tenor was born in Naples. He made his reputation in Europe, mainly in Italian opera, and then at New York's Metropolitan Opera, where he made over six hundred appearances. But what really brought him worldwide fame were his pioneer gramophone recordings, which earned him enormous sums of money. A film was made of his life, starring Mario Lanza.

PABLO CASALS
. . . .
(1876–1973)
Like many other artists of this century, the Spanish-born Catalonian cellist Pablo Casals was caught up in politics and war. He was already over sixty years old, with a distinguished career behind him, when, in 1939, at the end of the Spanish Civil War, he exiled himself from his country's new Fascist regime. Aged seventy-four, he founded the famous Prades Music Festival in southern France, later still settling in Puerto Rico, where he organized another festival. He also wrote his *Hymn to the United Nations,* conducting it at the U.N. Headquarters in New York, aged ninety-five.

FYODOR CHALIAPIN
. . . .
(1873–1938)
Chaliapin came from Kazan on the River Volga, then a remote provincial Russian town far from the social and artistic centers of Moscow and St. Petersburg. But by the age of twenty-one, he was already making a name for himself and went on to become the most acclaimed operatic bass of his time, appearing many times at London's Covent Garden Opera, La Scala, Milan, and the New York Metropolitan Opera. He virtually created the title role in Mussorgsky's *Boris Godunov,* combining his magnificent voice with a real flair for acting.

Frédéric Chopin

FRÉDÉRIC CHOPIN
. . . .
(1810–49)
Chopin was born in Warsaw and felt intensely patriotic toward Poland all his life. But his father was French, and, aged twenty-one, after a concert tour as a brilliant young pianist-composer, Chopin settled in Paris. The most famous episode in his otherwise quite private life was his love affair with the French writer George Sand (Aurore Dupin). A cold, wet winter spent with her in Majorca, and all the effort he put into composition, probably accelerated his tuberculosis, and after an exhausting concert tour of Britain, he died back home in Paris, aged thirty-nine.

BING CROSBY
. . . .
(1903–77)
Harry Lillis Crosby – Bing came from a cartoon character he loved as a boy – was already playing drums and singing at school. Abandoning law school, he joined the Rhythm Boys vocal group to sing with the famous Paul Whiteman band. With a recording contract, he began to change his singing style, moving from Dixieland jazz to the new sentimental crooning of swing, which made his fortune. From the 1930s and for the next forty years, Bing Crosby sold millions of records, made thousands of radio broadcasts and dozens of films (including the hugely successful 'Road' films with Bob Hope and Dorothy Lamour), his finely controlled voice and easy-going charm carrying him through every change of fashion in popular entertainment. He also showed business flair, investing in baseball and golf (his favorite pastime). His brother Bob was also a successful singer and bandleader.

MILES DAVIS
. . . .
(born 1926)
In contrast to most jazz musicians, Miles Davis was born into a prosperous, middle-class family and studied at the prestigious Juilliard School of Music in New York. He is also set apart from many of his colleagues by the remarkable length and variety of his career. Leaving Juilliard, he joined up with Charlie Parker and the startling innovations of bebop. He soon branched out on his own, however, initiating the 'cool' jazz style. So he has continued for nearly fifty years, forming new groups, creating new styles, adding flugelhorn and electric keyboards and guitars to his already unique trumpet playing and featuring other such exotic instruments as the Indian sitar and tabla drums. After Parker, he worked with a host of other jazz stars, including Gil Evans, Gerry Mulligan, John Coltrane, Herbie Hancock, Chick Corea and Keith Jarrett. Miles Davis' bands have been widely influential, and he is usually credited with the innovation of the 'jazz-rock' hybrid during the late 1960s.

Claude Debussy

Antonin Dvořák

CLAUDE-ACHILLE DEBUSSY

(1862–1918)

After a youthful visit to Russia, playing the piano for Tchaikovsky's patroness Madame von Meck, and a spell in Rome as the winner of a coveted music prize, France's greatest composer settled in Paris, close to his birthplace at St. Germain-en-Laye. Of striking appearance, with dark hair falling across a prominent forehead, Debussy had an intermittently turbulent love life. Otherwise he remained fairly aloof and fastidious, though quite able to speak his mind as an articulate music critic. His one great love was for his little daughter 'Chou Chou.' This was overshadowed by his illness from cancer and by depression brought on by the World War I. He died a few months before the end of the war (Chou Chou dying soon after, from influenza).

ANTONIN DVOŘÁK

(1841–1904)

Dvořák had a passion for trains, spending hours at railroad stations, or sending someone to collect engine numbers for him. His father was the butcher in a small Bohemian village, but Dvořák's musical talents were encouraged, and he proceeded to study and work in Prague. He shared with Smetana the nationalist sentiments that eventually led to the creation of Czechoslovakia, but his espousal by Brahms drew him closer to the German symphonic style. His music, echoing his basically sunny disposition, was soon very popular in Germany, Britain and the United States. He visited the U.S. with his family, at the height of his fame, before returning home to the directorship of the Prague Conservatory.

SIR EDWARD ELGAR

(1857–1934)

Elgar was over forty years old before he enjoyed real success with *The Dream of Gerontius* and the *Enigma Variations*. Suddenly, he was hailed as England's greatest composer, and as a great musical patriot, when someone else added the words of 'Land of Hope and Glory' to one of his melodies. His noble and dignified bearing as an Edwardian gentleman enhanced this image. But World War I, the loss of his wife, and the radically changed post-war world left him depressed and disillusioned, despite all the honors heaped upon him. He died, back in his hometown of Worcester, within sight of his beloved Malvern Hills. Today, Elgar's music seems to evoke a world that vanished in 1914.

EDWARD 'DUKE' ELLINGTON

(1899–1974)

Ellington's father was a butler in Washington, D.C. His sobriquet of 'Duke' was given to him by a childhood friend. By the end of the 1920s, he was already a top bandleader; and drawing on some of the best individual talents in jazz, while adapting his style to changing fashions, he grew in fame and esteem during the next forty years. A man of quiet charm and discretion, 'Duke' acted like a cultural ambassador for his country during many foreign tours with his band and was several times an honored guest at the White House, back in the city where he was born.

'Duke'Ellington's Orchestra

MANUEL DE FALLA

(1876–1946)

The difference between the man and his music could hardly be greater than in the case of Manuel de Falla. The music is alive with the color and fire of Spain. The composer was a diminutive, monk-like figure, deeply religious, and a hypo-chondriac. He was born in Cadiz, studied in Madrid with Felipe Pedrell, the great authority on Spanish folk music, then moved to Paris, where he met Debussy and Ravel and began to enjoy success as a composer. His fame reached its height just after World War I with Diaghilev's production of the ballet *The Three-Cornered Hat*. For the last twenty years of his life, Falla worked on *L'Atlantida*, a huge choral piece about the legendary continent of Atlantis, dying in Argentina before he could finish it.

KIRSTEN FLAGSTAD

(1895–1962)

Norway's Kirsten Flagstad is remembered as the greatest of all Wagnerian sopranos. She was, in fact, nearly forty years old before news of her singing began to spread beyond Scandinavia. First at the Bayreuth Festival, then in New York and London, her inter-pretations, notably of the roles of Isolde and Brunnhilde, were henceforth regarded as definitive. Gracefully retiring from the stage in 1953, she returned home to direct the Norwegian State Opera.

WILHELM FURTWÄNGLER

(1886–1954)

Principal conductor for many years of the Berlin and Vienna Philharmonic orchestras and the Bayreuth Festival, Furtwängler is remembered for his deeply-felt interpreta-tions, especially of Beethoven and Wagner. He became embroiled with the Nazis, hoping vainly to protect the integrity of German music against their excesses. He also composed symphonies and other concert works.

GEORGE GERSHWIN

(1898–1937)

Gershwin's ethnic and musical background was very similar to that of Irving Berlin (see above). Born Jakob Gershovitz, the son of Russian-Jewish immigrants to America, he began as a house pianist, plugging the latest songs in New York's music publishing district (Tin Pan Alley). His own first hit song was *Swanee*, thanks largely to vaudeville singer Al Jolson; through the 1920s and 1930s, often in collaboration with his lyricist brother Ira (Israel), he was Broadway's premier composer of stage musicals, reveling in the fame and fortune that came his way. But he was also ambitiously writing jazz-inspired symphonic works, culminating in his opera *Porgy and Bess*. Gershwin was only thirty-nine years old when he died, with little warning, from a brain tumor.

GILBERT AND SULLIVAN

Librettist W.S. Gilbert (1836-1911) and composer Sir Arthur Sullivan (1842-1900) formed perhaps the most famous partnership in musical theater. Both had distinguished careers of their own before they embarked, largely at the behest of London impresario Richard D'Oyly Carte, on their hugely successful series of comic operettas. Satirizing the fashions and institutions of Victorian England, as popular now as ever, these operettas include *Trial by Jury, HMS Pinafore, The Pirates of Penzance, Patience, Iolanthe, The Mikado, Ruddigore* and *The Gondoliers*. Ironically, their relationship was not a very happy one. Gilbert was a peppery character, while Sullivan thought the operettas rather beneath his dignity. It is, incidentally, unusual in such collaborations for the librettist's name to come first.

TITO GOBBI

(born 1915)

Gobbi was the outstanding Italian baritone of his generation, appearing at all the major opera houses around the world, and setting new vocal and dramatic standards in such great Verdian roles as Rigoletto, Iago and Falstaff. His most famous role of all was that of the evil police chief Baron Scarpia in Puccini's *Tosca*, singing opposite Maria Callas (see above) in the title role. Later in his career, Gobbi also showed talent and flair as an opera producer and a teacher.

GEORGE FRIDERIC HANDEL

(1685–1759)

The composer of *Messiah* was born in the Saxon town of Halle, in the same year as, and not very far from, J.S. Bach. In contrast to his great German contemporary, Handel led a colorful and adventurous life. From a humble job as a violinist in Hamburg, he moved swiftly to Italy, where he met Corelli and A. Scarlatti, learning much from them about both instrumental music and opera. After a brief return to Germany, he moved on again, this time to London, then the biggest and richest city in the world. There he settled (later taking British nationality), making and losing money in the tough competitive world of opera. Later, in response to changing fashions, he scored new successes with some of his oratorios. A large, choleric man, he suffered a serious stroke in later years, brought on by the stresses of his life, but recovered, and died in London, honored with a monument in Westminster Abbey. Like Bach, he went blind in old age.

FRANZ-JOSEPH HAYDN

(1732–1809)

Haydn came from a family of rural craftsmen living on the borders of modern Austria and Hungary. He was a choirboy and a humble music teacher in Vienna before joining the musical establishment of the aristocratic Austro-Hungarian Prince Paul Esterházy. He served the latter and his successor, Prince Nikolaus, for thirty years, during which time his fame as a composer spread across Europe. He was subsequently fêted wherever he went, to Paris, London and Oxford, before returning to Vienna, where he died after a long, successful and, on the whole, happy life.

JIMI HENDRIX

(1942–70)

The short life of guitarist Jimi Hendrix is a testament to the huge rewards and dire perils of the pop music world. Born into a poor black family in Seattle, he taught himself guitar, before enlisting in the U.S. Army. Back in civilian life, he toured the U.S. with several groups. Moving to London, in 1967, with his new-formed trio, the Jimi Hendrix Experience, he became an overnight sensation, with his incandescent playing and such gimmicks as setting fire to his guitar. This brilliant but wild image shot him to international stardom. Punishing schedules, emotional strains, pressures of racial politics and drugs destroyed him almost as rapidly as he rose to fame, and he died in 1970, not yet thirty years old.

FRANZ LISZT

(1811–83)

Hungarian-born Franz (Ferencz) Liszt was the most sensational virtuoso of them all – a young pianist of phenomenal ability and striking good looks, over whom women screamed and fainted. He had many love affairs, notably with the notorious Lola Montez, the French Countess Marie d'Agoult (their daughter Cosima married Wagner) and the Russian Princess Carolyn Sayn-Wittgenstein. But as a serious musician and creative artist, Liszt then turned away from the limelight, settling for some years in the small German town of Weimar, to compose and to give generous help to Berlioz, Wagner and many others. Later in life, he entered the Church, though his reputation as a lover stayed with him to the end of his venerable days.

GUSTAV MAHLER

(1860–1911)

Born in Bohemia but of Austrian nationality, Mahler was an inspired conductor of the Hamburg Opera, the Vienna Opera and then of the New York Philharmonic Orchestra, raising standards in orchestral playing and opera production, and confirming the image of the conductor as an autocrat and a martinet. Intense and neurotic, he was at the same time composing his huge, complex and emotional symphonies and song cycles. The strain was too much for his weak heart, however, and it killed him. His widow, Alma, later married the famous German architect Walter Gropius. Mahler's music has been dubbed 'the last farewell of modern man to the beautiful fading dream of Romanticism'.

DAME NELLIE MELBA

(1861–1931)

Helen Milhall was born near Melbourne, Australia, adopting her stage name from that city. She became the most celebrated soprano of her generation, singing principally at London's Covent Garden Opera and New York's Metropolitan Opera, sometimes with considerable control in such matters as casting and staging. She sang with Caruso (see above), and like him also made some pioneer recordings, notably as Mimi in Puccini's *La Bohème*. *Peach Melba* (peaches and ice-cream) is named for her.

Sir Yehudi Menuhin

(born 1916)

Aged just sixteen, American-born Yehudi Menuhin recorded Elgar's Violin Concerto with its silver-haired composer. Such an unlikely partnership highlights the amazing breadth of Menuhin's career. By the time he made his historic recording with Elgar, he was already an international violin virtuoso, sometimes performing with his almost equally gifted pianist sister Hephzibah. Bartók wrote a sonata especially for him. Settled in England, he directed the Bath Festival and founded a music school. From jazz with fellow violinist Stephane Grappelli to concerts with Indian sitarist Ravi Shankar (see below), Menuhin's interests and energy have known no bounds.

Olivier Messiaen

(born 1908)

In the winter of 1941, seated at a battered upright piano in a German P.O.W. camp, Messiaen joined in the first performance of his *Quatuor pour la fin du temps* (Quartet for the End of Time). Even his time as a soldier and prisoner-of-war hardly impinged upon his life as a mystic and one of this century's most original composers. Born in Avignon in southern France, Messiaen studied at the Paris Conservatoire. He then took the post of organist at the Paris church of La Trinité, combining this job as a working musician with his absorption in mysticism and a musical reinterpretation of birdsong. Apart from the interruption of the war years, so his life has continued, culminating in an extraordinary opera about the life of St. Francis of Assisi. He has also been the teacher of other eminent composers, including Boulez, Stockhausen and Xenakis.

Claudio Monteverdi

(1567–1643)

Monteverdi was born in Cremona, famous also as the home of the Stradivaris and other famous violin-makers. His first post was with the Duke of Mantua (a member of the Gonzaga family, one of the dynasties that ruled over Renaissance Italy), accompanying his employer on military expeditions and writing madrigals for him, as well as the pioneering opera *Orfeo*. The second part of Monteverdi's career took him to Venice, as *Maestro di Cappella* (director of music) at St. Mark's, then probably the most prestigious musical appointment in Europe. Surviving an outbreak of the plague, he divided his time between church music and more operas (Venice being one of the first centers of opera), dying esteemed and honored, at what was in those days a venerable age.

Ferdinand 'Jelly Roll' Morton

(1890–1941)

In an interview he recorded for the Library of Congress, 'Jelly Roll' Morton claimed to have invented jazz. This was not true, of course, but he certainly was one of the great jazz pioneers, born in New Orleans at just the right time and place. In New Orleans itself, then in Chicago, pianist Morton led some of the best early jazz bands, including the famous Red Hot Peppers, with whom he made some classic recordings. Overtaken by the rise of the big swing bands, and in poor health, he moved to California, where he died.

Wolfgang Amadeus Mozart

(1756–91)

Born in Salzburg, Austria, Mozart was a child prodigy.

He spent much of his childhood and youth, often with his violinist-composer father Leopold and sister Maria Anna, traveling around fashionable Europe, from London to Rome, playing or directing his own music. At the age of 22, he became court organist to the Archbishop of Salzburg, but clashed with the prelate and settled in Vienna, where he married the singer Constanze Weber (related to the composer Carl Maria von Weber) and embarked on a largely freelance career. Mozart enjoyed some success, notably with his operas, and earned the highest praise from his friend Haydn. But neither he nor Constanze could manage their affairs properly, and they were frequently short of money. Mozart died in Vienna, aged thirty-five, and was buried in an unmarked grave, though accounts of his final sad state may be exaggerated.

Ignacy Paderewski

(1860–1941)

The Polish-born Paderewski was a rare example of the artist-politician (Verdi, briefly, was another). He was the world's most fêted pianist in the early years of this century, his thick shock of hair and demeanor exciting the romantic notion of a musician as much as his actual playing. He also worked tirelessly for his country and was elected its first prime minister when Poland became an independent nation at the end of World War I. Sadly, he died in exile in New York, when his country had been torn apart again by the Soviet Union and Nazi Germany.

Niccolo Paganini

(1782–1840)

The Genoese-born Paganini was the supreme virtuoso of

the violin, as Liszt was of the piano. He made many European tours, astounding audiences with his playing and fascinating them with his rather strange, saturnine appearance (people said he was in league with the Devil). At a more serious level, he greatly advanced violin technique, such as pizzicato and staccato playing, as exploited in his own *Caprices* and other compositions. He also wrote some charming pieces for the guitar. A generous man to his colleagues, Paganini lost a lot of money invested in a Paris casino and ballroom.

Charlie Parker

(1920-55)

Charlie Parker, known to everyone in the jazz world as 'Bird,' is another example, like Jimi Hendrix, of brilliance burning itself out through drink and drugs. Born in Kansas City, he took up the saxophone while he was at school, practicing hard and modeling himself on such masters as Lester Young. He played in some of the best big bands, including those of Earl Hines and Billy Eckstine, before he and trumpeter Dizzy Gillespie set the jazz world ablaze with their revolutionary new bebop style, largely worked out in private sessions in New York in the mid-1940s. 'Bird's' fame subsequently took him on more commercially-orientated tours of the U.S. and Europe, leading to a sense of creative frustration that fueled his addiction to drugs and alcohol. By 1950 his greatest days were already behind him, although he was still capable of bursts of brilliance almost up to the time of his tragically premature death. Soon after he died, such was his god-like status, graffiti reading 'Bird Lives' appeared on New York walls.

ELVIS PRESLEY
(1935–77)

The teenage Elvis Presley paid four dollars to record a song for his mother's birthday. So began the recording career of the greatest of all pop idols. Brought up in rural Mississippi and Tennessee, his boyhood acquaintance with gospel and blues singing gave him the edge over other early rock 'n' roll performers when he started recording in the mid 1950s. With the astute Colonel Tom Parker as his manager, he was soon a national and then international star. Films followed, with Parker also orchestrating a multimillion dollar industry in Presley souvenirs. By 1960, after two years' army service, the old dynamic 'Elvis the Pelvis' slipped into an easier, glossier routine. He was on drugs, and his marriage broke up. Today his home, Graceland, in Memphis, Tennessee, is almost a national shrine.

MAURICE RAVEL
(1875–1937)

Stravinsky called Ravel a 'Swiss watchmaker'; his father was French-Swiss, and Maurice loved clocks and mechanical toys. He was born in the Basque region of southern France, but spent most of his life in Paris. Small and dapper, but also quite shy, Ravel nevertheless soon became famous, which set him up as a kind of rival to Debussy, to the irritation of them both. Rejected for military service in World War I, Ravel volunteered to drive an army truck, experiencing the horrors of Verdun. After the war he achieved even greater fame with his celebrated *Bolero*. But soon afterward, he was hurt in a car crash, which left him brain damaged and made further composition virtually impossible for the last sad years of his life.

THE ROLLING STONES

The Rolling Stones (principally Mick Jagger, Brian Jones, Keith Richard) turned out to be a prophetically good title for a group that, in name at least, has gone on rolling across the brutally tough landscape of pop music. They began in 1962 and three years later had created the hard-edged rock style that sent them to the top of the charts. Drama on and off-stage – drugs charges, the drowning of Brian Jones in his swimming pool, a fatal stabbing at a concert – kept them in a glare of publicity. With the 1970s they acquired a jet-setting image, losing much of their earlier drive. But still the Stones rolled on, Mick Jagger's charisma making him, in the hackneyed but true phrase, a legend in his own lifetime.

GIAOCCHINO ROSSINI
(1792–1868)

Rossini was known as 'Signor Crescendo' because of his stylistic trick of gradually building his music up to a thrilling climax. The device served him well through nearly forty operas in twenty years, many of them big successes. Such a punishing work-rate, though it made him rich, also left Rossini nervously exhausted. He settled in Paris, composing only a few more works (no more operas) during the next thirty-eight years and, when he felt well enough, leading the life of a gourmet. A famous dish is named after him.

RAVI SHANKAR
(born 1920)

Virtuoso sitarist and composer Ravi Shankar is India's most celebrated musician of modern times. Born in the northern province of Uttar Pradesh at the time of Indian independence (1947) he became a director of All India Radio, doing much to restore national pride in Indian classical music. He has also written music for several outstanding Indian films. Abroad, he appeared at such prestigious events as the Edinburgh Festival and United Nations concerts in New York, and founded a school of Indian music in Los Angeles. One of his closest friends has been Yehudi Menuhin (see above). His elder brother, Uday, made his own mark as a dancer and choreographer.

JEAN (JOHAN) SIBELIUS
(1865–1957)

Just as 'Land of Hope and Glory' turned Elgar into a patriotic hero for the English, so *Finlandia,* written when Finland was struggling for independence from Tsarist Russia, made Sibelius a hero in his own country. He was even awarded a state pension on the strength of this and other patriotic pieces. He continued to compose copiously, including much programatic and incidental music, as well as the seven symphonies by which he is chiefly acclaimed today. During the last thirty years of his long life, however, he produced hardly anything more (despite rumors of a new symphony), living in retirement in a large, secluded house not far from Helsinki.

FRANK SINATRA
(born 1915)

Born in Hoboken, across the Hudson River from New York City, Frank Sinatra first sang with a group called The Hoboken Four. But his career really started when he sang with Harry James and then with the Tommy Dorsey band, the latter's smooth trombone playing helping to shape his own dreamy vocal style, projecting him as the first great teenage idol. When swing gave way to rock 'n' roll, Sinatra shrewdly broadened his style, aided by such top arrangers as Nelson Riddle and Quincy Jones. Simultaneously, he blossomed as a screen actor, making over fifty films, including *From Here to Eternity, On The Town* and *High Society*. He also founded his own record company. Thus for nearly fifty years, 'Ole' Blue Eyes' stayed at the very top of show business, alongside Bing Crosby, whom he first attempted to emulate. His daughter Nancy has made her own mark as a singer.

Bessie Smith

BESSIE SMITH
(1895–1937)

According to everyone who heard and saw her, Bessie Smith fully earned her title of 'Empress of the Blues.' Born in Chattanooga, Tennessee, and the protégée of another great blues singer, Ma Rainey, she was already a star in her early twenties, a beautiful young black woman with an exceptionally strong and expressive voice. After a move to New York, she embarked on a touring show, 'Harlem

Frolics,' traveling around the country in her own luxury pullman car as the highest-paid black artist up to that time. The arrival of swing, radio and talking pictures in the late 1920s were blows to her kind of performance, but she continued to record and tour, until she died in the hospital after a car crash.

$\mathcal{I}$GOR STRAVINSKY
(1882–1971)

Stravinsky's father was a leading singer at the Russian Imperial Opera. Igor himself studied with Rimsky-Korsakov in St. Petersburg and was then commissioned by the great impresario Diaghilev to write music for three new ballet productions in Paris, *The Firebird, Petrushka* and *The Rite of Spring.* These propelled him to international fame and notoriety. After the Russian Revolution in 1917, Stravinsky and his family settled first in France and then in the United States, where he became an American citizen. Changes in the style of his own music accompanied these moves, keeping him in the forefront of the artistic world for half a century. Undersized and in poor health for much of the time, he outlived nearly all his contemporaries. He died in New York, but was buried in Venice, close to the grave of Diaghilev, to whom he first owed his fame and success.

$\mathcal{D}$AME JOAN SUTHERLAND
(born 1926)

Born in Sydney, Australia, Joan Sutherland studied singing first in her home city and then in London. Though she made her operatic debut in 1947 and sang some impressive roles, it was her performance in Donizetti's *Lucia di Lammermoor* at London's Covent Garden in 1959 that really established her. Thereafter she rivaled

Callas (see above) as the great Italian *bel canto* soprano of the age, noted for her purity of tone. She also toured Australia with her own opera company.

$\mathcal{T}$ORU TAKEMITSU
(born 1930)

Like Ravi Shankar in India, the Japanese composer Toru Takemitsu has done much to break down the barriers between Oriental and Western music. Born in Tokyo, he began teaching himself music soon after World War II, taking a keen interest in such current Western developments as *musique concrète,* electronic and aleatory methods of composition. With Japanese colleagues he founded the *Jikku Kobo* (Experimental Workshop) and began combining traditional Japanese styles with Western techniques. In 1959, Stravinsky pronounced his *Requiem for Strings* a masterpiece. Takemitsu later worked with the American John Cage at the East-West Center in Hawaii. Another accolade was a commission for the piece *November Steps* for the 125th anniversary celebrations of the New York Philharmonic Orchestra.

$\mathcal{P}$ETER (PYOTR ILYICH) TCHAIKOVSKY
(1840–93)

Russia's most famous composer studied law before turning to music, first in St. Petersburg and then in Moscow. Tchaikovsky was a rather neurotic man, ridden with guilt about his homosexuality, which probably drove him into a disastrous and very brief marriage. He was, at the same time, a hard-working and generally successful composer, touring Europe and the U.S. as conductor of his own

music, supported for many years by a patroness, Nadejda von Meck. But his homosexuality haunted him, and it is now believed it was on this account that he committed suicide by taking poison, just days after the première of his finest symphony, the *Pathetic.*

$\mathcal{A}$RTURO TOSCANINI
(1867–1957)

Toscanini, the most illustrious of conductors, came from Parma, near Verdi's birthplace. He was an orchestral cellist before stepping in at short notice to direct a performance of *Aida.* He later conducted the première of Puccini's *Turandot.* Disliking the Fascist regime in his own country, he went to the U.S., where the NBC Symphony Orchestra was formed especially for him. Toscanini established the custom of conducting from memory (in his own case because of myopia). He was also the epitomy of the tyrannical conductor, drilling an orchestra to perfection, though his fierce reputation was sometimes exaggerated.

$\mathcal{G}$IUSEPPE VERDI
(1813–1901)

In Italy, Verdi is as much a national hero as soldiers and statesmen are elsewhere. He was the son of an innkeeper, born near Parma, and was taught music first by the local organist, then by himself. While he was still struggling as an opera composer, his first wife and two young children all died, which nearly broke his spirit. But his next opera, *Nabucco,* was a big success, and the course of his life was set. From then on, his fame and stature increased with each new opera. He was also identified with the *Risorgimento,* the movement for Italian unity and independence, and was elected

to the first Italian parliament. Aged fifty-seven, Verdi planned to retire to his estate after the success of *Aida.* But more than ten years later, he was persuaded to work on *Otello,* and close to eighty years old, he followed it with *Falstaff.* He left his fortune to the musicians' home he had already founded in Milan.

Richard Wagner

$\mathcal{R}$ICHARD WAGNER
(1813–83)

Born in Leipzig, Wagner's career, first as conductor, then as composer, took him from Russia to London and Paris, then to Switzerland and Italy, before returning to his native Germany. In addition to composing his immense operas and music-dramas, he wrote numerous theoretical books and essays. He was also involved in politics, had various love affairs, married twice (the second time to Liszt's daughter Cosima), and was embroiled with the emotionally unstable King Ludwig II of Bavaria, who helped him build his own opera house at Bayreuth. Profligate with other people's money, nervous, hypersensitive and egocentric in the extreme, Wagner achieved almost all his aims. He died in Venice, but his body was brought back with much pomp to his home in Bayreuth.

Glossary

Absolute music Music that supposedly exists purely for its own sake, with no emotional or other extra-musical connotations.

Absolute pitch Ability to sing or identify a note without reference to the pitch of another note. Hence *relative pitch*, the ability to sing or identify a note after reference to another.

A cappella (It. 'in the church style') Vocal music without instrumental accompaniment.

Accelerando (It.) Getting faster.

Accent (1) Regular stress or emphasis on a rhythmic beat. (2) Emphasis on a particular note(s), marked >.

Accidental Specifically flattened or sharpened note, not included in the key of a particular piece of music.

Accompaniment Instrumental, choral or keyboard music supporting a solo voice or instrument(s).

Acid rock Rock music evoking the effects of LSD ('acid') or other hallucinogenic drugs.

Acoustics (1) Science of sound. (2) Architectural properties of a concert hall or room as they affect the sound of music played in it.

Adagio (It.) Slow tempo; a piece of music so performed.

Ad lib, ad libitum (L. 'at pleasure') Tempo and expression to be decided by performer. Hence also, to improvise.

Aeolian mode *See* MODES

Air or **ayre** Simple tune for instrument or voice. *See also* ARIA.

Alberti bass Common form of left-hand accompaniment in eighteenth-century keyboard music, consisting of simple broken chords. Named after Italian composer Domenico Alberti (*c*.1710–40).

Aleatory music (L. *alea*, 'dice') Music in which random or chance elements determine its course.

Alla marcia (It.) In march style.

Allegretto (It.) Not quite as fast as *allegro*.

Allegro (It.) Fairly fast tempo.

Allemande (Fr. 'German') Old German dance in four beats to the bar, often in baroque or classical suites.

Alto (It.) Lowest range in pitch of boys' and women's voices; also applied to the pitch range of some instruments. *See also* CONTRALTO and COUNTERTENOR.

Ambrosian chant Early type of church PLAINSONG introduced by Ambrose, Bishop of Milan, in the 4th century AD.

Andante (It. 'walking') A medium tempo, slower than *allegro*, faster than *adagio*, walking pace.

Andantino (It.) Slowish tempo, but slightly faster than *andante*.

Animato (It.) Lively, animated.

Anthem A choral composition, sometimes with soloists, sung at church services. Also, a national song.

Antiphony (Gk. 'sounding across') Music, usually choral, in the form of lead and response between two groups of singers. Hence **antiphon** for a type of church music.

Appoggiatura (It. 'leaning') Type of melodic ornamentation, with one note leading to or 'leaning on' the next, more important, note.

Arabesque Highly ornamented passage or short piece, by analogy with Arabic or Islamic decorative design. Also, specific movement in ballet.

Arco, con – (It. 'bow,' 'with the bow') Direction to strings (violin, etc.) to play with the bow.

Aria (It. 'air' or 'song') Structured piece for solo voice with instrumental accompaniment, usually in opera or oratorio.

Arioso (It.) Melodious, in style of aria. Song-like recitative.

Arpeggio (It. 'harp-like') Individual notes of a chord played in succession, as on a harp, rather than at the same time.

Arrangement Adaptation of part or all of a composition for voices and/or instruments other than those for which it was first written.

Ars Antiqua (L. 'old style') Early style of medieval polyphony, which developed in the thirteenth century.

Ars Nova (L. 'new style') Often complex style of fourteenth-century polyphony which succeeded the *Ars Antiqua*.

Atonality Quality of having no definite key center or tonality, as in TWELVE-TONE or other SERIAL MUSIC. *See* TONALITY (2).

Augmentation 'Stretching' a melodic line or part by increasing the time values of its notes. Common device in COUNTERPOINT.

Bagatelle (Fr. 'trifle') Short instrumental piece, often for piano.

Ballad A narrative song. Also, an eighteenth- or nineteenth-century drawing-room song.

Ballade (Fr., 'ballad') Instrumental piece, usually for piano, in romantic style.

Ballad opera English dramatic form with spoken dialogue alternating with songs.

Ballet (Fr.) Dance art form developed in France from court dances and transferred to the stage, now taking many forms and styles.

Ballett Piece for voices, similar to a madrigal, but usually with dance-like rhythm.

Bar *See* METER.

Barcarolle (It.) Venetian gondolier's song, or piece inspired by one.

Baritone Medium range of male voice, overlapping bass and tenor.

Baroque In music, period from about 1600 to 1750, in which new styles of musical expression were developed. Vaguely analogous to extravagant architectural style of period.

Bass (1) Lowest male voice. (2) Lowest part in a musical composition. (3) Low-pitched member of an instrumental family. *See also* CLEF.

Basso continuo *See* CONTINUO.

Beat (1) Regular musical pulse, especially when 'beaten out' rather than implied. (2) Indication of pulse by conductor. (3) In rock, jazz, etc., 'beat' can mean a basic rhythm pattern. (4) Throbbing effect heard when two notes forming a dissonance are sounded together.

Bebop, bop Improvisational jazz style, based largely on fragmented melodic phrases, generally fast and frenetic.

Bel canto (It. 'beautiful singing') Lyrical style of singing, emphasizing beauty of tone, especially in eighteenth- and nineteenth-century Italian opera.

Binary form Simple musical form in two sections. The first usually moves from the home key to a related one. The second returns to the home key.

Bitonality Simultaneous use of two keys in a piece of music.

Blues Basic jazz form, usually in twelve bars, with corresponding changes in harmony, based on the flattened or diminished third and seventh notes of the scale. So-called 'blue notes' refer to these.

Bolero (Sp.) Spanish dance originally accompanied by singing and castanets.

Boogie or **boogie woogie** Jazz form derived from the BLUES, primarily for the piano, with distinctive left-hand chords or figurations.

Bossa nova Latin American dance, from Brazil, relaxed, sometimes almost soporific in style.

Bourrée Old French dance, often included in baroque suites.

Breve (from L., 'short') In the Middle Ages, a note of half the length of a 'long,' which was the second longest time value after the 'maximus' or 'double long.' The long dropped out of use, the breve became rare and today the longest note normally used is the semibreve or whole note.

Cabaletta (It.) Name given to simple, popular types of operatic songs; bravura conclusions to arias or duets.

Caccia (It. 'chase,' 'hunt') Old type of vocal or instrumental piece like a round or canon (i.e. the melody 'chases' itself).

Cadence (L. *cadere*, 'to fall') Two chords bringing a piece of music to a close or leading to a new section (a kind of musical punctuation). The 'Amen' at the end of hymns and psalms is an example. Types of cadence include the 'perfect,' 'plagal,' 'imperfect,' and 'interrupted.'

Cadenza (It. 'cadence') Passage (or gap), usually in a concerto, allotted to the soloist, usually introduced by a cadence, or something like it.

Cajun Jazz-rock style named after the French-speaking *Acadians* (Cajuns) of Louisiana.

Cakewalk Early jazz-based dance style.

Calando (It.) Becoming quieter and slower.

Canon Type of contrapuntal piece, similar to a round, in which a melody is taken up by different voices or instruments in turn. Thus the melody should harmonize with itself.

Cantabile (It.) In a flowing, expressive, singing style.

Cantata (It. 'sung') Vocal composition for soloist(s), choir or chorus.

Canticle Sacred song, other than a psalm.

Cantilena (It. 'small song') Smooth, melodious writing for voice or instruments.

Cantillation Unaccompanied chanting in free rhythm, especially in Jewish worship.

Cantor (1) Leading singer in a Jewish synagogue. (2) Choir director in German Lutheran church.

Cantus firmus (L. 'fixed song') In polyphony, a set melody around which other contrapuntal parts are woven.

Canzona (It. 'song') Name applied to various types of song or, sometimes, instrumental pieces. Hence **canzonetta** or **canzonet**, 'little song.'

Capriccio (It. 'caprice') Piece of music, usually quite lively and in an improvisational style.

Carillon (Fr.) Set of bells, played manually or mechanically.

Carol Originally a dance, then a type of popular song; now associated with Christmas and other religious festivals.

Castrato (It.) Adult male singer whose voice was prevented from breaking by castration; practice now ceased. *Castrato* vocal parts now often sung by a COUNTERTENOR.

Catch Vocal round or canon. The singers have to 'catch,' or join in, at just the right moment.

Cavatina (It.) Slow operatic aria, or similarly slow, song-like instrumental piece.

Chaconne (Fr.) Piece of music, originally a dance, in which a bass part (GROUND BASS) is constantly repeated, with variations upon it. **Passacaglia** is very similar.

Chamber music Originally, music to be played in a room (chamber). Today, it means music for small instrumental ensembles, but not piano music.

Change ringing Art of ringing a peal of bells (usually eight) through a series of permutations.

Chanson (Fr. 'song'). Various types of French song, for solo voice or ensemble; but *mélodie* is the term usually applied to French art-song, i.e. the equivalent of German LIED.

Charleston Early jazz-based dance style.

Chorale German Lutheran hymn tune. Hence **chorale prelude**, a type of composition based on such a tune.

Chord Simultaneous sounding of two or more notes of different pitch.

Choro Originally a Brazilian instrumental ensemble, now describing a general Latin American popular instrumental style.

Chorus (1) Choir. (2) Composition or part of composition where each part is sung by several voices. (3) Song refrain. (4) Second and usually most familiar part of show-tune, preceded by the 'verse.' (5) Section of jazz solo, usually same length as initial theme.

Chromatic scale (Gk. *chromos*, 'color') Twelve-note scale, i.e. all the notes on a piano from one note to its equivalent an octave higher or lower. Hence **chromaticism**, music that is constantly modulating through the keys instead of staying in one key.

Classical music Music with emphasis on form, especially sonata form; strictly applied to the period 1750 to 1800. **Neo-classicism** is 20th-century music favoring a return to classical principles.

Clef Signs in notation (originally a letter) to establish the pitch of notes. There are, principally, the treble and bass clefs, but also a third, moveable clef sign, the alto or tenor. The word means 'key' but must not be confused with key itself.

Coda (It. 'tail') Passage added to end of a piece or movement, i.e. in sonata form, to emphasize conclusion.

Coloratura (It. 'coloring') Ornamental style in vocal music. A soprano whose voice is well adapted to this is a coloratura soprano.

Common time *See* TIME SIGNATURE.

Compound time Rhythmic beat in which SIMPLE TIME is multiplied, e.g. by changing two beats in the bar to two groups of three beats, or six beats in the bar.

Con brio (It.) With spirit, vigor.

Concertante (1) Work for solo instruments and orchestra, but closer in form to a classical-style symphony (*sinfonia concertante*). (2) The smaller group or solo instruments in a *concerto grosso*.

Concerto (It. 'together'). Originally a composition for two or more contrasted groups of instruments, primarily the **concerto grosso** or 'great concerto.' From the classical period on, more often a work, usually in three movements, for one or sometimes two solo instruments and orchestra. More recently, the concerto for orchestra has featured individual instruments, or groups of instruments, playing in turn.

Concert pitch Standard of pitch to which instruments are usually tuned. The note used for tuning is A above middle C, the frequency of which has been established internationally as 440 hertz (cycles per second).

Conductus Type of polyphonic church composition in Middle Ages, in which the *cantus firmus* was either a secular melody or original. Forerunner of the MOTET.

Consort Old English word for a complete group or family of instruments (i.e. viols). A broken consort included instruments of different groups.

Continuo (It.) Type of accompaniment, usually for keyboard, and usually following the bass line of the music (**basso continuo**), prevalent in baroque and some classical music. Figured bass indicates *continuo* harmonies, similar in intent to chord signs in dance and pop music. Once known as 'thorough bass' or 'through bass' in England.

Contralto (It.) Lowest-pitched female voice.

Contrapuntal *See* COUNTERPOINT.

Counterpoint (L. *punctus contra punctum*, 'note against note') Type of polyphonic music, weaving or fitting two or more melodies together, or weaving the same melody around itself. FUGUE and CANON are the two most important contrapuntal forms.

Countertenor High male voice of similar range to female contralto. Another name for male alto.

Courante (Fr.) French court dance, often included in baroque suites.

Cover version In pop and rock music, new versions of an existing recorded number; often a form of musical plagiarism.

Crescendo *See* DYNAMICS.

Crooning Soft, generally sentimental vocal style, popular in dance band SWING.

Crotchet European term for a basic note unit in counting time; a quarter of a whole note, hence the more logical term **quarter-note**.

Csárdás A national Hungarian dance, with slow and quick sections.

Cyclic or **cyclical form** Piece with movements connected by common musical ideas that recur.

Da capo (It. 'from the head') Direction to repeat a piece from the beginning, or in operatic aria a piece so repeated. *D. C. al fine* means repeat from beginning to end. *D. C. al segno* means repeat from the beginning to the section marked with the sign.

Descant Decorative part, sometimes improvised, added above a melody. Also English name for soprano recorder.

Diatonic (Gk. 'through the notes') Pertaining to Western-type music based on the 12 major and 12 minor scales.

Diminuendo *See* DYNAMICS.

Disco music Pop or rock music for discotheque

dancing, reduced largely to a strong, solid beat.

Divertimento (It.), **divertissement** (Fr.) Light instrumental composition with several movements, like a suite, intended to entertain or 'divert.' A *divertissement* in ballet is a dance-interlude not organically connected to the main work.

Dixieland Name for early or 'traditional' jazz band style, or imitations of this. From Jonathan Dixie, an American slave trader.

Dodecaphonic music *See* TWELVE-NOTE COMPOSITION.

Dorian mode *See* MODES.

Downbeat (1) Lowering of hand or conductor's baton in beating time. (2) Accented beat of bar (indicated by downbeat movement).

Drone Sustained notes played by, for example, drone strings or the drone on a bagpipe, which form a continuous accompaniment to the melody.

Duet Piece for two voices or instruments, or for two players on one keyboard instrument.

Dumka Ukrainian and Slavonic folk-ballad.

Duple time Basically two beats to the bar.

Dynamics Gradations of sound volume, indicated principally by the following Italian terms: *pianissimo* (*pp*), very quiet; *piano* (*p*), quiet; *mezzo-piano* (*mp*), fairly quiet; *mezzo-forte* (*mf*), fairly loud; *forte* (*f*), loud; *fortissimo* (*ff*), very loud. Also, *crescendo* (*cresc*), getting gradually louder; *diminuendo* (*dim*), getting gradually quieter.

Echo chamber Electronic device much used in early pop and rock 'n' roll.

Écossaise (Fr.) French dance, supposedly Scottish in origin.

Eighth-note See QUAVER.

Exposition (1) In SONATA FORM, first part of a movement, in which main themes are stated. (2) In FUGUE, section in which all the 'voices' or 'parts' make their first entries.

Expression marks In notation, signs which guide a player's interpretation of a piece. They cover most aspects of performance that cannot be exactly notated, like tempo, phrasing, accent, dynamics.

Falsetto (It.) Highest register of a man's voice, sometimes used comically to imitate a woman or child, seriously cultivated by countertenors.

Fandango Lively Spanish-Latin American dance.

Fanfare Musical flourish, usually for trumpets or other brass instruments.

Fermata (It. 'held') Pause sign placed above a note to prolong its length.

Figured bass *See* CONTINUO.

Fingering Use of fingers to play an instrument; more specifically, numbered indications of fingering for keyboard players.

Flamenco Spanish style

of folk song and dance, also style of guitar playing associated with it.

Flat Sign in notation indicating that a note is lowered in pitch by a half-tone. A double flat lowers the pitch by a whole tone. People are said to play or sing 'flat' when the pitch of their notes is slightly lower than true.

Folk music, folk-song Traditional music of a particular people, culture or nation, passed down by oral tradition.

Form Plan, design or procedure of a piece of music. *See* BINARY FORM; BLUES; CANON; CHACONNE; CHORUS; CONCERTO; CYCLIC FORM; FANTASIA; FUGUE; RONDO; SONATA FORM; SUITE; SYMPHONY; TERNARY FORM; VARIATION FORM.

Forte *See* DYNAMICS.

Fortissimo *See* DYNAMICS.

Foxtrot Jazz-based dance, once popular in ballroom dancing.

Frottola Fifteenth- and early sixteenth-century song style, preceding the madrigal.

Fugue (Fr. 'flight') Highly developed contrapuntal form. Starts with *exposition*, in which each part enters in turn with short melody or *subject*, followed by *episodes* where the music changes key, and *stretti*, where the time between entries is 'squeezed together.' **Double** – A fugue founded upon two subjects.

Fundamental Denoting or relating to the principal or lowest note of a harmonic series.

Funk Term in jazz and rock music with many meanings, but can describe a strong, earthy, physical quality of singing or playing; possibly from an old-English word meaning 'smoky, steamy, dirty.'

Galliard (from It. *galgiarda*) Lively, three-beats to the bar, Renaissance and Tudor dance, originally from Italy.

Gavotte Old French dance, in two beats to the bar, sometimes included in baroque and classical suites.

Gebrauchsmusik (Ger. 'music for use') Music by some earlier twentieth-century composers, especially Paul Hindemith and Kurt Weill, based on popular idioms and intended to be easily understood or instructive.

Gigue French name for an old British dance, the jig, often included in baroque and classical suites.

Glee Short, unaccompanied choral piece; hence the name Glee Club for some amateur choirs.

Glissando (It. from Fr. 'gliding') (1) On keyboard, rapid scale passage played by sliding back of thumb or fingers along keys. (2) Similar effect produced by 'sweeping' harp strings. (3) Continuously falling or rising sound on instruments without fixed notes, i.e. violin.

Gospel Pop and rock music style, mainly vocal, based on the often frenetic gospel singing in some churches.

Grave (It.) Slow, solemn tempo or mood.

Grazioso (It.) Gracefully.

Gregorian chant Style of PLAINSONG as revised by Pope Gregory in 6th century AD. Since then the standard chant of Roman Catholic Church.

Griot Traditional West African minstrel, whose style influenced calypso and other types of Afro-American music.

Ground bass *See* CHACONNE.

Guidonian hand Mnemonic for notes of scale, introduced by Guido d'Arezzo in eleventh century, which allotted different notes to the tips and joints of fingers and thumb. *See* HEXACHORD, and TONIC SOL-FA.

Habanera Latin American, specifically Cuban, dance, similar to TANGO.

Half-note *See* MINIM.

Harmonics Higher notes (also called partials or overtones) produced by vibrating string or air column in addition to basic note or FUNDAMENTAL.

Harmony The sound of chords, and by extension, progressions of chords or accompanying notes that are a significant addition to melody. The study of harmony has been of great importance in Western music; not so much in other musical cultures.

Heavy metal Strident, much-amplified style of rock music.

Hexachord Group of six consecutive notes of diatonic scale, taken as a

unit for learning sight-singing in Middle Ages. Introduced by Guido d'Arezzo in eleventh century.

Highlife General term for jazz-based dance music of West Africa.

Hillbilly music White American folk music originally from Appalachians.

Homophony (from Gk. 'same voice') (1) Music in unison as opposed to in harmony. (2) Style of music in which one part has the lead, the other parts being subsidiary and generally moving in step with the lead. Opposite of POLYPHONY.

Hook lines In rock and pop music, title words and melody of a number constantly repeated.

Hornpipe Lively old English dance, traditionally accompanied by an instrument made from animal horn.

Hymn Song of praise to a deity, primarily but not exclusively associated with Christianity.

Impromptu (1) Improvised piece of music. (2) Written composition with improvised character.

Improvisation Art of spontaneous music-making, i.e. ability to conceive and play music without writing it down beforehand.

Incidental music Music composed to supplement and point up stage drama.

In nomine (L. 'in the name of') Type of sixteenth- and seventeenth-century English contrapuntal composition based on a

PLAINSONG theme, usually for viols.

Instrumentation Instruments used in a piece of music; not the same thing as orchestration.

Interlude (1) Short piece inserted between two sections of an entertainment, i.e. play or opera. (2) Instrumental passage between verses of a hymn or lines of a verse.

Intermezzo (It. 'in the middle') (1) Operatic or dramatic interlude. (2) Movement in sonata, symphony, etc. (3) Name sometimes used for short, independent pieces.

Interval Difference in pitch between two notes. Common examples of intervals in Western diatonic music are: the fifth (i.e. C to G), augmented fifth (C to G sharp), the third (C to E), the minor third (C to E flat), the minor or diminished seventh (C to B flat). Intervals in other musical cultures may be measured in fractions of a half-tone.

Intonation Singing or playing accurately in tune.

Invention Name given by J. S. Bach to his two-part contrapuntal compositions for keyboard.

Inversion (1) Changing relative position of the two notes of an INTERVAL. (2) A melody is inverted when it is turned upside down so that upward intervals become equivalent downward intervals and vice versa.

Ionian mode *See* MODES.

Isorhythm (Gk. 'equal rhythm') Repeated rhythmic pattern or sequence, independent of melody line, used in medieval polyphony.

Janissary music Turkish military music, and Western music influenced by it, noted for its percussion.

Jazz Afro-American music, originating in the southern states and among the strongest forces in the music of this century. *See also* BEBOP, BLUES, DIXIELAND, RAGTIME, SPIRITUAL

Jig *See* GIGUE.

Jongleur Traveling musician and entertainer in medieval France.

Juju African pop music style, featuring guitars, drums and vocals, centred on Nigeria. **Yoruba Pop** or **Yopop** is an up-tempo version of it.

Kapellmeister (Ger. 'chapel master') Director of music at a German or Austrian church or court. Today, any musical director.

Key (1) In Western diatonic music, designation of the twelve major and twelve minor scales (C major, C minor, E flat major, and so on). The key signature at the beginning of a piece of notated music indicates the sharps or flats (if any) relevant to a particular scale. (2) Individual lever operating the mechanism on any keyboard instrument.

Kwela Black South African music, based on blues and other jazz styles.

Lambada Latin American, mainly Brazilian, dance style, often sexually suggestive.

Ländler South German folk dance in triple time. Forerunner of WALTZ, but slower.

Largamente (It.) Broadly, largely.

Largo (It. 'broad') Very slow, stately tempo.

Laudi spirituali Popular Italian devotional songs of Middle Ages and Renaissance, probably forerunners of oratorio.

Ledger or **leger lines** Short additional lines above or below stave, for notes beyond range of stave.

Legato (It. 'bound') Playing so that notes are smoothly connected, opposite of STACCATO.

Leitmotiv *See* MOTTO THEME.

Lento (It.) Slow, but not as slow as LARGO.

Libretto (It. 'little book') The text of an opera or oratorio.

Lied (Ger. 'song', plural *Lieder*) German, mainly nineteenth-century art-song.

M

Madrigal Polyphonic song for small group of singers, popular in Renaissance Italy and Tudor England.

Maestro di cappella (It. 'chapel master') Director of music.

Major *See* DIATONIC; KEY; SCALE.

Marcato (It.) Marked, accented.

March Military music to accompany marching, many marches are written specially for parades, a few for concert performance. **Slow march**, intended for a funeral or other solemn occasion.

Masque English, mainly seventeenth-century, stage entertainment, with elements of opera and ballet.

Mass A musical setting of the parts of the Eucharistic service sung by the choir or congregation. *See also* REQUIEM.

Mazurka Polish folk dance, in three beats to the bar.

Meistersinger (Ger. 'master singers') German singers, traders and craftsmen, who flourished in guilds from fourteenth to sixteenth centuries; the successors of the noble MINNESÄNGER.

Melisma (Gk. 'song') Musical phrase of several notes sung to one syllable.

Melodrama In specific musical sense, use of spoken voice against musical background.

Mento Caribbean, principally Jamaican, style of dance, similar to RUMBA.

Merengue Originally Caribbean folk dance style, now absorbed into Afro-Caribbean music.

Meter In rhythm, regular grouping of beats in measures or bars. In written music, meter is shown by a TIME SIGNATURE and by vertical bar-lines.

Mezzo, mezza (It.) Half, medium.

Mezzo-forte *See* DYNAMICS.

Mezzo-piano *See* DYNAMICS.

Mezzo-soprano Medium range of female voice, overlapping SOPRANO and CONTRALTO.

Mezza-voce Half the power of voice(s) or instrument(s).

Microtone Any INTERVAL smaller than a half-tone, i.e. a quarter-tone.

Minim British term for time value of one half of a whole note, or semibreve.

Minnesänger (Ger. 'love-singers') German aristocratic bards or minstrels, roughly contemporary with the French troubadours and trouvères.

Minor *See* DIATONIC; KEY; SCALE.

Minstrel Musical entertainer of the Middle Ages and later.

Minuet (Eng.), **minuetto** (It.) Court dance in three beats to the bar, sometimes included in a baroque suite; more especially the third movement (with a central 'trio' section) of a classical symphony.

Modes System of scales, derived from Classical Greece, used in Western music up to about 1600. With reference to the piano, the principal modes, as we now know them, encompass the white notes from C to C (Ionian), D to D (Dorian), E to E (Phrygian), F to F (Lydian), G to G (Mixolydian), A to A (Aeolian). Thus each has its own special arrangement of tones and half-tones, unlike the uniform progressions in pitch of the diatonic major and minor scales. Indeed, the tonal arrangement of a mode matters more than the actual pitch of the notes. But note that we can speak of a piece of music being in a major or a minor mode.

Modulation Change of key.

Moderato (It.) Moderate tempo.

Molto (It.) Much or very, as in *allegro molto* (very fast).

Monody (Gk. 'single voice') Style of music with emphasis on one melody line, in contrast to polyphony.

Monothematic Piece of music with only one theme or melody.

Mordent Musical ornamentation of three rapid notes, applying mainly, but not exclusively, to keyboard music.

Moresca Dance from Moorish Spain.

Morris dance English folk dance in two or four beats to the bar, possibly derived from the Moorish-Spanish MORESCA.

Motet Primarily a polyphonic choral piece, usually for the Church.

Motive (Eng.), **Motif** (Fr.), **Motiv** (Ger.) Nucleus, or smallest unit of a melody.

Motto theme A usually quite brief melodic, rhythmic or harmonic phrase, sometimes used to reinforce a sense of unity to a symphony or other large-scale work. The German **Leitmotiv** (leading motive) was developed by Wagner. The French **idée fixe** has similar connotations.

Movement Single or self-contained piece of music belonging to a symphony, concerto or other larger work, though such movements may sometimes be linked.

Mute Various devices to soften and modify the tone of some stringed and brass instruments.

N

Natural (1) Sign in notation indicating that a note is neither sharpened or flattened. (2) Word describing brass instruments that consist of a simple tube, with no valves or other mechanism.

Neo-classicism *See* CLASSICAL MUSIC.

Neume *See* NOTATION.

Nocturne (Fr.) Dreamy, romantic piece evocative of night.

Nonet Composition for nine voices or instruments.

Notation Any system of writing down music. Staff notation is the principal system in Western music. There is also tablature (diagramatic indications of fingering to secure particular notes or chords); TONIC SOL-FA (letters or syllables to represent pitched notes); and neumes (signs written above or below words to be sung, used in early Western music and in some other musical cultures).

Note (1) Single sound of specific duration and pitch. (2) Symbol representing this.

Note-row *See* TWELVE-NOTE COMPOSITION.

O

Obbligato (It. 'obligatory') Instrumental accompaniment to song, etc., having musical importance of its own.

Octave Interval formed by two notes, of which the upper has twice the frequency of the lower. So-called because the upper note is the eighth note of a diatonic scale commencing on the lower note.

Octet Composition for eight voices or instruments.

Opera (L. 'works') Musical stage drama, originally, in Italy, *dramma per musica*. It takes various forms and styles: *opera seria* (It. 'serious opera'), *opera buffa* (It. 'comic opera'), *opéra-comique* (Fr. opera with spoken dialogue), *singspiel* (Ger. opera with spoken dialogue), grand opera, Wagnerian music-drama, operetta (It. 'little opera') or light opera.

Opus (L. 'work') Musical composition, often designated by its opus or publication number.

Oratorio Extended setting usually of religious text for chorus, solo singers and orchestra.

Orchestra Large and mixed body of instruments. Hence orchestration, the discipline and art of writing for the instruments of an orchestra.

Organum Earliest form of polyphony, in which two or more melodic lines proceed at a constant interval of pitch.

Ostinato (It. 'obstinate') Constantly repeated musical phrase, often as an accompaniment.

Overdrive Sound effect in rock music, produced by electrical feedback.

Overtone *See* HARMONICS.

Overture (from Fr. *ouverture*, 'opening') (1) Orchestral introduction to opera or other stage or vocal work. (2) A concert overture is an independent piece for concert performance.

Palm wine Style of West African dance music, mostly for guitars, named after a local type of beer; forerunner of JUJU , from the 1950s onward, derived from rock 'n roll, but broadening into many styles.

Part One performer's music in an ensemble; a single line in a musical score. Hence, part-song, piece for five or more voices.

Partita (It.) (1) A variation. (2) Set of pieces; similar to baroque SUITE, but not restricted to dance forms.

Part-song *See* PART.

Pasodoble (Sp. 'double step') Lively Spanish dance, with two beats to the bar.

Passacaglia (It.) *See* CHACONNE.

Passepied (Fr. 'pass-foot') Lively French dance with three or six beats to the bar, included in some early French ballets.

Passing note In harmony, melodic note that 'passes through' a chord while not being an integral part of it.

Passion Special type of ORATORIO, based on the gospel accounts of Christ's trial and crucifixion.

Pastoral (Eng.), **pastorale** (It., Fr.) (1) Musical stage work with rural and mythological theme. (2) Instrumental piece which evokes the countryside.

Pause *See* FERMATA.

Pavan (Eng.), **pavana** (It.), **pavane** (Fr.) Stately sixteenth-century dance. Originally Italian, popular in Spain and England.

Pedal (1) Sustained bass note over changing harmonies. (2) Keyboard on an organ played with the feet. (3) Pedals of a piano, for dynamic effects.

Pentatonic scale (Gk. *pente*, 'five') Five-note scale, usually corresponding to the black notes on a piano, widely used in oriental and folk music.

Pesante (It.) Heavy, heavily.

Phrase Section of a melody, roughly analogous to part of a sentence divided by commas. Hence phrasing, playing a melody with due observance of its phrases; and phrase marks, as used in notated music.

Phrygian mode *See* MODES.

Pianissimo *See* DYNAMICS.

Piano *See* DYNAMICS.

Pitch Highness or lowness of a note, as defined by its frequency (rate of vibrations of its sound waves). *See also* ABSOLUTE PITCH; CONCERT PITCH.

Pizzicato, pizz (It.) Direction that strings (violin, etc.) should be plucked rather than bowed (*arco*).

Plainsong, plainchant Earliest form of Western church music, sung in unison and in free rhythm, i.e., according to the inflection of the words. *See also* AMBROSIAN CHANT; GREGORIAN CHANT.

Polka Popular nineteenth-century dance, originating in Bohemia.

Polonaise French name for stately Polish dance.

Polyphony (from Gk., 'many voices') Music having several independently moving parts; particularly applied to vocal music of the Middle Ages and Renaissance. Opposite of HOMOPHONY. *See also* COUNTERPOINT.

Polyrhythm Simultaneous use of several rhythms.

Polytonality Simultaneous use of several keys.

Pop music General term for much dance music from the 1950s onward, derived from rock 'n' roll, but broadening into many styles.

Portamento (It. 'carrying') The gliding up or down between two pitched notes, pertaining to the voice or stringed instruments.

Prelude (1) Introductory piece of music, similar to an overture. (2) Independent piece of music, often for a keyboard instrument.

Presto (It.) Fast tempo; hence **prestissimo**, very fast.

Program music Music intended to evoke extra-musical ideas, events and images; opposite of ABSOLUTE music.

Punk Anarchic, often deliberately crude, style of rock music.

Quadrille Communal or ballroom dance, similar to a SQUARE DANCE.

Quarter-note *See* CROTCHET.

Quarter tone Interval of half a half-tone.

Quartet Composition for four voices or instruments; but string quartet implies special type of work, similar in form to a symphony.

Quaver, eighth-note British and American terms for time value of one-eighth of a semibreve or whole note.

Quintet Composition for five voices or instruments.

Raga or **rag** (Hin. 'color', 'feeling') Wide variety of scales pertaining to Indian classical music, though different in function from Western diatonic scales. By extension, music based on these.

Ragtime Early jazz style, notably for the piano, so-called because of 'ragged' or syncopated rhythms.

Rai North African, specifically Algerian, style of rock music.

Rallentando (It.) Becoming slower.

Rap Type of rock music, relying on rapid-fire words, often married to disco tape or turntable manipulation.

Recapitulation *See* SONATA FORM.

Recitative (Eng.), **recitativo** (It.) In opera, style of musical declamation between speech and song.

Reggae Style of rock music, originally from Jamaica, with syncopated beat, associated with the black Rastafarian religious movement.

Register (1) Tonal qualities pertaining to the pitch range of a voice or instrument. (2) Set of organ pipes controlled by a particular stop; hence registration, the technique of using the stops on an organ.

Relative pitch *See* ABSOLUTE PITCH.

Répétiteur (Fr. 'repeater') The chorus-master of an opera-house who rehearses (repeats) the singer.

Reprise (Fr.) Repeat, or return to, a particular section of music.

Requiem Musical setting of the mass for the dead.

Rest In notation, signs indicating periods of silence corresponding to the time values of particular notes.

Rhapsody Piece of music, often for the piano, of a romantic and improvisational character.

Rhythm The organization of music in *time,* as opposed to its organization in *pitch* (tonality). Establishment of relative durations and time-positions of notes.

Rhythm and blues, R 'n' b Pop and dance music style, derived from blues and other jazz forms.

Ricercare (It. 'seek out') Contrapuntal piece in which the composer 'seeks out' exercises or devices in COUNTERPOINT.

Riff Brief, repeated phrase, much used in jazz and swing.

Ritardando (It.) Getting gradually slower.

Ritornello (It. 'little return') A regularly repeated passage, as between the verses of a song, also much in evidence in baroque music.

Rock music, rock Closely associated with pop music, but generally distinguished from pop by strong rhythms, harsher sounds or more esoteric styles.

Rock 'n' roll Early type of pop music, based on HILLBILLY, BLUES, BOOGIE and other styles; the basis also for much rock music.

Rococo (from Fr. *rocaille,* a type of decorative rock work) Eighteenth-century musical style, elegant and fanciful, like contemporary art and architecture. *Style galant* means much the same thing.

Romantic music Music, mainly nineteenth-century, in which emotional or other extra-musical content takes precedence over form; as opposed to CLASSICAL MUSIC.

Rondo (It. 'round') Musical form in which a principal theme alternates with contrasting themes or episodes.

Round *See* CANON.

Rubato (It. 'robbed') Style of playing with certain rhythmic freedom ('robbing' the time value of some notes) for expressive purposes.

Rumba Latin American dance, originally from Cuba, fairly fast and energetic.

Sabra Recent style of Israeli popular music, with Arabic overtones.

Salsa Latin American dance style, originating in Colombia.

Samba Latin American, specifically Brazilian, dance.

Saraband Slow, stately Spanish dance, often included in baroque suites.

Scale (It. *scala,* 'steps') Sequence or progression of notes ascending or descending by certain pitch intervals, as melodic or harmonic basis for piece of music. The diatonic scales providing the basis for much Western-style music are uniformly ordered in sequences of eight tones and half-tones, one order for the twelve major scales, a different order for the minor scales. *See also* CHROMATIC SCALE; KEY; MODES; PENTATONIC SCALE; RAGA; TETRACHORD; TWELVE-NOTE SCALE; WHOLE-TONE SCALE.

Scat singing Non-verbal kind of singing, often using nonsense words and sounds, popular in jazz.

Scherzo (It. 'joke') Instrumental piece, not necessarily humorous, often a movement in a symphony, sonata or other large-scale work.

Score Written or printed music with all the parts of a composition set out. Scoring is also another name for orchestrating a piece of music.

Scotch snap Rhythmic figure of a short on-the-beat note, followed by a longer one; found in some Scottish folk music.

Semibreve, whole note British and American terms for the longest time value in common use, equivalent to two minims or four crotchets. *See* BREVE.

Semiquaver, sixteenth-note British and American terms for time value of a sixteenth of a semibreve or whole note.

Semitone, half-tone With reference to the piano, the pitch interval between two adjacent notes (i.e. C to C sharp, E to F, B flat to B).

Septet Ensemble of, or composition for, seven voices or instruments.

Sequence (1) Repetition of a melodic phrase, or harmonic movement, at successively higher or lower pitches. (2) Chord sequence: movement of chords, harmonic progression.

Serenade Strictly, music to be sung or played at night or evening; more generally a relatively lightweight instrumental or orchestral piece.

Serial music Method of composition in which, if strictly adhered to, every aspect of the music, including pitch, rhythm and volume, is worked out according to a predetermined plan or series. The series can be repeated, inverted, reversed, augmented or diminished, etc., as long as mathematical relationships are preserved. *See also* TWELVE-NOTE COMPOSITION.

Sextet Ensemble of, or composition for, six voices or instruments.

Sforzando, sf., sfz. (It. 'forcing') Direction for note or chord to be strongly accented. Sudden force.

Sharp Sign in notation indicating that a note is raised in pitch by a half-tone. A double sharp raises the pitch by a whole tone. People are said to play or sing 'sharp' when the pitch of their notes is slightly higher than true.

Siciliano (It.) Old Italian, probably Sicilian, dance in six beats to the bar, sometimes included in baroque suites or as movements in sonatas, etc.

Simple time Two or four straight beats to the bar. *See also* COMPOUND TIME.

Sinfonietta (It.) Small-scale symphony.

Singspiel (Ger. 'sing-play') Originally musical stage drama with spoken dialogue and interpolated songs.

Ska Jamaican-based style of pop music, rhythmically close to REGGAE.

Skiffle Pop music style with folk music and HILLBILLY roots.

Soca Style of Afro-Caribbean dance music.

Solfeggio (It.), **solfège** (Fr.) *See* TONIC SOL-FA.

Solmization Sight reading from syllabic names or sounds, such as TONIC SOL-FA.

Solo (It. 'alone') Piece or part of a piece for performance by an individual singer or instrumentalist.

Sonata (It. 'sounding') Instrumental composition (sounded rather than sung); originally many kinds of instrumental piece, then the baroque-style trio sonata, and, in its best-known form, a work for one or two instruments in the classical mold of two or three movements.

Sonata form Not to be confused with SONATA; the form of a single piece of music, basically in three linked sections: *exposition* (usually with two contrasted themes), *development,* and *recapitulation.* The form employed in many first movements (sometimes other movements also) of classical or classical-style symphonies, concertos, string quartets, sonatas, etc.

Song Relatively short vocal piece, taking many forms including *strophic form* (the same melody repeated with each verse or stanza). A song-cycle is a group of songs usually linked by some overall image or idea.

Soprano (1) The highest range of female voice. (2) High, or highest-pitched, member of a family of instruments.

Sostenuto (It.) Sustained.

Sotto voce (It. 'under the voice') Barely audible.

Soukous Afro-Caribbean pop music, generally relaxed and easy on the ear.

Soul Pop or rock music style, mainly vocal, secular relation to GOSPEL, but generally more even-paced.

Spiccato (It. 'separated') In string playing, rapid STACCATO effect produced by bouncing the bow on and off the strings.

Spiritual Primarily black American religious song, one of the sources of jazz. There are also some 'white' spirituals.

Sprechgesang, sprechstimme (Ger. 'speech-song') Vocal delivery halfway between speech and song, much used by Schoenberg and his disciples.

Square dance Communal dance in HILLBILLY style, derived from British folk music, popular in rural North America.

Staccato (It. 'detached') Direction for notes to be played in detached, separated manner.

Indicated by dot above (or below) the note.

Staff, stave In notated music, horizontal five-line grid on the lines and spaces of which musical notes are written as an indication of pitch. *See also* LEDGER LINES.

Stop (1) To alter the playing length (and so the pitch) of a string by pressing on it with a finger. (2) Knob or lever on an organ controlling supply of air to a section of pipes.

Study (Fr. *étude*) Piece written primarily to develop or display some aspect of technique.

Style galant See ROCOCO.

Subject Term for the themes in sonata form, fugue and other musical forms.

Suite (Fr. 'following') Originally, a group (succession) of pieces, mostly based on courtly dances; more generally, any group of pieces (movements), or a selection of the music from an opera, ballet or other larger-scale work.

Suspension In harmony, sustaining a note from one chord into the next, often creating a dissonance or discord.

Swing Dance music, derived from jazz, rhythmically based on a slurring syncopation.

Symphonic poem, Tone poem Romantic-type orchestral work of descriptive nature, usually in one movement.

Symphony (Gk. 'sounding together') (1) Orchestral or instrumental interlude in a choral or stage work. (2) An overture or *sinfonia*. (3) An orchestral work, usually in four movements, dating from the classical period. A few of such

symphonies have vocal or choral parts also.

Syncopation Strictly, changing the accent or stress of a rhythm; more generally, misplacing beats or slurring them so as to distort the rhythm.

𝒯

Tablature *See* NOTATION.

Tacet (L. 'silent') Indication in notated music that a particular part in a score is silent for a whole movement.

Tala (Hin.) A measure or rhythmic cycle in Indian music.

Tango Latin American, originally Argentinian, dance style, with strongly accented rhythm.

Tarantella (It.) Lively Italian dance in six beats to the bar, traditionally associated with the tarantula spider.

Temperament Tempering or tuning mostly keyboard instruments, especially equal temperament, adjusting the pitch of notes so that music in any key is equally accessible to the player.

Tempo (It. 'time', plural *tempi*) Speed of pulse or beat in music. *See* ADAGIO; ALLEGRETTO; ALLEGRO; ANDANTE; ANDANTINO; LARGO; LENTO; MODERATO; PRESTO; PRESTISSIMO; VIVACE. *See also* ACCELERANDO; RALLENTANDO.

Tenor Highest natural (i.e. not falsetto) range of male voice. Also applied to instruments of similar range, like tenor horn, tenor saxophone.

Ternary form Piece of music in three basic sections, the third being a repetition, or near repetition, of the first.

Tessitura (It. 'texture') Most natural range of notes of a voice or instrument.

Tetrachord (Gk. 'four') Scale of four notes, originally the tuning of the strings on a Greek lyre. Historical basis of eight-note modes and diatonic scales.

Tie, bind Curved line in notation connecting two or more notes of the same pitch, so that they sound as a continuous note.

Tierce de Picardie (Fr. 'Picardy third') Major chord ending a piece in an otherwise minor key.

Timbre (Fr.) Tone quality or 'color,' especially characteristic sound of a particular instrument.

Time signature In notation, numerals at the start of a piece of music indicating both the number (top) and value (bottom) of beats to the bar. Common time is four quarter-note beats to the bar, i.e. 4/4, also represented by the symbol C, though historically this does not stand for 'common.'

Toccata (It. 'touch') Primarily a keyboard piece, usually in one movement, intended to demonstrate a player's sense of touch and control; though the name has been applied to other fairly rapid, staccato-like instrumental or orchestral pieces.

Tonality (1) General aspect of music concerned with pitch relationships of notes, i.e. melody, harmony, scales, etc., as opposed to rhythm, dynamics and timbre. (2) More

specifically, music having tonality is organized around a 'central' note or tonic, and has a sense of being in a particular scale or key. ATONALITY is the opposite of this.

Tone *See* TIMBRE.

Tone poem *See* SYMPHONIC POEM.

Tonic The first, leading or key note of a diatonic major or minor scale.

Tonic sol-fa System of notation, based on the mnemonic use of syllables, corresponding to the notes of a diatonic scale, do, ray, me, fa, so, la, te, do. The system also includes punctuation marks for rhythm. Note that in this system the syllables can apply to any scale; but continental sol-fa systems (Fr. *solfège*, It. *solfeggio*) always apply the syllables to the same notes, starting with do for C.

Transcription Arrangement of a composition for instrument(s) other than that for which it was originally written.

Transition Passage that joins one theme to another in a composition.

Transposition 'Translation' of a composition into a key other than that in which it was originally written.

Treble (1) High voice, usually of children ('boy soprano'). (2) Highest part in a musical composition. (3) High-pitched member of an instrumental family. *See also* CLEF.

Tremolo (It. 'trembling') On bowed stringed instruments, rapid repetition of a single note or of two adjacent notes, with back and forth strokes of the bow.

Trill Musical ornamentation, the rapid alternation between two notes a tone or half-tone apart. Also called a **shake**.

Trio (1) Composition for three instruments or voices. (2) Name applied to a baroque-type sonata, usually for three stringed instruments plus keyboard continuo. (3) Name loosely applied to the central section of a MINUET or SCHERZO in a classical-style symphony, string quartet or sonata.

Triple time Basically, three beats to the bar.

Triplet Rhythmic group of three evenly spaced notes played in the time of one or two beats, shown by a '3' under or over the notes.

Troppo (It. 'too much') But usually qualifying the opposite, i.e. *allegro ma non troppo, allegro* but not too much, moderate.

Tutti (It. 'all') Instrumental or orchestral passage for all players.

Troubadour Medieval poet-musician of southern France in eleventh to thirteenth centuries.

Trouvère (Fr. 'finder') Medieval poet-musician of northern France in eleventh to thirteenth centuries.

Twelve-note scale Scale or 'series,' using all twelve notes of the chromatic scale in a particular sequence, and implying equal importance for each note, unlike the tonal hierarchy implicit in the diatonic scales. Hence **twelve-note** or **dodecaphonic** (Gk. 'twelve-tones') music, based on such a scale. *See also* SERIAL MUSIC.

U

Unison Everybody playing or singing the same note, or, more loosely, playing or singing the same note an octave apart.

Up-beat (1) Raising of hand or conductor's baton in beating time. (2) Unaccented beat of bar (indicated by up-beat movement).

V

Variation form Strictly, theme and variation form, in which a theme is first played and then varied, that is, submitted to a sequence of musical changes. The CHACONNE and PASSACAGLIA are specific types of variation form. The RHAPSODY, too, can be loosely in variation form.

Vibrato Rapid up and down deviation from pitch of note, achievable on bowed and fretted stringed instruments, wind instruments and voices.

Villanella Fifteenth- and sixteenth-century Italian part-song.

Virtuoso Instrumentalist or singer of outstanding technique.

Vivace (It. 'lively,' 'brisk') Tempo equal to *allegro*, or faster.

Voice (1) For various ranges, *see* SOPRANO; TREBLE; MEZZO-SOPRANO; CONTRALTO: ALTO; TENOR; BARITONE; BASS; COUNTERTENOR. *See also* TESSITURA. (2) An instrumental part or line, as in a fugue.

Voluntary Organ solo played as PRELUDE to, or during, a church service.

W

Waltz Ballroom dance in three beats to the bar, developed from the old German and Austrian LÄNDLER.

Whole-note *See* SEMIBREVE.

Whole-tone scale with reference to the piano, a scale based on whole-tone intervals, i.e., C-D-E-F sharp-A flat, etc.

Y

Yodeling Singing style alternating between normal and falsetto voice.

Z

Zouk Style of Afro-Caribbean rock music.

Recommended Reading

The following publications, listed alphabetically according to author or editor(s), are excellent sources of reference for many of the aspects of music covered or touched upon in this book:

Ian Carr, Digby Fairweather, Brian Priestley, *Jazz: The Essential Companion*, London, Grafton Books, 1987

Iain Chambers, *Urban Rhythms: Pop Music and Popular Culture*, Basingstoke, Macmillan, 1985

John Collins, *African Pop Roots: The Inside Rhythms of Africa*, London, Foulsham Press, 1985

Colin Cripps *Popular Music in the 20th Century*, Cambridge, Cambridge University Press, 1988

David Ewen, *All the Years of American Popular Music*, London and Eaglewood Cliff, USA, Prentice Hall, 1977

Paul Griffiths, *A Guide to Electronic Music*, London, Thames & Hudson, 1979

Phil Hardy and Dave Laing, *The Encyclopedia of Rock*, London, Macdonald Orbis, 1987

Earl of Harewood (ed), *Kobbe's Complete Opera Book* (10th edn), London, Bodley Head, 1987

Christopher Hogwood, *Music at Court*, London, Gollanz, 1980

Michael Kennedy (ed), *The Concise Oxford Dictionary of Music* (3rd edn), London, Oxford University Press, 1980

Barry Kernfeld (ed), *The New Grove Dictionary of Jazz* (2 vols), London, Macmillan, 1988

Jennifer Lindsay, *Javanese Gamelan*, Kuala Lumpur, Oxford University Press, 1979

Ruth Midgley (ed), *Musical Instruments of the World*, London, Paddington Press, 1976

Michael Raeburn and Alan Kendall (eds), *Heritage of Music*, (4 vols), New York, Oxford University Press, 1989

Dafydd Rees (ed), *The Guinness Book of Rock Stars*, London, Guinness Publications, 1989

Timothy Ryback, *Rock Around the Bloc: A History of Rock Music in Eastern Europe and the Soviet Union*, New York, Oxford University Press, 1990

Curt Sachs, *The History of Musical Instruments*, London, Dent, 1968

Stanley Sadie (ed), *The New Grove Dictionary of Music and Musicians* (20 vols), London, Macmillan, 1980

John Sealey and Krister Malm, *Music in the Caribbean*, London, Hodder and Stoughton, 1982

David Toop, *The Rap Attack: African Jive to New York Hip Hop*, London, Pluto Press, 1984

Index